How To Make
A Fortune
In Import/Export

an Entrepreneur Press book

How To Make
A Fortune
In Import/Export

by Howard R. Goldsmith

RESTON PUBLISHING COMPANY, INC.
Reston, Virginia
A Prentice-Hall Company

Copyright © 1980 by The Entrepreneur Press
All Rights Reserved

ISBN: 0-8359-2962-0
0-8359-2961-2 (pbk)

Library of Congress Catalog Number: 79-91207

10 9 8

Printed in the United States of America

Contents

Section Four—Appendices

Figures

Foreword

If you've ever looked for an inexpensive, all-in-one-place, step-by-step guide to import/export, your search is over now. *How to Make a Fortune in Import/Export* answers all the questions you've ever thought of asking plus a lot more that probably haven't occurred to you as yet.

Whether you're an old pro, or just starting in the exciting import/export game, the wealth of information in this handbook can save you years of research and a fortune in costly mistakes.

This comprehensive guide covers such essentials as finding profitable products to import or export, buying at the "right" price, pricing goods for resale to maximize your profits, establishing and using credit in international business deals, documentation, shipping restrictions, duties and tariffs, customs declarations, as well as proven success formulas and "insider" tricks-of-the-trade.

While the opportunity for substantial wealth and profits is an undeniable attraction of the import/export business, there are many other benefits that you can also enjoy. Travel to exotic foreign lands; the excitement of major world-trade centers—London, Paris, Rome, Hong Kong, Tokyo, Berlin—the list goes on and on. Think of it: International travel—a tax-deductible expense. And don't overlook the noble element of promoting peace as a worldwide, good-will ambassador.

All of this and more can be yours in the import/export business. To get the best possible start, begin reading this all-inclusive guide today!

Donald M. Dible
Fairfield, California

To Sherri
for all her understanding

Acknowledgment

The information contained in this book has been gathered from many sources: major banks, government agencies, international organizations and associations, and personal experiences. Sifting through, refining, and editing this material has been a time-consuming labor of love.

I offer my thanks and appreciation to Joan Rogers for her assistance in editing and commenting on the manuscript. Without her aid, this book might never have been completed.

Howard R. Goldsmith
Los Angeles, September 1979

Section One

Introduction

Chapter One

Importing/Exporting: Is It for You?

The purpose of this book is to acquaint you, the novice, with the fundamentals of the export and import business, so that you can successfully operate such an enterprise. It is assumed that you have (1) little or no background in the field, (2) limited finances, (3) a full-time (40-hour-per-week) job, and (4) the desire to develop your own business.

If you've considered entrepreneurship before, you've probably discovered that many new business ventures require large amounts of capital and long-term, burdensome commitments on the part of the entrepreneur. In addition, real profit—extra money in your pocket beyond your salary—after the new business starts up is often five to ten years down the road. Some 80% of new businesses fail within the first five years of their existence; they simply run out of capital before they make a profit.

Such statistics might understandably turn you away from starting your own business if you are the sort who hesitates to mortgage possessions, work 80 hours a week, and deal constantly with creditors, competitors, insurance agents, personnel regulations, and the business tax system in order to make a go of your venture. What you want is a more promising opportunity—one which requires less capital, less commitment, more reliable promise for profit, and one which you can handle by yourself.

Few operations today offer greater potential for self-employment than international trade. It is a profession that, in the beginning, requires some of the same characteristics demanded of the entrepreneur in other fields—knowledge, skill, determination, stick-to-it-iveness—but to start with it requires them in lesser quantities, depending on the time you have to invest and the level of success you'd like to reach. It also works well as a solitary moonlight effort; the competition is considerably less than in numerous other business undertakings; and it requires a minimum of start-up financing.

Moonlighting

As a beginner, you can plan to start your import/export business in the evenings after work and on weekends. Writing letters; reviewing catalogs, samples, and price lists; and studying magazines and newspapers can all be done in your spare time. Only when your import/export income considerably exceeds your salary for a substantial period of time should you consider giving up your job. For example, your annual salary is $15,000. After two years, your average annual income from your import/export business is $25,000. You should continue working at your regular job.

Competition

According to reliable sources both in government and private industry, there are relatively few people (10,000 or less) engaged in international trade in the U.S. For a country of over 200 million people, this number is relatively small. Average net return for the majority of traders is in the $40,000 plus range, and a few top people are earning $100,000 per year.

Funding

Import/export offers a tremendous opportunity for big money with a small investment. The estimated two-year start-up cost, based on mid-1979 prices, is $1500 to $4000 for stationery, books, postage, telephones, and other such incidentals.

Let's consider some more specific aspects.

Exporting: Your Chances of Success

Most American firms do not export because of trade barriers (high tariffs, special taxes, etc.), while some are too busy with the domestic market, and many others are just afraid of the unknown. This situation offers you, the individual, a unique business opportunity rarely found in today's competitive marketplace. By providing an export service to firms either not exporting at all, firms just thinking about the export market, or firms that have failed in the past, you can develop a lucrative business. The opportunities in this area are fantastic! Consider the following:

1. Three out of five U.S. exporters have less than 100 employees; many have less than 10.

2. Exporters keep more than 4 million people employed—40,000 workers for every $1 billion of exports.

3. 95% of all U.S. firms sell only domestically.

4. Of the 300,000 U.S. manufacturers, less than 15,000 are exporting.

5. Most industrial nations export 15% to 25% of their Gross National Product. Exporting accounts for less than 10% of the U.S. GNP.

It is almost a truism that products sold successfully in the U.S. can be sold profitably abroad. Products marked "MADE IN USA" command a reputation of high quality, style, and state-of-the-art technological superiority.

Many American items sold abroad cost more than those produced locally, yet they quickly penetrate the market. In Europe, people are trading BMW's and Mercedes for American-made cars such as Pontiac Firebirds. The American cars (with taxes and freight charges) are more expensive than their European counterparts, and provide Europeans with status symbols, just as expensive European cars do for U.S. purchasers.

You can capitalize on the popularity of American products overseas if you have chosen your products and markets carefully and with some imagination.

Importing: Your Chances of Success

Currently the U.S. imports around $100 billion in goods, representing 5% of the total purchases made by industry and private consumers. This 5% is comprised of all types of merchandise. Coffee, rubber, petroleum products, iron and steel, and clothing are only a few of the best-known items.

It is estimated that more than 1 million workers are directly supported by the activities connected with importing. Each year, this business develops as conditions change in the U.S. and abroad. Recently, for example, the Zenith Company, a manufacturer of televisions and radios, moved a major part of their production facilities to the Far East in order to take advantage of cheaper labor costs and be competitive with foreign imports, and now they import their own products. However, many if not all manufacturers, when first importing products, go through an intermediary such as an import merchant, commission house, agent, broker, or wholesaler. You can be that intermediary.

As with exports, many companies are afraid to handle transportation, documentation, and finance when dealing with suppliers overseas. Again, if you select products and study the market well, you can find many opportunities to profit from products you sell to both the consumer and the industrial markets.

Now before you learn about selecting products, studying markets, and proceeding through proper channels, you should do a bit of self-examination. The next section will help you focus that examination.

Preparing Yourself to Be an Importer/Exporter

Like other trades, the import/export business makes certain demands upon its practitioners. Some of them, like initiative, responsibility, and problem-solving, it makes in common with other businesses. Others are special. The greater your needs and desires for success, the more important all these qualities become.

Before you make a firm decision to start your own import/export firm, you should consider whether your personality can deal both with the problems of starting any new business and with the unique demands of international trade.

Below is a questionnaire. Read it carefully, and try to test yourself objectively. The test isn't very scientific. It is only meant to make you think about yourself and your basic nature. After rating yourself, ask a friend to have you rated anonymously by several people who know you—people who can and will evaluate you objectively. The results may startle you, but consider them seriously. Remember: you are considering risking your money and your time; you are considering making contractual promises to others. You are starting something, and you should be able to finish it.

Rating Scale for the Potential Importer/Exporter

Instructions: After each question, place a check mark on the line at the point closest to your answer. The mark doesn't have to be directly over an answer because your rating may lie somewhere between two answers. Be honest with yourself.

1. Are you a self-starter?

I do things my own way. Nobody needs to tell me to get going.	If someone gets me started, I keep going all right.	Easy does it. I don't put myself out unless I have to.

2. Can you stick with it?

If I make up my mind to do something, I don't let anything stop me.	I usually finish what I start.	If a job doesn't go right, I turn off. Why beat your brains out?

3. How good an organizer are you?

I like to have a plan before I start. I'm usually the one to get things lined up.	I do all right unless things get too goofed up. Then I cop out.	I just take things as they come.

4. Can you take responsibility?

I like to take charge of and see things through.	I'll take over if I have to, but I'd rather let someone else be responsible.	There's always some eager beaver around wanting to show off. I say let him.

5. Can you make decisions?

I can make up my mind in a hurry if necessary, and my decision is usually ok.	I can if I have plenty of time. If I have to make up my mind fast, I usually regret it.	I don't like to be the one who decides things. I'd probably blow it.

6. Can people trust what you say?

They sure can. I don't say things I don't mean.	I try to be on the level, but sometimes I just say what's easiest.	What's the sweat if the other person doesn't know the difference?

7. Are you patient?

I have no difficulty hanging in there, without letting it bother me, until I get things straightened out. I can wait.	I'm ok with a minor delay now and again, but I can't stand foul-ups.	If things don't happen the way I expect them to right *now,* I get very upset.

8. Are you tactful?

I'm concerned about the other person's feelings and I'm particularly careful if another's background is different from mine.	I don't want to hurt anyone's feelings, but sometimes I do when I'm under pressure.	I don't always think, or care, about what I say.

9. Are you reasonably imaginative?

I often think up new, effective ways to get things done.	Once in a while I have a good idea.	I expect others to think of a new or different approach.

10. Are you interested in foreign affairs?

I regularly read about international events in news and business publications.	I listen to the 6 o'clock news and sometimes I'm conscious of international situations.	I think the most important events are right here at home—foreign affairs don't interest me.

   You have completed the questionnaire. Are most of your check marks on the left-hand side of the page? That's where they should be. But look them over carefully and be sure none of them is on the left-hand side because of wishful thinking. Compare your answers with those given by the people who know you. If you have weak points, admit to them. You may be able to compensate by training yourself or by obtaining help from a source outside yourself. But if you are weak in too many traits, self-employment and the import/export business are probably not for you.

Now let's consider why some of these qualities are important.

The first six items on the questionnaire deal with *drive,* which has been isolated as an important component of success in any business. Drive is made up of responsibility, vigor, initiative, and perseverence. If you desire to do so, you can develop the drive and the personal capacities that will help you improve your effectiveness and increase your chances of success. Much of the development of such drive depends on setting goals for yourself. That is, you must decide specifically how successful you want to be ("I'll make $10,000 from the new business next year"; "By June 30, I'll convince that manufacturer to let me export his products.") The chapters that follow will help you to define reasonable goals in the import/ export business.

The next four items on the questionnaire deal with the additional qualities needed by the importer/exporter. They are patience, tact, imagination, and an interest in foreign affairs.

Patience heads the list of special qualities. In shepherding merchandise to its destination, you will often enough deal with mail delays, poor routing, strikes, and revolutions, any of which can thoroughly test your reserves of entrepreneurial grit. You may also line up an excellent prospect—say a Japanese customer for yachts— only to discover a requirement your U.S. manufacturer can't meet or can't certify— Japan requires that all pleasure boats eligible for importation be able to withstand a drop of 20 feet. You must be calm enough not to develop a nervous tic because a shipment is late or lose your temper with the Japanese authority who explains to you the standards for imported pleasure boats.

Tact, as well as patience, will serve you well in the import/export business. In most transactions, you will be dealing with overseas agents and suppliers whom you've never met. This lack of a close relationship—you can't just drop by to discuss an order—can sometimes cause misunderstandings. Also, you will be dealing with businessmen from other cultures that have standards and customs very different from the ones with which you grew up. Misunderstandings can result from a cultural distance as well as from a physical one, and you must be alert to this danger and take steps to ward it off.

You will also need a dose of *imagination.* Difficulties in exporting to one part of the world may create possibilities for importing from that area. Reevaluation of currencies, changes in governments, and war all contribute a variety of unique circumstances offering profit potential to the imaginative trader. You must be able to analyze a changing marketplace and adapt your product and your selling approach to a variety of situations and potential customers. And sometimes you must have a talent for, as the saying goes, turning a lemon into lemonade.

To bolster your imagination, you need to keep up on the changing situations—that is, you need an *interest in foreign affairs.* For example, early in 1979, the deposal of the Shah of Iran and the ensuing economic collapse virtually halted business activity relating to Iran. In addition, it is quite common for countries in political and economic turmoil to put restrictions on currency. If you read about trouble in a certain area with which you are planning to do business, check with your local Department of Commerce office or with the international department of your bank—they will have the most up-to-date information.

In addition to listening to the news and reading magazines like *Time* or *Newsweek*, the new importer/exporter should become familiar with publications that tell more about the international business climate. These include: *Business Week*, the *Wall Street Journal*, the *New York Times*, and possibly the *Journal of Commerce*. These should be available in your local library, or you can subscribe to them; they will keep you well informed about world trade situations.

More specific information about import and export opportunities can be had from the *Trade Channel Magazines, Made in Europe*, and *Trade Opportunities in Taiwan*. Many other publications of this type could be useful to you, and you can review them at your local Department of Commerce office.

One thing that did *not* appear on the questionnaire was an item about *skill in a foreign language*. Perhaps you wondered about this omission; perhaps you have been worried that a foreign language was necessary and that you lacked it. You aren't alone. Americans on the whole have not been trained as linguists, and many, therefore, fear that their lack of knowledge of another language might prevent them from ever being successful in the import/export trade. Not true! Most transactions involving U.S. businessmen are carried out in English—residents of foreign countries are far better trained in languages than Americans are, and English is widely known. Another language can be helpful to you, but it is not necessary to your success as a trader. If you receive a request for information and the request is written in a foreign language, however, you must answer in that language. For this purpose, professional translation services are available in most large cities.

You have now considered the potential the import/export trade has to offer, and you have considered some of the qualities that you will have to possess or develop. You've decided you're made of the right raw material, and you'd like to explore the import/export business a bit further. Read on! Chapter 2 describes the first simple, inexpensive steps you must take to set up your new business.

Chapter Two

First Steps:
Setting Up Your Business

If you have never been in business for yourself before, you should read this chapter carefully. From the beginning, you want to impress your customers with your professionalism. You also want to set up your office and record-keeping in the most efficient ways possible, so they will help rather than hinder you as your business grows. The basic guidelines in this chapter can start you on the road to success before your first customer has signed a contract.

Establishing the Right Image

Because your business will be conducted almost exclusively through the mails, always use a conservatively designed letterhead—the simpler, the better. A sample letterhead appears in Figure 2-1. Include your company name (for example, XYX Trading Company, American Importing Company), address (including U.S.A. after the state), cable address, and bank. Generally, for overseas use, either 11 or 13 pound rag sheet, with *Air Mail* imprinted, is recommended.

The reason for using a light sheet is the high cost of mailing. Simulated parchment might look nice, but postage is expensive, and doubling the weight of your paper could double your postage costs. At this writing, air mail rates are 31¢ for the first one-half ounce outside of the U.S., Canada, and Mexico. For mail weighing above two ounces, the rate drops to 26¢ for each one-half ounce or fraction of each one-half ounce. In Central America, Bermuda, the Bahamas, Columbia, Venezuela, the Caribbean Islands, Miquelon, and St. Pierre, the rate is 25¢ per one-half ounce up to and including two ounces; then 21¢ for each additional half ounce. When calculating air mail charges, always figure any fraction of the next one-half ounce as a full ounce. Also buy a postage scale for convenience and to avoid excessive or insufficient postage. The amount of money saved will more than justify the cost.

Figure 2-1. Acceptable Letterhead

字 盛 股 份 有 限 公 司

Taiwan Develon Corporation

IMPORTER, EXPORTER, & AGENTS
2ND FL., 109 ROOSEVELT ROAD SEC. 2,
P. O. BOX 30-331 TAIPEI
TAIWAN, REPUBLIC OF CHINA

CABLE ADDRESS:
"DEVELONNS" TAIPEI
TELEPHONE
3415626, 3219627

In addition to lightweight airmail stationery, purchase a standard 20-pound white bond paper for domestic use. Buy small quantities of each type of stationery (no more than 1000 sheets and envelopes) because you will be adding the names of organizations and associations to your letterhead and will have to have your stationery regularly reprinted.

Always have your letters professionally typed if you cannot do an adequate job yourself. You will be judged as a company on the appearance and content of your letters since your business will be conducted through the mails. Be sure to discuss specific terminology or phrasing with your typist. Transactions have been terminated because of typing errors as simple as forgetting to put U.S. in front of the dollar ($) sign. In this example, the difference between the Hong Kong and the U.S. dollar is so great that a misunderstanding might cancel a deal for clothes or toys.

When buying your stationery, order 1000 business cards, conservatively designed like your letterhead. These will be of use to you when you call on local manufacturers or distributors, customs personnel, and shipping companies.

Also contact Western Union for a cable address. Airmail letters usually take up to two weeks for delivery. If you need an immediate reply, having a cable address is a great convenience for you and your customers.

Whether you have an office or use a room in your home, you should rent a post office box. This will safeguard your correspondence even though you will need to pick up your own mail. Your business will be through the mails, and any delayed or lost inquiries *can and will be costly*.

As your business develops, you should add a telex unit. This is a direct-line machine enabling you to receive and send messages to your overseas suppliers and agents. When you obtain a telex, you should add your telex number to your company letterhead.

If you are working out of your home, change your personal phone listing to a business listing, or order a second, business only, phone. You will then automatically have a free listing in the yellow pages. If you live in an area where many volumes of the yellow pages exist, place your firm's name in all of them. The price is relatively low and the exposure is beneficial.

Also subscribe to an answering service or buy an answering machine. Let your pocketbook dictate what you can afford. *Warning:* never have children or friends act as your service. As a new business, you *must* present a professional image.

Open a business checking and savings account under your new company's name. This will make it simpler to control expenses and receipts for tax purposes and to review the progress of the company. The Small Business Administration publishes several booklets on bookkeeping for new businesses. You should contact the SBA, obtain copies, and review them. Your accountant or banker can also provide sound advice on financial record keeping.

Organizing Your Filing System

Setting up a filing system is one of the keys to long-term success for the beginner. *It forces you to organize.*

Figure 2-2. Cross-Referenced File Cards

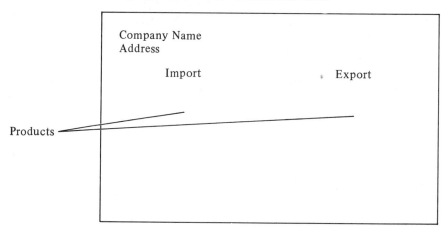

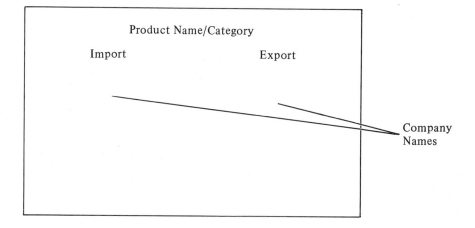

You begin with either a standard business desk with a file drawer, or a cardboard drawer from a stationery store. In the drawer, set up your folders by company for correspondence and price lists.

The next step is to cross-reference the company names and products. Purchase an index card box from a stationery store and set up the cards as shown in Figure 2-2.

Next, you should have storage facilities for samples. You don't need to rent a warehouse. Your facilities may consist of boxes, shelves, the hall closet, or anything else easy to organize. You should tag your samples with item number and supplier. This careful marking will make it easier to retrieve the specific article requested when an inquiry is received. You *must* have some way to pinpoint the whereabouts of your samples so that you do not needlessly waste time searching for them.

When you file a letter received from overseas, staple the envelope to it first. Foreign countries often have several towns with the same or similar names, and you may have to refer to the postmark to avoid confusion later. Postmarks also show foreign zip codes. Both envelope and foreign letterhead should show the special address sequence used in the originating country, since many countries use a different order than most Americans are accustomed to. Several sample addresses follow:

D-2000 Hamburg	(City)
Postfach 500749	(Post Office Box)
Holstenstrasse 224	(Street Address)
West Germany	(Country)
Electra House, Temple Place	(Street Address)
Victoria Embankment	(District)
London WC2R 3HP	(City, Zip Code)
England	(Country)
5-5 2-chome Minami-machi	(Street Address)
Mito, Ikasaki 310	(District, City)
Japan	(Country)

Finally, always keep a file copy of outgoing correspondence.

The guidelines set forth in this chapter apply to any business, not just the import/export business. It is essential, however, for you to consider them carefully, particularly if you have never before been in business for yourself, or if you have always depended upon another department to handle clerical duties. The next chapter discusses finding products to market. However, if your office procedures are poorly organized or nonexistent, even excellent, highly salable products can fail to bring you profits.

Chapter Three

Finding Products to Import and Export

Successful importing and exporting is really no more than matching products to markets. The extent to which you do this will determine your success as an import/export agent. Obviously it would be foolish to export a product if you have not considered its potential in the overseas market, and an excellent foreign market does you no good if you can't fill it with goods from the U.S. The same holds true for importing: an excellent product manufactured in Switzerland is of no benefit to you if you can't find a U.S. market for it, and an obvious consumer need in your neighborhood cannot be exploited without the right foreign market.

In finding products, then, you must explore general possibilities from both market and product aspects before you make specific decisions and follow them up with import/export contracts. If you promise a U.S. manufacturer that you will do your best to sell its products overseas, you should be fairly certain that you can, and you should be able to base your certainty on your knowledge of both the product and the foreign market. If you decide to import products to the U.S., you should know, again by your study of the product and the market, that you can sell the product profitably. In other words, you must do your homework—your market analysis—before you make commitments.

Matching Product to Market: The Importance of Market Research

Before you decide upon a product to import or export, you must prepare a market analysis to determine whether the product you are considering offers promise for profit. Or, if you have no specific product in mind, the analysis can show which products may be most profitable in which markets. Not every product can be successfully exported to every country. For instance, many foreign countries have domestic industries producing goods similar to those of U.S. manufactur-

14

ers. To protect these industries, the foreign country may use a high protective tariff, thereby making it unprofitable for you to export these goods to them. A market analysis can warn you, for example, not to export cuckoo clocks to the Black Forest area of Germany, where they are made, or watches to Switzerland. (The U.S. also restricts certain exports; see Chapter 12 for more information.)

There are many different types of information you should have before you make any kind of product decisions. You can begin in your local library. A list of some of the items you must research—and sources for those items—follows:

Information	*Examples of Sources*
Import statistics	United Nations, Organization for Economic Co-operation and Development (OECD) trade statistics; national trade statistics (from embassies).
Production statistics	Official statistical sources (from embassies), trade associations, *UN Statistical Yearbook* and *Monthly Bulletin of Statistics.*
Tariffs and quotas	Embassies, chambers of commerce.
Currency restrictions	Banks, embassies.
Sanitary restrictions	Embassies (consulates).
Political situation	Banks, press reports.
Economic situation	Banks, economic and financial journals and newspapers, IMF and OECD reports.
Consumption (of a product)	Official statistics, trade journals and commodity reviews, trade associations.
Identification of agents, importers, producers	Trade directories, trade associations, articles and advertisements in trade journals.
Information about specific companies	Banks, trade directories, press articles and advertising, company literature.
Credit terms	Banks.
Transport costs	Freight forwarders.
Packing requirements	Letters to purchasing offices of industrial users, to department store and supermarket buyers, to importers and so on.
Prices	Catalogues and price lists, advertising, trade press reports.
Features of competing products	Press advertising, catalogues and product literature, trade journal reports.
Leading trade journals	Press and media directories.
Population	Almanacs, statistical yearbooks.
Geographic features	Atlases, encyclopedias.

Once you have completed your basic studies and have narrowed down your product choices, you must look more closely at related *international trade and economic statistics.*

Why Do You Use Trade and Economic Statistics?

To do the type of market analysis you need for success in foreign trade, you must be able to understand and use trade and economic ststistics. Statistics can be extremely valuable in isolating attractive foreign markets. They are most useful for comparing several different markets for a particular product and for uncovering local conditions, such as high tariffs, that might prohibit profitable trade in that item.

It is very important that you be able to use statistics to answer these basic marketing questions:

1. Which products/services should be imported/exported to which country?

2. Are my import choices currently being sold to the U.S. or being manufactured here?

3. Which companies in my area are manufacturing my import choices? Does the local production of these goods prohibit their importation because locally made products offer too-strong competition?

4. Which countries offer the best markets for my export choices?

5. Are my export choices locally manufactured?

What Are Trade and Economic Statistics?

Statistics are not difficult to use, although a statistical compilation can be tedious and time consuming because of the quantity of data one must look through and decipher. Statistics are prepared by individual countries, groups within these countries, and regional and international organizations. By correctly analyzing statistics, one can find products for both importing and exporting. The following discussion will help you make the proper choices. (A section on the sources for statistical data is included in Appendix 12.)

There are two important types of statistics: *trade* and *economic.*

Trade statistics are totals (by quantities and/or monetary value and country of destination) of various product groups that move in international trade. They indicate which countries import significant quantities of your type of product and are, therefore, possible markets. They also indicate which countries export significant quantities of your type of products and are, therefore, the location of likely competitors for your markets.

If the statistics show a country that imports many products of your type, you should be encouraged for several reasons. First of all, *somebody* is buying the product. Second, because the country is buying imported products, its local producers are not effectively able to exclude outsiders (including U.S. traders, like you). Finally, that country's trade and other restrictions have not prohibited others from exporting to it, so there may be room for you, too.

Trade statistics can be very helpful in arriving at marketing decisions, but the importer/exporter must use them as a guide, not as a firm decision-maker.

Economic statistics provide data on important subjects besides imports and exports. These include population, income, industrial production by product category, consumption, appliance and automobile ownership, gold and foreign exchange reserves, and so forth. Economic statistics may be used to determine the location of consumers with a desired level of purchasing power and to locate countries where certain industries are well developed or where the consumption of certain products is significant. Like trade statistics, economic statistics don't always allow you to reach firm conclusions, but they can be valuable indicators.

Using Trade Statistics

The easiest method of using international trade statistics is by constructing an import/export grid. This grid identifies major importing countries and major exporting countries along one axis, and product categories along the other. The first step in preparing this grid is to obtain U.S. import/export figures for your product for perhaps the last three or four years. It is essential to consider statistics over a period at least this long to determine if any significant trends are present.

U.S. import/export statistics indicate the total amount, in U.S. dollars, of your product category which has been imported or exported for the years in question. A breakdown by country of origin or destination is given. From this breakdown, you will be able to determine which countries are importing from or exporting to the U.S. Figure 3–1 addresses U.S. exports of outboard motors.

Figure 3–2 illustrates a common grid, with exporters listed along the horizontal axis (across the top) and importers along the vertical axis (down the side). Many other configurations are possible, but for simplicity, this is a good model. The figures all refer to exports of sewing machines over a three-year period. Only those countries with significant dollar amounts are included; however, this Market Share Report from the Industry and Trade Administration of the U.S. Department of Commerce covered 14 principal exporting countries dealing in 90 foreign markets.

U.S. exporters captured varying percentages of the world markets, ranging from 5% to 25%. The fact that U.S. producers are supplying 5% or more to numerous markets illustrates the strength of the U.S.'s competitive position. From a high of 31% of Venezuela's imports to the 4% of Norway's, U.S.-exported sewing machines cover the globe.

In contrast, U.S. *importers* have bought most of their sewing machines from Japan (59%), followed by Italy (12%) and Germany (11%).

By checking these reports and others, the importer/exporter can determine not only several-year trends but also whether importing or exporting a particular product would be worthwhile.

This grid method is explained thoroughly in an International Trade Center booklet entitled *The Compilation of Basic Information on Export Markets,* sponsored by the General Agreement on Tariffs and Trade (GATT) in Geneva, Switzerland. (For ordering information, see "Guide to Information Sources," Appendix 12.) This manual illustrates about 30 different ways to analyze trade statistics, depending on your needs. It is a worthwhile introduction to this type of analysis and a useful addition to your library.

U.S. import/export figures are published by the Bureau of the Census in the form of numbered *Foreign Trade Reports,* issued monthly, with an annual supplement. The appropriate number is either FT-135 (U.S. imports) or FT-410 (U.S. exports), and a reference publication entitled *Schedule A* (for FT-135) or *Schedule E*

Figure 3–1. Exports of Outboard Motors from the United States, 1969

Country	Value ($000)	Country	Value ($000)
Canada	147	Spain	232
Mexico	1,021	Portugal	261
Guatemala	91	Malta	15
British Honduras	34	Italy	1,263
El Salvador	52	Yugoslavia	16
Honduras	41	Greece	87
Nicaragua	48	Turkey	55
Costa Rica	80	Cyprus	17
Panama	269	Iraq	19
Bermuda	29	Iran	26
Bahamas	405	Israel	19
Jamaica	184	Kuwait	33
Dominican Republic	44	Arabia	59
Leeward & Windward Is.	47	India	18
N. Antilles	118	Pakistan	75
French West Indies	172	Ceylon	109
Colombia	514	Thailand	50
Venezuela	1,364	Singapore	114
Guyana	52	Indonesia	224
Surinam	12	Philippines	158
French Guiana	66	Korea	40
Ecuador	90	Hong Kong	50
Peru	87	Japan	1,112
Bolivia	27	Australia	1,026
Chile	53	New Zealand	273
Brazil	991	Br. W. Pacific Is.	15
Paraguay	43	Fr. Pacific Is.	175
Uruguay	64	Tr. Terr. Pacific Is.	214
Argentina	799	Morocco	87
Sweden	2,259	Algeria	22
Norway	1,035	Ivory Coast	23
Finland	614	Ghana	100
Denmark	606	Nigeria	103
United Kingdom	866	Angola	59
Netherlands	479	Congo	86
Belgium	275	Ethiopia	22
France	1,209	Kenya	81
West Germany	999	Mozambique	92
Austria	129	Republic of South Africa	594
Switzerland	266	Zambia	41
		Other countries	174
		Total	23,129

Source: U.S. Department of Commerce, *Foreign Trade,* FT-410. December 1969.

Figure 3-2. United States Shares of Exports of Sewing Machines from 14 Supplier Countries to the World and to Selected Destinations, 1968 (in Percent of Total Import Market)

Destination	Total Exports from 14 Countries ($000)	United States	Japan	Germany	Italy	United Kingdom	Switzerland	Sweden	France	Netherlands	Other Reporting Countries
World	$343,676	10	33	24	12	9	6	2	2	1	1
United States	93,107	–	59	11	12	13	3	2	*	na†	*
Canada	15,407	32	26	7	5	26	5	1	*	na	–
Brazil	4,851	25	27	34	7	4	1	*	*	na	3
Costa Rica	486	52	19	11	3	5	11	na	1	na	*
Ecuador	935	6	55	10	24	4	1	1	*	na	–
Mexico	5,162	43	16	18	12	10	*	na	*	na	–
Venezuela	2,905	31	15	28	17	2	1	4	1	na	–
Belg./Lux.	7,709	11	11	27	13	2	15	2	2	16	*
France	23,332	7	6	56	13	6	10	*	–	2	1
Germany	21,238	13	35	–	16	10	7	2	5	9	4
Italy	13,452	9	1	76	–	5	3	*	1	3	1
Netherlands	10,408	12	19	45	9	2	5	4	1	na	3
United Kingdom	18,975	28	19	29	13	–	6	3	2	na	1
Denmark	3,427	6	22	32	8	6	14	9	1	na	1
Norway	3,738	4	1	23	8	3	20	40	*	na	2
Sweden	5,308	4	12	46	4	4	27	–	*	na	3
Austria	5,274	3	6	51	11	6	13	7	1	na	2
Switzerland	4,256	9	8	57	14	2	–	10	1	na	1
Ireland	2,044	10	27	17	3	43	1	*	*	na	–
Spain	3,516	11	2	49	20	9	5	*	2	na	3
Finland	3,005	4	1	31	18	9	11	24	*	na	2
USSR	3,356	1	24	18	48	1	*	na	9	na	–
Israel	1,527	17	28	31	11	2	7	na	2	na	1
Iran	3,382	1	49	21	15	7	5	1	1	na	1
Australia	9,203	13	33	13	6	15	18	2	1	na	*
So. Africa	6,663	15	25	19	16	8	11	1	5	na	*
Nigeria	988	1	29	12	30	14	*	*	12	na	*
Algeria	1,981	*	17	24	36	1	2	*	19	na	1
Japan	4,513	43	–	40	10	7	*	*	*	na	*
Malays/Sing.	2,289	3	74	7	5	10	1	*	*	na	–
Hong Kong	4,930	15	51	15	11	7	2	*	*	na	–
China (Taiwan)	4,044	2	91	2	3	*	2	na	na	na	–
Indonesia	1,102	1	97	1	na	1	*	na	na	na	–
Korea	3,312	5	89	4	1	na	1	*	na	na	*
Philippines	1,585	16	60	3	1	19	2	*	*	na	–
Thailand	2,685	2	72	16	1	15	*	na	na	na	*

Source: U.S. Department of Commerce, Market Share Report 70-90827, Commodity Series.
* Less than 1%.
† Not available or none.

(for FT-410) is the index *by* which you determine the numbered category that includes your type of product. These reports are on file in Department of Commerce field offices and in many libraries. They may be purchased on a subscription basis.

Your analysis should not end with a grid of U.S. imports/exports, for this can tell you nothing about those markets being served by exporters in other countries, particularly Western Europe and Japan. By using trade statistics from international organizations such as the Organization for Economic Cooperation and Development (OECD), 2 Rue André-Pascal, Paris 16, France, one can conduct two other types of analysis. The examples pictured in Figures 3-3 and 3-4, dealing with electromechanical hand tools, illustrate a form similar to the grid derived from the Foreign Trade Reports.

The first alternate analysis is to review U.S. imports of a product to see which countries are major exporters to the U.S. (use FT-135 reports, with *Schedule A*). Having obtained the names of countries exporting to the U.S., you can then assemble the export statistics of these countries to determine the other markets to which they are presently exporting. That is, a country exporting wicker baskets to the U.S. is a likely exporter of wicker baskets to other countries that import them.

Another approach is to obtain the import figures of those countries that import the greatest amounts of your product from the U.S. These import figures indicate the other countries serving the same markets. That is, if Sweden imports substantial quantities of canned fruit from the U.S., it is likely that Sweden also imports canned fruit from other countries that export it.

Problems with Trade Statistics

Although international trade statistics are extremely useful for identifying attractive products and markets and locating likely competitors, the difficulties and weaknesses of these figures warn against complete dependence on them. Consider the problems:

1. A number of categories of trade statistics both here and in foreign countries are simply too broad to be of value to anyone concerned with a specific product. Some import/export categories contain more than 100 different items, and producers of specialized products are likely to find such basket categories entirely useless. However, such figures can be used in reverse. That is, the absence of countries from such groups indicates the lack of a market.

2. Some countries do not publish trade statistics, and others are several years behind in issuing them.

3. Parts for both repair and assembly purposes are included with finished items in many categories. Such figures are likely to be misleading since a high percentage of the total may be parts destined for foreign assembly plants or to repair end items already in use.

4. Import/export figures are by necessity historical. They say nothing about new products, new marketing techniques, changes in trade restrictions, and other factors of importance. The results achieved by others may be a poor indication of your own trade possibilities.

5. Many exports are sent to free ports and foreign trade zones from which they are re-exported to other destinations. For example, Panama appears to be a much more significant market for U.S. products than it actually is because goods are shipped to the free port at Colon for shipment to other Central and South American markets.

However, in spite of the difficulties and weaknesses of using trade statistics, they are a valuable source of information for isolating attractive import/export markets and products.

Using Economic Statistics

A wide variety of economic statistics is available to aid the importer/exporter in preparing statistical profiles of one or more countries. The kinds of information required to construct a useful profile depends upon the particular product being exported or imported. For example:

1. An importer/exporter of items purchased by teenagers would be concerned about the size of the population by age group, per capita disposable income, and geographical distribution within a certain country; breakdowns in consumer spending among particular products; disposition of incremental income (additional income above basic expenses); and other economic statistics which may be obtained from a variety of sources.

2. The importer/exporter of coal mining machinery would be concerned about the levels of coal production, wage costs, fuel consumption, and so forth.

3. Other ways in which economic statistics may be used to isolate markets include using the number of wired homes to indicate the potential for electrical appliances and the number of motor vehicles to indicate the extent of the market for automotive accessories. (There is no sense in trying to sell electric hair driers in an area where homes have no electricity, or mag wheels to people who can afford only bicycles.)

The importer/exporter of consumer products should be extremely concerned with the disposition of incremental income—that is, how do people spend their extra money? The level of family purchasing power is rising rapidly throughout many parts of the world. Standards of living are rising and traditional spending patterns are being drastically altered. For example, one of the most obvious trends in shifting spending patterns is taking place in several European countries. Where families were content to use bicycles in the past, they switched to motor scooters several years ago and now many of these families are buying small automobiles. Even rising fuel costs have not offset the status of automobile ownership.

In other words, a certain level of spending on food, clothing, and housing is necessary to sustain a family. As family income rises above this basic level, expenditures on food, clothing, and housing are not increased proportionately. Instead, expenditures on appliances, automobiles, travel, and education are increased substantially or made for the first time.

Imports (c.i.f.)

Figure 3–3. Commodity Trade Data (Imports of Reporting Countries). Electro-Mechanical Hand Tools
Values (1000 U.S. Dollars)

Trade With	OECD Total	Canada	U.S.	Japan	OECD Europe	EEC	Belgium-Lux.	Netherlands	Germany	France	Italy	EFTA	United Kingdom
World	137029	26774	8547	2268	99440	58342	8014	8346	15935	20036	6011	34512	5047
OECD Total	*135337*	*26740*	*8466*	*2259*	*97872*	*58017*	*7915*	*8286*	*15881*	*19939*	*5996*	*33567*	*4225*
Canada	3215	–	3100	60	55	17	–	5	10	2	–	38	6
United States	30754	23272	–	1352	6130	4061	493	716	1032	1413	407	1598	689
Japan	5362	464	2817	–	2081	1327	37	306	398	370	216	594	353
OECD Europe	*96006*	*3004*	*2549*	*847*	*89606*	*52612*	*7385*	*7259*	*14441*	*18154*	*5373*	*31337*	*3177*
EEC	57559	653	1680	504	54722	30901	5792	4917	2115	13759	4318	20214	2126
EFTA	38294	2351	863	343	34737	21651	1592	2340	12318	4346	1055	11039	1003
Austria	363	10	–	2	351	212	5	41	159	5	2	136	3
Belgium/Lux.	622	–	–	1	621	537	–	308	98	109	22	64	6
Denmark	187	–	1	–	186	33	11	7	13	2	–	148	5
France	1604	8	2	1	1593	1048	558	107	295	–	88	205	68
Germany	43301	632	1671	398	40600	22613	4414	4019	–	10082	4098	15562	1523
Ireland	39	–	5	–	34	2	1	1	–	–	–	29	29
Italy	6368	3	4	104	6257	3115	258	483	1158	1216	–	2453	234
Netherlands	5664	10	3	–	5651	3588	562	–	564	2352	110	1930	295
Spain	113	–	1	–	112	58	–	1	8	49	–	54	18
Sweden	1103	130	104	2	867	440	30	63	192	71	84	374	41
Switzerland	17867	241	473	44	17109	12593	477	567	7871	2838	820	3846	951
United Kingdom	18713	1958	284	294	16177	8363	1067	1637	4082	1430	147	6498	–
Other Countries	62	12	1	1	48	10	2	5	1	2	2	38	4
Non-OECD Total	*1692*	*34*	*83*	*11*	*1564*	*323*	*98*	*59*	*54*	*98*	*14*	*941*	*818*
Sino-Soviet	648	–	–	–	648	301	98	59	45	93	6	50	4
USSR	52	–	–	–	52	16	7	–	–	4	5	–	–
Germany Sov. Zone	288	–	–	–	288	152	45	57	–	50	–	16	–
Poland	47	–	–	–	47	3	–	–	3	–	–	–	–
Czechoslovakia	244	–	–	–	244	129	46	2	41	39	1	31	1
Other Countries	17	–	–	–	17	1	–	–	1	–	–	3	3

Aust/N. Zeal/S. Afr.	*45*	–	–	*11*	*34*	*4*	–	–	*1*	–	*3*	*30*	*30*
Other Countries	45	–	–	11	34	4	–	–	1	–	3	30	30
Less dev. non-OECD	*999*	*34*	*83*	–	*882*	*18*	–	–	*8*	*5*	*5*	*861*	*784*
Yugoslavia	87	–	–	–	87	3	–	–	–	–	3	84	12
India	431	34	1	–	396	–	–	–	–	–	–	396	396
China Taiwan	27	–	27	–	–	–	–	–	–	–	–	–	–
Hong Kong	430	–	55	–	375	–	–	–	–	–	–	372	367
Other Countries	24	–	–	–	24	15	–	–	8	5	2	9	9

Figure 3–3 (continued). Commodity Trade Data (Imports of Reporting Countries). Electro-Mechanical Hand Tools Values (1000 U.S. Dollars) Imports (c.i.f.)

Trade With	Norway	Sweden	Denmark	Finland	Austria	Switzer-land	Portugal	Iceland	Ireland	Spain	Greece	Turkey	Yugo-slavia
World	2273	7163	5775	1526	5106	6095	1527	77	816	3609	1547	537	1626
OECD Total	*2273*	*7147*	*5772*	*1525*	*5080*	*6021*	*1524*	*77*	*815*	*3607*	*1521*	*268*	*1535*
Canada	–	3	19	10	–	–	–	–	–	–	–	–	–
United States	43	145	94	49	88	447	43	9	10	315	86	51	6
Japan	7	68	50	23	17	70	6	–	4	76	70	10	4
OECD Europe	*2223*	*6931*	*5609*	*1443*	*4975*	*5504*	*1475*	*68*	*801*	*3216*	*1365*	*207*	*1525*
EEC	1406	3435	2898	861	3734	4696	1058	11	167	2203	1062	164	1189
EFTA	817	3496	2711	582	1241	808	381	57	634	1010	303	43	336
Austria	1	–	1	–	–	130	1	–	1	1	1	–	23
Belgium/Lux.	–	1	3	7	14	31	2	–	6	2	–	12	23
Denmark	63	41	–	8	5	6	20	1	–	1	3	–	–
France	4	2	3	15	8	37	68	–	–	254	76	10	1
Germany	1177	2751	2093	520	2838	4075	585	9	146	1555	616	99	1064
Ireland	–	–	–	–	–	–	–	–	–	3	–	–	–
Italy	63	400	468	110	519	270	389	–	3	339	316	31	77
Netherlands	162	281	331	209	355	283	14	2	12	53	54	12	24
Spain	–	–	–	–	–	–	36	–	–	–	–	–	–
Sweden	26	–	157	63	29	53	5	1	5	25	3	19	18
Switzerland	253	935	814	190	626	–	77	2	31	554	75	8	270
United Kingdom	473	2493	1735	321	580	618	278	53	597	429	221	16	25
Other Countries	1	27	4	–	1	1	–	–	–	–	–	–	–
Non-OECD Total	–	*16*	*2*	*1*	*27*	*74*	*3*	–	*3*	*4*	*25*	*268*	*89*
Sino-Soviet	–	15	2	–	27	2	–	–	–	4	25	268	89
USSR	–	–	–	–	–	–	–	–	–	–	1	25	13
Germany Sov. Zone	–	3	1	–	11	1	–	–	–	–	13	107	70
Poland	–	–	–	–	–	–	–	–	–	–	8	36	1
Czechoslovakia	–	12	1	–	16	1	–	–	–	4	3	77	5
Other Countries	–	–	–	–	–	–	–	–	–	–	–	13	–

Aust./N. Zeal/S. Afr.	—	—	—	—	—	—	—	—	—	—	—	—	—
Other Countries	—	—	—	—	—	—	—	—	—	—	—	—	—
Less dev. non-OECD	1	1	—	72	—	3	—	3	—	3	—	—	—
Yugoslavia	—	—	—	72	—	—	—	—	—	—	—	—	—
India	—	—	—	—	—	—	—	—	—	—	—	—	—
China Taiwan	—	—	—	—	—	—	—	—	—	—	—	—	—
Hong Kong	1	1	—	—	—	3	—	3	—	3	—	—	—
Other Countries	—	—	—	—	—	—	—	—	—	—	—	—	—

Exports (f.o.b.)

Figure 3-4. Commodity Trade Data (Exports of Reporting Countries). Electro-Mechanical Hand Tools Values (1000 U.S. Dollars)

Trade With	OECD Total	Canada	United States	Japan	OECD Europe	EEC	Belgium-Lux.	Netherlands	Germany	France	Italy	EFTA	United Kingdom
World	158137	3441	23549	9163	121984	74807	569	6482	58115	2680	6961	46946	21629
OECD Total	125835	3273	15838	4784	101940	63170	546	6028	49738	1515	5343	38623	16226
Canada	12757	–	10790	46	1921	787		–	778	3	6	1134	892
United States	11383	3191	–	3603	4589	2150	8	19	2095	7	21	2418	390
Japan	2163	43	1080	–	1040	733	–	–	663	–	70	307	273
OECD Europe	99532	39	3968	1135	94390	59500	538	6009	46202	1505	5246	34764	14671
EEC	60016	6	2518	733	56759	33577	478	3885	25317	1008	2889	23120	9045
EFTA	33519	33	1237	260	31989	22205	49	2006	18151	180	1819	9720	4605
Austria	6014	–	52	10	5952	4479	3	420	3558	13	485	1473	719
Belgium/Lux.	7966	1	294	28	7643	5894	–	547	4584	502	261	1749	1243
Denmark	5081	–	66	10	5005	3039	4	301	2541	1	192	1966	861
Finland	1679	–	13	19	1647	925	–	215	630	6	74	722	336
France	20605	1	429	262	19913	15355	156	2660	11430	–	1109	4510	1652
Germany	15890	1	528	207	15154	2145	102	574	–	343	1126	12997	3908
Greece	1302	–	30	59	1213	930	–	48	563	72	247	283	189
Ireland	689	–	1	–	688	189	2	18	167	2	–	499	445
Italy	6024	1	50	213	5760	4756	3	104	4588	61	–	1002	128
Netherlands	9531	2	1217	23	8289	5427	217	–	4715	102	393	2862	2114
Norway	2538	–	16	–	2522	1601	–	138	1420	1	42	921	444
Portugal	1371	–	11	1	1359	937	1	13	654	63	206	390	274
Spain	3617	–	134	78	3405	2389	1	50	1855	229	254	1016	312
Sweden	6316	1	115	27	6173	3593	–	314	2988	11	280	2580	1444
Switzerland	6215	1	202	32	5980	5350	37	376	4614	49	274	629	527
Turkey	318	–	47	5	266	204	8	1	145	14	36	62	18
United Kingdom	4305	31	762	161	3351	2281	4	229	1746	36	266	1039	–
Other countries	71	–	1	–	70	6	–	1	4	–	1	64	57
Non-OECD Total	32232	165	7713	4378	19976	11577	23	453	8377	1165	1559	8316	5400
Sino-Soviet	1348	–	–	12	1336	1074	1	24	763	8	278	262	67

Poland	211	—	—	—	211	157	—	1	46	1	109	54	36
Czechoslovakia	647	—	—	—	647	530	—	1	507	1	21	117	28
Other countries	490	—	12	—	478	387	1	22	210	6	148	91	3
Aust./N. Zeal/S. Afr.	*9438*	*85*	*1058*	*1576*	*6719*	*2820*	*1*	*203*	*2203*	*28*	*385*	*3880*	*2842*
Australia	3790	54	604	550	2582	1134	—	126	815	—	193	1433	1027
New Zealand	975	17	165	122	671	160	—	14	146	28	192	511	477
South Africa	4673	14	289	904	3466	1526	1	63	1242	—	—	1936	1338
Less dev. non-OECD	*21446*	*80*	*3308*	*6137*	*11921*	*7683*	*21*	*226*	*5411*	*1129*	*896*	*4174*	*2491*
Yugoslavia	1947	—	1	8	1938	1364	—	45	1240	2	77	574	13
Algeria	391	—	—	—	391	316	—	2	55	246	13	75	6
Angola	216	—	2	15	199	98	—	2	53	19	24	101	67
Kenya	232	—	1	19	212	32	—	4	23	—	5	180	177
Mexico	1808	3	15	1319	471	318	—	—	311	—	7	153	31
Jamaica	225	28	—	126	71	—	—	—	—	—	—	71	71
Br. Terr Am.Nes	247	6	—	175	66	14	—	—	31	14	14	52	52
Colombia	521	—	—	441	80	31	—	—	—	—	—	43	3
Venezuela	1300	5	10	1006	279	224	—	4	171	1	48	49	10
Peru	198	—	13	108	77	47	—	1	31	10	5	30	20
Brazil	1781	—	48	652	1081	858	—	2	785	—	71	223	98
Chile	437	—	18	151	268	168	—	—	138	21	9	96	79
Argentina	908	—	18	336	554	330	—	6	216	23	86	223	183
Thailand	1155	—	895	63	197	116	—	—	109	1	6	81	50
Malaysia	228	—	126	12	90	39	—	2	27	5	5	51	19
Singapore	315	—	111	13	191	84	—	1	69	1	13	107	94
South Korea	509	—	409	77	23	19	—	—	16	3	—	4	—
China Taiwan	1005	—	958	27	20	19	—	—	19	—	14	1	1
Hong Kong	498	—	131	79	288	143	—	12	110	7	—	145	90
Philippines	309	—	78	116	115	55	—	—	55	—	60	60	54
Israel	902	4	48	116	734	397	2	53	265	17	86	337	229
Iran	822	—	20	31	771	660	1	1	569	3	—	111	49
US Dep.-Oceania	160	—	144	16	—	—	—	—	—	—	—	—	—
Other countries	5332	34	262	1231	3805	2351	18	91	1119	770	353	1407	1095

Figure 3-4 (continued). Commodity Trade Data (Exports of Reporting Countries). Electro-Mechanical Hand Tools Exports (f.o.b.). Values (1000 U.S. Dollars)

Trade With	Norway	Sweden	Denmark	Finland	Austria	Switzerland	Portugal	Iceland	Ireland	Spain	Greece	Turkey	Yugoslavia
World	36	1682	292	16	324	22918	49	—	NA	231	—	—	112
OECD Total	*33*	*1329*	*281*	*16*	*249*	*20456*	*33*	—	—	*147*	—	—	*86*
Canada	—	9	—	—	—	233	—	—	—	—	—	—	—
United States	—	26	1	—	2	1999	—	—	—	21	—	—	—
Japan	2	22	—	—	—	10	—	—	—	—	—	—	—
OECD Europe	*31*	*1272*	*280*	*16*	*247*	*18214*	*33*	—	—	*126*	—	—	*86*
EEC	3	553	60	8	192	13226	33	—	—	62	—	—	84
EFTA	28	626	217	8	52	4184	—	—	—	64	—	—	2
Austria	1	44	3	1	—	705	—	—	—	—	—	—	—
Belgium/Lux.	—	29	5	—	1	472	—	—	—	—	—	—	—
Denmark	4	208	—	1	—	891	—	—	—	—	—	—	—
Finland	1	156	35	—	15	194	—	—	—	—	—	—	—
France	—	57	3	—	—	2783	—	—	—	48	—	—	—
Germany	2	316	41	5	162	8533	30	—	—	12	—	—	—
Greece	—	14	2	—	1	77	—	—	—	—	—	—	—
Ireland	—	—	—	—	—	54	—	—	—	—	—	—	—
Italy	1	29	6	1	1	837	—	—	—	2	—	—	—
Netherlands	1	122	5	2	14	601	3	—	—	—	—	—	—
Norway	—	125	66	1	1	284	—	—	—	—	—	—	—
Portugal	—	4	1	—	1	110	—	—	—	32	—	—	—
Spain	—	46	—	—	2	656	—	—	—	—	—	—	—
Sweden	19	—	106	4	3	1004	—	—	—	—	—	—	—
Switzerland	1	57	3	1	40	—	—	—	—	1	—	—	82
Turkey	—	28	—	—	—	16	—	—	—	—	—	—	2
United Kingdom	2	32	3	—	6	995	—	—	—	31	—	—	—
Other Countries	—	5	1	—	—	1	—	—	—	—	—	—	—
Non-OECD Total	*4*	*351*	*10*	—	*71*	*2465*	*15*	—	—	*83*	—	—	*26*
Sino-Soviet	—	24	—	—	58	113	—	—	—	—	—	—	—

Poland	—	10	—	—	4	4	—	—	—	—	—	—	—	—
Czechoslovakia	—	8	—	—	35	46	—	—	—	—	—	—	—	—
Other Countries	—	6	—	—	19	63	—	—	—	—	—	—	—	—
Aust/N. Zeal/S. Afr.	—	43	—	—	—	995	—	—	—	*19*	—	—	—	—
Australia	—	39	—	—	—	367	—	—	—	*15*	—	—	—	—
New Zealand	—	—	—	—	—	34	—	—	—	4	—	—	—	—
South Africa	—	4	—	—	—	594	—	—	—	4	—	—	—	*26*
Less dev. non-OECD	4	284	10	—	13	1357	15	—	—	*64*	—	—	—	—
Yugoslavia	—	117	—	—	5	439	—	—	—	—	—	—	—	—
Algeria	—	11	—	—	—	58	—	—	—	—	—	—	—	—
Angola	—	1	—	—	—	21	12	—	—	—	—	—	—	—
Kenya	—	—	—	—	—	3	—	—	—	—	—	—	—	—
Mexico	—	14	—	—	—	108	—	—	—	—	—	—	—	—
Jamaica	—	—	—	—	—	—	—	—	—	—	—	—	—	—
Br. Terr Am.Nes	—	—	—	—	—	—	—	—	—	—	—	—	—	5
Colombia	—	1	—	—	—	39	—	—	—	6	—	—	—	—
Venezuela	—	—	2	—	—	37	—	—	—	6	—	—	—	—
Peru	—	—	—	—	—	10	—	—	—	—	—	—	—	—
Brazil	—	8	—	—	—	117	—	—	—	4	—	—	—	—
Chile	—	1	—	—	—	16	—	—	—	1	—	—	—	—
Argentina	—	3	—	—	—	37	—	—	—	—	—	—	—	—
Thailand	—	13	—	—	3	16	—	—	—	—	—	—	—	—
Malaysia	—	7	—	—	—	25	—	—	—	—	—	—	—	—
Singapore	—	2	1	—	—	11	—	—	—	—	—	—	—	—
South Korea	—	3	—	—	—	—	—	—	—	—	—	—	—	—
China Taiwan	—	—	—	—	—	42	—	—	—	—	—	—	—	—
Hong Kong	—	10	3	—	—	4	—	—	—	—	—	—	—	—
Philippines	—	2	—	—	—	103	—	—	—	—	—	—	—	—
Israel	—	4	1	—	—	46	—	—	—	—	—	—	—	—
Iran	—	15	1	—	—	—	—	—	—	—	—	—	—	3
US Dep.-Oceania	—	—	—	—	—	—	—	—	—	—	—	—	—	—
Other Countries	4	72	2	—	5	226	3	—	—	47	—	—	—	18

Therefore, importers/exporters of basic items such as food and clothing will not benefit from rising consumer incomes to the same extent as will importers/exporters of products suddenly in demand. In some cases, the explosion of demand in Western Europe will outstrip local production capacity, leaving at least temporary openings for exporters.

Product Considerations

The number of goods from which you as an importer/exporter can pick is virtually limitless. You may choose a specific product because you are familiar with it (perhaps you are an amateur chef who is knowledgeable about small kitchen implements) or because you live near a manufacturer (perhaps your home is across town from a manufacturer of phonograph records). Possibly your market analysis boded ill for kitchen implements and you must seek a different product, or possibly you had no product in mind until the market analysis suggested one to you. There are many reasons for choosing the product you do. Following are some considerations that have proven successful for many importers/exporters.

1. *Specialize.* In the past, individuals have tried to import/export items on a one-shot basis. They would trade in any or all types of goods and commodities. Generally, this proved disastrous because of a lack of expertise both in the goods and in their handling. Therefore, I suggest that you select your products with an eye to specialization. Plan on trading in one general type of merchandise (small kitchen implements, cutlery, and pots and pans would be one example of a workable group of products; you might be unwise, however, to try to mix cutlery and automobile accessories).

Specializing in a particular product or commodity also helps develop your reputation. If you have a good reputation, your name will be recognized throughout the industry. People will seek *you* out to represent their lines. You must avoid, however, handling products that are direct competitors—it is difficult, if not impossible, to treat the manufacturers of these products with equal fairness, and your reputation will suffer.

2. *Know your product line.* It is much easier to deal in materials with which you are familiar. Intimate knowledge of the best way to pack, ship, and market a certain product can benefit profits greatly.

3. *Work with local organizations.* As an exporter, you wish to provide a great deal of personal service to the manufacturers you represent; therefore, do not contact firms outside of your area. As an importer, you can build up contacts for your products by using local distributors.

4. *Stay small.* An individual starting out is usually better off dealing with small- to medium-sized manufacturers of light industrial or consumer goods. Stay away from large companies initially (Ford, General Foods, Texaco, etc.) because most have their own export departments or overseas subsidiaries. Any company already having overseas sales that comprise 15% to 20% of their total sales volume does not need your services.

Also, do not contact agricultural co-ops, weapons manufacturers, or sophisticated electronics equipment companies. Generally, their products require special export licenses, large amounts of capital, and a large network of support personnel.

5. *Consider yourself.* Whether you are importing or exporting, your individual circumstances should guide you. Everyone has special abilities and experiences that lend themselves to certain product categories. For example, if you are an electronics technician, you might consider dealing in consumer electronic products or possibly electronic testing equipment. On the other hand, never avoid a product category only because you aren't familiar with it. Your main job as an import/export agent is distributing and selling the goods—you can buy any technical expertise you need.

Let your marketing research be your first guide—let the public library, the U.S. Department of Commerce, and the local university dictate your final product choice.

6. *Choose either consumer or technical products.* Whether you choose to deal in consumer products or industrial goods, the basic techniques (documentation, financing, etc.) are the same for both importing and exporting. Any differences are dictated by the product itself. A fashion item may have a limited retail sales life; certain frozen foods have limited shelf lives, thereby necessitating special shipping and handling; highly technical items may require special repair facilities or, as with fashion goods, may have a limited sales life because rapid innovations in technology make them obsolete. Data processing equipment provides an example of this latter situation.

Product Potential Checklist

In doing your research, you should consider the following checklist for estimating import/export product potential. You should carefully review each item on this list as it pertains to the product or products you are considering.

Domestic market trade regulations. (Chapter 11 discusses controls, licenses, and documentation in more detail.)
- Country restrictions
- Currency and tax regulations
- Licensing and other requirements

Foreign market access. (This information can be found in country reports such as the *Overseas Business Reports*.)
- Tariffs and quotas of importing countries
- Currency restrictions
- Internal taxes
- Political factors

Foreign competition. (*Country Market Sectional Surveys* and *Global Market Surveys* will provide most of this information.)
- Domestic production, volume, and growth
- Reasons for success
- Strengths (size, special advantages)

Market size, pattern, and growth.   Again, refer to *Country Market Sectional Surveys* and *Global Market Surveys*.)

Price structure.   (For more information, write to U.S. embassies overseas and talk with international freight forwarders.)
- Prices to end users
- Trade markups
- Transport costs

Help in the Product/Market Search: The U.S. Department of Commerce

The U.S. Department of Commerce can assist both in analyzing markets and selecting products. It offers American exporters the world's best array of trade information services. The Department has assembled, for the convenience of business, three general classifications of international business information: foreign individual or company, product, and country. The information you need is available from the Trade and Industry Administration, an agency of the Department of Commerce. (A list of U.S. Department of Commerce district offices appears as Appendix 1.)

Importers/exporters requiring help should not hesitate to call the local office. Anyone who has never visited the local field office should do so and should ask the trade specialist to show samples of the wide variety of information kept available in the local files. For example, the following material is available:

Country Market Sectoral Surveys.   These in-depth reports cover the most salable products (10 to 15, usually) in a single foreign country. About 15 leading industrial sectors are considered, and information on about 50 leading markets is included. This report is extremely valuable for newcomers to exporting.

Global Market Surveys.   These are in-depth reports that cover up to 30 of the best foreign markets for a single U.S. industry. Each survey condenses extensive market research into individual country market summaries.

Market Share Reports.   These reports give a statistical picture of international trade in manufactured products, covering more than three-quarters of the total exported output of all free-world factories. They show trends in the movement of goods between countries over a period of several years. They also include data on imports of more than 1100 commodities by more than 90 countries and reflect both changing levels of these countries' import demand and shifts in the relative competitive position of exporting countries.

FT-410 (U.S. Exports) and Schedule E (Index).   From these monthly reports, you can learn which of some 169 countries have bought any of more than 3000 U.S. products. By checking U.S. exports or products for three or four years, you can determine which countries have the largest and most consistent markets. In some instances, the FT-410 statistics will also give you an indication of the average price for the product in a given market. All information is organized by Schedule E groupings (commodities by value and quantity).

Country Market Surveys. These are detailed and penetrating studies of the scope of the market for U.S. products in a country. They include banking, financial structure, natural resources, development, distribution facilities, industrial establishment, and trade practices. They also cover commodities analysis for that country.

Information about U.S. exports alone is not enough for a preliminary assessment. You must compare U.S. and foreign competition in the marketplace. Therefore, by using both *Market Share Reports* and the FT-410 series, you can select the best prospects for export, check to see where the product is manufactured (locally or not), and then decide whether it is feasible to market that product.

On the other hand, by analyzing these same reports, you might eliminate products you are considering *importing*. In actuality, these reports give you the total view of where products are going and our share of them.

Remember: All trade statistics are recapitulations of past history—they tell what *has* happened. The most current information can be had from your local U.S. Department of Commerce field office.

Other reports of interest available from the Department of Commerce include:

- *Commerce Business Daily* and *Business America*
- Foreign economic trends and their implications for the U.S.
- *Overseas Business Reports*
- Trade lists

Other Sources of Information

There are also several directories, available in your local library, that can be most helpful in locating producers of export products and purchasers/distributors of import products:

Thomas Register of American Manufacturers. Thomas Publishing Company, 1 Penn Plaza, New York, New York 10001.

National Directories for Use in Marketing. U.S. Small Business Administration, Washington District Office, Suite 250, 1030 15th St., N.W., Washington, D.C. 20417, and other SBA offices.

Midwest Manufacturers and Industrial Directory. Industrial Directory Publishers, Park Avenue Building, Detroit, Michigan 48226.

MacRae's Blue Book. MacRae's Blue Book Company, 100 Shore Drive, Hinfale, Illinois 60521.

If you follow the guidelines set forth in this chapter, making liberal use of data from informed individuals, organizations, trade and economic statistics, and the U.S. Department of Commerce, you should be able to assemble a short, workable list of products and a list of countries which seem to offer attractive prospects for those products.

Chapter Four

Importing/Exporting: Getting Started

Once you have chosen your products carefully, you must proceed through the right channels. Your next step is to establish those channels—to contact overseas agents and domestic manufacturers. Your ability to convince manufacturers that you can sell their products profitably will, to a great extent, determine your success in obtaining products to export. Similarly, to be successful with imports, you must display an ability to sell to local distributors.

You have completed your market research and have summed it up by making a list of the goods, with matching countries, that appear to offer the most potential for your import/export business. Now, next to each export product on your list, write the names of manufacturers that produce these products in your area, noting particularly any new firms. Generally, new companies are more apt to let you handle their overseas sales because they lack knowledgeable personnel and they need as many sales as they can get. (A good source for a list of new local companies is the local city or county clerk's office; most such offices sell lists of newly established businesses.) Then, next to each import product, list the names of distributors. You are now ready to solicit business actively by means of an international and domestic letter-writing campaign.

Making Overseas Contacts

Figure 4–1 shows a good example of a first-contact letter. *Be sure to indicate product categories you are interested in importing/exporting.* Send this letter to the chambers of commerce of all the countries in the world, and also write to local bi-national chambers of commerce, such as the American-Israeli Chamber of Commerce. (Your local chamber of commerce can supply names and addresses.) In addition, send letters to commercial attaches of foreign embassies (located in New York and in Washington, D.C.) and commercial attaches of U.S. embassies (obtain names and addresses from your local U.S. Department of Commerce field office).

Figure 4-1. Sample Text for First Contact Letter

Your letterhead
Date

Director
Chamber of Commerce (or U.N., Trade Association, etc.)
(City)
(Country)

Dear Sir:

As an export-import firm involved in many aspects of international
trade, we want to establish mutually profitable working arrangements
with similar businesses in (name of city). We deal primarily in (product
categories).

We would appreciate your supplying us with names and addresses of
appropriate firms who could represent us there, as we would represent
them in the United States.

Please publish a notice of our interest and offer in your next Chamber
of Commerce bulletin. This would also be appreciated.

Thank you for your generous assistance.

Sincerely Yours,

Finally, contact trade associations you feel would be important (see *Encyclopedia of Associations,* Gale Research Company, 700 Book Tower, Detroit, Michigan 48226). You might also contact the United Nations to learn of current projects or programs where bids are requested. (Send for the *Business Bulletin,* published monthly by the U.N.'s Development Program. It lists current opportunities for contractors. For detailed information on procedures and background for doing business with the U.N., ask for the "Guide to Firms and Organizations.")

You can reach some firms directly by answering ads in magazines and journals, such as *Business America, Trade Channel Magazines,* and *Made in Europe.* Figure 4-2 shows typical ads placed by companies that are looking either for U.S. representation (you as importer) or for exporters to provide specific merchandise for resale. (Copies of the magazines noted above can be found in the Trade and Industry Administration offices of the Department of Commerce and in many larger chambers of commerce, public libraries, and university libraries.)

You should send between 25 and 30 letters per day. This volume is the reason why the services of a professional typist are important. You must obtain a large number of replies in order to set up a large network of agents or distributors for your export products.

Figure 4-2. Typical Ads for Exporters and Importers

U.S.A.
Import
Manufacturers and exporters interested in doing business in the USA. Send for details of our "Americanization" promotion and distribution program. **Canyon Productions, P.O. Box 871, Palm Desert, California, 92260 USA.**

Export
Black African Rhinoceros Horns available, also variety of mold release agents for polyurethane foam plastic products. **Midam, P.O. Box 44552, Indianapolis, IN 46204, USA.**

Importers wanted for high quality low cost resistors, capacitors and other electronic components. Write immediately for descriptive literature and price list. **Sigler & Associates 655 E. Queen Street, Inglewood, Ca. 90301 USA.**

Dominican Rep.
Import
I am interested in receiving quotations from firms and exporters of the following articles: Glassware, Babywear, tapes, sandpaper, tacks for shoes, alarm clocks, 100% cotton sewing thread in cops, lamplight lampchimney, lampglass, black pencils, coloured pencils, wooden rulers, nail clippers, baby soothers, gloves, plywood, paper and all articles for export. **Commercial Zvelty United, P.O. Box 2303, Calle San Juan de la Maguana 188, Santo Domingo, Dominican Republic.**

Germany
Export
Lollipop sticks, beechwood sticks for all purposes, meat skewers, applicator sticks, softwood squares, softwood laths and sticks, candy-floss-sticks, rocket sticks, also coloured. Ask manufacturer for quotation. **R. Schulz-Dusenschoen 24 Luebeck, P.O. Box 2281 Germany.**

The Netherlands
Export
We supply and purchase all kinds of European and U.S.A. proprietary branded products. Specialists in cigarettes, tobacco-leaves and liquors owing to barterdeals offering rock bottom prices. Detailed inquiries invited. **R.P.M. International Merchants, P.O. Box 3133 Telex: 21634 promy nl., Rotterdam, The Netherlands.**

Nigeria
Import
We want to import Building Materials, Food Items, Chemicals, Automobile Spare Parts and Accessories, Printing Material, Stationery Goods & General Merchandise. We also require the services of confirminghouse and Buying agents. Contact: **Amichitrade Enterprise, 38 Balogun Square, G.P.O. 8873, Lagos, Nigeria.**

Before sending your first letter, review the following, which should apply to all of your future overseas business correspondence:

1. Write your letters in English. Most companies and organizations overseas have someone on their staff who can translate. However, if you receive replies in another language, answer in that language. Most large cities have foreign language translation and typing services.

2. Make sure your letterhead has U.S.A. on it. State and zip code are not sufficient for international mail travel.

3. Write your letters in standard English. Stay away from slang, colloquial expressions, and humor. The people who are receiving and reading your letters may have only a rudimentary understanding of English.

4. Check your postage carefully. A few cents shortage may delay a transaction weeks or perhaps months.

5. Never send currency through the mail. In certain parts of the world, it is common practice for postal employees to supplement their income by opening letters containing currency.

6. Send all your letters air mail and request a response the same way. All important documents (purchase orders, sales contracts, etc.) should be sent registered mail when possible.

7. Never send form letters. Since most of your business will be conducted by mail, you will be judged both by the content and the appearance of the letters you send.

8. If you are asked for metric specifications on a product, *always* reply as requested. The United States is the last stronghold of the Customary (English) measurement system. For only a few dollars, you can purchase a metric converter, or you can use the chart in Figure 4-3. If you cannot do the conversions yourself, ask the engineers where the product is manufactured to send you metric specifications.

9. When sending cables, follow the same general rules listed above for letters.

Making Domestic Contacts

To each of the local companies manufacturing the products you are interested in, send a "no-cost" letter. In it, state that, at no cost to them, you will market their products abroad. Make sure you write to the highest ranking marketing officer (vice president of Sales or Marketing, national sales manager, or the like) and request an appointment. If you receive no answer within two weeks, call for an appointment. *You must be very aggressive.*

Each week, try to make several appointments. It is beneficial to speak with the company's top executives, since they are the decision-makers.

At the meeting, first explain that you will represent the company free of charge. Emphasize that you can sell their products through your worldwide distributor network. This will not only increase their sales, but also lower their produc-

Figure 4-3. Metric Conversion Chart—Approximations

Symbol	When You Know	Multiply By	To Find	Symbol
		Length		
mm	millimeters	0.04	inches	in
cm	centimeters	0.4	inches	in
m	meters	3.3	feet	ft
m	meters	1.1	yards	yd
km	kilometers	0.6	miles	mi
		Area		
cm^2	square centimeters	0.16	square inches	in^2
m^2	square meters	1.2	square yards	yd^2
km^2	square kilometers	0.4	square miles	mi^2
ha	hectares ($10,000m^2$)	2.5	acres	
		Mass (weight)		
g	grams	0.035	ounce	oz
kg	kilograms	2.2	pounds	lb
t	tonnes (100kg)	1.1	short tons	
		Volume		
ml	milliliters	0.03	fluid ounces	fl oz
l	liters	2.1	pints	pt
l	liters	1.06	quarts	qt
l	liters	0.26	gallons	gal
m^3	cubic meters	35	cubic feet	ft^3
m^3	cubic meters	1.3	cubic yards	yd^3
		Temperature (exact)		
°C	Celsius temp.	9/5 (+32)	Fahrenheit temp.	°F
		Temperature (exact) to Metric		
°F	Fahrenheit temp.	–32 5/9 of remainder	Celsius temp.	°C
		Length		
in	inches	*2.5	centimeters	cm
ft	feet	30	centimeters	cm
yd	yards	0.9	meters	m
mi	miles	1.6	kilometers	km
		Area		
in^2	square inches	6.5	sq. centimeters	cm^2
ft^2	square feet	0.09	square meters	m^2
yd^2	square yards	0.8	square meters	m^2
mi^2	square miles	2.6	sq. kilometers	km^2
	acres	0.4	hectares	ha

Symbol	When You Know	Multiply By	To Find	Symbol
Mass (weight)				
oz	ounces	28	grams	g
lb	pounds	0.45	kilograms	kg
	short tons (2000 lb)	0.9	tonnes	t
Volume				
tsp	teaspoons	5	milliliters	ml
tbsp	tablespoons	15	milliliters	ml
fl oz	fluid ounces	30	milliliters	ml
c	cups	0.24	liters	l
pt	pints	0.47	liters	l
qt	quarts	0.95	liters	l
gal	gallons	3.8	liters	l
ft^3	cubic feet	0.03	cubic meters	m^3
yd^3	cubic yards	0.76	cubic meters	m^3

* in = 2.54 cm (exactly)

tion costs (see the discussion of marginal costing in Chapter 6 for an explanation of how production costs are lowered).

Be sure to bring a *sole agent contract* (Figure 4-4) with you to the meeting. *This is what you want them to sign.* This contract gives you the exclusive right to market their products overseas; it is similar to a manufacturer's representative contract.

One point to consider: commission rates vary from industry to industry. Make sure you check the industry standards *before* you meet with the company executive.

Appointing Overseas Distributors

Within a four- to eight-week period, you should receive responses from your overseas letters. The responses will resemble the illustration in Figure 4-5. Most will ask what lines of merchandise you carry and what you wish to import or export. They may ask for a sole agent contract. Many will send samples and catalogues of merchandise they wish you to import.

After reviewing the letters you receive from foreign firms seeking to act as your representative, write back to those that appear most promising (basing your judgment on the initial and any subsequent market analysis).

In most countries, people working in international trade can understand English. If your products require, however, a detailed piece of literature to explain operations or benefits, it may be wise to have this information printed in multiple languages (this need is especially critical in South America, where both Spanish and Portuguese are spoken). The most common non-English languages in foreign trade are French, Spanish, and German.

Figure 4-4. Sole Agent Contract

This agreement made and entered into by and between:

Company:
Address:

hereinafter called the Manufacturer

AND:

Your Company:
Address:

hereinafter called the Export Representative:

WITNESSETH

The Manufacturer appoints the Export Representative as its exclusive sales representative and export department in and for all countries of the world except the United States.

The Manufacturer agrees to pay the Export Representative a commission of (specify %) on all orders received, excluding the United States and (if another), with or without the Export Representative's intervention. Commission due and payable thirty (30) days after shipment of order.

The Manufacturer shall provide catalogues and samples for the Export Representative's overseas agents and distributors.

Export Representative shall have an obligation to appoint distributors for the sale of the Manufacturer's products.

The Manufacturer will refer copies of any correspondence between Manufacturer and others in the territory assigned to the Export Representative.

The Export Representative, through his agents and distributors, will make every effort to promote the sale of the Manufacturer's products.

This contract shall be in force for a period of five (5) years from this date and shall continue automatically at the end of that time unless cancelled in writing, with a six (6) month notice, by either party.

If there is no business generated in any twelve (12) month period from this date, either party can cancel the contract by notice in writing forthwith.

Signed: _____
                                  Manufacturer

Date: _____
Witnessed: _____
                                  Notary Public

Signed: _____
                            Export Representative

Date: _____

Figure 4-5. Typical Agent Letter

Date: _____

Dear Sir:

    We received your promotional letter describing the products (toys, apparel, etc.) you distribute. We wish to establish relations and are, therefore, desirous of making a mutually beneficial alliance with an import-export firm in (name the city).

    We handle several (toys, apparel, etc.) lines of products and would like to know what you have to offer and what your country needs in imports.

    We wish to enter into agreements for Sole Agency Contracts on specific lines and products.

    Anticipating your early reply.

Sincerely Yours,

_____

    If you did not receive the following information initially, request it before appointing your overseas representative. In the same vein, you would supply this information about yourself, if you were asked for it:

1. Products carried
2. Territory covered
3. Commissions expected
4. Number of salesmen
5. Functions performed (agent, importer, exporter, manufacturer, etc.)
6. Companies they do business with in the U.S.

    This last point is most important; you should appoint only representatives having a history of success with U.S. products. Contact the U.S. firms they are currently dealing with and ask the amount of business (in dollars and in units of merchandise) they are handling, the length of time they have been associated with the U.S. firm, and their credit reliability. This information can protect you from dealing with a disreputable agent. Conversely, you should give this type of information about your company's overseas agents and representatives freely to U.S. companies that ask for it.

    Remember: choose your overseas representatives carefully, and check their references thoroughly. Some of the largest companies never thoroughly checked their agents or distributors and have suffered because of it. For example, Ford Motor Company recently found that its Japanese licensees were selling Ford's Mustang II automobile for $10,000—almost twice the U.S. price. They were able to do this because the Japanese viewed American cars as luxury vehicles. The pricing, however, created an artificially high price for the car, limiting its market potential.

    For more detailed information about an overseas agent, you can have a credit check done through your bank (Dun & Bradstreet) or through your local Department of Commerce office (*World Traders Data Report*).

Appoint one agent per country, unless you have information indicating that an agent is able to sell in several countries. Multi-national dealers exist, for example, in the Middle East. Initially do not appoint more than one agent per country, just as you would not handle competing products of different manufacturers. It is important to treat your overseas agents fairly. Their ability and willingness to sell your products reputably will to a great extent determine your success in selling your products overseas.

There are several forms that import/export organizations can take. You will encounter these various forms in your correspondence with overseas traders, and you should be familiar with each type, both so you know how the organizations operate and so you can select the best form for your own business to take. Some of the forms are more suitable than others for the beginner. Chapter 5 discusses forms for export organizations and makes recommendations for the novice; Chapter 14 does the same for import forms.

Section Two

Exporting

Chapter Five

Export Organizations

There are several ways to organize an exporting firm. There are only two that the novice should consider, and these are discussed below. You will see these two forms, as well as others, in action as you gain experience as a trader.

Export agents have sales representatives in foreign countries who sell with catalogues and samples. When a sale is completed, the end user pays the export agent, not the exporter's overseas representatives. The agent in turn pays his or her representatives. When you are starting out, this arrangement can pose problems because you appear to have limited resources and experience.

Export management companies (once known as *combination export management companies*) handle the foreign business of several noncompeting domestic manufacturers. The export company acts, in effect, as the export department for the manufacturer and is paid either on a commission, salary, or buy-and-sell arrangement. This is the form that is generally most profitable for beginners.

If you are starting out in business and are low in capital reserves, you will probably need to begin on commission. Under this system, you receive a 7½% to 20% discount on the wholesale distributor price. The manufacturer is paid by the end user, and you are paid by the manufacturer. For example, if you were selling custom tire rims wholesale for $10, and you receive a 10% discount, the price of the rim to you as an exporter would be $9. Since you are working on a commission basis, however, your commission is the amount of the discount, or $1 per rim. When the end-user in a foreign country pays the manufacturer $10, the manufacturer pays you $1.

If the buy-and-sell approach is employed, you sell the manufacturer's product under your own name—you might buy the discounted $10 tire rim for $9 and resell it, adding on your export costs in arriving at your selling price. This approach involves sales and credit risks, packaging, shipping, and all correspondence. You, the export management company, purchase at the domestic net wholesale distributor price less a certain percentage equal to the manufacturer's domestic sales overhead.

As you develop your business, you may decide to change from a commission system to a buy-and-sell system. The buy-and-sell form is a good way to build up business, especially if you are dealing with small manufacturers who cannot afford to tie up their capital in the goods that you export. You buy the products directly from them and *you* assume all the risks.

You can expect to lose a client when his overseas sales reach 15% to 20% of his total sales volume. At this point, the manufacturer will usually develop an in-house export department. Losing a client in this way is evidence of your success, and a good reference from your lost client makes your task in seeking out new clients much easier.

After you have developed a clientele within a certain product area, join an export trade association, club, or organization. Aside from being good for your image as a serious member of the profession, your participation in these organizations might bring you more clients.

Appendix 8, Associations Fostering Foreign Trade, and Appendix 9, Foreign Trade Clubs, list organizations dealing with both importing and exporting. Many of them list their functions and addresses.

You have now selected your products, established a network of overseas contacts, and considered the form you want your business to take. The next chapter discusses pricing and selling of export products—without a prudent approach to these topics, your business cannot survive! (See Chapter 15 for a discussion of import pricing.)

Chapter Six

Pricing and Selling

After you have set up your overseas network by deciding with which overseas agents and distributors you will deal and have acquired several domestic manufacturers as clients, one day you will receive a request from a foreign representative asking for prices. You must be prepared to establish, or to help your domestic clients establish, a sound approach to pricing. The method generally used to price an export product effectively is called *marginal cost pricing.* Making up the marginal cost price are the following incremental costs:

1. *Costs to produce the export product* over and above costs to produce items sold domestically.
2. *Costs of selling in the foreign market,* such as advertising and credit.
3. *Costs of moving the goods* from factory to final destination.

The total of these costs represents a level below which prices cannot be set without incurring a loss.

It is extremely important for both you and the manufacturer to understand the benefits *you* can provide the manufacturer in selling abroad. By examining the following cost analysis, you can easily see how exporting can significantly improve profits.

Costs to Produce the Export Product

All manufacturing costs are either fixed or variable. *Fixed costs,* such as executive salaries, rent, and interest payments, change little with the volume of output. *Variable costs,* such as the costs of materials and sales, rise as the volume of output rises. The total cost of each item is generally computed by adding to its variable cost a share of total fixed costs.

Marginal costing includes variable costs, but not fixed costs, in the total cost of each item. That is, *margin* refers to the production capacity beyond the normal limits upon which fixed costs are based. Export products are manufactured within this margin.

For example, assume a small company was operating at 80% of its capacity and had *no alternative* for using the idle 20%. Futher assume that it had to maintain its present minimum work force, which also worked at 80% of capacity.

The factory costs of increasing production by 10% might include only raw materials and extra utilities. *No* other costs would increase. Note that labor can be treated as a fixed cost, since the additional output does not cause the payroll to rise.

The company could sell the 10% production increase without losing money if they recovered the materials cost and the increase in the utilities bill. Any amount greater than this would contribute to the payment of fixed costs, all of which would have been incurred whether production had been increased the 10% or not. If, in the absence of other sales alternatives, they could sell this 10% abroad by lowering the export price below the domestic sales price, it might be to their advantage to do so.

Costs of Selling in the Foreign Market

It is important to identify and include those out-of-pocket costs which result directly from trying to export a particular product. For example, if significant costs for new packaging or promotional literature are required to market an item overseas, these expenses should be costed directly into the specific export items and not into the entire product line. However, most of the time these costs are figured into the total projected sales volume for that item, as a fixed cost. The same is true for travel to foreign markets, advertising and promotion abroad, credit, and other costs that relate directly to the export item. These are really fixed costs which must be covered by the export sales. In determining the f.o.b. (free on board, meaning that you do not pay shipping charges) export price (this does *not* mean that you should *quote* f.o.b.), a projected export sales volume should be estimated and the fixed export costs for this period should be prorated over the number of items to be sold. (See "Terms of Sale," below, for definitions of some common abbreviations.)

Let the product determine the type of packaging and promotional literature needed. Consumer items such as toiletries and prepared foods need the same creative packaging displayed when these items are sold domestically. Most industrial items, such as food processing or computer equipment, need little in the way of packaging, but detailed explanatory literature is important. In both cases, when you receive a request for prices, send a price list with literature, samples (of small items), or pictures. If samples are requested, send them immediately. The requestor should be billed for the manufacturing costs only.

Cost of Moving the Goods

The last group of costs are those traditionally associated with exporting—the costs involved in moving the goods from the factory door to the ultimate foreign consumer. A few of these costs, such as certain types of general marine insurance policies, are fixed, but most of them, including tariffs, shipping, warehousing, commissions, and margins, are variable.

Pricing Summary

The following are the various elements of pricing which must be considered:

- Cost of manufacturing
- Export commission
- Foreign agent commission
- Foreign freight forward fee
- Freight to port
- Consular invoice
- Export packing

If necessary:

- Marine insurance
- Ocean freight

These elements are illustrated in a calculation sheet of export costs:

Cost of 250 dozen consumer products	$350,073
Export agent fee at 10%	35,046
Foreign agent commission at 5%	17,551
Freight forwarder's fee	150
Inland freight from factory to port	600
Consular invoice	5
Export packing	400
SELLING PRICE TO CUSTOMER	$403,825
Marine insurance	1,061
Ocean freight to Sydney, Australia based on volume c.i.f. to Sydney, Austrailia	1,000
SELLING PRICE IF MARINE INSURANCE AND OCEAN FREIGHT ARE NECESSARY	$405,886

Great care must be exercised in preparing a price quotation. You must be absolutely certain that you overlook nothing. Therefore, very carefully review all of your figures and double-check the calculations.

Start your price quotation letter by stating that your company is pleased to submit its firm, fixed price quotation for a specified period of time (usually, the manufacturer will give you a period of time the quote is valid). State that the shipping date will remain open until the order is received. If the overseas agent has requested samples or literature, send it by registered airmail to insure delivery.

Many times a seller is requested to submit a *pro forma invoice* with his quotation (see example in Chapter 18, Importing: Documentation). A pro forma invoice is not for payment purposes. It is only a model, which the buyer will use when applying for an import license or arranging for funds.

Figure 6-1. Standard Terms and Conditions

Prices quoted herein are firm for _____ (days, weeks, months) after _____ , 19___ . Delivery date will be quoted upon receipt of an order. Delivery of (product) can be made to shipside ____ days after receipt of order and receipt of a confirmed letter of credit. Terms of payment to our company: An irrevocable confirmed letter of credit issued by your bank and irrevocably confirmed by your bank's U.S. correspondent bank, or by our bank, _____ .
The prices covered in this quotation are in terms of currency of seller's country and are subject to change without notice unless exception is indicated. All orders received and accepted by us are contingent upon the acceptance of the order by the supplier, and deliveries are subject to delays caused by strikes, floods, fires, riots, the contingencies of transportation, unavoidable accidents, acts of God, or any other causes of delay beyond our control. Orders accepted by us are not subject to cancellation. Any taxes or consular fees imposed by any government authority on the sale of this order and not shown shall be paid by the buyer. All CIF quotations subject to present freight and insurance rates.

Before completing your quotation, check the current overseas prices for your product category to make sure you are competitive. It is common for overseas agents to check with several sources of a product before they place an order.

Finish your price quotation with a paragraph called "Terms and Conditions." Figure 6-1 shows a format which can be used and which will protect your interests when the deal is consummated.

Terms of Sale

It is very important that a common understanding exists regarding the delivery terms. In the U.S., it is customary to ship "f.o.b. factory," "freight collect," "prepay and charge," or "c.o.d.," but an entirely different set of terms is used in international business. Some terms sound similar, but they have different definitions. Some of the more common terms used in international trade are briefly defined below; more comprehensive lists appear in the glossaries at the end of this book.

c.i.f.: cost, insurance, freight to named overseas port of import. Under this term, the seller quotes a price including the goods, insurance, and all transportation and miscellaneous charges to the point of debarkation from vessel or aircraft.

c.&f.: cost and freight to named overseas port of import. Under this term, the seller quotes a price including the cost of transportation to the named point of debarkation.

f.a.s.: free along side at named U.S. port of export. Under this term, the seller quotes a price, including service charges and delivery of the goods along side the vessel.

Figure 6‑2. Export Purchase Order.

EXPORT ORDER

THE XZ EXPORT CORPORATION
1005 Beaver Street
New York, N.Y. 10017
Telephone: 423-8005

TO: *TEMCO Mfg. Co.*
400 Lexington Ave.
New York, N.Y. 10001

Date: September 18, 19—
Order No.:   7131

Please enter our order for the following for shipment *from mill not
later than September 28 to connect with S/S "PARIS" loading October 5,
19—.*

Goods	*Sugar*
Packing	*In 6-ply export paper bags*
Quantity	*10,000 (ten thousand) bags*
Price	*$1.76 per bag*
Terms of Delivery	*FAS Steamer New York Harbor*
Terms	*Net cash vs. your invoices and clean S/S Dock*
	Receipt
Reference	*Telephone conversations—September 15 and 17*

Port Marks:

BISON   Number Pkgs. *Not necessary to number*
SÃO PAULO   *shipping pkgs*
Via SANTOS

—INSTRUCTIONS—

Please render your invoices in sextuplicate, showing thereon all port
marks, numbers of packages, etc. Any condition arising preventing scheduled delivery or delaying scheduled delivery should be brought to our attention immediately. All marking and packing instructions must be rigidly
adhered to as foreign country of destination regulations are excessively
strict. Your failure to observe our instructions in this regard may result
in fines or duty penalties for which we must hold you responsible.

THE XZ EXPORT CORPORATION

_____

(Authorized Signature)

f.o.b.: free on board. There are a number of classes of f.o.b. Here are three:

f.o.b. named inland port of origin

f.o.b. named port of exportation

f.o.b. vessel (named port of export)

In all classes of f.o.b., the price quoted includes loading the product onto the carrying vessel, but not shipping it.

ex (named point of origin), e.g., ex factory, ex warehouse, etc.: Under this term, the price quoted applies only at the point of origin, and seller agrees to place the goods at the disposal of buyer at the agreed place on the date or within the period fixed. All other charges are for the account of the buyer.

In quoting, make your terms meaningful. A price for industrial machinery quoted "f.o.b. Saginaw, Michigan, not export packed" would be unacceptable to prospective foreign buyers, who would have no way to determine with any accuracy what the export packing costs would be in Saginaw and would not know the freight charges from Saginaw to the port of export.

Always quote c.i.f. whenever possible; this means something abroad. It shows the foreign buyer what it costs to get your product into a port in his country or in a nearby port.

If you need assistance in figuring the c.i.f. price, a freight forwarder will be glad to help you. Furnish him with a description of your product and the weight and cubic measurement when packed. He can then compute the c.i.f. price and usually will not charge you for this service.

Most of the information for your price quotation will come from your freight forwarder. He will also make most of the necessary shipping arrangements and handle your insurance needs. Other services offered by these people are discussed in later chapters.

When your customer accepts your quote, he will send you a purchase order and open a letter of credit in your favor (letters of credit are further discussed in Chapter 7). Examine the purchase order you receive. Make sure it conforms to your price quote.

Next, contact the manufacturer and inform him of the terms and conditions of the purchase order. Make arrangements with him for delivery close to the ship's departure date. (A sample export purchase order appears in Figure 6-2.)

Finally, have your foreign freight forwarder prepare all documents for shipping. After the goods are shipped, the freight forwarder will give you the documents necessary for you to receive payment from the bank. In order to receive payment, it is very important that you have complied with all requirements listed in the letter of credit.

Normally, you will be billed by the manufacturer, the freight forwarder, and the shipping (trucking, airline) company within 30 days. You must calculate and then pay commission to your overseas agent(s).

Chapter 7 deals in more detail with the methods of payment.

Chapter Seven

Methods of Payment

Because exporting requires international financial arrangements and agreements, many would-be exporters hesitate to become involved, or try and become confused. Actually, export terms of sale and payments are quite simple and differ only slightly from domestic financing. The general concepts are about the same and the methods similar. In either situation, the seller wants to be assured that the buyer will pay, and the buyer wants to be certain that he receives what he pays for.

There are three types of export financing—short, medium, and long term. Short term covers 180 days or less; medium term, 181 days to five years; and long term, five years or more. This discussion is limited to short term financing, inasmuch as the beginner is usually not in a position to offer better terms.

There are five categories of short term financing:

1. Cash with order or in advance of order
2. Letters of credit
3. Documentary drafts
4. Open account
5. Consignment

Cash with Order or in Advance of Order

The best terms possible are receiving cash in advance or with orders—you have payment before the goods have left your hands. However, unless there is an extraordinarily favorable sellers' market or a situation where the seller dominates that market, most overseas customers will be reluctant to pay in advance. There are times when insisting upon some cash in advance is prudent—if a foreign customer orders a specially designed piece of equipment which you do not normally carry, you should require him to give you a 25% deposit against the total cost of the item before manufacturing begins. By and large, very little business is conducted in this manner.

Letters of Credit

It goes without saying that you, the exporter, want to be paid as quickly as possible, whereas your overseas customer may well want to defer payment for as long as possible. The answer, of course, is credit.

Since World War II, U.S. exporters have usually insisted upon letters of credit that were equivalent to cash on shipment. As late as 1963, one-half of all U.S. exports were sold on a letter-of-credit basis; the remainder was sold on open account or draft collection terms. In many Third World countries, letters of credit are not used because the governments restrict the outflow of currency, and insisting upon this form of payment may jeopardize your sale.

A letter of credit (illustrated in Figure 7-1) is a financing instrument opened by a foreign buyer with a bank in his locality. The letter of credit stipulates the purchase price agreed upon by the buyer and seller, the quantity of merchandise to be shipped, and the type of insurance coverage to protect the merchandise during shipment. The letter of credit names the seller as beneficiary (that is, you are the party who gets paid) and identifies the definite time period the terms remain in force. Finally, the letter of credit directs the buyer's bank to transmit credit (payment) to the seller's bank via cable or airmail when all the stipulated conditions have been met.

A letter of credit assures the seller of the solvency of his buyer. Most letters of credit are "irrevocable and confirmed" by the seller's bank in the U.S. before they are accepted by the seller. This confirmation obligates your bank to pay you once you have met all the stated conditions in the particular letter of credit.

There are two simple considerations when using letters of credit:

1. Specify as fully as possible to your buyer the amount of credit (payment) needed, the length of time for which this amount is valid, whether partial shipments are acceptable, and any other requirements or necessary documents.

2. When the letter of credit is delivered to you through your local bank, check to see that you can meet all provisions specified. If not, request an amendment by the foreign buyer before proceeding.

Letters of credit are most often used when initiating business with a new account, when a check of the importer's credit reveals it would be unwise to make shipment on a less secure basis, or when large purchases are made by an unknown buyer. When dealing with established accounts, letters of credit can become burdensome, especially considering the competitive financing terms available today. For example, a European company recently made a large sale of aluminum cable to a Mexican company, even though their price was higher than that of a competing U.S. firm. The deciding factor in closing the deal was not the price but the loan made by the European company, with the assistance of its government, to finance the installation over an extended period of time. This story illustrates a common practice in international trade—you can close more sales if you offer better terms. To be successful, you must offer your established accounts something better than letter of credit terms.

Figure 7-1. Letter of Credit

Zelch Bank of Kansas
0024 Main Street
Kansas City, Kansas

Overseas Exporting Company
10223 Won Street
Wichita, Kansas

Gentlemen:

We have received a letter dated January 6, 1979 from the Wandt
Bank of Munich, Germany advising us to inform you that a letter
of credit No. x124 has been opened in your favor for US $8,500
(Eight Thousand Five Hundred and No/100 US Dollars) from the
account of German Importers, Munich, Germany to be paid at
sight on Zelch Bank of Kansas. This credit expires July 12, 1979,
Kansas City, Kansas.

Documents to accompany draft(s):

Commercial Invoice in Triplicate.

Negotiable Insurance Policy and/or Underwriter's Certificate,
endorsed in blank, covering marine and war risks.

Full set of clean "on board" ocean Bill of Lading made out to
order of shipper blank endorsed marked "Freight Prepaid" and
notify German Importers/111 Rheinstrasse, Munich, Germany.

Evidence of shipment of 600 dozen musical instruments CIF
Bremerhaven, Germany.

Partial shipments permitted.

If your relationship with your customer is good, other methods of financing
can make business transactions easier. You might want to consider two special
types of letter of credit that offer you more flexibility:

1. *Revolving letter of credit.* Useful when shipping a variety of goods to
an established customer. It normally runs for an extended period of time,
and provides for immediate replenishment of funds drawn against it.

2. *Assignable letter of credit.* The same as the normal letter of credit, except that it includes the phrase "and/or assigns" following the name of the
beneficiary. This allows the exporter to finance his domestic purchase by using the overseas buyer's credit. That is, you agree that payment from the letter of credit may be made to your U.S. supplier. This is a way for an exporter to conduct business with little or no capital.

Documentary Drafts

Drafts are a popular and common method of financing exports. A draft is a written instrument drawn by one party (the overseas importer) ordering a second party (the bank) to pay a certain sum of money to a third party (you, the exporter) at sight or at some definite future time. Before World War II, drafts settled a majority of U.S. export transactions. Since the war, letters of credit have become more popular because of their safety factors (payment is guaranteed because your local bank assumes payment responsibility) and their ease of control by monetary authorities (governments can control money leaving their country by not allowing banks to issue letters of credit or by authorizing banks to issue them only within certain financial limits, such as $0-$50,000).

When using drafts, you and the buyer usually agree beforehand that the transaction will be on a sight basis or perhaps on a 60- or 90-day deferred payment basis. The overseas importer orders his merchandise directly from you, and you arrange to ship the goods. You then take your shipping documents and your own draft, drawn on the importer, to your bank. Your U.S. bank forwards all documents to their correspondent bank overseas. This overseas bank notifies the importer when the documents arrive. If terms are payment at sight, this arrangement would be called a *sight draft document against payment,* and the importer would be required to pay immediately to obtain the shipping documents so he can pick up the goods.

However, if the importer has agreed to "accept" the draft, he or she is permitted to obtain the documents and the merchandise while not being obliged to make payments until the draft matures. The importer will, of course, have established credit locally and made arrangements with his or her bank prior to undertaking the shipment.

Two other types of drafts are used less frequently: *time drafts* and *date drafts.* They are used to give the buyer better financing because they are forms of deferred payment made in terms of either a time lapse in shipping (the merchandise is not shipped until a specified date), invoicing (billing is delayed for a specified period of time), or payment (payment is not required until a specified time has elapsed, say 120 days).

Open Account

In open account financing, the overseas importer neither provides letters of credit nor honors drafts. The only requirement is that the importer pay the balance on his account periodically, or within a certain period of time after the purchase.

Open account financing is usually used between large companies and their subsidiaries (for example, Ford Motor Company and Ford of Europe). As might be expected, this arrangement requires the exporter to have full confidence in his overseas buyer. Some open-account arrangements are on a monthly basis for outstanding bills. However, other types of arrangements (quarterly, semi-annually) are common. Many Third World nations do not allow open accounts in international trade because they could not control their balance of payments if money were to flow freely in and out of the country.

Consignment

When goods are exported on consignment, the exporter is not paid until the goods are sold in the overseas marketplace. Consignment is rarely used between independent exporters and foreign importers. There is too much risk for the exporters because they are not paid until all goods are sold. Also, most exporters feel that, when an importer has his money tied up in inventory, he will make a greater sales effort.

Dealing with Foreign Currency

Generally, a U.S. exporter or importer will have no trouble with currency because the U.S. dollar is one of the most accepted currencies in world trade. However, at times it may be necessary to accept orders and quote prices in other currencies, such as the Spanish *peseta,* the Japanese *yen,* or the Greek *drachma.* If you are faced with this situation, you should contact your bank.

Banks buy and sell convertible currency for spot (immediate) or future delivery. You, as an importer, may contract with a bank to buy the currency for future delivery at a fixed rate of exchange because you know that, at some future time, you must make payment in a foreign currency. Conversely, as an exporter you may protect yourself by contracting to sell to a bank, at a fixed rate of exchange, the foreign currency proceeds you expect on a given date. These contracts provide a "hedge" against currency fluctuation. That is, importers and exporters avoid the risk of fluctuating exchange rates and can better determine their true costs and profits when they enter into such a contract. The bank does not charge interest on these contracts because no payments are due in advance of the due date of the contract.

Chapter Eight

Using Credit in World Trade

The methods of payment described in Chapter 7 can involve varying credit terms. It is important to your success in exporting that you understand the use of credit in overseas transactions.

Factors Affecting Your Use of Credit

First, competition is becoming more intense, and U.S. exporters and banks now must offer attractive terms if they are going to compete with traders of other nations.

Second, when you become better acquainted with buyers overseas, and as these buyers prove their credit worthiness, you should be more willing to extend longer credit terms.

Third, longer terms have been made less risky for American exporters because of the export credit insurance now available through the U.S. government in association with the insurance industry. Without doubt, this protection against political and commercial risks of doing business abroad has helped many exporters, especially those new to foreign marketing, to be more competitive than before.

How to Get Credit Information about Your Buyers

There are several sources of credit information. Your bank is in an excellent position, either directly or through its correspondents, to obtain credit information for you. In addition, it is not uncommon for one exporter to check with another exporter to find out what his or her experience has been in selling to a particular foreign buyer on credit. The U.S. Department of Commerce also maintains information on thousands of buyers around the world. *World Traders Data Reports* (WTDRs) are available through the Department's district offices. Such private credit institutions as Dun and Bradstreet offer an international service as well.

Figure 8-1. Financing Sources

	Purpose	Loans	Guarantees and Insurance	Who Can Borrow	Where the Money Must Be Spent	Private Participation in Agency Loans	Must Seek Private Capitol First
Overseas Private Investment Corporation (OPIC)	Facilitate the use of private capitol in less developed nations	Dollars at commercial rates and terms or in local currency for 5–15 years	Political risk against war, revolution, or insurrection	US citizens, firms, or foreign firms 95% US owned	Proceeds in dollars spent in US. Other currencies where loan originated	Yes	No
International Finance Corporation (IFC)	To finance only private firms contributing to underdeveloped nations	Any firm contributing to underdeveloped countries. Also capital stock investments	Can underwrite capital stock subscriptions	Private firms in member countries	Member countries and Switzerland	Yes	Yes
International Monetary Fund (IMF)	To encourage stability, expansion and growth in world trade	Foreign exchange transactions for member nations	N/A	Governments of members	No limitations	None	No
World Bank	Finance projects in less developed countries	Lends in most currencies, 5–35 years, government guarantees required except for IFC loans	Guarantees part or whole loans	Governments of members	Member countries and Switzerland	Commercial Banks	No
International Development Association (IDA)	Same as World Bank	To 50 years without interest	Same as World Bank	Same as World Bank	Same as World Bank	No	Yes
Inter-American Development Bank	To accelerate economic growth in Latin America	Lends in currencies of members	Can guarantee loans	Public or private groups in member countries	Worldwide	Yes	Yes

Organization	Purpose	Terms	Coverage	Eligibility	Geographic	Notes	
Foreign Credit Insurance Association (FCIA)	To protect US-based exporters and interested financial institutions against losses	Exporter can assign policy to bank to obtain receivables financing	Commercial risk and political risk coverage, war, riot, and revolution	Any US exporter with FCIA policy can make application for export receivables bank financing	N/A	N/A	N/A
Private Export Funding Corporation (PEFCO)	Financing exports of US goods through loans to foreign importers	Lends dollars for short, medium, and long term periods. Must have export-import bank approval	Does not guarantee or insure loans	Foreign private enterprises, governments, and agencies	Dollars must be spent to buy US goods	Loans money only in conjunction with private lenders (banks, etc.)	Yes
Export-Import Bank (EXIMBANK)	To promote US exports through loans and assistance in financing, guarantees and insurance	Dollars only: agricultural commodities to 12 months also long term loans 5–20 years	Provides political and credit guarantees to US and foreign financial institutions	Purchasers of US exports	United States	Encourages commercial and other institutions to participate	Yes
Agency for International Development (AID)	Promote economic and social development in underdeveloped nations	Up to 40 years long with 10-year grace period	Similar to HEW housing guarantees	Governments and government agencies of underdeveloped nations	United States or underdeveloped nations	None	Yes

Where to Find Financing for Your Export Sales

Many sources of financial assistance are open to you. First, of course, is your own working capital or bank line of credit—that is, *you* might loan money in the form of credit to your overseas customer. Use of your own facilities may, however, restrict your total cash availability even if you were to establish a separate export line of credit with your bank.

Probably the best solution is to contact a bank—about 250 U.S. banks have qualified international banking departments. Perhaps no other country in the world offers such a wide choice of financial institutions that are prepared to provide international financing and marketing assistance to exporters.

Commercial banks with active international departments have specialists fully familiar with particular foreign countries and experts in different types of commodities and transactions. These banks, located in all major U.S. cities, maintain a wide network of correspondent relationships with smaller banks throughout the U.S. This banking network enables any exporter to find assistance (for yourself or your overseas customer) directly or indirectly for export financing needs. These larger banks also maintain correspondent relationships with banks in most foreign countries or operate their own overseas branches, providing a direct channel to your overseas customer.

Exporters should also be aware of factoring houses that deal in accounts receivable of American exporters. Factors may charge higher fees than banks, but they will purchase your receivables, often without recourse (that is, if your buyer fails to pay them, it is their loss, not yours), assuring you of prompt, although discounted, payment for your export sales.

The U.S. government also participates in the financing of America's exports. The Export–Import Bank of the United States (Eximbank) offers direct loans for large projects and equipment sales that usually require longer term financing. It cooperates with commercial banks in the United States and abroad in providing a number of financial arrangements to help U.S. exporters offer credit to their overseas buyers. It provides export credit guarantees to commercial banks that in turn finance export sales. Further information about Eximbank can be had from:

Export–Import Bank of the United States
811 Vermont Avenue, N.W.
Washington, D.C. 20571

In addition to help from Eximbank, the exporter can also turn to the Foreign Credit Insurance Association (FCIA), which provides insurance to American exporters to enable them to extend credit terms to their overseas buyers. The insurance is against commercial credit and political risk loss, thereby making it possible to secure financing from commercial banks and other lending institutions at lower rates and on a more liberal basis than would otherwise be the case. For more information about the FCIA, contact:

Foreign Credit Insurance Association
One World Trade Center, 9th Floor
New York, New York 10048

Information on both organizations can also be had from your U.S. Department of Commerce district office.

In addition to Eximbank and FCIA, there is an export credit sales program operated by the U.S. Department of Agriculture's Commodity Credit Corporation (CCC). Under this program, U.S. exporters may apply for export financing of eligible commodities purchased either from privately owned stocks or CCC inventories. If you need further information, contact:

Assistant Sales Manager
Commercial Export Programs
Foreign Agricultural Service
U.S. Department of Agriculture
Washington, D.C. 20250

or your local U.S. Department of Commerce district office.

Finally, the U.S. exporter can obtain financing for overseas borrowers through the Private Export Funding Corporation (PEFCO). These loans must be guaranteed by the Export–Import Bank. If you need further information, contact:

Executive Vice President
Private Export Funding Corporation
280 Park Avenue
New York, N.Y. 10017

A list of financing sources appears in Figure 8–1.

Chapter Nine

Free Help for the Exporter

The export business is unique among businesses in that you, the exporter, have access to more free advice and assistance than in any other type of venture. There are several groups anxious to help you because your success furthers theirs:

- Industry and Trade Administration, U.S. Department of Commerce
- Foreign freight forwarders/custom house brokers
- U.S. banks
- Chambers of commerce
- International trade associations
- Transportation companies (Pan Am, TWA, etc.)

Industry and Trade Administration

The Industry and Trade Administration of the U.S. Department of Commerce is very interested in your success because it helps the federal government to increase exports for reasons of balance of payments (the U.S. suffered nearly a $30 billion trade deficit in 1977). The Administration has offices in 43 cities in the U.S. (for a listing, see Appendix 1). Each of them offers the exporter detailed information about the following:

Trade missions. The Administration sponsors teams of business leaders who travel abroad to promote U.S. trade and investment and to exchange business proposals with their foreign counterparts.

Trade centers. Permanent overseas showcases for U.S. goods are placed in major foreign cities, such as London, Frankfurt, Milan, Stockholm, Bangkok, and Tokyo.

Sample display service. Samples are displayed overseas for U.S. firms seeking agents or distributors in such countries as Lebanon, Thailand, Kenya, and the Philippines.

Mobile trade fairs. Traveling exhibits, organized jointly by U.S. manufacturers and carriers, are supported by the U.S. Department of Commerce.

Commercial exhibitions. U.S. product exhibits at international trade fairs abroad help American firms make sales and find new agents.

Agency index. Aimed at prospective foreign buyers, this index lists local distributors of U.S. products.

Foreign traders index. Information on more than 150,000 foreign importing organizations in 135 countries is stored in a computerized file.

Export mailing list service. U.S. firms wishing to make export contacts may obtain lists of foreign organizations interested in specific products or product groups. The lists, selected by computer from the Foreign Traders Index, is available either on pressure-sensitive mailing labels or in standard printout format.

(From this source, I obtained a list of importers of office products. Then I sent out a piece of promotional literature describing several items that were quite competitive. The response was enthusiastic and resulted in several large orders for my company.)

Data tape service. U.S. firms with computer facilities may purchase magnetic tapes containing information on all firms in selected countries or in all countries covered in the Foreign Traders Index.

Trade list service. The names and addresses of foreign distributors, agents, purchasers, and other firms, classified by products they handle and services they offer, are made available to U.S. firms.

Trade contact survey. This survey helps U.S. businesspeople find foreign firms specifically interested in their products and services.

(An associate of mine in the medical supply business used the trade contact survey effectively in setting up distributors in Western Europe. The results, $500,000 in sales during the first year, were very gratifying.)

World trade directory reports. These reports describe operations of a foreign company—products, size and reputation, capital, annual turnover.

Commercial newsletter. The newsletter informs over 50,000 businesspeople in 50 nations of new U.S. products, research, and economic trends.

Investment in developing countries. American private capital strengthens economic progress and opens new opportunities for trade.

Licensing. U.S. manufacturers enter into agreements for manufacture of their products by overseas firms, in return for royalties.

America weeks. The U.S. Department of Commerce supports special sales promotions of U.S. consumer products by overseas department stores.

GATT negotiations. The U.S. has joined in negotiations in Geneva for trade liberalization.

Regional export expansion councils. Public-spirited business leaders work with Department of Commerce field offices to promote U.S. export expansion.

Publications. Hundreds of Department of Commerce publications provide current information on business conditions and opportunities abroad.

Foreign trade zones. The Department of Commerce has established numerous duty-free trade zones for manufacturing and marketing. Locations include New York, New Orleans, San Francisco, Seattle, Mayaguez, Toledo, and Honolulu. (See Chapter 22 for more information.)

Piggyback program. The Department of Commerce supports cooperative exporting, where products of firms not equipped to sell abroad are "carried" to market by established exporters.

Business counseling services. Department of Commerce district offices offer guidance, in-depth counseling, and scheduling of appointments with officials in various agencies. This is a one-stop service designed to give the businessperson a maximum amount of information in a minimum of time.

Many states also provide aid through their export councils or departments, which work to foster the sale of products from that state (see Appendix 7 for state trade promotion offices).

Private industry eager for the exporters' business also offers free assistance. Consider the following sources:

Freight Forwarders, Custom House Brokers

This area of foreign trade has generally caused the most problems and therefore discouraged many hopeful traders. In searching for a reliable, service-oriented company, check with your local international bank and other import/export companies. Many are listed in the yellow pages—so be thorough in your search. Remember: these companies will provide routing and scheduling information, book ocean cargo or air freight space, prepare all necessary shipping documentation, handle shipping insurance, arrange for warehousing and storage, etc. For the services performed, the rates are quite reasonable. Always review charges, however, before completing a transaction. (See Appendix 5 for a list of freight forwarders and custom house brokers.)

U.S. Banks

If your current bank has no international department, have your branch manager recommend two or three alternatives. Ask other companies in foreign trade for recommendations. Also, check with the local international trade association.

Remember: You are a potentially important customer. Go where you will receive the best *service.* The banking officer you are dealing with is just as important as the institution.

The services offered include:

- Working capital loans
- Short-term advances against shipping and collection documents
- Direct loans to foreign importers by U.S. banks
- Handling of letters of credit and drafts
- Reference checks on overseas firms
- Help in establishing credit reliability
- Assistance in locating markets for your products, using the bank's economic studies of certain areas

(See Appendix 6 for list of banks doing international business.)

There are many other places, such as those described below, where one can find help in solving foreign trade problems. You should, however, use the U.S. Industry and Trade Administration, your freight forwarder, and your local bank before you contact any of the others. These three will provide the most help in the least amount of time.

Chambers of Commerce

Most cities in the U.S. have a chamber of commerce. The larger cities have departments to help local business people in exporting. They generally will have a reference library of books and magazines dealing with imports/exports, or they can refer you to one. Many of the organizations have world trade committees to promote the sale of goods from each area. Also, they have guest speakers from time to time to discuss current overseas business developments. (See Appendix 10 for a list of U.S. and foreign chambers.)

International Trade Associations

There are more than 25 cities that now have World Trade Centers, many within the U.S. Normally, wherever you find a World Trade Center, there is a trade association nearby. There are many types of trade associations or clubs:

Export managers associations are generally made up of individuals who own or export for themselves, or of large companies that export. Many combination export management people belong to these groups. Often, manufacturers will contact them looking for someone to handle their overseas business.

Foreign trade associations often have as members heads of major corporations and city officials. They invite foreign speakers.

Freight forwarding organizations are usually comprised of people in the freight business. They, like the other associations, have speakers discussing different aspects of international trade relating to transportation.

Importing associations are a variety of different clubs usually representing special product groups, such as metals, shoes, etc. (See Appendix 9 for a list of importing associations.)

Transportation Companies

Some airlines (TWA, Pan Am) provide all types of assistance to clients. They publish reference materials on shipping, where to find products, and the like. (See Appendix 5 for a list of these companies.)

Chapter Ten

Preparing Goods for
the Foreign Market
and for Shipment

Whether you are acting as the export department for a manufacturer or shipping under your own label, you should make certain the merchandise is properly prepared both for its destined foreign market and for shipping.

There are four phases of preparation: engineering, production, packing, and marking. The first of these, engineering, is part of the homework you must do before you offer products for sale overseas.

Engineering

It may be necessary to modify a product in order to sell it successfully overseas. Modifications may make a product conform with country regulations, historical preferences, or local customs; or facilitate movement, reduce costs, or compensate for possible differences in electrical current and/or measurement standards.

The most common mistake American exporters make is failing to consider these overseas differences. They tend to think that any product that has sold well in the U.S. will sell well in the same form in other countries. This error is best illustrated by the domestic car manufacturers' approach to selling overseas. Because of great success within the home market, little or no effort was made to build a vehicle that could be used in multiple areas of the world—that is, a universal car. However, by examining the sales of cars like the Volkswagen and the Toyota, one can see opportunities that American manufacturers failed to address. Only the advent of stricter smog control regulations and the rising cost of fuel have brought about changes in Detroit's thinking regarding design and performance. Although in some instances American cars are status symbols, the typical large American car has difficulties navigating narrow European roads. As a soldier in Germany, I often saw

American vehicles in ditches or in accidents because during intense fog or rain they were unsuitable for the conditions.

A business associate of mine, in the electronics field, was more flexible than the domestic auto firms just described. Before committing himself to shipping a large quantity of modular components for receivers and transmitters, he obtained a catalog of these products from a friend in Germany. By closely examining the equipment described within that magazine, he stripped down his product to meet the more basic needs of the European market, thus saving both himself and his distributor from a potentially disastrous marketing error.

Thus, to avoid problems of "fit," have your overseas distributor or agent send you local catalogs and pictures of products similar to yours. You must know what has been selling successfully in your market. Then you can help your manufacturers conform with customs, regulations, and standards used overseas. You must be prepared to modify.

Other considerations:

1. Many foreign countries use different electrical standards than those in the U.S. It is not unusual to find phase, cycle, or voltages, both in home and commercial usage overseas, that would damage equipment designed for use in the U.S., or that would impair its operating efficiency. These will sometimes vary even within a given country. This knowledge will let the exporter know if it is necessary to substitute a special motor and/or arrange for a different drive ratio to achieve a desirable operating RPM or service factor.

2. Many items of equipment must be graduated in the metric system to allow them to be integrated with other pieces of equipment or to allow work to be completed in the standard of a country.

3. As freight charges are usually assessed on a weight or volume basis, whichever provides the greater revenue for the carrier, some consideration must be given to shipping an item disassembled, rather than assembled, in order to lower delivery costs. Also, this may be necessary to facilitate movement on narrow roads, streets, through doorways or elevators which could otherwise cause transit problems.

4. Local customs or historical preference regarding size, color, speed, source, or grade of raw materials, etc., are other reasons why a redesign might be considered. In addition, many foreign governments have established mandatory standards. These will usually be specified with the request for quotation.

Production

The most important thing to remember about production is to process overseas orders promptly—as promptly as domestic orders would be processed. It is much more difficult to explain, in a different language, to someone halfway around the world, the reason for a delayed shipment than to someone locally. If a shipment is delayed, it may be necessary to extend the expiration date of a letter of credit. This is an added expense to the buyer, one he won't appreciate, especially if it happens often.

Packing

Packing is a critical element of your export business. If the product doesn't arrive at its destination in good condition, it is almost as if your product hadn't arrived at all. Both manufacturers and freight forwarders can help with proper packing, since they have had experience with shipping hazards and with the specific product, respectively. Following is a basic packing guide to introduce you to alternative methods of preparing your products for shipment.

Exterior Containers

Fibreboard Boxes (Cartons)

The most common economical container continues to be the fibreboard box. This is understandable as shippers seek efficient, but cheaper and lighterweight containers.

It comes closest to fitting the description of the ideal shipping container, which is light in weight, of low cost, but able to withstand normal transportation hazards and protect the contents against loss or damage during transportation. The fibreboard box frequently measures up to most of these requirements in domestic transportation, but fails frequently in overseas movements when proper selection procedures are not followed. It must be recognized that all commodities cannot be suitably packed in fibreboard boxes. Moreover, all fibreboard boxes are not suitable overseas containers. This is particularly true because increases in moisture content of corrugated fibreboard adversely affect its stiffness and compressive strength.

Figure 10-1. Fibreboard Boxes (Cartons)

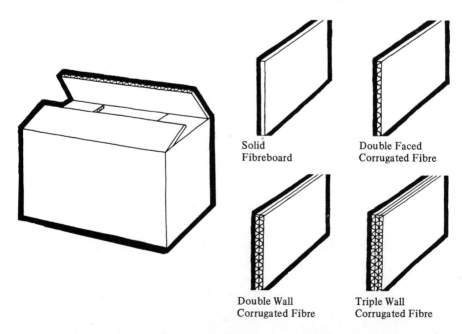

Solid
Fibreboard

Double Faced
Corrugated Fibre

Double Wall
Corrugated Fibre

Triple Wall
Corrugated Fibre

First, the shipper must determine whether or not a fibreboard container is a suitable one for the particular commodity to be shipped, bearing in mind the item's vulnerability as well as the handling and transportation hazards to be encountered. If the answer is "yes," he must then proceed to use the fibreboard container subject to the following:

1. The underlying factors in the selection of the fibreboard box are resistance to compression, resistance to puncture, strength on the score lines, and probably the most important—resistance to moisture absorption. Impregnated and multiwall boxes are the most practical. Never use corrugated fibreboard boxes with a bursting test strength of less than 275 lbs. per square inch (for exporting).

2. Flaps should be stapled or glued with a water resistant adhesive applied to the entire area of contact between the flaps. For further protection, all seams can be sealed with a water resistant tape.

3. Keep weight of contents within load limits specified in the box maker's certificate which appears on the box. The imprinted certificate should appear on one exterior face of every carton. It indicates bursting strength, size limit, and weight limit. (Figure 10-2)

4. Reinforce with two tension straps applied at right angles and crisscrossing at top and bottoms, or with two girth straps of filament tape.

5. When the nature of the contents permits, the load should support the walls of the container. Otherwise, the container selected should have sufficient resistance to compression to prevent collapse when placed in the bottom tier of a pile of similar boxes. NEVER OVERLOAD.

6. Full height partitions should be utilized to separate fragile items within the same fibreboard box and/or to increase the stacking strength of the box.

Figure 10-2. Box Certificate

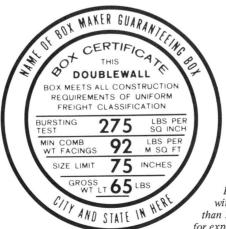

DO NOT use fibreboard with a bursting test of less than 275 lbs. per square inch for export shipping containers.

Figure 10-3. Nailed Wood Boxes

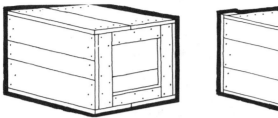

7. Do not overlook economies and additional security offered by unitizing or palletizing, or by overpacking several fibreboard boxes in consolidation containers.

8. Remember, highly pilferable merchandise is never safe in fibreboard boxes.

Nailed Wood Boxes

The nailed wood box (Figure 10-3) is one of the most satisfactory containers for overseas shipments for commodities of moderate weight.

Among its particular advantages is its ability to support superimposed loads; its ability to contain difficult loads without undue distortion or breaking open; the protection it affords contents from damage due to puncture, breakage or crushing; and, finally, the fact that it permits interior blocking to hold the contents in place, thus allowing the container to be turned on its side or upside down. The following recommendations should be considered in selecting the nailed wood box:

1. Boxes should be made up of seasoned lumber with moisture content between 12 per cent and 18 per cent. Knots should not be over one-third the width of the board and specifically should not interfere with nailing. Bad cross graining should also be avoided.

2. Consult appropriate tables for selection of proper sizes of lumber and nails. Boxes with two or four cleats on each end are particularly recommended for overseas shipment. (Figure 10-4)

3. Load properly. Many a well designed box fails because the load is not properly fitted within the container. Unless the item to be packed is irregular in shape, do not permit any voids or dead space. If the load must be kept upright, equip the box with lift handles, skids, top peaks or gables, or some similar device to assure the box being stowed and handled in an upright position. AVOID OVERLOADING.

4. Reinforce the boxes with adequate tension metal straps placed one-sixth of the distance from the ends, unless containers are in excess of 48 inches in length or over 250 pounds. Then, three or more straps should be used, with one for each additional 24 inches. Staples should be used to hold strapping in place when boards are five-eights of an inch in thickness or greater.

Figure 10-4. Lumber and Nail Tables for Nailed Wood Boxes

Weight of Contents (Pounds)		Number of End Cleats	BELOW MEASUREMENTS IN INCHES											
			LOAD SUPPORTS CONTAINER WALLS						LOAD GIVES LITTLE OR NO CONTAINER SUPPORT					
			SOFTWOOD			HARDWOOD			SOFTWOOD			HARDWOOD		
Over	Less		Thickness sides, top & bottom	Thickness ends	Thickness and width of cleats	Thickness sides, top & bottom	Thickness ends	Thickness and width of cleats	Thickness sides, top & bottom	Thickness ends	Thickness and width of cleats	Thickness sides, top & bottom	Thickness ends	Thickness and width of cleats
0	50	2	3/8	5/8	5/8 X 1 3/4	3/8	5/8	5/8 X 1 3/4	1/2	3/4	3/4 X 2 1/4	1/2	5/8	5/8 X 1 3/4
		4	3/8	5/8	5/8 X 1 3/4	3/8	5/8	5/8 X 1 3/4	1/2	5/8	5/8 X 2 1/4	1/2	5/8	5/8 X 1 3/4
50	100	2	1/2	3/4	3/4 X 2 1/4	3/8	5/8	5/8 X 1 3/4	1/2	3/4	3/4 X 2 1/4	1/2	5/8	5/8 X 1 3/4
		4	1/2	3/4	3/4 X 2 1/4	3/8	5/8	5/8 X 1 3/4	1/2	5/8	5/8 X 2 1/4	1/2	5/8	5/8 X 1 3/4
100	250	2	5/8	3/4	3/4 X 2 1/4	1/2	3/4	3/4 X 2 1/4	5/8	3/4	3/4 X 2 5/8	1/2	3/4	3/4 X 2 1/4
		4	5/8	5/8	5/8 X 2 1/4	1/2	5/8	5/8 X 2 1/4	5/8	3/4	3/4 X 2 1/4	1/2	5/8	5/8 X 2 1/4
250	400	2	3/4	13/16	3/4 X 2 5/8	5/8	3/4	3/4 X 2 1/4	3/4	1 1/16	1 1/16 X 3 1/4	5/8	13/16	13/16 X 2 3/4
		4	3/4	13/16	3/4 X 2 5/8	5/8	3/4	3/4 X 2 1/4	3/4	3/4	1 1/16 X 3 1/4	5/8	3/4	3/4 X 2 3/4
400	600	4	13/16	13/16	13/16 X 2 5/8	5/8	3/4	3/4 X 2 1/4	13/16	13/16	1 1/16 X 3 1/4	3/4	13/16	13/16 X 2 3/4
600	800	4	13/16	1 1/16	1 1/16 X 3 1/4	13/16	1 1/16	1 1/16 X 3 1/4	13/16	1 1/16	1 1/16 X 3 1/4	3/4	13/16	13/16 X 2 3/4
800	1000	4	1 1/16	1 5/16	1 5/16 X 4 1/8	1 1/16	1 5/16	1 5/16 X 4 1/8	1 1/16	1 5/16	1 5/16 X 4 1/8	7/8	1 1/16	1 1/16 X 3 3/8

NAILS—Cement coated nails are preferred for their increased holding power. The size of the nail depends on the thickness of the wood (see above). Use 6d for 5/8", 7d for 3/4", 8d for 13/16", 9d for 1-1/16" & 12d for 1-5/16". Do not use nails into wood less than 5/8". Spacing of nails (fastening sides, tops & bottom to the ends) varies with the size of the nail. Space 6d 2", 7d 2-1/4", 8d 2-1/2", 9d 2-3/4", and 12d 3-1/2". (If nailing into end grain, reduce spacing by 1/4".)

WOOD—Fir, pines, poplar, cottonwood, cedar, hemlock and larch are included in the softwood category. Hardwoods include ash, elm, cherry, oak, hard maple and hickory.

5. DO NOT USE SECOND-HAND BOXES. They are deficient in strength and do not permit detection of pilferage.

6. Boxes should be equipped with corrugated fasteners or similar devices where contents are substantially valued and susceptible to pilferage.

7. Boxes should be lined with a waterproof barrier material, sealed at the edges with a waterproof tape or adhesive, to protect both the contents and the interior packing material.

Crates

There are two general types of crates—the open or skeleton crate and the fully sheathed crate. Both types are dependent upon properly constructed frameworks. While the drawings (Figure 10-5) illustrate the comparative strength of frame members of open crates under vertical compression, the same principles apply to sheathed crates, as they also require diagonal bracing to make them rigid. Keep in mind that sheathing is provided to protect the contents against exposure to the elements.

The open crate can be used where contents are virtually indestructible and packing is required only to facilitate handling and stowage. It also serves well as an overpack to consolidate fibreboard boxes or to provide unit pack stiffness to resist crushing. Three-way corner construction should be reinforced with diagonals.

Consider these points in sheathed crate construction.

1. Provide a SUBSTANTIAL framework, i.e., corner posts or vertical end struts, edge or frame members, intermediate struts and diagonal braces.

2. Large crates are usually stowed in lower holds, hence must bear great superimposed weights. Insure top strength by frequent top joists under sheathing (never more than 30" apart). DON'T depend on end grain nailing ALONE to hold these joists. Provide joist support positioned directly under the joists' ends.

3. Reinforce floor at load bearing points when between skids or sill members.

4. Design for vertical sheathing: sides and ends.

5. On skid-type crates terminate end sheathing at flooring to permit entry of forklifts. Terminate side sheathing ½" short of skid bottoms to prevent tearing away of sheathing when crate is dragged sideways.

6. On sill-type crates provide lengthwise rubbing strips at base to facilitate handling and prevent tearing adrift of sheathing when the crate is dragged.

7. Where skids are used, be sure they are of sufficient dimensions and an adequate number provided. Skid ends should always be chamfered.

8. Reduce cube and interior bracing problems by providing maximum disassembly of the carried item. Spares and disassembled parts should be adequately secured to the crate interior. In so doing, aim at a low center of gravity.

9. Supplement weak end grain nailing of interior bracing by back-up cleats.

10. Line crate interiors (except bottom) with a good grade waterproof barrier material. Ventilate crates containing machinery or other items suscepti-

Figure 10–5. Crates

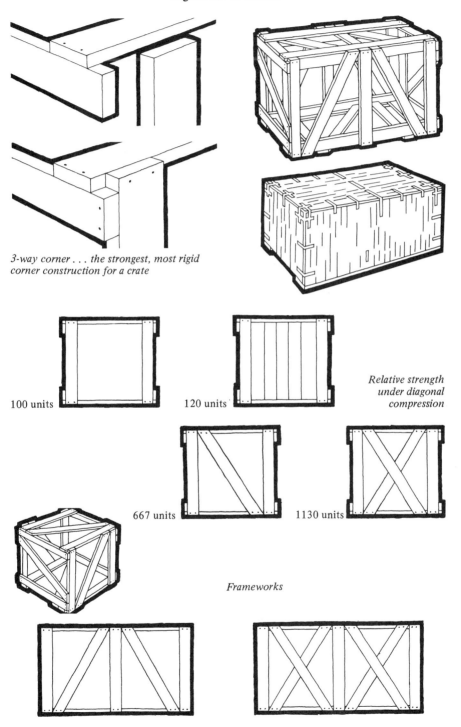

3-way corner . . . the strongest, most rigid corner construction for a crate

100 units

120 units

Relative strength under diagonal compression

667 units

1130 units

Frameworks

ble to damage from condensation, with baffled vents or louvre plates covering ventilation hole clusters at ends or sides. Also, space floor boards 3/8" apart. Consider use of crate top coating where open freight car or open storage may be encountered.

11. Corners of all crates should be reinforced with lengths of 1" flat nailed strapping applied so as to tie together all their faces at each corner.

12. Assure yourself that handling facilities are available for your crate at destination and at intermediate points. Provide consignee with opening instructions to reduce accidental damage in unpacking.

Wirebound Boxes and Crates

Wirebound boxes and crates (Figure 10-6a) have shown themselves useful for a large variety of products not affected by minor distortions of the container, and where the possibility of pilferage is not a primary concern. It is an ideal container for overpacks of solid or corrugated fibreboard boxes (cartons). If the wirebound container is not completely filled or if the contents may be affected by possible distortion of the container, interior blocking or bracing, properly applied, should be used. The ends of wirebound containers should be reinforced to adequately resist the forces that may be applied during handling, thus preventing damage to contents.

Shippers should AVOID OVERLOADING and should not use boxes too large for their contents. Other considerations are:

1. Veneer and cleats should be full thickness, straight grained and sound, free from knots, decay, mildew or open splits. Sound knots not more than 1½" in diameter and less than one-third the width of the piece of veneer are allowable. Wire should be free from rust and scale.

2. Ideal staple spacing is 2½" on crates; 2" on boxes. A minimum of two staples per slat is recommended.

3. Mitered cleats provide greater resistance to rough handling than tongued and grooved cleats.

4. Observed care in effecting closures to avoid wire fatigue. Use special closure tools.

Figure 10-6. (a) Wirebound Boxes and Crates (b) Cleated Plywood Boxes

(a)   (b)

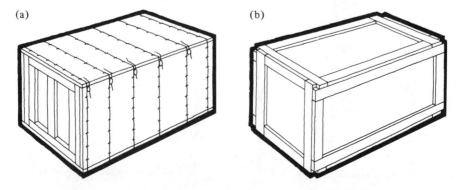

5. Consult appropriate tables and your box supplier for specifications for export type containers.

6. Where contents are susceptible to pilferage or exceed 150 lbs., apply one tension strap around top, bottom, and ends. If over 250 lbs., apply two additional straps 3" from each end around top, bottom and sides; also consider applying straps over intermediate cleats.

7. Line box interior with good grade of waterproof barrier material, properly sealed.

Cleated Plywood Boxes

Properly assembled and used, cleated plywood panel boxes (Figure 10–6b) have many uses in foreign trade. Their lightness and comparative strength particularly recommend them for air freight shipments. Shippers may abuse these containers, however, by using second-hand units, overloading, applying strapping improperly, allowing long unsupported panels or failing to properly nail the box closed. Thin panels invite damage to contents through punctures. Follow these points in plywood shipments.

1. Consult appropriate tables to avoid overloading, to determine proper nail spacing and to find correct dimensions of plywood and cleats. NEVER USE SECOND-HAND BOXES.

2. Reject rotten, split or otherwise defective cleats.

3. Apply intermediate cleats to all panels in excess of 24".

4. Apply strapping only over edge and/or intermediate cleats for maximum support. Strapping which spans unframed areas is easily broken; may injure handlers. Employ stapling to hold banding in place on the cleats.

5. Don't overlook lining with adequate waterproof or vaporproof barrier material, where contents are susceptible to water damage.

Steel Drums

New steel drums (Figure 10–7a) are generally excellent for export. Second-hand drums, unless thoroughly reconditioned and tested, may give trouble because of fatigue caused by dents at the chime and previous damages to closures. Also consider the following:

1. Closures must be made as prescribed by the manufacturer. Back up friction type covers of drums as well as cans or pails with soldering or spot welding at three or more points.

2. Be sure adequate seals are used on locking levers and sealing rings of open end drums. Failure of seals may result in accidental opening of covers.

3. Consider use of tamperproof seals at filling and dispensing holes.

4. Make frequent spot checks of automatic filling machinery by weighing filled drums. Shortages may occur at the source.

5. Do not re-use single or one trip containers.

6. For hazardous or dangerous substances, be sure the drums are approved for the carriage of the intended cargo.

Fibre Drums

Fiber drums (Figure 10–7b) are gaining importance in the export picture. Before using, however, it should be determined that open storage en route is not contemplated. Considerations for fibre drums include:

1. High density materials should not be packed into fibre drums.

2. Fiber drums should be filled to capacity in order to add rigidity to the packages.

3. It is advisable to settle or de-aerate materials—particularly light fluffy powders—during the filling operations. Use of a vibrator or mechanical settler is recommended. Bag-lined drums can be de-aerated simply by manually compressing the filled bag.

4. Keep size of drum compatible with weight of contents to avoid overloading.

5. Closures are important. Be sure sealing rings and locking levers are properly in place and will not be accidentally jarred or pulled loose.

6. Handle with mechanical equipment or roll on bottom chimes. Fibre drums are not designed to roll on sidewalls. Avoid cutting and chafing of sidewalls.

Barrels, Casks or Kegs

The wooden barrel (Figure 10–7c) has been a workhorse of overseas trade, dating back to ancient times. Selection of the wrong barrel for your product can result in leakage, contamination, breakage and many other headaches. The following are basic recommendations:

1. Tight (liquid) barrels should be stored bung up. Request stowage on bilges. Slack (dry) barrels should be stored on ends. Never store or ship slack barrels on their side.

2. Provide reinforcing head cleats running from chime to chime at right angles to headpieces. Cleat thickness should never be greater than chime depth.

3. Use tongue and groove staves with a suitable liner where the contents, such as dry chemicals and powders, may sift. Make sure barrel wood and liner material will not contaminate contents.

4. Keep voids in slack barrels to a minimum. Use headliners (strips of coiled elm fastened inside chime) to give barrel heads added strength.

5. Where tight barrels are employed, hoops should be fastened with not less than three hoop fasteners (dogs) per hoop. Provide for inspection at interim transit points to check for leakage where practicable. If contents are carried in brine, re-brining at interim points may save contents of leaking units.

Multi-Wall Shipping Sacks

Multi-wall shipping sacks or bags (Figure 10–8a) are being used more and more for packaging of powdered, granular and lump materials, particularly dry chemicals.

Figure 10-7. (a) Steel Drums (b) Fibre Drums (c) Barrels, Casks or Kegs

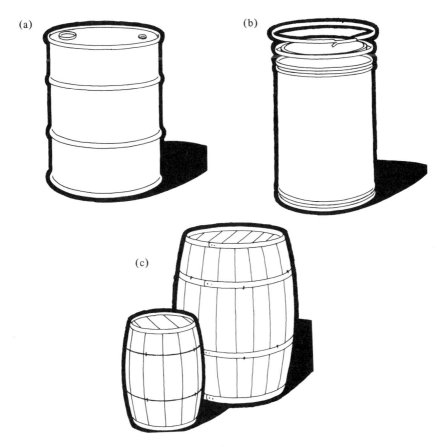

These sacks are flexible containers generally made up from two walls or plies of heavy duty kraft paper to a maximum of six. Often, they are made in combination with special coatings, laminations, impregnations, or even plies of textile material such as burlap to give them additional strength and added protection to their contents. Because of the flexibility of these containers, special attention must be given to the use of flexible waterproof or moistureproof barriers in their construction.

There are several types of bags used, the most common being the pasted bottom or sewn bottom open-mouth, and the pasted valve or sewn valve. The pasted bottom and sewn bottom open mouth type bags are closed after filling, by sewing through all plies with a strip of tape incorporated into the sewn end in such a way that it folds over the end of the sack to control sifting. They can also be closed by gluing. The valve type bags are closed by manually folding over an external paper sleeve or by the check-valve action of an inner paper sleeve when the bags are full. The internal pressure of the contents causes this, and care must be taken that the bags are sufficiently filled to exert this pressure. It must be recognized that slight leakage will nevertheless occur, particularly when the bags are handled.

The use of these bags for overseas shipments should be limited. This type of container, more than any other, must be adapted to the requirements of the commodity they contain. This requires careful research and intelligent selection. It is recommended that the loaded bag does not exceed 50 lbs. Consideration must be given to the value of the product as well as to its hygroscopic properties and chemical and physical characteristics. Utmost consideration must be given to in-transit hazards, such as atmospheric conditions or exposure to the elements, number of transfers, handling and warehouse facilities. Of major importance is the question as to whether the contents of the sack will be subjected to contamination if the bags are ruptured or if foreign matter can filter in through the stitching holes.

A good practice for the shipper is to include a supply of open mouth refill or overslip sacks with each shipment.

The number of refill sacks should not be less than one per cent of the number of sacks in the shipment and preferably three per cent. The refill sacks should be imprinted with instructions for their use as well as identification of the commodity which they will carry. Overslip sacks should be slightly larger than the original sack and constructed of the same number and kind of plies.

Palletizing of a number of sacks, adequately shrink-wrapped and/or banded to the pallet, has been particularly effective in reducing damage and pilferage, and forces use of mechanical handling equipment.

Bales

A well made bale (Figure 10-8b) may be expected to outturn reasonably well in most export trades. Bear in mind, however, that all bales are subject to pilferage, hook hole and water damage. They are, therefore, not recommended for highly valued commodities. To minimize losses, follow these recommendations:

1. Where contents may be subject to damage from strapping pressure, use a primary wrap of fibreboard material.

Figure 10-8. (a) Multi-Wall Shipping Sacks (b) Bales

(a)

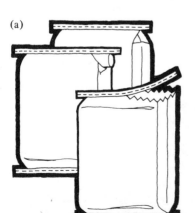

(b)

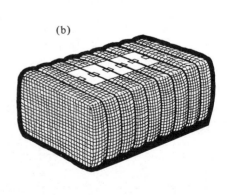

Figure 10-9. Cushioning Characteristics (1)

Type Material	Abrasion Resistance	Resilience	Compression	Absorption	Water Resistance	(2) Dusting	Damping Quality (3)
Bound Fibre	Poor	High	Low	Low	High	High	Fair
Cellulosic	Good	Medium	High	(4)	(4)	High	Excellent
Fibrous Glass	(4)	High	Low	Low	High	Low	Fair
Wood Excelsior	Poor	Medium	High	High	(4)	High	Excellent
Hair Felt	(5)	Medium	Low	(5)	(5)	Low	Poor
Solid Fibreboard	Poor	Medium	Low	Low	High	Low	Poor
Wax Shredded Paper	Poor	Low	High	High	Low	High	Excellent
Wrapping Paperboard	Good	Low	High	High	Low	Low	Excellent
Cellular, Plasticized, Polyvinyl Chloride	(4)	High	Low	Nil	High	Low	Good
Rigid or Elastic Polyurethane Foam	(6)	(6)	(6)	(6)	Low	None	(6)
Chemically Blown Cellular Rubber	Good	High	Low	(6)	(6)	Low	Fair
Latex Foam Sponge Rubber	Good	High	Low	High	Low	Low	Fair
Paper Honeycomb	Energy dissipating medium only.						
Corrugated Fibreboard	Used primarily as a die cut, cells pads and trays.						

(1) These ratings are general in nature. Any characteristic can be varied in a customized mode.
(2) Dusting describes the extent of material breakdown in small or dustlike particles in transit.
(3) Damping quality reflects the ability of the material to progressively diminish vibrations or oscillation.
(4) This material is manufactured under different specifications that vary the degree of named characteristics.
(5) Used mainly as padding for large heavy items. Often glued in place.
(6) This is a foam-in-place material that can vary in make-up to meet requirements.

2. Use an inner wrap of creped or pleated waterproof paper. This type paper is necessary to provide moisture protection and to give with bale distortions without tearing.

3. Provide heavy outer wrap of burlap or similar cloth able to stand heavy abrasions in transit.

4. Provide "ears" at corners of small bales to facilitate handling without hooks. Bale weights under 300 lbs. are less apt to be handled with hooks.

5. A minimum of four flat tension bands should be used. Apply tightly at the maximum bale compression to avoid slipping of end bands.

6. Stencil all shipping and cautionary marks on bale. Do not use tags.

Cushioning

Fragile and brittle items must be suspended or protected against shock and vibration by a cushion that gradually increases resistance against item movement. Selection of the correct cushioning material depends on the item's size, weight, shape, surface finish and the built-in shock resistance. See Figure 10-9 for cushioning characteristics.

Unit Loads

Many products or commodities can be economically palletized or unitized (Figures 10-10 and 10-11) to facilitate handling, stowage and protection of cargo. Often, packing costs can be significantly reduced by palletizing and unitizing. Pallet and unit loads offer the following additional advantages:

- Handling of palletized or unitized loads requires use of mechanical handling equipment—reducing the manual handling damage hazard.
- Eliminates the multiple handling of individual items—further reducing possible damage from manual handling.
- Reduces opportunity for pilferage and theft and permits early detection of tampering.
- Speeds loading and unloading of trailers, boxcars, intermodal containers, barges, ships, and aircraft.
- Facilitates application of waterproofing protection to the load; the overwrap applied accompanies the load for the entire journey.
- Reduces incidence of lost or strayed items.
- Facilitates checking and inventory of shipment.

Palletizing is the assembly of one or more packages on pallet base and securing the load to the pallet.

Unitizing is the assembly of one or more items into a compact load, secured together and provided with skids and cleats for ease of handling.

Palletizing Cargo

There are four "standard" pallets that accommodate the different modal/intermodal containers most frequently used in international commerce. The sizes,

Figure 10-10. Palletizing Cargo

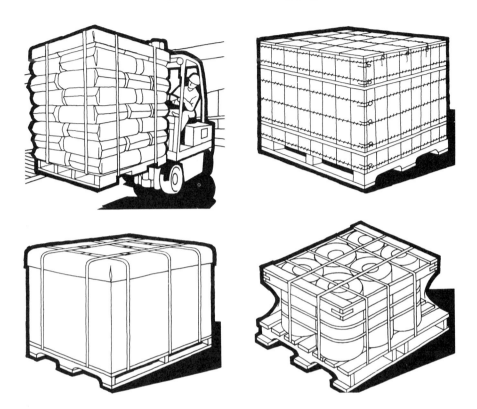

in inches, of these pallets are 45 x 54 (114 x 137 cm), 45 x 45 (114 x 114 cm), 45 x 33.75 (114 x 83 cm), and 40.91 x 49.09 (104 x 125 cm).

Select the pallet that:

1. best utilizes the space of the intermodal transportation to be used.

2. best utilizes the uniform unit package dimensions of the item to be shipped.

3. limits the weight of the palletized load to 2200 pounds (1000 kg).

Assemble the individual unit packages on the pallet base without an overhang. The load pattern should minimize voids and be interlocking.

Insert spacers between the rows or layers of irregularly shaped items. Adhesives can be used between cartons in a uniform load.

Secure the load tightly and firmly by using horizontal and vertical strapping. Plastic shrink wrap can be used to stabilize and protect palletized loads.

Provide stacking protection to the top of the pallet by using a lumber, plywood or fibreboard cap. Loads that are susceptible to compression must also be supported with vertical framing.

Palletized loads susceptible to water damage can be protected by shrink wrap or stretch wrap, overwrapping with barrier material, or consolidated shipping in a weathertight container.

Unitizing Cargo

Assemble individual items into one unit by bolting, nailing, or strapping together.

Provide load with skids to facilitate handling by forklift.

Provide vertical cleats on sides of load to facilitate handling by cargo sling.

Figure 10–11. Unitizing Cargo

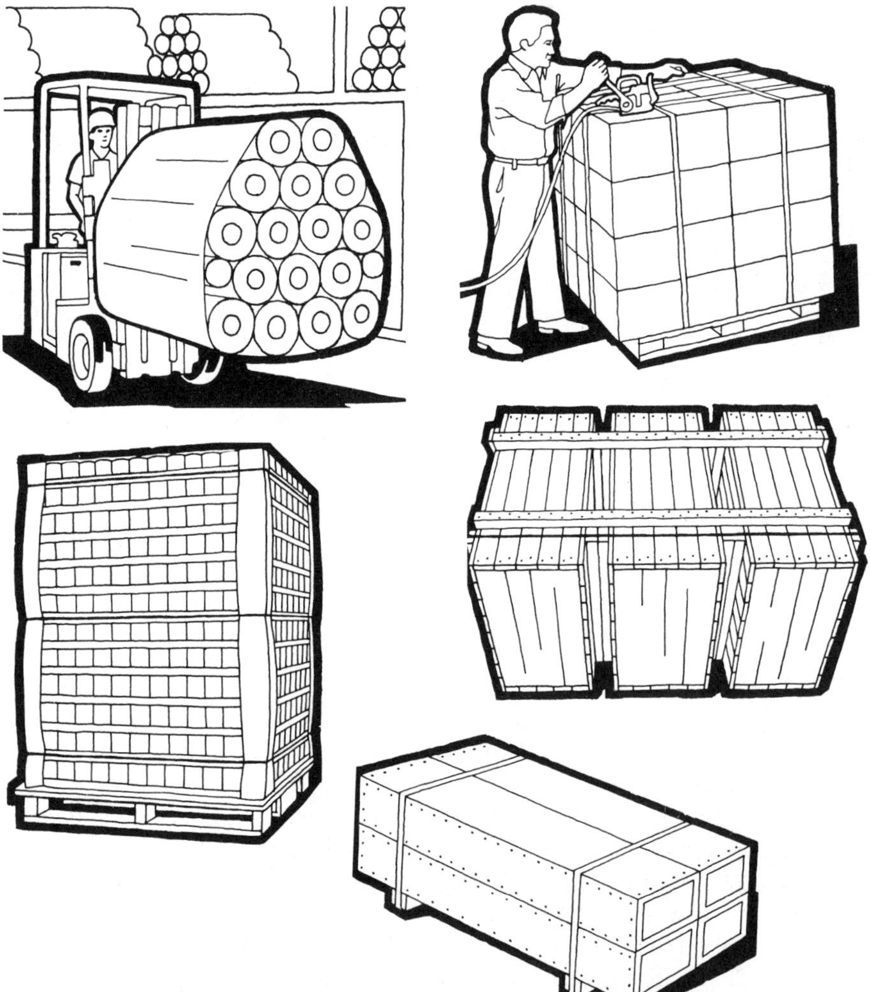

Provide water damage protection by using plastic shrink wrap or stretch wrap on individual items before assembly into unit load.

Apply shrink wrap or stretch wrap to entire load.

Use waterproof paper or plastic film overwrap.

Sources of Help

If the manufacturer you are working with is unfamiliar with correct packing methods, contact your freight forwarder for the name(s) of export packing companies to handle your goods. These firms are experts in their field.

Marking

The primary purpose of marking is for the identification of the shipment, enabling the carrier to forward it to the ultimate consignee. Old marks, advertising and other extraneous information only serve to confuse this primary function for freight handlers and carriers. Follow these fundamental marking rules:

1. Unless local regulations prohibit, use blind marks; particularly where goods are susceptible to pilferage. Change them periodically to avoid familiarity by handlers. Trade names, consignees' or shippers' names should be avoided as they indicate the nature of the contents.

2. Consignee (identification) marks and port marks showing destination and transfer points should be large, clear and applied by stencil with waterproof ink. They should be applied on three faces of the container, preferably side, and/or ends, and top. Legibility is of utmost importance. Letters should be a minimum of 2" high.

3. If commodities require special handling or stowage, the containers should be so marked, and this information should also appear on the bills of lading.

4. Cautionary markings must be permanent and easy to read (use the languages of both the origin and destination countries). The use of stencils is recommended for legibility—do not use crayon, tags or cards. Figure 10-12 gives an example of marking on an export pack.

If the manufacturer you are working with is unfamiliar with the correct marking procedures, contact your freight forwarder for the name(s) of export packing companies to handle your goods. These firms are experts in marking as well as packing.

Non-Hazardous Pictorial Markings

It is recommended that handling instructions always be printed on the exterior pack in the language of the destination country. It is not unusual for a shipment to be handled by another country along the transport path or by freight handlers that cannot read. These potential problems can best be overcome by pictorial markings. The seven symbols depicted under the heading of "International" in

Figure 10-12. Example of Markings

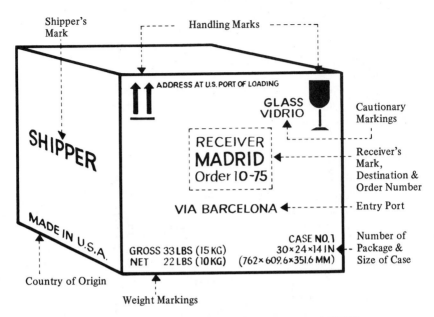

Shipper's Mark
Handling Marks
ADDRESS AT U.S. PORT OF LOADING
GLASS VIDRIO
Cautionary Markings
SHIPPER
RECEIVER MADRID Order 10-75
Receiver's Mark, Destination & Order Number
VIA BARCELONA
Entry Port
MADE IN U.S.A.
Country of Origin
GROSS 33 LBS (15 KG)
NET   22 LBS (10 KG)
CASE NO.1
30×24×14 IN
(762×609.6×351.6 MM)
Number of Package & Size of Case
Weight Markings

LARGE PACKAGES SHOULD HAVE MARKINGS ON TWO SIDES

Figure 10-13 represent markings that have been accepted by the International Organization for Standardization. The other three symbols under the U.S. caption are additional markings that have been accepted by the American National Standards Institute, but are not yet included as international standards.

Cautionary markings in various languages appear in Figure 10-15.

Hazardous Materials

Unilateral state regulation of international commerce is impractical in today's interdependent world. Procedures that are acceptable in one country and forsaken in another inhibit world trade through embargo or unacceptable delay in cargo reaching its ultimate destination. The labels shown in Figure 10-14 are the hazardous material (dangerous goods) identifications adopted by many IMCO (United Nations) member countries to smooth the flow of these type materials in waterborne commerce. The color coding, symbol, and the class number (when displayed) are universal.

These labels simply provide a visual signal of dangerous goods in transport. They will cause special handling along the transport path, including embargo, if the commodity is not authorized for carriage. Dangerous goods regulations almost always also require special documentation and packing under strict criteria. Routing through named entry ports is also a frequent requirement. Consequently, when negotiating for entry into foreign trade of these items, always require a complete explanation of the applicable rules.

Figure 10–13. Non-Hazardous Markings

INTERNATIONAL

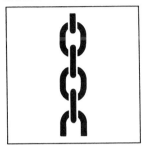

Sling here

Fragile, Handle with care

Use no hooks

This way up

Keep away from heat

Keep dry

Center of gravity

U.S. STANDARDS

Do not roll

Hand truck here

Keep away from cold

Figure 10-14. Hazardous Materials (Color of solid or shaded area in parentheses)

Class 1
Explosives
(Orange)

Class 1
Explosives
(Orange)

Class 2
Non-Flammable
Gases (Green)

Class 2
Flammable
Gases —OR—
Class 3
Flammable Liquids
(Red)

Class 4
Flammable Solids
(Red & White Stripe)

Class 4
Spontaneously
Combustible
Substances (Red)

Class 4
Water Reactive
Substances
(Blue)

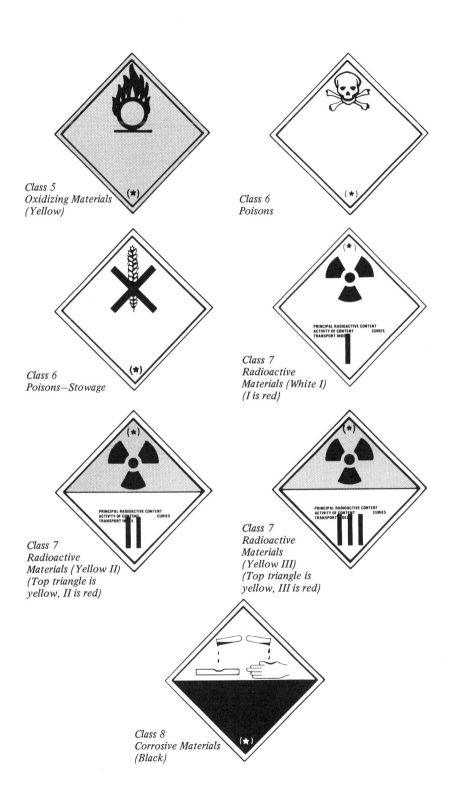

Class 5
Oxidizing Materials
(Yellow)

Class 6
Poisons

Class 6
Poisons–Stowage

Class 7
Radioactive
Materials (White I)
(I is red)

Class 7
Radioactive
Materials (Yellow II)
(Top triangle is
yellow, II is red)

Class 7
Radioactive
Materials
(Yellow III)
(Top triangle is
yellow, III is red)

Class 8
Corrosive Materials
(Black)

PRINCIPAL RADIOACTIVE CONTENT
ACTIVITY OF CONTENT   CURIES
TRANSPORT INDEX

Figure 10–14 (continued). Hazardous Materials (Classes)

Hazard Classes. The below table of "Hazard Class Numbers" defines the numbers frequently displayed on the labels (shown on the previous two pages) in the space denoted by the star in parentheses.

Class	Description
1	Explosives (Class 1.1, 1.2 and 1.3) Explosives (Class 1.4 and 1.5)
2	Non-Flammable and Flammable Gases
3	Flammable Liquids
4	Flammable Solids (Readily combustible) Spontaneously Combustible Substances Water Reactive Substances
5	Oxidizing Materials (Oxidizing maters and/or organic peroxides)
6	Poisonous Materials (Class A, B & C poisons or toxic substances) Poisonous Materials (Harmful stow away from foodstuffs)
7	Radioactive Materials (White I, Yellow II or Yellow III)
8	Corrosive Materials (Acids, corrosive liquids/solids & alkalines)
9	Miscellaneous Hazardous Materials (Those materials which present a danger in transport. No specific label authorized.)

Important: Do not assume that compliance with domestic regulations will automatically qualify a shipment for passage through enroute countries and entry into the destination port. Requirements that are not met can easily be the difference between profit and loss.

If the material may be hazardous then in addition to all known required markings and labels furnish pertinent chemical or physical data. This will expedite foreign freight relabelling by forwarders.

Export Insurance

Export shipments are usually insured against loss or damage in transit by ocean marine insurance. Inland marine policies cover shipment to the point of departure whether seaport, airport, or rail terminal inside the U.S. Two types of policies are popular in international trade:

1. Special (one-time) cargo policy, which insures a single shipment.

2. Open and blanket cargo policies, which are in continuous effect and automatically insure all cargo moving at the seller's risk.

The one-time cargo policy is, of course, more expensive since the risk cannot be spread over a number of different shipments. However, if your export business is infrequent, it may be wise to obtain this type of coverage.

Open and blanket cargo policies are similar. The open policy remains in force until it is cancelled, covering all shipments of the exporter in transit within speci-

Figure 10-15. Cautionary Markings

English	French	German	Italian	Spanish	Portuguese	Swedish
Handle With Care	Attention	Vorsicht	Attenzione	Manéjese con Cuidado	Tratar Com Cuidado	Varsamt
Glass	Verre	Glas	Vetro	Vidrio	Vidro	Glas
Use No Hooks	Manier Sans Crampons	Ohne Haken handhaben	Manipolare senza graffi	No Se Usan Ganchos	Não Empregue Ganchos	Begagna inga krokar
This Side Up	Cette Face En Haut	Diese Seite oben	Questo lato su	Este Lado Arriba	Este Lado Para Encima	Denna sida upp
Fragile	Fragile	Zerbrechlich	Fragile	Frágil	Fragil	Ömtäligt
Keep in Cool Place	Garder En Lieu Frais	Kuehl aufbewahren	Conservare in luogo fresco	Manténgase En Lugar Fresco	Deve Ser Guardado Em Lugar Fresco	Förvaras kallt
Keep Dry	Protéger Contre Humidité	Vor Naesse schuetzen	Preservare dall' umidita	Manténgase Seco	Não Deve Ser Molhado	Förvaras torrt
Open Here	Ouvrir Ici	Hier oeffnen	Aprire da questa parte	Ábrase Aquí	Abrir Por Este Ponto	Öppnas här

Prepared by Marine and Aviation Services Dept, Insurance Co. of North America.

fied geographical trade areas. Premiums are paid "as they go" because the amounts can be determined only when the goods are shipped.

Blanket policies are closed contracts. The insured exporter pays a lump sum premium that is fixed in advance. The premium is based on the estimated total amount of shipping expected. It can be adjusted depending on whether the coverage exceeded the originally insured amount or fell below it.

Generally, the open (or floating) policy is more popular with U.S. exporters because:

1. If the exporter fails to report that goods have been forwarded from the place of shipment, he is automatically covered.

2. The rate schedule attached to this policy gives the premium charge for various commodities and merchandise so that the exact insurance amount can figure into the c.i.f., or landed, sales price.

Your freight forwarder will normally handle your insurance or will recommend someone for you to use. The forwarder's rates are very competitive, since he can offer insurance services along with shipping and transportation.

Chapter Eleven

Documentation and Licensing

Documentation is very important in processing an order. The papers accompanying a shipment tell what is being shipped, to whom, and how. Figure 11-1 shows the paper flow connected with an export transaction.

Papers show the approval of the U.S. government and sometimes of the government of the receiving country, and they provide either or both countries with the raw data that makes up trade statistics. Special care should be given in the preparation of the documents to avoid difficulties at the time of shipment. In foreign trade, there is no element of the casualness sometimes present in transactions taking place in the U.S. marketplace. If the documentation for a foreign shipment is wrong in even a small element, the shipment may be refused by customs at the U.S. port of exit or the foreign port of entry; it may be delayed; it may be lost. It is not as easy to correct documentation errors for foreign shipments as it is for shipments within the U.S. A recent *Business Week* article emphasized the problem in U.S. exports to France. American firms repeatedly send incorrect documentation, so French importers cannot get shipments out of customs; one or two such experiences would be enough to dry up an otherwise promising market.

Obviously, it is necessary for the exporter to understand the necessary documentation. There are two basic types of documents to be considered: shipping documents and collection documents.

Shipping Documents

Shipping documents consist of *export licenses* and *export declarations*. Export licenses are also of two types: *validated licenses* and *general licenses*, along with alterations and special cases.

Validated export licenses. These licenses apply to products that the U.S. government wants to control closely: strategic goods (articles of war), items in short supply (copper, certain chemicals), goods affected by foreign policy (computers to the U.S.S.R.). A validated export license amounts to special permission to sell such products overseas, or special permission to sell more ordinary products to countries

Figure 11–1. Export Steps

Shipper

1 Prepares Domestic Bill of Lading for movement of cargo to pier, and sends copy to his forwarder along with packing list.

2 Checks Bill of Lading:
   - number of packages
   - marks and numbers
   - description of cargo
   - foreign destination
   - gross weights of each package shipped
   - local party to be notified

3 Marks cargo plainly to show:
   - gross and net weights
   - cubic measurement
   - foreign destination
   - identification marks
   - country of origin

Motor Carrier

4 Secures interchange agreement with steamship company on containers.

5 Accepts cargo for transit to the port.

6 Advises freight forwarder or shipper's local representative of cargo's arrival.

7 Obtains the following information from forwarder or representative:
   - name of vessel
   - sailing date
   - pier number and location
   - location of any special permits needed to clear hazardous or oversize cargo for acceptance by ocean terminal.

8 Obtains Dock Receipt from forwarder or other representative to accompany cargo.

9 Contacts terminal operator to make appointment for special handling or equipment, if required, at least 24 hours before delivery.

Forwarder

10 Provides Dock Receipt and special permits, if any, to delivering motor carrier.

11 Checks Dock Receipt for completeness:
   - name of shipper
   - name of vessel
   - ports of loading and discharge
   - number and type of packages
   - description of cargo
   - gross weight, dimensions, and cubic measurement of each package
   - marks and numbers
   - shipper's export declaration number, if required.

Driver

12 Moves his truck on line upon arrival at pier.

Terminal Operator

13 Issues pass to driver at gate house.

14 Checks driver's papers:
   - Dock Receipt
   - Permits

15 Calls driver for unloading.

16 Assigns driver a checker and an unloading spot.

Driver

17 Unloads his vehicle (using extra pier labor is optional, at rates specified in the Terminal Conference tariff.)

18 Obtains signed copy of Dock Receipt, and receipt for extra labor, if used.

Terminal Operator

19 Retains original of Dock Receipt.

Driver

20 Surrenders gate pass at gate house.

Terminal Operator

21 Forwards Dock Receipt to steamship company.

Steamship Company

22 Issues Ocean Bill of Lading to shipper or his agent.

upon which the U.S. has placed trade restrictions. Obtaining this special permission is frequently time-consuming and costly. There are thousands of products that do not require a validated license, and all but 20 countries in the world can receive these products, as far as the U.S. is concerned. Particularly for the new exporter, there is little point in dealing in restricted items or with restricted countries. It is best to concentrate on the many items that require only a general export license, and to sell these items to importers in nations with which the U.S. has good and open trade relations.

Your local Department of Commerce office can give you a current list of goods and countries requiring validated export licenses, and Chapter 12 provides an introduction. Skimming Chapter 12 can give you an idea of the scope of U.S. trade relations with other countries. Obtaining some familiarity with these relations should be part of your homework, to be done before you select the products to export and while you are doing market research.

General export licenses. Perhaps 90% or more of the items exported require a general license. There are several types of general licenses that cover all items not requiring a validated license. Figures 11-2 and 11-3 show an application for an export license; Figure 11-4 shows the license itself. (Figures 11-2 through 11-3 are grouped together at the back of the chapter.)

Normally, actual licensing is handled by your freight forwarder; however, it is wise to ask the local Department of Commerce which type of license is required before you quote an order, since the fee varies. Checking ahead of time will save considerable time and effort, and familiarity on your part can forestall errors by others. You should also be familiar with the following, in order to facilitate planning:

Time needed for acquiring licenses. Most applications, amendments, and re-export requests are acted upon within two weeks after receipt in the Office of Export Administration. Those involving strategic commodities, sensitive areas, and/or other security or policy problems may, however, require a longer processing time. When processing time extends in excess of 90 days, the Office of Export Administration will advise the exporter of the circumstances requiring the additional time and give an estimate of when action will be taken. Since a premature request for information may actually interrupt the normal processing of such documents and therefore cause unnecessary delay, the applicant should, unless an emergency exists, wait from three to five weeks from the date the document was mailed before requesting information. The request for status is made on a special form, shown in Figure 11-5.

Amendments and Extensions. A change that constitutes an essentially new transaction, such as a change in ultimate consignee, destination, or commodity, requires a new license. Where the change is not significant, however, a license may be amended (e.g., a price increase, extension of validity period, addition of another commodity, etc.). Individual licenses that are issued with the normal one-year validity period may be extended for six months if complete shipment cannot be made against the license during the original validity period. Figure 11-6 illustrates the form used when amendments are necessary.

Emergency clearances. There may be times when there is an urgent reason for an application to receive immediate attention. In justifiable emergencies, the

Office of Export Administration (and certain Department of Commerce district offices), when requested to do so by the applicant or his authorized agent and at the applicant's or agent's expense, will send a telegram authorizing clearance of the shipment. Usually, such special clearance can be handled within one working day. The validity of a license issued under this special processing procedure expires on the last day of the month following the month of issuance. Because a license issued on an emergency basis is expected to be used immediately, the validity of such licenses may not be extended.

Exports by mail. When shipping by mail, a Shipper's Export Declaration (Figure 11-7) should be presented to the postmaster at the time of each commercial mailing valued over $250. Either the validated license number, or the general license symbol along with the phrase "Export License Not Required," must be marked on the address side of each parcel. Parcel post packages are subject to inspection by customs officers at various international mail points, and packages that do not comply with this marking requirement may be returned to the sender or may be seized by Customs. Exports by mail must also conform to Post Office Department regulations as to size, weight, permissible contents, etc.

Reexports. The reexport of U.S. commodities, in whole or in part, from the original country of destination to another country may be made without further recourse to the Office of Export Administration *only if* (a) the destination control statement on the shipping documents specifically names the countries to which the Office of Export Administration authorizes the reexport; (b) the commodity is exportable directly from the U.S. to the new country of destination under an appropriate general license authorization; (c) the reexport is to a destination to which direct shipment from the U.S. is authorized under an unused outstanding validated export license; or (d) the reexport is specifically authorized under a special licensing procedure. In all other instances, the approval of the Office of Export Administration is required before reexport may be made.

In order to obtain authorization to reexport commodities previously exported, Request to Dispose of Commodities or Technical Data Previously Exported, Form DIB699P (Figure 11-8), should be submitted to the Office of Export Administration.

If the form is not readily available, a letter request may be submitted setting forth all the facts surrounding the proposed reexport, with a certification by the applicant that the facts are true as stated, and that he or she will be strictly accountable to the Office of Export Administration for the use of the authorization to export if the request is granted.

Parts and components. The use of U.S.-origin parts, components, and materials in the manufacture abroad of commodities that will be exported from the country of manufacture to any other country requires prior authorization of the Office of Export Administration, unless either the U.S.-origin parts and components or the foreign-produced commodity, were they of U.S. origin, could be shipped from the U.S. to the new country of destination under General License G-DEST. A request for such authorization should include a description of both the components and the end product, the relative value of each, the country(ies) of ultimate destination, the ultimate consignee, if known, and any other pertinent information.

Once the required license is obtained by the freight forwarder, a general license symbol is stamped on the shipper's export declaration (described below). The freight forwarder generally handles licensing (as well as export declaration and shipping instructions), but it is wise for you to be aware of general requirements and procedures, as well as instances requiring special licensing.

Special licensing procedures. In addition to individual export licenses, described above, the Office of Export Administration provides certain simplified procedures under which one license application can cover a number of transactions. The most widely used are:

Project license. A single license covering the export of all commodities requiring validated licenses that are needed for certain large-scale operations such as construction projects, petroleum development projects, etc.

Periodic requirements license (PRL). A single license authorizing the export to one or more consignees, in a single country with which the U.S. has good trade relations (see Chapter 12), of an estimated one year's requirements of commodities identified by the symbol "P" in the "Special Provisions List" column of the Commodity Control List (CCL; see Chapter 12 for a description).

Time limit license (TL). A license covering shipments of unlimited quantities of commodities to one or more ultimate consignees in a single country in the Western Hemisphere. Commodities identified by the symbol "R" in the "Special Provisions List" column of the CCL are not eligible under the time limit license procedure.

Distribution license. A single license authorizing exports during one year of certain commodities to consignees in specified countries with which the U.S. has good relations. The consignees must have been approved in advance as foreign distributors or users.

Service supply license (SL). A license that enables persons or firms in the U.S. or abroad to provide prompt service for equipment (a) exported from the U.S., (b) produced abroad by a subsidiary, affiliate, or branch of a U.S. firm, or (c) produced abroad by a manufacturer who uses parts imported from the U.S. in the manufactured product. It permits the export of spare and replacement parts to consignees in certain approved countries.

Foreign-based warehouse procedure. A license that permits a qualified U.S. exporter to obtain, without supplying the supporting documents previously mentioned, licenses to export commodities to be stocked abroad for sale in approved countries. The distribution of the U.S. commodities must be under the control of a distributor approved by the Office of Export Administration, and each customer to whom the commodities are distributed must also be approved by the Office.

Application of licenses. The export licensing controls described above are administered by the Department of Commerce and apply to (1) exports of commodities and technical data from the U.S.; (2) reexports of U.S.-origin commodities and technical data from a foreign destination to another foreign destination; (3) U.S.-origin and components used in a foreign country to manufacture a foreign end-product for export; and (4) in some instances, the foreign produced direct product of U.S.-origin technical data.

These licensing controls do not extend to exports by U.S. subsidiaries, affiliates, or branches in foreign countries if the commodities exported are (1) of foreign manufacture, (2) contain no U.S. materials, and (3) are not based on restricted U.S. technology. However, the Treasury Department does control certain transactions by U.S. nationals (including foreign subsidiaries or branches of U.S. firms) involving foreign-origin commodities destined for Country Groups Q, S, W, Y, or Z (Country Groups are described in Chapter 12). Such transactions may be subject to the Transaction Control Regulations, the Foreign Assets Control Regulations, the Cuban Assets Control Regulations, or the Rhodesian Sanctions Regulations. Complete information on Treasury controls may be obtained from the Office of Foreign Assets Control, U.S. Department of the Treasury, Washington, D.C. 20220.

The controls established by the Office of Export Administration are published in the *Federal Register* and in the U.S. Department of Commerce *Export Administration Regulations*. However, a portion of the material appearing in the *Export Administration Regulations*, the Commodity Control List, is incorporated in the *Federal Register* by reference only.

Subscriptions to the U.S. Department of Commerce *Export Administration Regulations* and supplementary U.S. Department of Commerce *Export Administration Bulletins* may be ordered from the Superintendent of Documents, U.S. Government Printing Office, Washington, D.C. 20402; from any U.S. Department of Commerce district office; or from Room 1605, U.S. Department of Commerce Building, 14th and E Streets, N.W., Washington, D.C. 20230. Subscribers will receive the basic *Export Administration Regulations*, and all supplementary *Export Administration Bulletins* issued until the next edition of the *Export Administration Regulations*. A subscription is an inexpensive way to build up an information library on export regulations.

Shippers export declaration. This document has a dual purpose. The government uses it to help move shipments through U.S. Customs because it shows the proper authorization for shipment—that is, general or validated export licenses. In addition, the shipping information and description of the merchandise that it contains becomes part of the statistics upon which the FT-410 reports (Schedule B—Commodity) are based. Explicit shipping instructions are usually included with the above documents. The freight forwarder generally handles licensing, export declaration, and shipping instructions. It is wise, however, for you to be aware of general requirements and procedures, as well as instances requiring special treatment.

Collection Documents

Collection documents are the documents which are submitted to the importer or the importer's bank in order to receive payment. Collection documents may vary from country to country in method of receiving payment and mode of shipping. Documents may even vary from importer to importer. There are several general types of documents:

Commercial invoices. As in a domestic shipment, good business practice dictates that a commercial invoice (Figure 11-9) include the full address of the shipper, seller, and consignee, if different; the respective reference numbers; date of the order; shipping date; mode of shipment; delivery and payment terms; a complete description of the merchandise; prices, discounts, and quantities.

In addition, on an export order, it is customary to indicate the origin of the goods, and the export marks. If payment is to be against a letter of credit, reference to the bank and the corresponding credit or advice numbers must be given.

Some countries require special certification, sometimes in the language of that country, incorporated in the invoice. Information about these statements may be obtained from any Department of Commerce district office.

In some instances, it is necessary for the seller to sign his invoices and even have them notarized or countersigned by his chamber of commerce, or both. Many times it is also necessary to have them visaed by the resident consul of the country of destination. Again, this information may be obtained from Department of Commerce district offices.

Consular invoices. A few foreign countries, notably Latin American, require a special form of invoice (Figure 11-10) in addition to the commerical invoice. These documents must be prepared in the language of their country and on official forms sold by the respective consulates. They are then visaed by resident consul, thereby certifying to their authenticity and correctness. It is recommended that the shipper's forwarder prepare these documents at time of shipment.

Certificates of origin. Even though the commercial invoice may contain a statement of origin of the merchandise, a few countries require a separate certificate (Figure 11-11) sometimes countersigned by a chamber of commerce and possibly even visaed by their resident consul at the port of export. These may be on a special form of the foreign government, while in other cases, a certificate on the shipper's own letterhead will suffice. Statements of origin are required to establish possible preferential rates of import duties under a most favored nation arrangement.

Inspection certificates. In order to protect themselves, many foreign firms request a certificate of inspection (Figure 11-12). This may be either an affidavit by the shipper or by an independent inspection form, as dictated by the buyer, certifying to the quality, quantity, and conformity of goods in relation to the order.

Bills of lading. These may be overland (truck or rail), air, or ocean bills of lading (Figure 11-13), depending on destination or terms of sales. As in a domestic shipment, there are two basic types—"straight" or nonnegotiable, and "shipper's order" or negotiable, bills of lading. The latter is used for sight draft or letter of credit shipments. This shipper must endorse the original copy of the "order" bill of lading before it is presented to the bank for collection. The endorsement may either be "in blank" or "to the order of" a third party such as the negotiating bank. The letter of credit will stipulate which endorsement to use. With the exception of ocean shipments, only one original bill of lading is issued by the carrier. Any number of original ocean bills of lading may be issued depending upon the requirements of the buyer. Normally, all original copies are endorsed and submitted to the bank.

According to the rules set forth by the International Chambers of Commerce governing foreign trade terms, documents, etc., on draft or letter of credit shipments, the only bill of lading that is acceptable is one that is marked "CLEAN ON BOARD," which means that the carrier has not taken any exception to the condition of the cargo or packing and that the merchandise has actually been loaded aboard the carrying vessel.

Dock receipts, warehouse receipts, etc. In cases where the shipper is not responsible for moving the merchandise to the foreign destination, but to the U.S. port of export instead, these documents may be requested. They are exactly as their name implies, a receipt to the effect that the stipulated merchandise has been received at the pier or a warehouse for further disposition.

Certificate of manufacture. This document is used when a buyer intends to pay for the goods prior to shipment but the lead time for the manufacture of the products is lengthy and the buyer does not desire to allocate the money so far in advance. If the seller feels that the buyer is a good credit risk, he will proceed with the manufacture of the products with perhaps only a down payment. After the merchandise is ready, the seller prepares a certificate stating that the ordered goods have been produced in accordance with the contract and have been set aside for the account of the buyer. Commercial invoices and packing lists are sent as supporting documents. As soon as payment and shipping instructions have been received, the merchandise is shipped.

Insurance certificates. Where the seller provides ocean marine insurance, it is necessary to furnish insurance certificates, usually in duplicate, indicating the type and amount of coverage involved. Here again, these are negotiable documents and must be endorsed before submitting them to the bank.

The seller can arrange to obtain an open cargo policy to cover all of his foreign shipments or he can use the open cargo policy which his forwarder maintains.

These are the basic documents involved in foreign shipments. However, a country or individual may require additional ones, and they will be specified either in the order or letter of credit. Special care should be taken when reviewing the order or letter of credit to assure that all of the documents required are furnished in the manner prescribed to avoid rejection and other difficulty.

As mentioned previously, freight forwarders as well as other traffic management firms are capable and willing to prepare these documents for the shipper at moderate cost. Let them!

Another word of caution: shipping documents must be presented for collection within certain time limits after shipment or they will be considered "stale" and the bank will reject them. It will then be necessary to contact the buyer for permission to honor these late documents before the bank will release payment. It is equally important to make sure the shipment is made within the specified time indicated in the letter of credit, otherwise the credit will expire and it may not be possible to receive payment. In most cases it will be possible to arrange for the buyer to pay for the shipment, but serious delays may be experienced.

Information regarding the documents required and assistance in their preparation may be obtained from any Department of Commerce district office. Illustrations of forms discussed in this chapter follow. (UNZ & Co., 190 Baldwin Ave., Jersey City, N.J. 07306 provides an excellent catalog of forms with indications of their use and instructions for filling them out. Beginners will find it helpful and should write the company for a copy.)

Figure 11-2. Application for Export License

FORM DIB-622P (REV. 3-75)
(FORMERLY FC-419)
Form Approved OMB No. 41-R-0735

CONFIDENTIAL — Information furnished herewith is deemed confidential and will not be published or disclosed except in accordance with provision of Section 7(c) of the Export Administration Act of 1969, as amended.

U.S. DEPARTMENT OF COMMERCE
DOMESTIC AND INTERNATIONAL BUSINESS ADMINISTRATION
BUREAU OF EAST-WEST TRADE
OFFICE OF EXPORT ADMINISTRATION
WASHINGTON, D.C. 20230

APPLICATION FOR
EXPORT LICENSE

DATE RECEIVED (Leave Blank)

CASE NO. (Leave Blank)

DATE OF APPLICATION

APPLICANT'S TELEPHONE NO.

1. APPLICANT'S NAME

STREET ADDRESS

CITY, STATE, ZIP CODE

2. PURCHASER IN FOREIGN COUNTRY
(If same as ultimate consignee, state "SAME AS ITEM 3"; if same as intermediate consignee, state "SAME AS ITEM 4.")

NAME

STREET ADDRESS

CITY AND COUNTRY

3. ULTIMATE CONSIGNEE IN FOREIGN COUNTRY

NAME

STREET ADDRESS

CITY AND COUNTRY

4. INTERMEDIATE CONSIGNEE IN FOREIGN COUNTRY.
(If none, state "NONE"; if unknown, state "UNKNOWN.")

NAME

STREET ADDRESS

CITY AND COUNTRY

5. COUNTRY OF ULTIMATE DESTINATION

6. APPLICANT'S REFERENCE NUMBER

7. (a) QUANTITY TO BE SHIPPED

(b) COMMODITY DESCRIPTION AS GIVEN IN COMMODITY CONTROL LIST (Include characteristics such as basic ingredients, composition, type, size, gauge, grade, horsepower, etc.)

(c) EXPORT CONTROL COMMODITY NUMBER AND PROCESSING NUMBER

(d) TOTAL SELLING PRICE AND POINT OF DELIVERY (Indicate F.O.B., F.A.S., C.I.F., etc.)

UNIT PRICE	TOTAL PRICE

TOTAL

8. FILL IN IF PERSON OTHER THAN APPLICANT IS AUTHORIZED TO RECEIVE LICENSE

NAME

STREET ADDRESS

CITY, STATE, ZIP CODE

9. IF APPLICANT IS NOT THE PRODUCER OF COMMODITY TO BE EXPORTED, GIVE NAME AND ADDRESS OF SUPPLIER.
(If unknown, state "UNKNOWN.")

Figure 11-3. Application for Export License (continued)

10. END USE OF COMMODITIES COVERED BY THIS APPLICATION. DESCRIBE FULLY.

11. IF APPLICANT IS NOT EXPORTING FOR HIS OWN ACCOUNT. GIVE NAME AND ADDRESS OF FOREIGN PRINCIPAL AND EXPLAIN FULLY.

12. ADDITIONAL INFORMATION *(Attach separate sheet if more space is needed.)*

13. APPLICANT'S CERTIFICATION. — The undersigned applicant hereby makes application for a license to export and certifies as follows: That all statements herein, and in any documents or attachments submitted in support hereof, are true and correct to the best of his knowledge and belief; and that (a) he has read the instructions on the fifth copy of this application and is familiar with the U.S. Department of Commerce Export Administration Regulations; (b) this application conforms to such instructions and regulations; (c) unless Item 14 is completed, he negotiated with and secured the export order directly from the purchaser or ultimate consignee or through his or their agents abroad; (d) all parties to the export transaction, the exact commodities and quantities, or the exact technical data, and all other terms of the order and other facts of the export transaction are fully and accurately reflected herein; (e) documents and records evidencing the order and other facts of the export transaction to which this application relates will be retained by him for 2 years from whichever is later: the time of (i) the export from the United States, or (ii) any known reexport, transshipment, or diversion, or (iii) any other termination of the transaction, whether formally in writing or by any other means, and made available to the Department of Commerce upon demand; (f) any material or substantive changes in the terms of the order or other facts of the export transaction as reflected in this application or any certification made in connection therewith, whether the application is still under consideration or after a license has been granted, will be reported promptly by him to the Department of Commerce; and (g) if the license is granted, he will be strictly accountable for its use in accordance with the Department of Commerce Export Administration Regulations and all terms and conditions specified on the face of the license.

Type or Print	SIGN HERE IN INK _____
_____ (Applicant *(Same as Item 1)*)	(Signature of person authorized to execute this application.)

Type or Print _____
(Name and title of person whose signature appears on the line to the left)

14. ORDER PARTY'S CERTIFICATION (See § 372.6 (c) of the *Export Administration Regulations*.) — The undersigned order party certifies to the truth and correctness of Item 13 (d) above, and that he has no information concerning the export transaction that is inconsistent with, or undisclosed by the application and agrees to comply with Items 13 (e) and 13 (f) above.

Type or Print	SIGN HERE IN INK _____
_____ (Order Party)	(Signature of person authorized to sign for the Order Party)

Type or Print _____
(Name and title of person whose signature appears on the line to the left)

This license application and any license issued pursuant thereto are expressly subject to all rules and regulations of the Department of Commerce. Making any false statement or concealing any material fact in connection with this application or altering in any way the validated license issued, is punishable by imprisonment or fine, or both, and by denial of export privileges under the Export Administration Act of 1969, as amended, and any other Federal statutes.

FOR OFFICIAL USE ONLY

ACTION TAKEN	VALIDITY PERIOD	AUTHORITY	RATING		END USE CHECK	RE-EXPORT	SUPPORT DOCUMENT	DV	TYPE OF LICENSE	TECH DATA
☐ APPROVED										
☐ REJECTED	MONTHS									
DOCUMENTATION										

_____   _____   _____   _____
(Licensing officer)   (No.)   (Date)

_____   _____
(Review officer)   (Date)

NOTE: Submit the first four copies of this application, Form DIB-622P (with top stub attached), to the Office of Export Administration, Room 1617M, Domestic and International Business Administration, U.S. Department of Commerce, Washington, D.C. 20230, retaining the quintuplicate copy of the form for your files. Remove the long carbon sheet from in front of the quintuplicate copy. Do *not* remove any other carbon sheets. See Special Instructions on back of quintuplicate. Reproduction of this form is permissible, providing that content, format, size, and color of paper and ink are the same.

ORIGINAL
0 E A FILE COPY

Figure 11-4. Export License

FORM DIB-628 (REV. 3-75)

EXPORT LICENSE

U.S. DEPARTMENT OF COMMERCE
DOMESTIC AND INTERNATIONAL BUSINESS ADMINISTRATION
BUREAU OF EAST-WEST TRADE
OFFICE OF EXPORT ADMINISTRATION

Not approved unless the official validation stamp appears hereon.

VALIDATION

LICENSE NUMBER

License is hereby granted to the licensee named herein, upon the terms and provisions stated herein, to export from the United States the articles, materials, technical data, or supplies herein described. This license is granted in reliance on representations heretofore made by the licensee to obtain it and is expressly subject to all export control laws, regulations, rules, and orders. It is not transferable without written permission from the Office of Export Administration.

1. LICENSEE

2. PURCHASER

3. ULTIMATE CONSIGNEE IN FOREIGN COUNTRY

4. INTERMEDIATE CONSIGNEE

5. COUNTRY OF ULTIMATE DESTINATION

6. APPLICANT'S REFERENCE NO.

QUANTITY	DESCRIPTION OF COMMODITIES	EXPORT CONTROL COMMODITY NUMBER AND PROCESSING NUMBER	UNIT PRICE	TOTAL PRICE

Figure 11-5. Request for Status

FORM IA-743-A
(REV. 4-70)

U.S. DEPARTMENT OF COMMERCE
BUREAU OF INTERNATIONAL COMMERCE
OFFICE OF EXPORT CONTROL
WASHINGTON, D.C. 20230

Form Approved; Budget Bureau No. 41-R1463

REQUEST FOR, AND ADVICE ON, STATUS OF PENDING APPLICATION, AMENDMENT, OR REEXPORT REQUEST

INSTRUCTIONS - This page is to be filled out by applicant or applicant's agent. Please submit, in duplicate, to Office of Export Control (Attn: 854). One copy will be returned with the appropriate advice noted on the reverse side.

Requestors should allow the period of time set forth in §370.11(b) of the Export Control Regulations to expire before requesting advice on progress of an application, amendment, or reexport request. No action will be taken on earlier requests, unless an emergency exists and is explained. A status request should relate only to one application, amendment, or reexport request.

Name of Applicant Address (Street, City, State, Zip Code)		1. Date
2. Date of application, amendment, or reexport request (Specify type)	3. Requestor's Ref. No.	4. Case No. (If known)
5. Country of ultimate destination	6. Name of ultimate consignee	
7. Commodity description		

NOTE:

- An Export License must be returned immediately to the Office of Export Administration, Room 1617M, Domestic and International Business Administration, U. S. Department of Commerce, Washington, D.C. 20230, (a) when it has been fully used, (b) when it has expired, or (c) when it has been determined that it will not be used or will no longer be used.

- Each shipment made against this license shall be entered on the reverse and licensee must sign prior to returning it.

- A Destination Control Statement is required to be shown on all bills of lading, air waybills, and commercial invoices. (See Export Administration Regulations § 386.6.)

TOTAL

8. Export Control Commodity No.

9. Processing No.

10. Dollar value

11. Is telegraphic/telephonic reply desired at requestor's expense?

Telegraphic ☐ Yes ☐ No   Telephonic ☐ Yes ☐ No

Telephone No. _____ Area Code _____

12 Applicant's signature

13. Signature and address of authorized agent *(If not applicant)*

14. Remarks

USCOMM-DC 22247-P70

Figure 11-6. Request for Notice of Amendment Action

FORM DIB-685P (Formerly IA-763)
(Revised 4-74)

U.S. DEPARTMENT OF COMMERCE
DOMESTIC AND INTERNATIONAL BUSINESS ADMINISTRATION
BUREAU OF EAST-WEST TRADE
OFFICE OF EXPORT ADMINISTRATION

FORM APPROVED. OMB NO. 41-R1186

REQUEST FOR AND NOTICE OF AMENDMENT ACTION

THIS SPACE FOR OFFICIAL USE ONLY

VALIDATION

1. CASE NO.	3. LICENSE NO.	
2. APPLICANT'S REFERENCE NO.	4. EXPIRATION DATE OF LICENSE	

5. RETURN COPY OF AMENDMENT NOTICE TO

☐ APPROVED   ☐ REJECTED

_____ _____
(Signature of licensing officer)   (Date)

REASON FOR REJECTION

6. NAME OF LICENSEE	
7. COUNTRY OF ULTIMATE DESTINATION	8. DATES OF PREVIOUS EXTENSIONS (If any)

13. AMEND LICENSE TO READ AS FOLLOWS:

9. COMMODITY DESCRIPTION

10. EXPORT CONTROL COMMODITY NO.	11. PROCESSING NUMBER

12. FACTS NECESSITATING AMENDMENT

14. HAS THIS REQUEST BEEN PREVIOUSLY REJECTED OR IS IT PENDING IN ANY COMMERCE DEPARTMENT OFFICE?

IF YES, EXPLAIN ON SEPARATE SHEET. ☐ YES ☐ NO

15. SIGNATURE

_____
(Licensee)

BY _____
(Authorized agent)   (Title)   (Date)

Figure 11-7. Shipper's Export Declaration

Form No.
7525-V
(12-10-73)

U.S. DEPARTMENT OF COMMERCE - SESA, BUREAU OF THE CENSUS - D18A, BUREAU OF EAST-WEST TRADE

SHIPPER'S EXPORT DECLARATION
OF SHIPMENTS FROM THE UNITED STATES

Export Shipments Are Subject To Inspection By U.S. Customs Service and/or The Office of Export Control

READ CAREFULLY THE INSTRUCTIONS ON BACK TO AVOID DELAY AT SHIPPING POINT

Declarations Should be Typewritten or Prepared in Ink

Form Approved: O.M.B. No. 41-R0397

CONFIDENTIAL For use solely for official purposes authorized by the Secretary of Commerce. Use for unauthorized purposes is not permitted. (Title 15, Sec. 30.91(a) C.F.R.; Sec. 7(c) Export Administration Act of 1969, as amended, P.L. 91-184).

Authentication (When required)

Do Not Use This Area	District	Port	Country	(For customs use only)

FILE NO. (For Customs use only.)

1. FROM (U.S. Port of Export)

2. METHOD OF TRANSPORTATION (check one):
☐ Vessel ☐ Air ☐ Other (Specify)
(INCL. FERRY)

2a. EXPORTING CARRIER (If vessel, give name of ship, flag and pier number. If air, give name of airline.)

3. EXPORTER (Principal or seller — licensee)   ADDRESS (Number, street, place, state)

4. AGENT OF EXPORTER (Forwarding agent)   ADDRESS (Number, street, place, state)

5. ULTIMATE CONSIGNEE   ADDRESS (Place, country)

6. INTERMEDIATE CONSIGNEE   ADDRESS (Place, country)

7. FOREIGN PORT OF UNLOADING (For vessel and air shipments only)

8. PLACE AND COUNTRY OF ULTIMATE DESTINATION (Not place of transshipment)

(9)	(10)	(11)	(12)	(13)	(14)	(15)
MARKS AND NOS.	NUMBER AND KIND OF PACKAGES, DESCRIPTION OF COMMODITIES, EXPORT LICENSE NUMBER, EXPIRATION DATE (OR GENERAL LICENSE SYMBOL). (Describe commodities in sufficient detail to permit verification of the Schedule B commodity numbers assigned. Do not use general terms.)	SHIPPING (Gross) WEIGHT IN POUNDS (required for vessel and air shipments only)	SPECIFY "D" OR "F"	SCHEDULE B COMMODITY NO. (Include Commodity Control List italicized digit, when required)	NET QUANTITY IN SCHEDULE B UNITS (State unit)	VALUE AT U.S. PORT OF EXPORT (Selling price or cost if not sold, including inland freight, insurance and other charges to U.S. port of export) (Nearest whole dollar; omit cents figures)

These commodities licensed by U.S. for ultimate destination .... Diversion contrary to U.S. law prohibited.

VALIDATED LICENSE NO.   OR GENERAL LICENSE SYMBOL

16. BILL OF LADING OR AIR WAYBILL NUMBER

17. DATE OF EXPORTATION (*Not required for shipments by vessel*)

18. THE UNDERSIGNED HEREBY AUTHORIZES .... (Name and address—Number, street, place, State)
TO ACT AS FORWARDING AGENT FOR EXPORT CONTROL AND CUSTOMS PURPOSES.

(DULY AUTHORIZED
BY OFFICER OR EMPLOYEE)

EXPORTER

▶ 19. I CERTIFY THAT ALL STATEMENTS MADE AND ALL INFORMATION CONTAINED IN THIS EXPORT DECLARATION ARE TRUE AND COR-RECT. I AM AWARE OF THE PENALTIES PROVIDED FOR FALSE REPRESENTATION. (*See Paragraphs I (c), (e), on reverse side.*)

Signature............................ For............................ (Name of corporation or firm, and capacity of signer: e.g., secretary, export manager, etc.)
(Duly authorized officer or employee of exporter or named forwarding agent)

Address............................

▶ Declaration should be made by duly authorized officer or employee of exporter of forwarding agent named by exporter.
a. If shipping weight is not available for each Schedule B item listed in column (13) included in one or more packages, insert the approximate gross weight for each Schedule B item. The total of these estimated weights should equal the actual weight of the entire package or packages.
b. Designate foreign merchandise (reexports) with an "F" and exports of domestic merchandise produced in the United States or changed in condition in the United States with a "D". (*See instructions on reverse side.*)

Do Not Use This Area

Figure 11-8. Request to Dispose of Commodities or Technical Data Previously Exported

FORM DIB-699P (7-76)
OMB No. 41-R1569

U.S. DEPARTMENT OF COMMERCE
DOMESTIC AND INTERNATIONAL
BUSINESS ADMINISTRATION
BUREAU OF EAST-WEST TRADE
OFFICE OF EXPORT ADMINISTRATION
WASHINGTON, D.C. 20230

CASE NO. (Leave Blank)

CONFIDENTIAL - Information furnished herewith is deemed confidential and will not be published or disclosed except in accordance with Section 7 of the Export Administration Act of 1969.

REQUEST TO DISPOSE OF
COMMODITIES OR TECHNICAL
DATA PREVIOUSLY EXPORTED

1. DATE OF REQUEST

2(a). APPLICANT'S REF. NO.

2(b). APPLICANT'S TELEPHONE NO.

3. APPLICANT'S NAME

STREET

CITY, STATE,
ZIP CODE

4. COMMODITIES OR TECHNICAL DATA PREVIOUSLY EXPORTED
UNDER:

VALIDATED LICENSE NO. _____

CASE NO. _____

GENERAL LICENSE (specify type) _____

5. NEW ULTIMATE CONSIGNEE

NAME

STREET

CITY AND COUNTRY

6. ORIGINAL ULTIMATE CONSIGNEE

NAME

STREET

CITY AND COUNTRY

7. I (WE) HEREBY REQUEST AUTHORIZATION TO: ☐ REEXPORT ☐ SELL
☐ OTHER (Specify)
THE FOLLOWING: (If this request is being submitted on behalf of another firm or individual, explain in Item 10 below.)

8.(a) QUANTITY	(b) DESCRIPTION OF COMMODITY OR TECHNICAL DATA	(c) EXPORT CONTROL COMMODITY NO. AND PROCESSING NO.	(d) DOLLAR VALUE

9. END USE OF COMMODITIES OR TECHNICAL DATA BY NEW ULTIMATE CONSIGNEE *(Describe fully)*

10. ADDITIONAL INFORMATION *(Attach separate sheet if more space is needed)*

11. APPLICANT'S CERTIFICATION - I(We) certify that the above statements are true to the best of my (our) knowledge and belief. If authorization is granted, I(We) will be strictly accountable for its use in accordance with the Export Administration Regulations and all terms and conditions specified on the authorization.

Type or Print _____
(Applicant   *(Same as Item 3)*)

SIGN HERE IN INK _____
(Signature of person authorized to execute this request)

Type or Print _____
(Name and title of person whose signature appears on line to left)

FOR OFFICIAL USE ONLY

SPECIAL CONDITIONS

ACTION TAKEN	AUTHORITY	RATING					
		END USE CHECK	RE-EX-PORT	DV	SUPPORT. DOCUMENT	TECH. DATA	TYPE OF LICENSE
☐ APPROVED							
☐ REJECTED							

_____ _____
(Licensing officer)   (No.)   (Date)

DOCUMENTATION

_____
(Review officer)   (Date)

NOTE: Submit Form DIB-623P or FC-420 (Application Processing Card) and the first four copies of this request to the Office of Export Administration, Room 1617M, Domestic and International Business Administration, U.S. Department of Commerce, Washington, D.C. 20230 retaining the quintuplicate for your files. This form may be reproduced provided the content, format, size and color of paper and ink are the same.

ORIGINAL
O E A CASE FILE COPY

Figure 11-9. Commercial Invoice

COMMERCIAL INVOICE

| SHIPPER/EXPORTER | DOCUMENT NO. |
| | EXPORT REFERENCES |

| CONSIGNEE | FORWARDING AGENT - REFERENCES |
| | POINT AND COUNTRY OF ORIGIN |

| NOTIFY PARTY | DOMESTIC ROUTING/EXPORT INSTRUCTIONS |

PIER OR AIRPORT		
EXPORTING CARRIER (Vessel/Airline)	PORT OF LOADING	ONWARD INLAND ROUTING
AIR/SEA PORT OF DISCHARGE	FOR TRANSSHIPMENT TO	

| PARTICULARS FURNISHED BY SHIPPER | | | |
| MARKS AND NUMBERS | NO. OF PKGS. | DESCRIPTION OF PACKAGES AND GOODS | GROSS WEIGHT | MEASUREMENT |

DELIVERY TERMS

NET INVOICE VALUE	AMOUNT INSURED
$	$

See addendum attached for detailed summary of billing and packing.

CERTIFICATIONS

Form No. 80-325
Printed and Sold by Unz & Co., Division of Scott Printing Corp., 190 Baldwin
Ave., Jersey City, N.J. 07306 — N.J. (201) 795-5400 / N.Y. (212) 344-2270 Signed
Toll Free (800) 631-3098

Figure 11-10. Consular Invoice

DA 59

DECLARATION OF ORIGIN—
for the export of goods to the
REPUBLIC OF SOUTH AFRICA

Supplier (name, address, country) ....

Consignee (name, address, country) ....

NOTE TO IMPORTERS

This declaration, properly completed by the supplier, must be furnished in support of the relative bill of entry where goods qualify for and are entered at the rate of duty lower than the general rate

Particulars of transport ....

Customs date stamp

1	2	3	4	5	6	7
Item No.	Marks and numbers	No. and desc. of packages	Description of goods	Country of origin	Gross Mass	Invoice No./ Ref.

I, (name and capacity) ....

duly authorised by the supplier of the goods enumerated above hereby declare that—

1. the goods enumerated opposite item(s) .... in column 1 above have been wholly produced or manufactured in the country stated in column 5 in respect of such goods from raw materials produced in that country;

2. the goods enumerated opposite item(s) .... in column 1 above have been wholly or partly manufactured from imported materials in the country specified in column 5 in respect of such goods; and

2. 1 the final process of manufacture has taken place in the said country;

2. 2 the cost to the manufacturer of the materials wholly produced or manufactured in the said country plus the cost of labour directly employed in the manufacture of such goods is not less than .... per cent of the total production cost of such goods;

2. 3 in calculating the production cost of such goods only the cost to the manufacturer of all materials plus manufacturing wages and salaries, direct manufacturing expenses, overhead factory expenses, cost of inside containers and other expenses incidental to manufacturing, used or expended in the manufacture of such goods have been included and profits and administrative, distribution and selling overhead expenses have been excluded.

....
Place   Date   **Signature of Deponent**

Form No. 10 - 659   Printed and Sold by Unz & Co., Division of Scott Printing Corp., 190 Baldwin Ave., Jersey City, N.J. 07306 — N.J. (201) 795-5400 / N.Y. (212) 344-2270 Toll Free (800) 631-3098

Figure 11-11. Certificate of Origin

CERTIFICATE OF ORIGIN

SHIPPER/ EXPORTER	DOCUMENT NO.
	EXPORT REFERENCES

CONSIGNEE	FORWARDING AGENT - REFERENCES
	POINT AND COUNTRY OF ORIGIN

NOTIFY PARTY	DOMESTIC ROUTING/EXPORT INSTRUCTIONS

PIER OR AIRPORT		
EXPORTING CARRIER (Vessel/Airline)	PORT OF LOADING	ONWARD INLAND ROUTING
AIR/SEA PORT OF DISCHARGE	FOR TRANSSHIPMENT TO	

		PARTICULARS FURNISHED BY SHIPPER		
MARKS AND NUMBERS	NO. OF PKGS.	DESCRIPTION OF PACKAGES AND GOODS	GROSS WEIGHT	MEASUREMENT

The undersigned _____ (Owner or Agent), does hereby declare for the above named shipper, the goods as described above were shipped on the above date and consigned as indicated and are products of the United States of America.

Dated at _____ on the _____ day of _____ 19 ____

Sworn to before me this _____ day of _____ 19 ____

_____
SIGNATURE OF OWNER OR AGENT

The _____, a recognized Chamber of Commerce under the laws of the State of _____, has examined the manufacturer's invoice or shipper's affidavit concerning the origin of the merchandise, and, according to the best of its knowledge and belief, finds that the products named orginated in the United States of North America.

Secretary _____

Form No. 80-335—   Printed and Sold by Unz & Co., Division of Scott Printing Corp., 190 Baldwin Ave., Jersey City, N.J. 07306—N.J. (201) 795-5400 / N.Y. (212) 344-2270 Toll Free (800) 631-3098

Figure 11–12. Inspection Certificate

CUSTOMS FORM JUL 67 7512

Form Approved.
Budget Bureau No. 48-R212.7.

Entry No. ....
Port ....
Date ....

TRANSPORTATION ENTRY AND MANIFEST OF
GOODS SUBJECT TO CUSTOMS INSPECTION
AND PERMIT

BUREAU OF CUSTOMS

Entry No. ....

Class of Entry
(I. T.) (Wd. T.) (Wd. Ex.) (T. E.) (Drawback, etc.)

PORT OF ....

DIST. No. ....   PORT CODE NO. ....   FIRST U. S. PORT OF UNLADING ....   DATE ....

Entered or imported by .... to be shipped

in bond via ....   (C. H. L. number)   (Vessel or carrier)   (Car number and initial)   (Pier or station)

District Director of Customs at ....   Final foreign destination .... consigned to

Consignee ....   (For exportations only)

Foreign port of lading ....   B/L No. ....   (At customs port of exit or destination)   Date of sailing ....

(Above information to be furnished only when merchandise is imported by vessel)

Imported on the ....   Flag ....   on ....   via ....

(Name of vessel or carrier and motive power)   (Date imported)   (Last foreign port)

Exported from ....   on ....   Goods now at ....

(Country)   (Date)   (Name of warehouse, station, pier, etc.)

MARKS AND NUMBERS OF PACKAGES	DESCRIPTION AND QUANTITY OF MERCHANDISE NUMBER AND KIND OF PACKAGES (Describe fully as per shipping papers)	GROSS WEIGHT IN POUNDS	VALUE (Dollars only)	RATE	DUTY

G. O. No. ....

CERTIFICATE OF LADING FOR TRANSPORTATION IN BOND AND/OR LADING FOR EXPORTATION FOR

.... (*Port*)

WITH THE EXCEPTIONS NOTED ABOVE, THE WITHIN-DESCRIBED GOODS WERE:

Delivered to the Carrier named above, for delivery to the District Director of Customs at destination sealed with Customs seals Nos. ....

or the packages (were) (were not) labeled, or corded and sealed.

.... (*Inspector or warehouse officer*)

.... (*Date*)

Laden on the—

.... (*Vessel, vehicle, or aircraft*)

which cleared for—

on .... (*Date*)

as verified by export records.

.... (*Inspector*)

.... (*Date*)

I truly declare that the statements contained herein are true and correct to the best of my knowledge and belief.

Entered or withdrawn by ....

....

....

To the Inspector or Warehouse Officer: The above-described goods shall be disposed of as specified herein.

.... *For the District Director of Customs.*

RECEIVED from the District Director of Customs of above district the merchandise described in this manifest for transportation and delivery into the custody of the customs officers at the port named above, all packages in apparent good order except as noted hereon.

....

.... *Attorney or Agent of Carrier.*

Figure 11-13. Bill of Lading

SHORT FORM BILL OF LADING
(Non-Negotiable Unless Consigned To Order)

NAME OF CARRIER

SHIPPER/EXPORTER (2) (COMPLETE NAME AND ADDRESS)	DOCUMENT NO. (5)
	EXPORT REFERENCES (6)
CONSIGNEE (3) (COMPLETE NAME AND ADDRESS)	FORWARDING AGENT-REFERENCES (7) (COMPLETE NAME AND ADDRESS)
	POINT AND COUNTRY OF ORIGIN (8)
NOTIFY PARTY (4) (COMPLETE NAME AND ADDRESS)	DOMESTIC ROUTING/EXPORT INSTRUCTIONS (9)

PIER/TERMINAL (10)

VESSEL (11) FLAG	PORT OF LOADING (12)	ONWARD INLAND ROUTING (15)
PORT OF DISCHARGE FROM VESSEL (13)	FOR TRANSSHIPMENT TO (14)	

PARTICULARS FURNISHED BY SHIPPER

MARKS AND NUMBERS (16)	NO. OF PKGS. (17)	DESCRIPTION OF PACKAGES AND GOODS (18)	GROSS WEIGHT (19)	MEASUREMENT (20)

FREIGHT AND CHARGES PAYABLE AT

	PREPAID	COLLECT
TOTAL		

PREPAID ☐   COLLECT ☐

RECEIVED the goods or the containers, vans, trailers, pallet units or other packages said to contain goods herein mentioned, in apparent good order and condition, except as otherwise indicated, to be transported, delivered or transhipped as provided herein. All of the provisions written, printed or stamped on either side hereof are part of this bill of lading contract.

IN WITNESS WHEREOF, the Master or agent of said vessel has signed _____ bills of lading, all of the same tenor and date, one of which being accomplished, the others to stand void.

_____
FOR THE MASTER

BY _____   B/L NO.

DATED

Form 80-320 —   Printed and Sold by Unz & Co., Division of Scott Printing Corp., 190 Baldwin Ave., Jersey City, N.J. 07306 — N.J. (201) 795-5400 / N.Y. (212) 344-2270 Toll Free (800) 631-3098

Chapter Twelve

Country Groups and Commodity Controls

In addition to the licensing procedures described in Chapter 11, the U.S. government controls exports by separating all the countries of the world into Country Groups. The government looks upon some of these more favorably, for political reasons, than upon others. Products can be exported freely to some, with more difficulty (special licensing) to others, and not at all to others. Which products are affected? The cross-reference to the Country Group list is the Commodity Control List (CCL), which indicates which products require which licenses to go to which countries.

Country Groups

All destinations for exports (excluding Canada) are divided into the following Country Groups. Canada is not included in any Country Group since exports to that country normally are controlled only in specific short supply or foreign policy situations.

Group Q— Romania
Group S— Southern Rhodesia
Group T— All countries of the Western Hemisphere, except Cuba
Group W— Poland
Group Y— Albania, Bulgaria, Czechoslovakia, East Germany, (Soviet Zone of Germany and East Berlin), Estonia, Hungary, Latvia, Lithuania, Outer Mongolia, People's Republic of China, and the USSR
Group Z— North Korea, North Vietnam, South Vietnam, Cambodia, and Cuba
Group V— All other countries, except Canada

Briefly, the policies relating to the licensing of exports to various Country Groups are:

1. *U.S. Possessions:* No export authorization is required for shipments of commodities or technical data intended for use or consumption by persons in Puerto Rico or U.S. territories, dependencies, and possessions. Such shipments are considered domestic shipments.

2. *Canada:* As a general rule, no commodities or technical data require export licenses to Canada for consumption in Canada. Whenever commodities or technical data do require a validated export license for Canada, that requirement is shown in the Export Administration Regulations.

3. *Cuba* (in Country Group Z): U.S. restrictions on trade with Cuba have been in effect since 1960. Under the embargo, exports to Cuba are kept to an absolute minimum consistent with humanitarian considerations. Commodities meeting the provisions of certain general licenses, such as GIFT and BAGGAGE, may be sent to Cuba, as may publications, periodicals, and technical data exportable under General License GTDA. All other exports require validated export licenses, and applications therefore are generally rejected.

4. *North Korea, North Vietnam, South Vietnam, and Cambodia* (in Country Group Z): There is an embargo on commercial shipments to these countries. However, personal baggage, publications, periodicals, and technical data exportable under General License GTDA may be shipped to these areas.

5. *East European Communist Countries and People's Republic of China* (in Country Group Y): For the past several years, the U.S. government has consistently followed a policy of permitting some nonstrategic trade with the USSR and other East European Communist countries, and more recently with the People's Republic of China. Commodities that are essentially peaceful in nature are subject to General License G-DEST. Where a validated license is required, the proposed transaction is reviewed carefully to determine whether the transaction would contribute significantly to the military potential of the countries mentioned above in a way that would be detrimental to the U.S. national security. Included in this review are such considerations as:

a. Is the commodity designed for, intended for, or could it be applied to a significant military use?

b. Does it contain unique or advanced technology that is extractable?

c. Would it promote the military-industrial base of the country of destination?

d. For nonmilitary commodities, can non-U.S. sources supply a comparable item or an adequate substitute?

e. Are the quantities and types of equipment normal for the proposed use?

f. Is the equipment an integral part of a larger package and therefore unlikely to be used for other than the stated purpose?

6. *Romania* (in Country Group Q): and *Poland* (in Country Group W): Exports to Romania and Poland are also restricted for reasons of national security, but the restrictions are less severe than for exports to other Eastern European countries.

7. *Southern Rhodesia* (in Country Group S): In conformity with the United Nations Security Council's Resolutions of 1965, 1966, and 1968 condemning the refusal of the present regime in Southern Rhodesia to take steps to offer self-determination to the majority African population, the United States has imposed a near total embargo on trade with that country. Validated licenses are required for all exports except commodities or technical data meeting the provisions of certain general licenses, and documentary motion picture film and certain printed materials that may be shipped under General License G-DEST. Validated licenses are issued only for commodities or technical data specifically intended for particular medical, humanitarian, or educational uses.

8. *Other Countries* (Country Groups T and V): The Department of Commerce generally approves applications to export to T and V countries. Applications for T and V destinations are required primarily to assure that the commodity to be exported will not be diverted to an unauthorized or restricted destination. It should be noted, however, that in support of the United Nations Security Council's Resolutions of 1963 condemning the Republic of South Africa's apartheid policy, the United States prohibits exports to the Republic of South Africa and South-West Africa (Namibia) of arms, munitions, military equipment and materials, and materials and machinery for their manufacture and maintenance. The Department of Commerce therefore generally rejects applications for related items under its jurisdiction when there is a likelihood of military end use. Otherwise, export controls to the Republic of South Africa and South-West Africa (Namibia) are the same as for other destinations in these Country Groups. A more limited list of commodities is similarly restricted from export to certain near eastern countries, or to Portugal and its African territories.

Commodity Controls

The Commodity Control List is the key to determining whether a specific shipment is exportable under an established general license authorization, or whether a validated export license (for which an application must be filed), is needed. For all of the commodities licensed by the Bureau of East-West Trade, the CCL shows the destinations for which each commodity requires a license document. It also shows whether any special requirement must be met in connection with the submission of a license application.

The CCL is keyed to the Schedule B Commodity Classification System, which is known to most exporters because it must be used to prepare the Shipper's Export Declaration.

Using the Commodity Control List

Each commodity on the CCL is identified in the first column by its Export Control Commodity (ECC) Number. This number is composed of the first one to five digits of the seven-digit Schedule B (*Schedule B, Statistical Classification of Domestic and Foreign Commodities Exported from the United States,* available from the U.S. Government Printing Office) commodity classification number applicable to the commodity and by italicized digits in parentheses indicating the sequence of that entry among all those entries that have the same preceding digit(s). This number is followed by a code letter indicating the country groups for which a validated license is required. (In the example set forth below for Capacitance strain gages designed for operation at temperatures of plus 600° F and over, this code letter is "J," indicating that a validated license is required to export this commodity to Country Groups Q, S, W, Y, and Z.)

To determine whether a specific commodity requires a validated license, first find the Schedule B number under which it is classified. (If assistance is necessary, it is obtainable from the Foreign Trade Division, Bureau of the Census, Washington, D.C. 20233.) Then, using that number as the key, locate the commodity on the CCL. As an example, the Schedule B number for Capacitance strain gages is 729.5266; the ECC Number is, therefore, 7295 *(48)*. The CCL shows that for No. 7295 *(48)*, a validated license is required for shipments to Country Groups Q, S, W, Y, and Z, while exports to Country Groups T and V can be made under General License G-DEST. However, the column titled "GLV $ Value Limits" shows that individual dollar-value shipments of these gages may be made in amounts up to $100 to Country Group Q under the provisions of General License GLV. There is no GLV value shown for Country Groups T and V since shipments of these gages to T and V destinations are exportable under General License G-DEST. No GLV value is shown for Country Groups S, W, Y, or Z since General License GLV is *not* applicable to those destinations.

Section Three

Importing

Chapter Thirteen

Import Organizations

The import business is one of the oldest trades, dating back to a period when people bartered for goods—a period before the invention of money. The trade was and still is open to anyone with the perseverance and willingness to learn the mechanics. Importing is not limited to the exotic paraphernalia found in the local "Import Plus" store. Overseas manufacturers provide the U.S. market with a vast array of both consumer and technical products. By using your ingenuity and doing a thorough job of market research, you can tap what constitutes a $100 billion gold mine. Consider the following examples.

- More than a dozen name-brand foreign cars are sold in the U.S. As with domestic cars, whole lines of accessories are made to enhance the vehicles' appearance. Such auto accessories are fine products for the novice importer, as are accessories for recreational vehicles, mopeds, and bicycles.
- Foreign-made wearing apparel, food, and home furnishings continue to be popular in the U.S. *Made in Europe* magazine can give you an idea of current styles and prices.
- Health and beauty products from Europe have great appeal for the American consumer; they form a product category of excellent potential for the novice.
- Electronics is a growing industry abroad, as it is in the U.S. The novice should investigate electronic products both for consumer and technical markets.
- Industrial factory equipment, such as drill presses and lathes, are often well made by overseas manufacturers and can easily attract U.S. buyers. Many U.S. plants have not modernized since World War II, so opportunity abounds for the right product in the right locale.

Magazines such as *International Entrepreneur*, which discuss new business opportunities, can provide the novice with ideas for products that are salable in the current marketplace. There are many other business-opportunity publications—you should check them out.

Importing and Exporting: Working Together

The beginner just getting involved in exporting can easily combine importing with it. Importing and exporting are just opposite sides of the same coin. Either can be operated independently, or they can work together. Neither is more profitable; importing, however, puts a greater burden on the novice because imported products must be distributed and sold. In contrast, the exporter functions as a middleman between the manufacturer and the overseas representative, who does the distributing and selling.

The following chapters review pricing, selling, financing, transportation, customs clearance, etc. as they pertain to importing. All are important, but the key to your import success is found in *marketing*. Finding products, identifying customers, promoting products, and selling them are the bases for a lucrative importing business. Expertise in financing can be found at your bank; transportation help comes from freight forwarders and transportation companies; documentation assistance is obtainable from a customshouse broker, and U.S. Customs itself will explain regulations. Do not let the technicalities of importing interfere with your marketing efforts. Pay the experts for what they know; save your time to sell your products.

Before pursuing the following chapters, you should quickly review the introductory chapters, particularly those on market research and on making overseas and domestic contacts. With importing just as with exporting, it is critical for the new practitioner to do his or her homework thoroughly before making commitments. There is always some risk involved in every business dealing, and it is every businessperson's responsibility to lessen the risk as much as possible by intelligent forethought. Consider also that, whereas previously you were thinking about trade from the standpoint of the exporter, who had to deal with the foreign importer, you have now switched places. To an exporter somewhere in the world, *you* are the foreign importer. Reviewing the exporting chapters with this in mind can greatly enhance your understanding of the import business.

Basic Organizations for an Import Firm

There are several types of import organizations with which the beginner should be familiar. Although you may start out as an import agent, expansion into an organization requiring capital and experience may be in the future.

Import agents generally buy on orders received, and as *commission agents* they either receive a fixed commission from the seller or act as brokers, collecting fees just for bringing two parties together.

When operating on fixed commissions, the agent usually checks the creditworthiness and intent of the U.S. buyer, delivers the documents, collects the proceeds, and remits them to the foreign exporter less a commission. At no time during the operation does the agent assume title for the goods.

Figure 13-1. Import Steps

Steamship Company

1 Notifies consignee two days prior to ship's arrival.

2 Provides freight release to terminal operator.

Broker

3 Obtains customs release, freight release; Department of Agriculture clearances, etc., before contacting motor carrier.

4 Forwards to motor carrier an original of the Domestic Bill of Lading and an Original Delivery Order, which authorizes pick-up of import cargo.

5 Checks Bill of Lading for completeness:
   • number of packages
   • description of cargo
   • marks and numbers
   • inland destination
   • gross weights of each commodity shipped
   • consignee

6 Checks Delivery Order for completeness:
   • forwarder's name
   • shipper's name
   • ultimate consignee's name
   • motor carrier making pickup
   • vessel
   • arrival date
   • voyage number
   • ocean bill of lading number
   • pier number and location
   • marks and numbers
   • number of packages
   • description of goods
   • gross weights
   • legible signatures

7 Guarantees with terminal operator loading charges and demurrage.

Motor Carrier

8 Secures interchange agreement with steamship company on containers.

9 Ascertains expiration of free time and availability of cargo for pick-up before dispatching driver to pier.

10 Provides driver with original and copy of Delivery Order before departure for pier.

11 Contacts terminal operator to make appointment, if required, at least 24 hours before pick-up.

12 Checks Bill of Lading and Delivery Order for completeness, as above.

13 Dispatches truckman to the pier.

Terminal Operator

14 Issues pass to driver at gate house.

15 Checks Delivery Order for completeness and legibility, as above.

16 Verifies motor carrier's credit rating for loading charges.

17 Makes arrangements for payment of demurrage, if any has accrued.

18 Directs driver to pier customs office.

Customs

19 Verifies driver's papers against prelodged customs permits.

20 Stamps Delivery Order or tally sheet.

Terminal Operator

21 Calls driver for loading.

22 Assigns checker and loading spot.

Customs

23 Performs all necessary functions prior to the release of cargo.

Terminal Operator

24 Loads cargo onto vehicle with pier personnel. Checker notes exceptions and shortages.

25 Retains original Delivery Order.

Driver

26 Assists in and/or supervises load-
    ing of his vehicle.

27 Signs tally and loading ticket.
    Exceptions and shortages noted.

28 Reports back to delivery office, if
    required.

29 Retains copy of Delivery Order.

30 Surrenders gate pass at gate house.

Motor Carrier

31 Advises broker of completion of
    cargo pick-up.

When the agent acts as broker, you normally represent the seller. However, during extraordinary periods (war, bad weather), both buyer and seller may pay for the agent's services (providing munitions during wartime is a good example).

Most import agents have small organizations with fewer than 10 employees. They keep catalogues and samples of non-competitive lines to show to their local clients. This is the best form for the beginner, since it protects you from risk.

Most large buyers, however, prefer to deal with a merchant who has a local stock of merchandise. This way, the buyer can see exactly what he is getting, and there is no delay in delivery. Commodity merchants especially prefer access to a local stock because most trade on the exchanges and want to provide excellent pricing and quick delivery. The beginner, if he wishes, can use the money and connections gained from commissions for setting up a warehouse with showrooms and sales staff, and thereby become an import merchant.

Import merchants have warehouse facilities and a fairly large sales staff. They may specialize in one commodity (coffee, tea, spices, textiles, and other traditional imports), buying and selling the goods on their own behalf, or they may act as a broker, never taking title to the goods. That is, they may buy only on orders received. They are the oldest type of U.S. importing organization, and are plentiful in the established eastern and western seaports.

Import distributors are very popular when the product requires backup support (farm machinery, computers, or anything else where sales must be closely supported with good service). These firms are usually fairly large organizations that are sometimes directly or indirectly owned by a foreign manufacturer. Many of the Japanese consumer electronic firms have set up this type of company to handle all U.S. distribution. Most such firms have large warehousing facilities, service departments, showrooms, and sales staff.

Usually advertising and promotion play an important role in these operations. In some cases, the foreign source controls sales promotion, and in other instances the import division does it all.

As with the import merchant, many distributors specialize in certain goods. For example, representing a half dozen noncompeting food lines is a common practice.

International trading companies are usually found in Europe and Japan. Generally, they are large organizations with good marketing coverage and financial stability. In Japan, they control the domestic distribution networks for many types of products, and exporters must sell through them.

Manufacturers sometimes import to augment their product lines. The manufacturer who imports is usually a large company, like U.S. Steel, which relies on a continuous flow of raw materials from overseas. Usually a permanent division of that corporation is stationed overseas. The larger steel, petroleum, and copper companies provide examples of this type of importer.

Usually, the type of organization appears on the firm's letterhead. When dealing with foreign import organizations, do not be surprised if the same company or family name appears repeatedly from letterhead to letterhead. In many parts of the world, certain families dominate a particular industry, so that all functions regarding that product are under one company or family name.

Steps Along the Way

Whatever import organization you select, you must be prepared to follow your imports through a series of steps in order to bring them into the U.S. A comprehensive list appears in Figure 13-1, showing what is expected of each of the services you'll deal with.

Chapter Fourteen

Pricing and Selling

Once you, the beginning importer, have selected the product or product category in which you plan to deal, and have considered the domestic contacts (wholesalers, manufacturer's representatives) you must make in order to sell the merchandise, you can approach the pricing of imports in more detail. Before you offer anything for sale, you should analyze your costs carefully, just as you would before quoting a price on an export order. As it does for the exporter, a cost analysis helps to select products that offer the greatest potential for profit.

Let's say that, after completing your international product research, you decide that women's handbags ought to sell well in your area. At this point, you write to the overseas distributors or manufacturers to obtain a price list, pictures, samples (if available), delivery prospects, and terms.

When writing for prices, ask for the c.i.f. (cost, insurance, freight) price to your nearest port (or airport, as the case may be). This will make your landed cost (cost of getting merchandise to your nearest port) computations simpler because insurance and freight are included in the price. If, however, f.o.b. terms are the only terms available, ask your foreign freight forwarder for the cost of transporting goods to your locale. Very often, the exporter will only give you an f.o.b. price, and you must handle shipping and customs through your freight forwarder or customhouse broker. Finally, make certain your pricing is current—check the date on the price list.

When the handbag samples arrive, take them to department stores, specialty shops, and boutiques and compare them to the domestic products. Speak with local manufacturer's representatives and buyers regarding the market for these handbags.

Then prepare a landed cost survey, which is very similar to the cost survey you prepared when you quoted your export order. This alerts you to the product's profitability or lack of same, so you can adjust your price or decide whether to import. A survey prepared for women's handbags follows:

LANDED COST SURVEY
for XYZ Importing Co.
New York, NY

Supplier: John Houser, Southampton, England
Quantity: 100 handbags

GROSS SALES PRICE	$2778.00
Less Cash Discount (10%)	277.80
Net Sales Price	2500.20
LANDED COST	
Purchase Price (100 @ $25 each)	2500.00
Packing (1 per case)	—
Inland Freight to Foreign Port	—
Insurance (Marine & War Risk - $4280 @ $1.10 per $100 valuation)	47.08
Ocean or Air Freight or Parcel Post truck or rail (Southampton to NY)	1350.00
Brokerage Costs at Coast or Border	.40.00
Inland Freight in U.S.	—
Duty (Customs) ($2500 @ 15%)	375.00
Tax (IRS or other)	—
Brokerage Clearance Fees	45.00
Reforwarding from Broker	—
Banking Charges - Letter of Credit ($2500 @ ¼% minimum)	10.00
TOTAL LANDED COSTS (EX. Dock, NY)	1867.08
EXPENSES	
Repacking	—
Freight Out (Truck)	50.00
Advertising	—
Interest	—
Postage	10.00
Total Expenses	60.00
TOTAL LANDED COSTS AND EXPENSES ($2500 + 1867.08 + 60)	$4427.08

Unit Cost: Approximately $44.27 each
Suggested Selling Price: $77.47
Net Profit: $3319.92

Keep in mind when pricing that reselling a 25-cent item for $2.50 is difficult, if not impossible, in today's marketplace. Balance of trade, reevaluation of the dollar, and so on have made exaggerated profits unrealistic. If possible, stay with items that offer a reasonably steady profit.

For mail order items, a minimum of 150% mark-up after calculating shipping costs is needed. When dealing with wholesale quantities on high cost-per-unit items, 50% to 75% is reasonable. On occasions, 25% to 45% is sufficient, but be leery when the mark-up is too low. Each item should be judged on its individual merit. Mark-ups differ depending on the item and one should (and indeed cannot afford to) generalize.

In large corporations, a traffic manager or his clerk would be responsible for handling these calculations. You, the individual, can receive all the specialized help you need from your banker and your custom house broker. U.S. Customs is also helpful, and import regulations are spelled out in detail in a book entitled *Custom House Guide*, published by Budd Publications, New York.

Before you complete a transaction for fashion goods, sophisticated equipment, or anything requiring exacting specifications (close tolerance, special materials, etc.), stipulate in your letter of credit, purchase order, and/or draft instructions that a certificate of inspection is required for the overseas exporter to be paid. This will provide a safeguard to insure that you receive what you are paying for.

It is extremely important for the beginner *not* to buy anything without a domestic purchase order in hand. That is, never order an item from overseas that you have not already sold to a domestic source. Adhering to this rule will save you both money and headaches. Once you have built up sufficient sales, warehousing becomes practical—but not until that point. How do you build up sufficient sales? By means of a good distributor network.

Distribution

As an exporter, you had only to ship the goods; the foreign importer handled the end distribution. Importing presents an aspect that never troubles the exporter —you, as an importer, must sell or somehow distribute products to the end users. There are several ways of distributing or selling products; not all of them work for the beginner.

Retail store. Most people consider a retailing operation because their contact with imported merchandise is limited to the consumer area. For the beginner, this approach poses difficulties for two reasons. The beginner usually lacks both retail management experience and the necessary funds.

Direct mail. This is the industry term for the type of advertising most consumers refer to as "junk mail." Despite its unpopularity, properly done it is an effective sales technique, particularly for single products or product categories. It is very costly, however, and is best left to experts with generous advertising budgets.

Mail order. This sales approach is different from direct mail because the sellers, large organizations, generally stock many different types of items, not just items from a single product category, and illustrate them in catalogues. Familiar examples are Sears, Fingerhut, and Speigel. These operations have many of their own overseas buying offices and contacts for importing. If you have a unique consumer idea, it is definitely worth the try to contact one of these large mail-order concerns.

Distribution Network. One avenue available to the beginning importer is a broad network of wholesalers, manufacturer's representatives, jobbers (these are also sometimes known as dealers or distributors), and mass merchandisers or retailers. By contacting members of these trades, you can become part of the distribution network, which looks like this:

1. Consumer products→manufacturer→wholesaler→retailer→public.
2. Industrial products→manufacturer→manufacturer's representative→distributor→end user.

You can find the names of manufacturer's representatives, wholesalers, and mass merchandisers dealing in your product or product category in the following directories:

Manufacturers Agents Annual Directory. The Agent and Representative, 626 North Garfield Ave., Alhambra, CA 91802.

Directory of Manufacturers Agents. (Useful for contacting industrial distributors.) McGraw-Hill Book Co., 1221 Avenue of the Americas, New York, N.Y. 10022.

Verified Directory of Manufacturers Representatives, 8th ed. Manufacturers Agent Publishing Co., 663 Fifth Ave., New York, N.Y. 10022.

Major Mass Market Merchandisers. The Salesman's Guide, Inc., 1182 Broadway, New York, N.Y. 10001.

Market Guide of Mass Merchandisers. Dun & Bradstreet, Inc., 99 Church St., New York, N.Y. 10008.

Sheldons Jobbing Trade Annual, 92nd ed. Pheton-Sheldon Publications, Inc., 32 Union Square, New York, N.Y. 10003.

Directory of Industrial Distributors (1971–1972). Industrial Distribution, McGraw-Hill Book Co., 1221 Avenue of the Americas, New York, N.Y. 10020.

Your local library should be able to provide copies of some or all of these publications. Write to those prospective distributors that deal in your product category. In your letters, state what you are offering—a picture if possible, price, delivery, discounts, how packaged and shipped, and how long the offer is in effect.

This is the basic technique in marketing your imported goods.

Chapter Fifteen

Financing Imports

The beginning importer is in a better position than the beginner in many other business fields. You can start with virtually no capital, simply by acting as a commission merchant and not ordering anything that does not already have an eager buyer at home. After operating in this fashion for a time, during which you develop a better sense of what you can sell and how you can sell it, you may begin using commissions to finance your own import ventures. If you are successful on this limited scale and have also built a functional distribution network that you know works for your product line, you may eventually wish to finance larger overseas purchases than what your bank account permits. When you reach this point, you must consider how best to approach your banker to finance your imports.

When you first visit your banker, be prepared to give an accurate statement of your net worth. Have a definite proposal neatly typed—something like the landed cost survey in Chapter 14—and include a cost and profit analysis. The more information you can give on your prospective customers, the better. That is, you must prove to the banker that you have done your homework and that you know what you are doing.

You should also include a personal financial statement. Shown in Figure 15-1 is a sample. There are many publications available to help you prepare your financial statement, and a visit to your accountant may be the best solution. If you are considering borrowing money to expand your business, your accountant can offer suggestions that will far exceed his fee in savings to you.

Remember that bankers are not mysterious. They are businesspeople just like you are, except that they are in the business of lending money for the purpose of financing attractive proposals. The suggestions they make can save considerable expense and time. If they refuse your request, you should consider objectively the reasons for the refusal and ask yourself if the venture you are proposing is indeed as attractive as you believe it to be.

If possible, go to a bank where you have established previous good credit and where the bankers know you. If you have been working with exports through the

Figure 15-1. Personal Financial Statement

PERSONAL FINANCIAL STATEMENT

As of _____ 19___

Received at _____ Branch

Name _____ Years _____

Address _____ Employed by _____

Position _____ Age _____ Name of Spouse _____

If Employed Less Than
1 Year, Previous Employer _____

The undersigned, for the purpose of procuring and establishing credit from time to time with you and to induce you to permit the undersigned to become indebted to you on notes, endorsements, guarantees, overdrafts or otherwise, furnishes the following (or in lieu thereof the attached) which is the most recent statement prepared by or for the undersigned as being a full, true and correct statement of the financial condition of the undersigned on the date indicated, and agrees to notify you immediately of the extent and character of any material change in said financial condition, and also agrees that if the undersigned, or any endorser or guarantor of any of the obligations of the undersigned, at any time fails in business or becomes insolvent, or commits an act of bankruptcy, or dies, or if a writ of attachment, garnishment, execution or other legal process be issued against property of the undersigned or if any assessment for taxes against the undersigned, other than taxes on real property, is made by the federal or state government or any department thereof, or if any of the representations made below prove to be untrue, or if the undersigned fails to notify you of any material change as above agreed, or if such change occurs, or if the business, or any interest therein, of the undersigned is sold, then and in such case, all of the obligations of the undersigned to you or held by you shall immediately be due and payable, without demand or notice. This statement shall be construed by you to be a continuing statement of the condition of the undersigned, and a new and original statement of all assets and liabilities upon each and every transaction in and by which the undersigned hereafter becomes indebted to you, until the undersigned advises in writing to the contrary.

ASSETS	DOLLARS	cents	LIABILITIES	DOLLARS	cents
Cash in B of _____ (Branch)			Notes payable B of _____ (Branch)		
Cash in _____ (Other—give name)			Notes payable _____ (Other)		
Accounts Receivable-Good			Accounts payable		
Stocks and Bonds (Schedule B)			Taxes payable		
Notes Receivable-Good			Contracts payable _____ (To whom)		
Cash Surrender Value Life Insurance			Contracts payable _____ (To whom)		

Assets

Autos _(Year-Make)_ _____ _(Year-Make)_ _____

Real Estate (Schedule A) _____

Other Assets (describe)

1. _____
2. _____
3. _____
4. _____
5. _____

TOTAL ASSETS

Liabilities

Real Estate indebtedness (Schedule A) _____

Other Liabilities (describe)

1. _____
2. _____
3. _____
4. _____

TOTAL LIABILITIES

NET WORTH

TOTAL

ANNUAL INCOME

Salary _____

Salary (wife or husband) _____

Securities Income _____

Rentals _____

Other (describe)

1. _____
2. _____
3. _____
4. _____
5. _____

TOTAL INCOME

and ANNUAL EXPENDITURES (Excluding Ordinary Living Expenses)

Real Estate payment (s) _____

Rent _____

Income Taxes _____

Insurance Premiums _____

Property Taxes _____

Other (describe-include instalment payments other than real estate)

1. _____
2. _____
3. _____

TOTAL EXPENDITURES

LESS-TOTAL EXPENDITURES

NET CASH INCOME (exclusive of ordinary living expenses) _____ bank and have therefore previously checked it out in terms of the service the banking officers give you, you are more likely to receive better attention and more help than if you choose a bank with which you have never dealt.

You may have some difficulty obtaining financing the first time you want it. A method that has proved successful, however, is to approach your banker with a sizable purchase order from a reputable company. If the banker believes the customer has credit reliability and the order appears to be good, he may issue you a "back-to-back" letter of credit on the strength of that order. (Letters of credit are discussed in detail in Chapter 7). This way, you will avoid paying for the goods either until they are shipped or until they have arrived in the U.S., and your capital will not be tied up for a long period of time.

Chapter Sixteen

Transporting Imports

When you are exporting products, you are responsible for packing and shipping them properly and for meeting any particular requirements set by your overseas buyer. For assistance, you often rely on your freight forwarder or transportation company for packing and shipping.

When you are importing goods, you usually rely on the overseas exporter to provide you with the same service—he quotes you a c.i.f. price and is responsible for moving the merchandise to a U.S. port of entry. It is from that point that you, or someone acting for you, takes possession of the goods and moves them to their final destination. Since you have been apprised by the overseas exporter of the carrier, the date of shipment, and the expected date of arrival, you can arrange for the transportation services you need.

In some instances, however, you may have to make shipping arrangements yourself for goods from overseas, in which case you must rely more heavily on the services of a freight forwarder. Very often, your overseas supplier sends you only f.o.b. prices (though you, as an exporter, would always strive to quote c.i.f. prices and arrange for shipping to your overseas buyer). If this occurs, you must notify the exporter of the freight forwarder that you will be using; the freight forwarder will provide you with costs, handle the overseas shipment, and deliver it wherever you wish.

Methods of Transportation

On television and in popular magazines, one often sees pictures of ships marked EXXON or Texaco and of trucks marked with the name of some particular store. As a beginner, of course, you cannot afford to own the transportation. You will rent space on ships, planes, trucks, and trains, and you will use the parcel post system. The type of transportation you require will be determined by the quantity, cost, and size of each shipment, the distance it must travel, and the nature of the goods. For example, importers of perishables must make certain they obtain overseas transportation and rapid dispatch at the pier on arrival in order to prevent spoilage. Obviously, close attention must be paid to routing and scheduling dates. Importers of seasonal merchandise must likewise make sure that schedules are met. As anyone who has worked in a department or specialty store knows, sales promotions generally run on time. Late goods are usually returned to the vendors because most sales contracts have a clause specifying arrival dates.

Your location also has a direct bearing on transportation. The closer you are to the docking site or airport, the easier it is to supervise the movement of the goods. The further you are from a metropolitan port, the more dependent you are on the freight forwarder or customhouse broker. Generally, an importer enters into a contract with a broker so that, regardless of where the goods land, the broker can handle the entry documentation and delivery of goods to the ultimate buyer.

Ocean freight. The majority of goods from foreign countries, excluding Canada and Mexico, come by ocean freight. It is the most economical way to ship large quantities.

Steamship companies charge by weight or measurement, depending on which produces the greatest revenue. Therefore, articles such as fishing weights would probably be charged by weight, whereas modular housing would be charged by size (cubic feet).

Air freight. Air freight is becoming more popular as rates are reduced. Speed of delivery is a major attraction, but in addition it is often easier to ship fragile, expensive items by air, since less packaging is required for security during air shipment and since most such items are lightweight (watches, for example, or art work).

Air freight rates are based on the commodity shipped and the distance traveled. Within these constraints, weight and volume, as with ocean freight, will determine the final cost. Rates are normally set on a sliding scale. As the weight goes up from the minimum, the price per pound goes down.

As with passenger transportation, air carriers are trying to increase the use of their cargo services. To this end, freight forwarders are allowed to pool the shipments of smaller shippers, thus taking advantage of the lower rates applied to large quantities. The freight forwarders, acting in this instance as consolidators, book several shipments to one destination, then book the cargo on an air carrier to obtain the best rates. They then pass on the savings to the shippers.

Quotations from air carriers are from airport to airport. You should compare air quotations with ocean freight plus truck or rail quotations, considering also delivery schedules and the nature of the goods, before you make a final decision.

Parcel post. Samples and other small, inexpensive packages are best dispatched by parcel post. Air parcel post is best, since it speeds delivery by two or three weeks.

Truck and rail. From Canada or Mexico, for all but small shipments, truck and rail are better than air. Occasionally, due to customs formalities, air might be faster from Mexico.

A call to a truck carrier will give you the latest rates. Trains require carload lots, so it might be advisable to check with a local inland freight forwarder for better rail rates.

Insurance

All shipments should be insured either by yourself or by the shipper. If you have obtained c.i.f. pricing from your supplier, you will not have to worry about insurance, since it is included in the price you pay for the merchandise. Consider, however, that there are some insurance coverages taken out by foreign sellers which U.S. importers do not find satisfactory. Therefore, before you accept a deal with a c.i.f. price, check to see that the coverage meets your needs.

If you make infrequent purchases from a particular source, the price you pay may not include insurance. In such cases, or if the offered coverage is unacceptable, you should obtain an open marine policy from a local company or through your customs broker. (Since 90% of import shipments come by sea, such policies are generally termed "marine," although they usually cover other means of transportation as well.)

Generally, it is easier to process a claim through a U.S. insurance company. Also, it is preferable to have one company underwrite all risks for collection purposes. Most marine insurance companies, however, will not grant an open policy until your volume and experience is established. Therefore, you will have to arrange coverage through your broker or rely on the foreign shipper.

Regardless of how you acquire marine insurance, you must have protection against "General Average Agreement," which, simply stated, means that if the ship on which your freight is being carried sustains damage, or if any other cargo is damaged due to collision, fire, etc., the ship owner has the option of collecting a share of the damage from each firm that has cargo on board. This claim becomes a lien on your cargo, and any such lien must be satisfied before you can obtain your cargo.

Finally, you should also acquire an open inland marine policy, which covers shipments of goods after discharge at seaport, international airport, or rail terminal to their ultimate destination inside the U.S.

Chapter Seventeen

Documentation

Just as the U.S. government controls to which foreign countries exports are freely sent, it controls from which countries imports are freely received. It also levies an import tax, called a *duty*, on certain classes of items, and it collects data for trade statistics. These ends are accomplished by means of the *customs invoice*, also called a *commercial invoice*, and several other documents, which tell U.S. Customs what a shipment contains, where the products were manufactured, and how much they are worth.

Document Preparation and Handling

Before a shipment can move through Customs, the importer *must* have the correct documentation. Many of these documents should be familiar to the reader who has reviewed Chapter 11, which deals with export documentation. The *customs invoice* is the most important of several documents normally supplied by the shipper or exporter. Other documents are three copies of the original *bill of lading* or air bill and, if requested, an *insurance certificate* and a *certificate of origin*. When a shipment has a total worth of U.S. $500 or more and is subject to duty on an *ad valorem* (see Chapter 18 for an explanation) basis, a *special customs invoice* (Figure 17-1) is needed.

Normally, arrangements for all documentation are handled through the banks. The letter of credit and purchase order will state what documents are necessary, as well as the amount of money required for the transaction. These documents can be sent to the importer or his forwarder—they are never sent directly to Customs.

Each shipment should have only one consignee (that is, it should be addressed just to you). U.S. Customs prefers that invoices be in English, but an invoice properly prepared in the language of the exporter is acceptable. There is no particular, required form for the customs invoice, as long as it meets standard commercial practices and the government requirements listed below:

1. Description of merchandise
   a. The name by which each item of merchandise is known to the trade in the country of production or exportation

b. The grade or quality of each item of merchandise

c. The marks, numbers, or symbols under which each item of merchandise is sold by the seller or manufacturer to the trade in the country of exportation

d. The marks and numbers of the package in which merchandise is packed

2. The quantities in the weights and measures of the country or origin or that of the U.S.

3. The purchase price of the merchandise in the currency of purchase or, in the case of non-purchased material, the price that the seller would have received or was willing to receive in the currency in which the transactions are usually made.

4. The currency used, in the case of purchased merchandise.

5. All charges upon the merchandise, itemized by name and amount when known to the seller or shipper or all charges by name included in invoice prices when amounts for such charges are unknown to the seller or shipper.

6. All rebates, drawbacks, and bounties, separately itemized, allowed upon the exportation of the merchandise. Any rebate or grant given the manufacturer must also be itemized on the invoice by name and amount.

7. Any costs for items such as dies, molds, patterns, engineering work, financial assistance, etc., which assist in production but are not included in invoice price. If "assists" were involved, also state by whom they were supplied, if they were supplied without cost, if they were rented, or if they were invoiced separately. If they were invoiced separately, attach a copy of the invoice.

8. Where current home consumption prices are higher than current export prices, an explanation of the difference should be made. (This information is important so that foreign suppliers do not sell their goods at a lower price than in their own country—otherwise known as "dumping"—thereby obtaining an unfair advantage over U.S. manufacturers.)

9. If merchandise is imported from a country having a currency for which two or more rates of exchange have been certified by the Federal Reserve Bank of New York, the exact exchange rate or rates used in converting the U.S. dollars received for such merchandise into foreign currency should be shown on the invoice. If the dollars had not been converted at the time the invoice was prepared, the invoice should so state and should indicate the rate at which the dollars will be converted.

10. In the case of certain special classes of items, additional information must be shown on the customs invoice. The classes are diverse, including such items as beads (invoice must tell length of string, size of beads in millimeters, and material of which beads are composed), fish livers (invoice must tell if livers contain extra oil, and if so, what kind), and boiled wool (invoice must certify that a certain boiling process was followed in the country of origin). The importer should check with the U.S. Customs Office for details and exact requirements.

Figure 17-1. Special Customs Invoice

DEPARTMENT OF THE TREASURY
UNITED STATES CUSTOMS SERVICE
19 U.S.C. 1481, 1482, 1484

SPECIAL CUSTOMS INVOICE
(Use separate invoice for purchased and non-purchased goods.)

Form Approved.
O.M.B. No. 48-RO342

1. SELLER

2. DOCUMENT NR. *

3. INVOICE NR. AND DATE *

4. REFERENCES *

5. CONSIGNEE

6. BUYER (if other than consignee)

7. ORIGIN OF GOODS

8. NOTIFY PARTY *

9. TERMS OF SALE, PAYMENT, AND DISCOUNT

10. ADDITIONAL TRANSPORTATION INFORMATION *

11. CURRENCY USED

12. EXCH. RATE (if fixed or agreed)

13. DATE ORDER ACCEPTED

14. MARKS AND NUMBERS ON SHIPPING PACKAGES	15. NUMBER OF PACKAGES	16. FULL DESCRIPTION OF GOODS	17. QUANTITY	UNIT PRICE		20. INVOICE TOTALS
				18. HOME MARKET	19. INVOICE	

22. PACKING COSTS	
23. OCEAN OR INTERNATIONAL FREIGHT	
24. DOMESTIC FREIGHT CHARGES	
25. INSURANCE COSTS	
26. OTHER COSTS (Specify Below)	

21. ☐ If the production of these goods involved furnishing goods or services to the seller (*e.g., assists such as dies, molds, tools, engineering work*) and the value is not included in the invoice price, check box (21) and explain below.

27. DECLARATION OF SELLER/SHIPPER (OR AGENT)

I declare:

(A) ☐ If there are any rebates, drawbacks or bounties allowed upon the exportation of goods, I have checked box (A) and itemized separately below.

(B) ☐ If the goods were not sold or agreed to be sold, I have checked box (B) and have indicated in column 19 the price I would be willing to receive.

(C) SIGNATURE OF SELLER/SHIPPER (OR AGENT):

I further declare that there is no other invoice differing from this one (unless otherwise described below) and that all statements contained in this invoice and declaration are true and correct.

28. THIS SPACE FOR CONTINUING ANSWERS

THIS FORM OF INVOICE REQUIRED GENERALLY IF RATE OF DUTY BASED UPON OR REGULATED BY VALUE OF GOODS AND PURCHASE PRICE OR VALUE OF SHIPMENT EXCEEDS $500. OTHERWISE USE COMMERCIAL INVOICE.

*Not necessary for U.S. Customs purposes. Printed and Sold by Unz & Co., Division of Scott Printing Corp., 190 Baldwin Ave., Jersey City, N.J. 07306 — N.J. (201) 795-5400 / N.Y. (212) 344-2270 Customs Form 5515 (12-20-76)

Form No. 15-350

Figure 17-2. Pro Forma Invoice

Importers Statement of Value or the Price Paid in the Form of an Invoice

Name of shipper . . . . address . . . .
Name of seller . . . . address . . . .
Name of consignee . . . . address . . . .
Name of purchaser . . . . address . . . .

The merchandise (has) (has not) been purchased or agreed to be purchased by me. The prices, or in the case of consigned goods the values, given below are true and correct to the best of my knowledge and belief, and are based upon (check basis with an "X"):

(a) The prices paid or agreed to be paid (   ) as per order dated . . . .

(b) Advices from exporter by letter (   ) by cable (   ) dated . . . .

(c) Comparative values of shipments previously received (   ) dated . . . .

(d) Knowledge of the market in the country of exportation (   )

(e) Knowledge of the market in the United States (if U.S. value) (   )

Information as to value obtained from U.S. Customs pursuant section 141.83, CR. (   )

Check which of the charges below are, and which are not included in the prices listed in columns "D" and "E":

	Amount	Included	Not included
Packing			
Cartage			
Inland freight			
Wharfage and loading abroad			

	Amount	Included	Not included
Lighterage			
Ocean freight			
U.S. duties			
Total			

A	B	C	D	E	F	G
Case marks numbers	Manufacturer's item number symbol or brand	Quantities and full description	Unit purchase price in currency	Total purchase price currency	Unit foreign value in	Total foreign value

Country of origin

IF ANY OTHER INVOICE IS RECEIVED, I WILL IMMEDIATELY FILE IT WITH THE DISTRICT OR PORT DIRECTOR OF CUSTOMS.

Signature of person making invoice . . . .

Title and firm name . . . .

Date . . . .

Pro Forma Invoices

When a commercial customs invoice is required but is not available at the time a foreign shipment arrives at U.S. Customs, the *importer* (*not* the foreign exporter) may prepare a *pro forma* invoice. This "invoice" contains generally the same information required on the proper customs invoice, which is prepared by the exporter.

In addition to the pro forma invoice, the importer also must give a bond, which guarantees that he will file the required invoice with the district or port director of Customs within six months from the date of entry of this shipment. If the invoice does not arrive in that time, the importer will incur a liability under the bond.

The pro forma invoice is a device that speeds the movement of goods through Customs. It may be made out in substantially the form shown in Figure 17-2.

Installment Shipments

Installments of a shipment covered by a single order or contract and shipped from one consignor to one consignee may be included in one invoice if the installments arrive at the port of entry by any means of transportation within a period of not to exceed seven consecutive days. Otherwise, shipments must be invoiced separately.

An invoice to cover an installment shipment should be prepared in the same manner as an invoice for a single shipment, and obviously it must fit the invoicing requirements for the class of goods involved. If it is practical to do so, the invoice should show the quantities, values, and other invoice data with respect to each installment, and it should identify the carrier on which each installment was shipped.

Invoicing Errors

It is necessary for you, the U.S. importer, to be familiar with invoicing requirements so that you can assist the foreign exporters with whom you deal to fill out invoices properly. If your exporters make an error, *you* will pay the penalty that Customs imposes, and *you* will pay storage charges for the goods while Customs awaits the proper documents.

Prevention of invoicing errors can best be accomplished by a clear understanding of the terms of sale—that is, description of goods, quantity, price, currency, rebates, etc.—between buyer and seller. Most countries of the world have commercial invoice requirements similar to those described earlier in this chapter, and experienced foreign exporters should have no difficulty in providing the necessary material. Still, errors are made. The common errors made by foreign shippers are the following:

1. The shipper assumes that a commission, royalty, or other charge against the goods is a so-called "nondutiable" item and omits it from the invoice.

2. A foreign shipper who purchases goods and sells them to a U.S. importer at a delivered price shows on the invoice the cost of goods to him instead of the delivered price (which includes freight and insurance).

3. A foreign shipper manufactures goods partly with the use of materials supplied by the U.S. importer, but invoices the goods at the actual cost to the manufacturer without including the value of the materials supplied by the importer.

4. The foreign manufacturer ships replacement goods to his customer in the U.S. and invoices the goods at the net price without showing the full price less the allowance for defective goods previously shipped and returned.

5. A foreign shipper who sells goods at list price, less a discount, invoices them at the net price, and fails to show the discount.

6. A foreign shipper sells goods at a delivered price but invoices them at a price f.o.b. the place of shipment and omits the subsequent charges.

7. A foreign shipper states in an invoice of purchased goods that the current market value in the foreign country is the same as the purchase price, whereas there have been sales for home consumption or export at a higher price between the date of purchase and the date of exportation.

8. A foreign shipper indicates in the invoice that the importer is the purchaser, whereas he is in fact either an agent who is receiving a commission for selling the goods or a party who will receive part of the proceeds of the sale of the goods sold for the joint account of the shipper and consignee.

Further Information

This chapter does not pretend to answer all questions about invoices and other documentation. Chapter 18 continues the discussion, but the importer in need of assistance should contact a U.S. consular officer or Treasury representative, or a director or commissioner of Customs.

Chapter Eighteen

The Entry Process

The U.S. government regulates imports through the use of documents, physical inspection of shipments, and appraisal of goods. When a shipment arrives at a seaport or airport, Customs sends a notice to the importer or customhouse broker. Usually five days are allowed for an entry to be made—that is, for you or your broker to present the required documents, pay the duty, and collect the parcels. If entry is not made within five days, the goods are moved to a warehouse under Customs custody, and you are charged storage. If you have not removed your goods within one year, the government can auction the materials to pay for storage. Usually, this sale does not occur because the exporter notifies you of when and on what ship or flight the goods are being sent, so the shipment can be met without delay. The exporter (through the banks) sends you all the documents necessary for you to secure the goods at the pier.

From a commercial standpoint, all goods arriving at U.S. ports require a formal entry, with the exception of those valued at less than U.S. $250 or those that are not subject to internal revenue taxes.

There are four steps in the processing of import shipments:

1. entry, or filing of documents
2. appraisement and valuation—that is, setting the value of a shipment through examination
3. classification, or setting the duty rate
4. liquidation, or final determination of the duty

These functions are performed by two- and three-man teams of Customs officials. In the past, this process has taken as long as three months. Today, it usually takes less than a week.

Entry

Before an entry can be made, the importer or broker must be in possession of certain documents. The most common required documents are:

1. commercial customs invoice, which the exporter fills out
2. special (consular) customs invoice, which the exporter fills out for certain shipments
3. bill of lading, which the exporter fills out
4. entry form, which the importer fills out

On the entry form, you estimate the duty you will have to pay. You can then pay the collector of Customs immediately, or you may post a bond (minimum $10,000), which guarantees against your possible failure to pay duties, taxes, or penalties at a later date. Two types of bonds are employed:

1. term bond, which applies to entry though only one port
2. general term bond, which covers all U.S. ports

Surety may also be posted in the form of cash. For most situations, your customhouse broker's bond will provide the necessary coverage.

Because most transactions are financed through letters of credit, you must pay your bank to receive the documents you will need to clear Customs. The only document not supplied through the bank is the consular invoice, required for goods valued at U.S. $500 or more.

At this point, proper documentation in hand, you or your broker takes possession of the shipment from the carrier. Customs inspectors will then examine the goods. If the goods are perishable, or if the carrier, importer, or agent would in some way be inconvenienced, Customs can speed processing by issuing a special permit, Customs form II RC-450, for immediate release of the goods. Applications for this special permit should be made prior to the arrival of the goods. If the application is approved, the shipment is released immediately following arrival. The right to make entry must be filed in proper form within ten days of release of the shipment.

Caution. Bear in mind that the importer who files the above documents with Customs vouches for the truth of the documents, as well as of the entry and other documents which are filed with the entries. The presentation of any false documents, information, or statement (by whomever prepared) can subject the importer to severe penalties, whether or not the U.S. has been deprived of any revenue. These penalties are by statute equivalent to the domestic value of the imported merchandise, including all expenses of transportation and insurance and the duties applicable to the merchandise.

The importer is also subject to similar penalties for failure to disclose all details of the transaction pursuant to which the merchandise was exported to the U.S., including any financial aid or other assistance provided to the manufacturer or exporter, and full information as to the status of any agent involved in the transaction, including the amount of commission or other reimbursement paid to such agent.

Importers are entitled to purchase merchandise and have it valued for Customs purposes on the most favorable basis possible, *so long as full disclosure of the transactions is made to the Custom officials.* All documents should be carefully considered by the importer as to their accuracy and truthfulness before they are submitted to Customs.

It is apparent that importing merchandise into the U.S., especially from the Far East, can be complicated by language problems and by special characteristics of business in foreign countries. Importers are encouraged to consult their local Customs appraising officers for assistance, advice, and clarification of matters involving the valuation of their imported merchandise.

Appraisement and Valuation

After the proper documents are filed, Customs inspectors take a sample of the goods to the Customs plant, called the Appraiser Stores. Here, the sample is analyzed and its value is ascertained.

Classification

Next, the inspectors classify the items and set the duty rate—that is, the percentage of value that will be charged as duty.

Liquidation

Liquidation is the final determinaton of the exact amount of duty owed on the shipment. You will be notified if Customs officials disagree with your estimate of value and duty, which you stated on your entry form. Remember that you estimated value and duty on your entry form; Customs officials also make an initial judgment when they first obtain samples of the shipment. If the importer and Customs disagree, a protest can be filed within 90 days after the liquidation date with the U.S. Customs Court, whose decision is binding both on the importer and on Customs. Protests can delay entry for months. Most of the time, importers and Customs agree, and goods enter the U.S. within a week.

Liability for Duties

Duties or taxes on imports cannot be prepaid in a foreign country before exportation to the U.S. In the usual case, liability for the payment of duty becomes fixed at the time an entry is filed with the district director of Customs. The person or firm in whose name the entry is filed is the one who must pay. If the entry is made by a customhouse broker in his own name, he is exempt from paying any increased or additional duties found due on the goods, as long as he names the actual owner of the goods in the entry, obtains an owner's declaration in which the owner agrees to pay any increased or additional duties, and files the owner's declaration with the district director of Customs within 90 days of the date of entry, together with the owner's bond.

When Customs enters unclaimed goods for warehousing, the liability for the payment of duties may be transferred to any person who purchases the goods and desires to withdraw them in his or her own name.

Types of Entry

There are 22 different kinds of Customs entries. The following are the most prevalent:

1. *Consumption Entry* is the most common type. It is used when goods are intended for resale within the country or are brought directly into the importer's stock.

2. *Immediate Transportation Entry* is used when the importer desires to have his or her merchandise forwarded from the port of entry to an interior destination for Customs clearance. Usually the customhouse broker will arrange shipment under bond without appraisement.

3. *Warehouse Withdrawal for Consumption Entry* makes it possible to pay duty only on portions of a shipment at a time. The importer leaves the shipment in a Customs-bonded warehouse; the customhouse broker withdraws a portion of the goods as they are needed and pays duty only on that portion.

4. *Immediate Exportation Entry* allows goods to be routed via a U.S. port to a foreign country. The steamer pier may serve as a bonded warehouse when the transship period is short.

5. *Appraisement Entry* applies to household goods, new or used, that are not intended for sale. Immigrants' belongings, for example, are given this type of entry.

6. *Baggage Declaration and Entry* is filed when a U.S. citizen returns from a trip abroad.

Following acceptance of the entry and payment of duties, the shipment is examined to make certain it contains what you state it to contain, and then it is released, providing no legal or regulatory violations have occurred.

If you are planning to receive a large shipment, you will find the services of a customhouse broker extremely valuable. Small shipments coming through the mails usually do not require such services. The following two sections discuss the handling of both small and large shipments.

Mail, Parcel Post: Do It Yourself

Small shipments are best consigned to you by parcel post. Customs will simply clear the shipment and have the postman collect any duty owed. The mails are most useful for small, inexpensive objects because you save on shipping charges and there is no need to clear parcels valued at under $250 personally. The only requirement, made jointly by Customs and the Postal Service, is that all parcel post packages have, securely attached, a Customs declaration giving both an accurate description and the value of the contents. Commercial shipments must also be accompanied by a commercial invoice enclosed in (or securely attached to) the parcel bearing the declaration, and the package must be marked on the address side, "Invoice Enclosed." If the shipment contains more than one package, each package should be numbered and marked "Invoice in Package #___." Shipments that do not comply with these requirements will be delayed through Customs.

Packages other than parcel post (such as letter class mail), printed matter, commercial papers, and samples must be marked, on the address side, "May be opened for Customs purposes before delivery."

If the value of the mail importation exceeds $250, the addressee is notified to prepare and file documentation for a formal Customs entry at the nearest Customs port.

A nominal charge, currently $1, is collected from the addressee on all dutiable or taxable mail.

Ocean, Air, Truck: Hire a Customs Broker

Shipments on all three types of carrier require similar handling. All shipments should be consigned to you directly, marked to the attention of your Customs broker. Air and truck shipments should show on the airway bill or the freight bill that the shipment is to be sent to you "In Bond," consigned to your address.

As a beginning importer, you should depend heavily upon your broker for handling paperwork. Familiarity with the documentation is necessary, but the primary purpose of the importer is to sell merchandise, not to process paperwork.

Goods may be entered by the consignee named in the bill of lading under whch they are shipped (you), or the bill of lading may be endorsed over to a broker or carrier, who can then enter the goods. In most instances, entry is made by a person or firm certified by the carrier bringing the goods to the port of entry to be the owner of the goods for Customs purposes. (The broker will have all the paperwork you collected when you paid the bank for the goods: bill of lading, insurance certificate, etc. He will present these to the carrier to collect the goods.) The carrier will issue to the broker a carrier's "certificate," which may be no more than a duplicate bill of lading or a shipping receipt.

If you live close to the point of Customs clearance and regularly import shipments valued at less than $250, you can probably clear the parcels yourself, without posting bond with Customs. If you live some distance away, however, or if you import more expensive merchandise, you will find it less expensive, less trouble, and less time-consuming to employ a customhouse broker. He knows the Customs regulations and is familiar with the requirements of the local Customs office. He will post bond in your behalf, pay duty, clear the shipment, and forward the shipment to you. He will invoice you for all charges plus his nominal fee, which rarely exceeds $20 to $50 per $1,000 of merchandise value.

As with any business dealing, always precheck your broker's charges, freight costs, insurance, and Customs duty. Confirming costs in advance will avoid the disaster of extra charges being billed to you after you have sold the goods. Appendix 5 contains a list of freight forwarders and customhouse brokers. Always check with several of these firms and compare prices.

Dutiable Status

One of the basic determinations an importer must make when deciding whether to import an item is its duty status. All items are classified as either dutiable or free from duty.

There are three types of duty levied: *specific, ad valorem,* and *compound. Specific duties* are assessed as an amount per unit of item, such as 10¢ per pound or 5¢ per yard. *Ad valorem duties* are a fixed percentage: 10% of total value, 25%

of total value. The *compound duty* is a combination of specific and ad valorem duties. For example, wool valued at under $4 per pound is dutiable at 23½%, plus 25¢ per pound; wool worth over $4 per pound is dutiable at 23½%, just like the cheaper wool, but the specific rate jumps to 37½¢ per pound.

No comprehensive discussion of the rates of duty provided for in the Tariff Schedules of the U.S. could be attempted in a book of this limited scope. If you need information about the classification and rate of duty (or free status) of specified goods, you may write to the commissioner of Customs at the port of entry at which your goods will be entered.

When requesting information, you must supply the following information:

1. A complete description of the goods. Send samples, sketches, diagrams, or other illustrations if the goods cannot be described in writing.

2. The method of manufacture or fabrication.

3. Specifications and analyses.

4. Quantities and costs of the component materials—with percentages, if possible.

5. Whatever information you have as to the:

    a. Commercial designation of your goods in the U.S.

    b. Chief use of your goods in the U.S.

If you are positive that any of the foregoing will not be of use in determining the status of your goods you may disregard it, but omitting necessary information will delay a decision. Send samples along with the description whenever you can.

The decision you receive can be relied upon for placing or accepting orders for goods to be imported to the U.S. The decision will not be changed without prior public notice.

Full rates of duty, which are not listed here because they are constantly changing, apply to products of the following countries or areas, whether imported directly or indirectly:

Albania	Communist Korea
Bulgaria	Kurile Islands
China	Latvia
Cuba	Lithuania
Czechoslovakia	Outer Mongolia
Estonia	Southern Sakhalin
East Germany	Tanna Tuva
Hungary	Tibet
Communist Indochina	U.S.S.R.

Products of other countries are subject to reduced duty rates as set forth in the Tariff Schedules of the U.S.

Currency Conversion

The conversion of foreign currency for Customs purposes must be based on the New York market buying rate for the foreign currency involved, as determined and certified by the Federal Reserve Bank of New York.

The rates for widely used currencies are certified each day. Other rates are certified only by request of Customs officers, for the dates needed.

The date of exportation of the goods determines the rate of exchange to be used in converting foreign currency for Customs purposes. The currencies of certain foreign countries listed in the Customs Regulations are converted at a value measured by the buying rate first certified by the Bank for a day in the quarter in which the day of exportation falls. These include most but not all the more widely used foreign currencies. Ordinarily, conversions involving the currency of other countries will be made at the buying rate certified by the Bank for the particular day on which exportation occurred, even though a different rate may have been used in payment of the goods.

Temporary Free Importation

The importer should be aware that some goods, primarily samples and displays, may be admitted into the U.S. without the payment of duty, under bond for their exportation within one year from the date of importation. The categories are as follows:

1. Merchandise imported to be repaired, altered, or processed in the U.S., as long as the end product does not contain alcohol, perfume, or wheat; a complete accounting of articles made and any wastes is given to Customs; and the results of the processing are exported or destroyed within the bonded period.

2. Models of women's wearing apparel imported by manufacturers for use solely as models in their own establishment.

3. Samples solely for use in taking orders for merchandise; articles solely for examination with a view to reproduction (except printing plates); and motion picture advertising films.

4. Articles intended solely for testing, experimental, or review purposes (plans, specifications, drawings, photos, etc.). Such articles may be destroyed during the bonded period rather than exported.

5. Containers for covering or holding merchandise during transportation and suitable for reuse for that purpose.

6. Articles imported by illustrators and photographers for use solely as models in their own establishments, in the illustration of catalogs, pamphlets, or advertising matter.

7. Professional equipment, tools of trade, repair components for such equipment and tools, and articles of special design for temporary use in the manufacture or production of items for export.

8. Theatrical scenery, properties, and apparel for temporary use in theatrical exhibitions.

This law also allows for foreign residents to import articles such as cars, boats, works of art, films, and animals for their use while visiting the U.S., participating in an exhibition, lecturing, promoting business, etc.

If after a year the goods are not exported, the bond will be forfeited, or the articles seized, unless they are destroyed under Customs supervision or unless satisfactory proof of destruction is furnished to the district or port director of Customs with whom the Customs entry was filed.

Specific information regarding articles that can be imported free should be obtained from a commissioner of Customs.

Refunds

The exportation of imported goods after they have been released from Customs custody does not result in a refund of the duties paid on the goods. There are three exceptions:

1. When articles manufactured or produced in the U.S. with the use of imported merchandise are exported, a refund of 99% of the duties paid on the imported merchandise is refundable.

2. When the imported goods do not conform to the sample or specifications on the basis of which they were ordered, or were shipped without the consent of the consignee, the importer may secure a refund of 99% of the duties paid by returning the goods to Customs custody within 90 days (or longer if authorized) after they were released and exporting them under Customs supervision.

3. When imported goods found not to be entitled to admission into the commerce of the U.S. are exported under Customs supervision, a refund of the entire amount of duties paid on the rejected goods is allowable.

A refund of the entire amount of duties paid is allowable:

1. when imported goods are exported from a bonded Customs warehouse or from continuous Customs custody elsewhere than in a bonded warehouse within the warehousing period;

2. when the imported goods are withdrawn for supplies, maintenance, or repair for vessels and aircraft under certain conditions; and

3. when imported goods found not to be entitled to admission into the commerce of the U.S. are destroyed under Customs supervision.

A refund of the entire amount of duties may also be made when articles entered under bond under any provision of the Customs laws are destroyed under Customs supervision during the period of the bond and when articles in a Customs bonded warehouse are voluntarily abandoned to the government by the consignee.

Excess Goods and Shortages

Showing the contents of each package on the invoice, the orderly packing of the goods, the proper marking and numbering of the packages in which the goods are packed, and the placing of the corresponding marks and numbers on the invoice facilitate the allowance in duties for goods which do not arrive and the ascertainment of whether any excess goods are contained in the shipment.

If any package which has been designated for examination is found by the Customs officer to contain any article not specified in the invoice, and there is reason to believe that such article was omitted from the invoice with fraudulent intent on the part of the seller, shipper, owner, or agent, the contents of the entire package in which the excess goods are found are subject to seizure and possible forfeiture.

On the other hand, when no such fraudulent intent is apparent, penalties do not accrue, but the duties due, if any, on the excess goods will be collected.

When a deficiency in quantity, weight, or measure is found by the Customs officer in the examination of any package which has been designated for examination, an allowance in duty will be made for the deficiency.

Allowance in duty is made for deficiencies in packages not designated for examination, provided that before liquidation of the entry becomes final the importer notifies the district or port director of Customs of the shortage and establishes to the satisfaction of the director that the missing goods were not delivered to him.

Damage or Deterioration

Goods which are found by the Customs officer to have been entirely without commercial value at the time of arrival in the U.S. because of damage or deterioration are treated as a "nonimportation." No duties are assessed on such goods. When such damage or deterioration is present with respect to part of the shipment only, allowance in duties is not made unless the importer segregates the damaged or deteriorated part from the remainder of the shipment under Customs supervision.

When the shipment consists of fruits, vegetables, or other perishable merchandise, allowance in duties cannot be made unless the importer, within 96 hours after the unloading of the merchandise, and before it has been removed from Customs custody, files an application for allowance with the district or port director of Customs.

On shipments consisting of any article partly or wholly manufactured of iron or steel, or any manufacture of iron or steel, allowance or reduction of duty for partial damage or loss in consequence of discoloration or rust is precluded by law.

Tare

In ascertaining the quantity of goods dutiable on net weight, a deduction is made from the gross weight for tare. The following schedule tares are provided for in the Customs Regulations:

Apple boxes—8 pounds per box. This includes paper wrappers, if any, on the apples.

China clay in so-called half-ton casks—72 pounds per cask.

Figs in skeleton case—Acutal tare for outer containers plus 13% of the gross weight of the inside wooden boxes and figs.

Fresh tomatoes—4 ounces per 100 paper wrappings.

Lemons and oranges—10 ounces per box and 5 ounces per half box for paper wrappings, and actual tare for outer containers.

Ocher, dry, in casks—8% of the gross weight; in oil in casks—12% of the gross weight.

Pimientos in tins imported from Spain—

30 pounds for case of 6 tins, 3 kilos each

36.72 pounds, case of 24 tins, 28 ounces each

17.72 pounds, case of 24 tins, 15 ounces each

8.62 pounds, case of 24 tins, 7 ounces each

5.33 pounds, case of 24 tins, 4 ounces each

Sugar—2.5 pounds per bag for standard bags.

Tobacco, leaf not stemmed—13 pounds per bale.

For other goods dutiable on the net weight, an actual tare will be determined. An accurate tare stated on the invoice is acceptable for Customs purposes in certain circumstances.

If the consignee files a timely application with the district or port director of Customs, an allowance may be made in any case for excessive moisture and impurities not usually found in or upon the particular kind of goods.

Chapter Nineteen

Marking

U.S. Customs laws require that each imported article produced abroad be legibly marked in a conspicious place with the name of the country of origin (the country in which the article was grown, manufactured, or produced) in English so the ultimate U.S. purchaser can see it. A toy might be marked, for example, "Made in Venezuela."

Most established foreign export companies are familiar with U.S. marking requirements. However, if you are dealing in a unique item, say a new invention, you may save yourself much difficulty if you communicate marking information to your overseas source.

When Marking Is Not Required

The following articles and classes or kinds of articles do not require marking. However, the outermost containers in which such articles ordinarily reach the ultimate purchaser in the U.S. must be marked.

Art, works of
Articles entered in good faith as antiques and rejected as unauthentic
Bagging, waste
Bags, jute
Bands, steel
Beads, unstrung
Bearings, ball
Blanks, metal, to be plated
Bolts, nuts, and washers
Briarwood in blocks
Briquettes, coal or coke
Buckles
Burlap

Buttons
Cards, playing
Cellophane and celluloid
Chemicals, drugs, etc., in capsules, pills, etc.
Cigars and cigarettes
Covers, straw bottle
Dies, diamond wire, unmounted
Dowels, wooden
Effects, theatrical
Eggs
Feathers
Firewood
Flooring

Flowers, artificial, except bunches

Glass, cut for clocks, hand mirrors, etc.

Glides, furniture

Hairnets

Hides, raw

Hooks, fish

Hoops (wood), barrel

Laths

Leather, except finished

Lumber, sawed

Metal bars

Mica

Monuments

Nails, spikes, and staples

Natural products, such as vegetables and animals

Nets, bottle wire

Paper, newsprint, stencil, stock

Parchment and vellum

Parts for machines imported from same country as parts

Pickets, wooden

Pins, tuning

Pipes, iron or steel, and fittings

Plants, shrubs, and other nursery stock

Plugs, tie

Poles, bamboo

Poles, electric-light, telephone, etc.

Posts (wood), fence

Pulpwood

Rags

Railway materials

Ribbon

Rivets

Rope

Scrap and waste

Screws

Shims, trace

Shingles (wood), except red cedar

Skins, fur, dressed or dyed

Skins, raw fur

Sponges

Springs, watch

Stamps, postage

Staves (wood), barrel

Steel, hoop

Sugar, maple

Ties (wood), railroad

Tiles, not over 1 inch in greatest dimension

Timbers, sawed

Tips, penholder

Trees, Christmas

Weights, in sets

Wicking, candle

Wire, except barbed

Unless an article which you are importing to the U.S. is specifically named in the above list, it would be advisable for you to obtain advice from a district or port director of Customs, regional commissioner of Customs, or commissioner of Customs before concluding that it is exempt from marking.

The following items are also exempt from marking:

- items for use by the importer and not intended for sale (such as samples)
- items to be processed in the U.S.
- items obviously from a specific country

The following classes of articles are also exempted from marking to indicate the country of origin, although their containers must be marked:

- Articles which are incapable of being marked
- Articles which cannot be marked prior to shipment to the U.S. without injury

- Articles whicn cannot be marked prior to shipment to the U.S. except at an expense economically prohibitive of their importation
  - Crude substances
  - Articles produced more than 20 years prior to their importation

When the marking of the container of an article will reasonably indicate the country of origin of the article, the article itself is exempt from such marking. This exemption applies only when the articles will reach the ultimate purchaser in an unopened container. For example, dried flower sachets which reach the retail purchaser in sealed containers marked clearly to indicate the country of origin come within this exemption. Materials to be used in building or manufacture by the builder or manufacturer who will receive the materials in unopened cases likewise come within the exemption.

The following articles and their containers are not subject to the requirement of marking to indicate the country of their origin or to the special marking requirements set out in this chapter:

- Articles entered or withdrawn for immediate exportation or for transportation and exportation.
- Products of American fisheries which are free of duty.
- Products of possessions of the U.S.
- Products of the U.S. exported and returned
- Articles valued at not more than $1 which are passed without entry

When Marking Is Required

Except as specifically set out in the preceding section of this chapter, every other imported article must be marked legibly and in a conspicuous place in such manner as will indicate to an ultimate purchaser in the U.S. the English name of the country of origin of the article.

It is not feasible to state who will be the "ultimate purchaser" in every circumstance. Broadly stated, an "ultimate purchaser" may be defined as the last person in the U.S. who will receive the article in its imported form. Generally, if an imported article will be used in manufacture, the manufacturer is the ultimate purchaser. If an article is to be sold at retail, the American consumer is the ultimate purchaser. A person who subjects an imported article to a process which results in a substantial transformation of the article, even though the process may not result in a new or different article, may be an ultimate purchaser in certain circumstances; but if the process is a minor one which leaves the identity of the imported article intact, the consumer remains the ultimate purchaser.

If either an article or a container requires marking, the marking is considered adequate if it remains legible until the article reaches the ultimate purchaser.

If the imported article is combined with articles of different origin before delivery to the ultimate purchaser, the marking must clearly show that the origin is only that of the imported article and not that of any other article. For example, if bottles imported from England are to be filled in the U.S., they must be marked "Bottle made in England." Imported labels that are affixed to U.S. products should so indicate, as in "Label printed in Japan."

If the imported article is substantially changed in the U.S., as when bristles are inserted into imported hairbrush blocks or toothbrush handles, only the country of origin mark must appear.

Although it is permissible to mark articles (or their containers) with the name of the country of origin after importation, under Customs supervision, and at the expense of the importer, marking after importation almost invariably results in delay, inconvenience, and expense which could have been avoided had the articles (or their containers) been marked at the time of manufacture.

Special Marking Requirements

The following articles must be marked legibly and conspicuously by die stamping, cast-in-the-mold lettering, etching, engraving, or by means of metal plates attached by welding, screws, or rivets to the article. Details on these groups of items can be had by consulting the Tariff Schedules of the U.S., and the importer is advised to do so.

Knives of all kinds and their parts, including handles
Clippers, shears, and scissors of all kinds
Razors and blades
Pliers of all kinds
Surgical and dental instruments
Scientific and laboratory instruments
Drawing instruments
Thermostatic bottles, jars, etc.
Watch and clock movements, cases, and dials

Some articles (consult Tarriff Schedules) must be marked to show the name of the manufacturer or purchaser.

Gold and silver articles have certain marking requirements that are administered by the Department of Justice, Washington, D.C. 20530, which should be contacted with questions.

If you intend to import any of the above articles or articles possibly related to them to the U.S., you should request specific advice from a district or port director of Customs, a regional commissioner of Customs, or the commissioner of Customs as to the exact marking requirements.

If you are in doubt about whether your goods (or their containers) must be marked, how to mark them, what is to be regarded as the country of their origin, or if you need information on any other aspect of marking, contact the above Custom authorities.

Improper Marking

The U.S. government is obviously concerned about informing its citizens of the origin of the goods they purchase. It follows, therefore, that there are federal regulations against marking that gives the purchaser a false impression of origin. The regulations state that no imported article of foreign origin which bears a name or mark calculated to induce the public to believe that it was manufactured anywhere other than the country or locality in which it was in fact manufactured shall be admitted to entry at any customhouse in the U.S.

In general, the words "United States," the letters "U.S.A.," or the name of any city or locality in the U.S. appearing on an imported article or its container are deemed to be calculated to induce the public to believe that the article was manufactured in the U.S. unless the name to indicate the country or origin appears in close proximity to the name which indicates a domestic origin. For example, Columbian crockery called "Los Angeles" brand dinnerwear would be considered misleading unless a "Made in Columbia" mark appeared everywhere the brand name "Los Angeles" appeared.

An imported article bearing a prohibited name or mark is subject to seizure and forfeiture. However, upon the filing of a petition by the importer prior to final disposition of the article, the district or port director of Customs may release it upon the condition that the prohibited marking be removed and that the article or containers be properly marked. Or the article may be exported or destroyed.

If books are the articles being imported, the words "Printed in," followed by the name of the country of origin and the words "Printed by," followed by the name and address of the foreign printer and the name of the country of origin, or words of similar significance, should appear on the front or back of the title page or cover (not covered by a dust cover or jacket), or on a page near the front or back of the book.

Chapter Twenty

Government Import Restrictions

Chapter 12 discussed U.S. government export restrictions, which take the form of Country Groups and commodity controls. To the same end, as you read in Chapter 18, the government levies higher duties against goods from certain countries. This chapter discusses government protection of its citizens through a list of items whose importation is prohibited or restricted, controls over import quantities by means of import quotas, protection for U.S. industries in the form of the so-called antidumping regulations, and import "preferences" shown to developing nations.

Generally, import licenses are not required for merchandise entering the U.S. There are thousands of products that can be imported freely and with no restrictions, and the beginner is well-advised to concentrate on these. They are almost all types of consumer products found in retail stores, such as clothing, T.V.s, most automotive products, radios, all types of appliances, and gifts. Industrial products that can be imported freely include machinery, heating units, most food products, and construction equipment.

The following section discusses prohibited and restricted articles. It is unlikely that many of these articles would be of interest to the beginner, but a summary is included so you will know what products to avoid and what agencies to contact if you have questions.

Prohibited and Restricted Articles

The importation of certain articles is either prohibited or restricted. Their shipment to the U.S. may result in seizure or forfeiture. Many of these prohibitions and restrictions on importations are subject, in addition to Customs regulations, to the laws and regulations administered by one or more other government agencies, with which Customs cooperates in enforcement. Such laws and regulations may, for example, prohibit entry, limit entry to certain ports, restrict routing, storage, or use, or require treatment, labeling, or processing as a condition of release. Customs clearance is given only if these various additional requirements are met. The restrictions apply to all types of importations, including those made by mail and those placed in foreign-trade zones (discussed in Chapter 21).

A list of categories of restricted goods follows, along with the agency that administers the restriction. A local Customs office can give more information, as can the agencies themselves.

Alcoholic beverages and confectionary
Bureau of Alcohol, Tobacco, and Firearms
Department of the Treasury
Washington, D.C. 20226

Arms, ammunition, explosives, and implements of war
Bureau of Alcohol, Tobacco, and Firearms
Department of the Treasury
Washington, D.C. 20226

Automobiles and equipment
Environmental Protection Agency
Washington, D.C. 20460

Coins, currencies, stamps, and other monetary instruments
U.S. Secret Service
Department of the Treasury
Washington, D.C. 20223

Eggs and egg products
Veterinary Services
Animal and Plant Health Inspection Service
U.S. Department of Agriculture
Washington, D.C. 20250

Electronic products, radiation standards
Department of Health, Education, and Welfare
Food and Drug Administration
Bureau of Radiological Health
Rockville, Maryland 20857

Foods, drugs, cosmetics
U.S. Consumer Product Safety Commission
Washington, D.C. 20207

Products from certain Communist countries
Foreign Assets Control
Department of the Treasury
Washington, D.C. 20220

Animals
Bureau of Epidemology
Veterinary Public Health Service
Atlanta, Georgia 30333

Fruits, vegetables, plants, insects
Fruit and Vegetable Division
Consumer and Marketing Service
Department of Agriculture
Washington, D.C. 20250

and

Plant Protection and Quarantine Programs
U.S. Department of Agriculture
Hyattsville, Maryland 20782

Livestock and meat
Department of Agriculture
Hyattsville, Maryland 20782

Narcotics
Drug Enforcement Administration
Department of Justice
Washington, D.C. 20537

Pesticides and toxic substances
Environmental Protection Agency
Washington, D.C. 20460

Wild animals, endangered species
U.S. Fish and Wildlife Service
Department of the Interior
Washington, D.C. 20240

Wool, fur, textile, and fabric products
Federal Trade Commission
Washington, D.C. 20580

Milk and cream, viruses and serums, rags, brushes
Public Health Service
Department of Health, Education, and Welfare
Rockville, Maryland 20857

Import Quotas

Various import quotas, established by directives from the Committee for the Implementation of Textile Agreements, by legislation, and by presidential proclamations, are administered by the Commissioner of Customs. These quotas are of two types—tariff-rate and absolute. Figure 20-1 lists commodities that are affected.

Tariff-rate quotas. Tariff-rate quotas provide for the entry of a specified quantity of the quota product at a reduced rate of duty during a given period. For example, Australian beef was imported under this type of quota in order to reduce the domestic price to the consumer. There is no limitation on the amount of the product which may be entered during the quota period, but quantities entered in excess of the quota for the period are subject to higher duty rates. In most cases,

Figure 20-1. Examples of Import Quotas

Commodities Subject to Import Quotas
Administered by the Commissioner of Customs as provided for in the
Tariff Schedules of the United States

Tariff-rate Quotas	*Absolute Quotas*
• Cattle, weighing less than 200 lbs. each	• Animal feeds, containing milk or milk derivatives
• Cattle, weighing 700 lbs. or more each (other than dairy cows)	• Butter substitutes, containing over 45% butterfat, provided for in item 116.30, *Tariff Schedules of the United States,* and butter oil
• Whole milk, fluid, fresh, or sour	
• Fish, fresh, chilled, or frozen, filleted, etc., cod, haddock, hake, pollock, cusk, and rosefish	• Buttermix, over 5.5% but not over 45% by weight of butterfat
• Tuna fish, described in item 112.30, *Tariff Schedules of the United States*	• Cheese, natural Cheddar, made from unpasteurized milk and aged not less than 9 months
• Potatoes, white or Irish: certified seed or other than certified seed	• Cream, fluid or frozen, fresh or sour
	• Ice cream
• Wiskbrooms, wholly or in part of broom corn	• Milk and cream, condensed or evaporated
• Other brooms, wholly or in part of broom corn	• Cotton, having a staple length under 1-1/8" (except harsh or rough cotton having a staple of under 3/4", and other linters)
	• Cotton (other than linters) having a staple length of 1-1/8" or more
	• Cotton card strips made from cotton having a staple length under 1-3/16" and comber waste, lap waste, sliver waste, and roving waste, whether or not advanced
	• Fibers of cotton processed but not spun
	• Peanuts, shelled or not shelled, blanched, or otherwise prepared or preserved (except peanut butter)
	• Stainless steel sheets and strip, plates, bars and rods and alloy tool steel
	• Wheat fit for human consumption*
	• Milled wheat products fit for human consumption*
	• Sugars, syrups, and molasses described in items 155.20 and 155.30, *Tariff Schedules*

* Suspended indefinitely

products of Communist-controlled areas are not entitled to the benefits of tariff-rate quotas.

Absolute quotas. Absolute quotas are quantitative; that is, no more than the amount specified may be permitted entry during a quota period. This type of quota has been used to protect steel and other industries for political purposes. Some absolute quotas are global, while others are allocated to specified foreign countries. Imports in excess of a specified quota may be exported or detained for entry in a subsequent quota period.

General. The usual Customs procedures generally applicable to other imports apply with respect to commodities subject to quota limitations.

The quota status of a commodity subject to a tariff-rate quota cannot be determined in advance of its entry. The quota rates of duty are ordinarily assessed on such commodities entered from the beginning of the quota period until such time in the period as it is determined that imports are nearing the quota level. District directors of Customs are then instructed to require the deposit of estimated duties at the overquota duty rate and to report the time of official acceptance of each entry. A final determination of the date and time when the quota is filled is made, and all district directors are advised accordingly.

Other quotas. Quotas on certain other products are administered by specific agencies. Fuel oil and oil product quotas are administered by the Director, Oil Imports, Federal Energy Administration, P.O. Box 7414, Ben Franklin Station, Washington, D.C. 20461. Quotas on watches and watch movements are administered by Office of Import Programs, Special Import Programs Division, U.S. Department of Commerce, Washington, D.C. 20230. Dairy product quotas are administered by the Department of Agriculture. Detailed information can be had from the Import Branch, Foreign Agricultural Service, U.S. Department of Agriculture, Washington, D.C. 20250.

Antidumping Regulations

Dumping is the practice of selling foreign merchandise in the U.S. at less than fair value, thereby causing injury to domestic industries. The determination as to whether dumping is occurring is ordinarily based upon a comparison between the net, f.o.b. factory price to the U.S. importer and the net, f.o.b. factory price to purchasers in the home market. If the sales to the U.S. are on a c.i.f. delivered basis or on an f.o.b. seaport basis, the necessary deductions are made in order to arrive at an f.o.b. factory price. If the merchandise is not sold in the home market, or if the amount sold in the home market is so small as to be an inadequate basis for comparison, then comparison is made between the prices to the U.S. and prices for exportation to third countries. If the merchandise is sold only to the U.S. or if the merchandise sold in the home market or to third countries is not sufficiently similar to the merchandise sold to the U.S. to furnish a satisfactory basis for comparison, then comparison is made between the price to the U.S. and the constructed value. Constructed value is the sum of:

1. cost of materials, labor, and fabrication:

2. usual general expenses, such as factory and administrative overhead, and the usual profit realized in the manufacture of merchandise of the same general character; and

3. cost of packing and other expenses incident to preparing the merchandise for shipment to the U.S.

In most cases, an importer should be able to satisfy himself that merchandise is not being purchased at less than fair value by comparing net, f.o.b. factory prices to the U.S. with the net, f.o.b. factory prices in the home market or to third countries.

Preferences

A wide range of products, classifiable under approximately 2,750 different item numbers prefixed with A or A* in the Tariff Schedules of the U.S., may qualify for duty free entry if imported into the U.S. directly from any of the designated developing countries and territories. These countries are listed below; entries in the list may change from time to time.

Requests for information concerning the addition to, or deletion from, the list of eligible merchandise or countries should be directed to the Chairman, Trade Policy Staff Committee, Office of the Special Representative for Trade Negotiations, 1800 G St., N.W., Washington, D.C. 20506.

Independent Countries

Afghanistan	Dominican Republic
Angola	Egypt
Argentina	El Salvador
Bahamas	Equatorial Guinea
Bahrain	Ethiopia
Bangladesh	Fiji
Barbardos	Gambia
Benim	Ghana
Bhutan	Grenada
Bolivia	Guatemala
Botswana	Guinea
Brazil	Guinea Bissau
Burma	Guyana
Burundi	Haiti
Cameroon	Honduras
Cape Verde	India
Central African Empire	Israel
Chad	Ivory Coast
Chile	Jamaica
Colombia	Jordan
Congo (Brazzaville)	Kenya
Costa Rica	Korea, Republic of
Cyprus	Lebanon

Lesotho
Liberia
Malagasy Republic
Malawi
Malaysia
Maldive Islands
Mali
Malta
Mauritania
Mauritius
Mexico
Morocco
Mozambique
Nauru
Nepal
Nicaragua
Niger
Oman
Pakistan
Panama
Papua New Guinea
Paraguay
Peru
Philippines
Portugal
Republic of China (Taiwan)

Romania
Rwanda
Sao Tome and Principe
Senegal
Sierra Leone
Singapore
Somalia
Sri Lanka
Sudan
Surinam
Swaziland
Syria
Tanzania
Thailand
Togo
Tonga
Trinidad and Tobago
Tunisia
Turkey
Upper Volta
Uruguay
Western Samoa
Yemen Arab Republic
Yugoslavia
Zaire
Zambia

Dependent Countries and Territories

Afars and Issas,
    French Territory of the
Antigua
Belize
Bermuda
British Indian Ocean
    Territory
British Solomon Island
Brunei
Cayman Islands
Christmas Island (Australia)
Cocos (Keeling) Islands
Comoro Islands
Cook Islands
Dominica
Falkland Island (Malvinas)
    and Dependencies

French Polynesia
Gibraltar
Gilbert Island
Heard Island and
    McDonald Islands
Hong Kong
Macao
Montserrat
Netherlands Antilles
New Caledonia
New Hebrides Condominium
Niue
Norfolk Island
Pitcairn Island
Portuguese Timor
Saint Christoper-Nevis-
    Anguilla

Saint Helena
Saint Lucia
Saint Vincent
Seychelles
Spanish Sahara
Tokelau Islands

Trust Territory of the
  Pacific Islands
Turks and Chicos Islands
Tuvula
Virgin Islands, British
Wallis and Futuna Islands

Civil and Criminal Fraud Laws

Importers who submit false or fraudulent documents to Customs may have to forfeit their merchandise and pay a penalty equal to the domestic value of the merchandise. These strictures are provided by the Tariff Act of 1930. In addition, a criminal fraud statute provides a maximum of two years' imprisonment, or a $5,000 fine, or both, for each violation involving an importation or attempted importation.

Both of these fraud statutes were enacted by Congress to discourage persons from evading the payment of lawful duties owed to the U.S. They are enforced by special agents assigned to the Office of Investigations who operate throughout the U.S. and in the major trading centers of the world.

Chapter Twenty-One

Foreign Trade Zones

Manufacturers and exporters familiar with the advantages of continental free ports, free-trade zones, and entrepot (trade and shipment) facilities will be interested to learn that a number of foreign-trade zones have been established in the U.S. to encourage the consignment and reexport trade.

Foreign exporters planning to expand or open up new American outlets may forward their goods to a foreign-trade zone in the U.S. to be held for an unlimited period while awaiting a favorable market in the U.S. or nearby countries without being subject to customs entry, payment of duty or tax, or bond.

The zones provide similar advantages for U.S. importers. For example, apparel may be brought into and held in trade zones. The importer thus obtains flexibility—the stock can be labeled as it is sold. Should a customer cancel part of an order, the importer is not in the position of having to relabel stock in order to sell it to another store.

You might also wish to buy equipment in one country and sell it in another. Used machinery purchased in Europe might be stored in a U.S. foreign trade zone, refurbished there, and then sold in South America. The importer would only have to pay storage fees—no duty would apply.

Merchandise brought into foreign trade zones may be stored, sold, exhibited, broken up, repacked, assembled, distributed, sorted, graded, cleaned, mixed with foreign or domestic merchandise, otherwise manipulated, or manufactured. The resulting merchandise may thereafter be either exported or transferred into customs territory. When foreign goods, in their condition at time of entry into the zone or after processing there, are transferred into customs territory of the U.S., the goods must be entered at the custom house. If entered for consumption, duties and taxes will be assessed on the entered articles according to the condition of the foreign merchandise at the time of entry into the zone, if it has been placed in the status of privileged foreign merchandise prior to manipulation or manufacture, or on the basis of their condition at the time of entry for consumption, if the foreign merchandise was in nonprivileged status at the time of processing.

An important feature of foreign-trade zones is that the goods may be brought to the threshold of the market, making immediate delivery certain and avoiding possible cancellation of orders due to shipping delays after a favorable market has closed.

Production of articles in zones by the combined use of domestic and foreign materials makes unnecessary either the sending of the domestic materials abroad for manufacture or the duty-paid or bonded importation of the foreign materials into this country. Duties on the foreign goods involved in such processing or manufacture are payable only on the actual quantity of such foreign goods incorporated in merchandise transferred from a zone for entry into the commerce of the United States. If there is any unrecoverable waste resulting from manufacture or manipulation, allowances are made for it, thereby eliminating payment of duty except on the articles which are actually entered. If there is any recoverable waste, it is dutiable only in its condition as such and in the quantity entered.

A second notable feature under the zone act is the authority to exhibit merchandise within a zone. Zone facilities may be utilized for the full exhibition of foreign merchandise without bond, for an unlimited length of time, and with no requirement of exportation or duty payment. Thus, the owner of goods in a zone may now display his goods where they are stored, establish showrooms or his own, or join with other importers in displaying his merchandise in a permanent exhibition established in the zone; and, since he may also store and process merchandise in a zone, he is not limited to mere display of samples, but he may sell from stock in wholesale quantities.

The owner of foreign merchandise that has not been manipulated or manufactured in any way that would effect a change in its United States tariff classification had it been taken into customs territory may, upon request to the district director of Customs, have its dutiable status fixed and liquidated. This dutiable status will apply irrespective of when the merchandise is entered into customs territory and even though its condition or form may have been changed by processing in the zone, as indicated above.

Domestic merchandise may be taken into a zone and, providing its identity is maintained in accordance with regulations, may be returned to customs territory free of quotas, duty, or tax, even though while in the zone it may have been combined with or made part of other articles. However, domestic distilled spirits, wine, and beer, and a limited number of other kinds of merchandise, may not be processed while in the zone.

Savings may result from manipulations and manufacture in a zone.

For example, many products, shipped to the zone in bulk, can be dried, sorted, graded, or cleaned and bagged or packed, permitting savings of duties and taxes on moisture taken from content or on dirt removed and culls thrown out. From incoming shipment of packaged or bottled goods, damaged packages or broken bottles can be removed. Where evaporation results during shipment or while goods are stored in the zone, contents of barrels or other containers can be regauged and savings obtained, as no duties are payable on the portions lost or removed. In other words, barrels or other containers can be gauged at the time of transfer to customs territory, to insure that duties will not be charged on any portion of their contents which has been lost due to evaporation, leakage, breakage, or otherwise.

Savings in shipping charges, duties, and taxes may result from such operations as shipping unassembled or disassembled furniture, machinery, etc., to the zone and assembled or reassembling them there.

Merchandise may be remarked or relabeled in the zone to conform to requirements for entry into the commerce of the United States if otherwise up to standard. Remarking or relabeling that would be misleading is not permitted in the zone.

Substandard foods and drugs may, in certain cases, be reconditioned to meet the requirements of the Food, Drug, and Cosmetics Act.

There is no time limit as to how long foreign merchandise may be stored in a zone, or when it must be entered into customs territory, reexported, or destroyed.

Foreign merchandise in Customs bonded warehouses may be transferred to the zone at any time before the limitation on its retention in the bonded warehouse expires, but such a transfer to the zone may be made only for the purpose of eventual exportation or destruction.

When foreign merchandise is transferred to the zone from Customs bonded warehouses, the bond is cancelled and all obligations in regard to duty payment, or as to the time when the merchandise is to be reexported, are terminated. Similarly, the owner of domestic merchandise stored in internal revenue bonded warehouses may transfer his goods to a zone and obtain cencellation of bonds. In addition, domestic goods moved into a zone for export are considered exported upon entering the zone for purpose of excise and other internal-revenue tax rebates. A manufacturer, operating in customs territory and using dutiable imported materials in his product, may also obtain drawbacks of duties paid or cancellation of bond, upon transferring the product to the zone for export and complying with the appropriate regulations.

Thus, he does not need to wait until he finds a foreign customer, or until his customer is ready for delivery, to obtain these benefits.

Foreign-trade zones are listed below. Information as to rates and charges, and details as to how individual foreign-trade zones can be utilized, may be obtained by writing to the U.S. Foreign-Trade Zone Manager.

Zone No. 1. Brooklyn Navy Yard, Brooklyn, New York 11205
Zone No. 2. P.O. Box 60046, New Orleans, Louisiana 70160
Zone No. 3. Ferry Bldg., San Francisco, California 94111
Zone No. 5. P.O. Box 1209, Seattle, Washington, 98111
Zone No. 7. G.P.O. 2350, San Juan, Puerto Rico 00936
Zone No. 8. 3332 St. Lawrence Drive, Toledo, Ohio 43605
Zone No. 9. Pier 39, Honolulu, Hawaii 96817
Zone No. 10. (Bay County), 203 15th St., Bay City, Michigan 48706
Zone No. 12. P.O. Box 1988, McAllen, Texas 78501
Zone No. 14. Little Rock Port Authority, 7500 Lindsey Rd., Little Rock, Arkansas 72206

Zone No. 15. (Kansas City, Missouri)
Zone No. 17. (Kansas City, Kansas)
            2440 Pershing Road, Kansas City, Missouri 64108
Zone No. 16. Sault Industrial Park, Sault Ste. Marie, Michigan 49783
Zone No. 18. 2001 Fortune Drive, San Jose, California 95131
Zone No. 19. Omaha Douglas Civic Center No. 401, 1819 Farnam Street,
            Omaha, Nebraska 68102
Zone No. 20. (Portsmouth), 1600 Maritime Tower, Norfolk, Virginia 23510
Zone No. 21. (Dorchester County), P.O. Box 1498, Summerville, South
            Carolina 29483
Zone No. 22. Butler Drive, Lake Calumet Harbor, Chicago, Illinois 60633
Zone No. 23. 901 Fuhrmann Blvd., Buffalo, New York 14203
Zone No. 24. (Pittston), Eastern Distribution Center, Inc., Wilkes-Barre/
            Scranton Airport Terminal, Avoca, Pennsylvania 18641
Zone No. 25. P.O. Box 13136, Port Everglades, Florida 33316
Zone No. 26. Atlanta Foreign-Trade Zone, P.O. Box 1157, Shenendoah,
            Georgia 30265
Zone No. 27. Massachusetts Port Authority, 99 High Street, Boston,
            Massachusetts 02110
Zone No. 28. Industrial Development Commission, 1213 Purchase Street,
            New Bedford, Massachusetts 02740

General information on United States Foreign-Trade Zones may be obtained from any American Consulate abroad or from the Foreign-Trade Zones Board, Department of Commerce, Washington, D.C. 20230.

Summary

This book has outlined the basics of the import/export business. It can be complex, or it can be as routinely simple as most domestic transactions. Whether you enter the trade as an importer or as an exporter, whether you plan eventually to run a large operation or want always to keep the trade to a moonlighting effort, your tools will be the same: information, salesmanship, perseverance, and overseas contracts.

These are several points that this book has addressed and that you should remember as you develop your business:

1. Make long-term commitments. The closer you can work with your suppliers and overseas agents, the more profitable your business will become.

2. Do a thorough job of market research. Supply the right product for the right market.

3. Institute a simple and logical system of costing for your exports and imports.

4. Try to offer the best credit terms possible to your clients, and try to obtain the best credit terms possible for yourself.

5. Try to employ bilingual agents. It is much easier to deal with a foreign representative who speaks your language as well as his or her own.

6. As your business develops, visit your agents and customers overseas. Encourage them to visit the U.S.

7. Support your overseas sales with multilingual promotional literature and advertising. French, English, German, and Spanish are the languages you should consider.

8. Keep yourself abreast of local business conditions wherever your products are sold. Avoid a pushy, hard-sell approach. When importing, familiarize yourself with the trade practices of the industry or industries you deal with.

179

9. Never commit yourself to an arrangement you cannot fulfill. Nothing you can do does more harm than failing to live up to an agreement on pricing, delivery, or service.

10. Conform to all foreign rules and regulations.

The Appendices that follow this summary provide you with the names, addresses, and definitions you'll need to get started in the import/export trade. Now that you've read this book, the next step is up to you.

Section Four

Appendices

U.S. Department of Commerce District Offices

ALBUQUERQUE, N.M., 87102, 505 Marquette, N.W., Suite 1015 (505) 766-2386.

ANCHORAGE, 99501, 632 Sixth Ave., Hill Bldg., Suite 412 (907) 265-5307.

ATLANTA, 30309, Suite 600, 1365 Peachtree St., NE. (404) 881-7000

BALTIMORE, 21202, 415 U.S. Customhouse, Gay and Lombard Sts. (301) 962-3560.

BIRMINGHAM, ALA., 35205, Suite 200–201, 908 S. 20th St. (205) 254-1331.

BOSTON, 02116, 10th Floor, 441 Stuart St. (617) 223-2312.

BUFFALO, N.Y., 14202, Room 1312, Federal Bldg., 111 W. Huron St. (716) 842-3208.

CHARLESTON, W.VA., 25301, 3000 New Federal Office Bldg., 500 Quarrier St. (304) 343-6181 Ext. 375.

CHEYENNE, WYO., 82001, 6022 O'Mahoney Federal Center, 2120 Capitol Ave. (307) 778-2151

CHICAGO, 60603, Room 1406, Mid-Continental Plaza Bldg., 55 E. Monroe St. (312) 353-4450.

CINCINNATI, 45202, 10504 Federal Office Bldg., 550 Main St. (513) 684-2944.

CLEVELAND, 44114, Room 600, 666 Euclid Ave. (216) 552-4750.

COLUMBIA, S.C., 29204, Forest Center, 2611 Forest Dr. (803) 765-5345.

DALLAS, 75202, Room 7A5, 1100 Commerce St. (214) 749-1515.

DENVER, 80202, Room 165, New Custom House, 19th and Stout Sts. (303) 837-3246.

DES MOINES, IOWA, 50309, 609 Federal Blvd., 210 Walnut St. (515) 284-4222.

DETROIT, 48226, 445 Federal Bldg., 231 W. Lafayette. (313) 226-3650.

GREENSBORO, N.C., 27402, 203 Federal Bldg., W. Market St., P.O. Box 1950. (919) 378-5345.

HARTFORD, CONN., 06103, Room 610-B, Federal Office Bldg., 450 Main St. (203) 244-3530.

HONOLULU, 96813, 286 Alexander Young Bldg., 1015 Bishop St. (808) 546-8694.

HOUSTON, 77002, 2625 Federal Bldg./Courthouse, 515 Rusk St. (713) 226-4231.

INDIANAPOLIS, 46204, 357 Federal Office Bldg., 46 E. Ohio St. (317) 269-6214.

LOS ANGELES, 90049, Room 800, 11777 San Vicente Blvd. (213) 824-7591.

MEMPHIS, 38103, Room 710, 147 Jefferson Ave. (901) 521-3213.

MIAMI, 33130, Rm. 821, City National Bank Bldg., 25 W. Flagler St. (305) 350-5267.

MILWAUKEE, 53203, Federal Bldg., 517 E. Wisconsin Ave. (414) 224-3473.

MINNEAPOLIS, 55401, 218 Federal Bldg., 110 S. Fourth St. (612) 725-2133.

NEW ORLEANS, 70130, Room 432, International Trade Mart, 2 Canal St. (504) 589-6546.

NEW YORK, 10007, 37th Floor, Federal Office Bldg., 26 Federal Plaza, Foley Sq. (212) 264-0634.

NEWARK, N.J., 07102, Gateway Bldg. (4th floor) (201) 645-6214.

OMAHA, 68102. Capitol Plaza, Suite 703A, 1815 Capitol Ave. (402) 221-3665.

PHILADELPHIA, 19106, 9448 Federal Bldg., 600 Arch St. (215) 597-2850.

PHOENIX, ARIZ., 85004, 508 Greater Arizona Savings Blvd., 112 N. Central Ave. (602) 261-3285.

PITTSBURGH, 15222, 2002 Federal Bldg., 1000 Liberty Ave. (412) 644-2850.

PORTLAND, ORE., 97204, Room 618, 1220 S.W. 3rd Ave. (503) 221-3001.

RENO, NEV., 89502, 2028 Federal Bldg., 300 Booth St. (702) 784-5203.

RICHMOND, VA., 23240, 8010 Federal Bldg., 400 N. 8th St. (804) 782-2246.

ST. LOUIS, 63105. Chromalloy Bldg., 120 S. Central Ave. (314) 425-3302.

SALT LAKE CITY, 84138, 1203 Federal Bldg., 125 S. State St. (801) 524-5116.

SAN FRANCISCO, 94102. Federal Bldg., Box 36013, 450 Golden Gate Ave. (415) 556-5860.

SAN JUAN, P.R., 00918, 659 Federal Bldg. (809) 763-6363.

SAVANNAH, 31402. 235 U.S. Courthouse and Post Office Bldg., 12529 Bull St. (912) 232-4321.

SEATTLE, 98109, 706 Lake Union Bldg., 1700 Westlake Ave. North. (206) 442-5615.

Appendix Two

U.S. Ports of Entry

Following is an alphabetical list of the Customs ports of entry arranged
by States, including Puerto Rico and the Virgin Islands.
District shown in boldface; regional headquarters
shown in italic.

ALABAMA
Birmingham
Mobile

ALASKA
Alcan
Anchorage
Fairbanks
Juneau
Ketchikan
Kodiak
Pelican
Petersburg
Sand Point
Sitka
Skagway
Wrangell

ARIZONA
Douglas
Lukeville
Naco
Nogales
Phoenix
San Luis
Sasabe

ARKANSAS
Little Rock-N. Little
  Rock

CALIFORNIA
Andrade
Calexico
Eureka
Fresno
*Los Angeles-Long
  Beach*
Port San Luis
San Diego
*San Francisco-
  Oakland*
Tecate

COLORADO
Denver

CONNECTICUT
Bridgeport
Hartford
New Haven
New London

DELAWARE
Wilmington

**DISTRICT OF
COLUMBIA**
Washington

FLORIDA
Apalachicola

Boca Grande
Carrabelle
Fernandina Beach
Jacksonville
Key West
Miami
Orlando
Panama City
Pensacola
Port Canaveral
Port Everglades
Port St. Joe
St. Petersburg
Tampa
West Palm Beach

GEORGIA
Atlanta
Brunswick
Savannah

HAWAII
Honolulu
Hilo
Kahului
Nawiliwili-Port Allen

IDAHO
Easport
Porthill

ILLINOIS
Chicago
Peoria

INDIANA
Evansville
Indianapolis
Lawrenceburg

IOWA
Des Moines

KANSAS
Wichita

KENTUCKY
Louisville

LOUISIANA
Baton Rouge
Lake Charles
Morgan City
New Orleans

MAINE
Bangor
Bar Harbor
Bath
Belfast
Bridgewater
Calais
Eastport
Fort Fairfield
Fort Kent
Houlton
Jackman
Jonesport
Limestone
Madawaska
Portland
Rockland
Van Buren
Vanceboro

MARYLAND
Annapolis
Baltimore
Cambridge
Crisfield

MASSACHUSETTS
Boston

Fall River
Gloucester
Lawrence
New Bedford
Plymouth
Salem
Springfield
Worcester

MICHIGAN
Battle Creek
Detroit
Grand Rapids
Muskegon
Port Huron
Saginaw-Bay City
Sault Ste. Marie

MINNESOTA
Baudette
Duluth and Superior, Wis.
Grand Portage
International Falls-
  Ranier
Minneapolis-St. Paul
Noyes
Pinecreek
Roseau
Warroad

MISSISSIPPI
Greenville
Gulfport
Pascagoula
Vicksburg

MISSOURI
Kansas City
St. Joseph
St. Louis

MONTANA
Butte
Del Bonita
Great Falls
Morgan
Opheim
Piegan
Raymond

Roosville
Scobey
Sweetgrass
Turner
Whitetail
Whitlash

NEBRASKA
Omaha

NEVADA
Las Vegas
Reno

NEW HAMPSHIRE
Portsmouth

NEW JERSEY
Perth Amboy

NEW MEXICO
Albuquerque
Columbus

NEW YORK
Albany
Alexandria Bay
Buffalo-Niagara Falls
Cape Vincent
Champlain-Rouses
  Point
Chateaugay
Clayton
Fort Covington
Massena
New York
  Kennedy Airport
  Area*
  Newark Area*
  New York Seaport
  Area*
Ogdensburg
Oswego
Rochester
Sodus Point
Syracuse
Trout River
Utica

NORTH CAROLINA
Beaufort-Morehead
  City

*Under jurisdiction of an area director of Customs.

Charlotte
Durham
Reidsville
Wilmington
Winston-Salem

NORTH DAKOTA
Ambrose
Antler
Carbury
Dunseith
Fortuna
Hannah
Hansboro
Maida
Neche
Noonan
Northgate
Pembina
Portal
Sarles
Sherwood
St. John
Walhalla
Westhope

OHIO
Akron
Ashtabula
Cincinnati
Cleveland
Columbus
Conneaut
Dayton
Sandusky
Toledo

OKLAHOMA
Oklahoma City
Tulsa

OREGON
Astoria[1]
Coos Bay
Newport
Portland[1]

PENNSYLVANIA
Chester
Erie
Hamisburg
Philadelphia
Pittsburg
Wilkes-Barre/Scranton

PUERTO RICO
Aguadilla
Fajardo
Guanica
Humacao
Jobos
Mayaguez
Ponce
San Juan

RHODE ISLAND
Newport
Providence

SOUTH CAROLINA
Charleston
Georgetown
Greenville-
  Spartanburg

TENNESSEE
Chattanooga
Knoxville
Memphis
Nashville

TEXAS
Amarillo
Beaumont
Brownsville
Corpus Christi
Dallas/Ft. Worth
Del Rio
Eagle Pass
El Paso
Fabens
Freeport
Galveston
Hidalgo

Houston
Laredo
Lubbock
Orange[2]
Port Arthur[2]
Port Lavaca-Point
  Comfort
Presidio
Progresso
Rio Grande City
Roma
Sabine[2]
San Antonio

UTAH
Salt Lake City

VERMONT
Beecher Falls
Burlington
Derby Line
Highgate Springs/
  Alburg
Richford
St. Albans

VIRGIN ISLANDS
Charlotte Amalie,
  St. Thomas
Christiansted
Coral Bay
Cruz Bay
Frederiksted

VIRGINIA
Alexandria
Cape Charles City
*Norfolk-Newport
  News*
Reedville
Richmond-Petersburg

WASHINGTON
Aberdeen
Anacortes[3]
Bellingham[3]
Blaine

---

[1]Consolidated as the Columbia River port of entry.
[2]Consolidated as the Beaumont, Orange, Port Arthur, Sabine port of entry.
[3]Consolidated as the Port of Puget Sound.

Boundary
Danville
Everett[3]
Ferry
Friday Harbor[3]
Frontier
Laurier
Longview[1]
Lynden
Metaline Falls
Neah Bay[3]

Nighthawk
Olympia[3]
Oroville
Port Angeles[3]
Port Townsend[3]
Seattle[3]
South Bend-Raymond
Spokane
Sumas
Tacoma[3]

WEST VIRGINIA
Charleston

WISCONSIN
Ashland
Green Bay
Manitowoc
Marinette
Milwaukee
Racine
Sheboygan

Appendix Three

Customs Regions and Districts

Headquarters
U.S. Customs Service
1301 Constitution Ave., N.W.
Washington, D.C. 20229

Region I—Boston, Mass. 02110
DISTRICTS:
 Portland, Maine 04111
 St. Albans, Vt. 05478
 Boston, Mass. 02109
 Providence, R.I. 02903
 Buffalo, N.Y. 14202
 Ogdensburg, N.Y. 13669
 Bridgeport, Conn. 06609

Region II—New York, N.Y. 10048
New York District, which is coexten-
sive with New York Region, has
three administrative areas: Kennedy
Airport Area, Newark Area, and
New York Seaport Area.

Region III—Baltimore, Md. 21202
DISTRICTS:
 Philadelphia, Pa. 19106
 Baltimore, Md. 21202
 Norfolk, Va. 23510
 Washington, D.C. 20018

Region IV—Miami, Fla. 33131
DISTRICTS:
 Wilmington, N.C. 28401
 San Juan, P.R. 00903
 Charleston, S.C. 29402
 Savannah, Ga. 31401
 Tampa, Fla. 33601
 Miami, Fla. 33132
 St. Thomas, V.I. 00801

Region V—New Orleans, La. 70112
DISTRICTS:
 Mobile, Ala. 36601
 New Orleans, La. 70130

Region VI—Houston, Tex. 77002
DISTRICTS:
 Port Arthur, Tex. 77640
 Galveston, Tex. 77550
 Houston, Tex. 77052
 Laredo, Tex. 78040
 El Paso, Tex. 79985

Region VII—Los Angeles, Calif. 90053
DISTRICTS:
 Nogales, Ariz. 85621
 San Diego, Calif. 92188
 Los Angeles, Calif.,
  San Pedro, Calif. 90731

Region VIII—San Francisco, Calif. 94105

DISTRICTS:

San Francisco, Calif. 94126
Honolulu, Hawaii 96806
Portland, Oreg. 97209
Seattle, Wash. 98104
Anchorage, Alaska 99501
Great Falls, Mont. 59401

Region IX—Chicago, Ill. 60603

DISTRICTS:

Chicago, Ill. 60607
Pembina, N. Dak. 58271
Minneapolis-St. Paul, Minn. 55401
Duluth, Minn. 55802
Milwaukee, Wis. 53202
Cleveland, Ohio 44114
St. Louis, Mo. 63105
Detroit, Mich. 48226

Appendix Four

Customs Attaches
and Senior Representatives
in Foreign Countries

Canada

Senior Customs Representative
U.S. Consulate
Tour du Sud, Suite 1122
Complex des Jardins
Montreal 45B 1G1, P.Q.
Tel: 281-1456

England

Customs Attache
American Embassy, Room G94
24/32 Grosvenor Square
London W.1
Tel: 499-1212

France

Customs Attache
American Embassy, D Bldg.
58 Rue La Boetie, Room 211
75008 Paris
Tel: 265-7400, Ext. 8241

Germany

Customs Attache
American Embassy, Room 2069
5300 Mehlemer Aue
Bonn-Bad Godesberg
Tel: 89-3207

Hong Kong

Senior Customs Representative
American Consulate General
26 Garden Road
Hong Kong, British Crown Colony
Tel: 5-239-011, Ext. 243

Italy

Customs Attache
American Embassy
Via Veneto 119, Room 302
00187 Rome
Tel: 4674, Ext. 475

Japan

Customs Attache
American Embassy, Room 202
Akasaka I-chome, Minato-ku
Tokyo, 107
Tel: 583-7141, Ext. 7205

Mexico

Customs Attache
American Embassy
Paseo de la Reforma 305
Colonia Cuahtemoc
Mexico, D.F.
Tel: 553-3333

Taiwan

Customs Attache
2 Chun Hsiao West Road
Second Section
Taipei
Tel: 333-551, Ext. 224

Appendix Five

Customhouse Brokers and Freight Forwarders

ALABAMA

MOBILE, Alabama
John M. Brining
Suite 402, First Federal Savings Bldg.
Mobile, Alabama 36602

N.D. Cunningham & Co., Inc.
302 Commerce Bldg., P.B. Box 15
Mobile, Alabama 36601

Dodd, Sara Sanford
P.O. Box 1115
Mobile, Alabama

Provence & Co.
1 Stuart Circle
Mobile, Albama

CALIFORNIA

LOS ANGELES, California
Air-Sea Forwarders, Inc.
10425 La Cienega Boulevard
Los Angeles, Calif. 90045

American Consolidators Corp.
3689 Bandini Boulevard
Los Angeles, Calif. 90023

Global Forwarding, Inc.
Number One Global Way
Anaheim, Calif. 92803

Arizona Theater Service, Inc.
1525 West 23rd Street
Los Angeles, Calif. 90007

Jet Air Freight
900 West Florence Avenue
Inglewood, Calif. 90301

Bekins International Lines, Inc.
1335 South Figueroa Street
Los Angeles, Calif. 90015

California Cartage Express
4366 East 26th Street
Los Angeles, Calif. 90023

California Western Freight Association
d/b/a Western Freight Association
2102 Alhambra Avenue
P.O. Box 54037
Los Angeles, Calif. 90031

Coast Carloading Co.
2110 Alhambra Avenue
P.O. Box 54293
Terminal Annex
Los Angeles, Calif. 90054

De Witt Freight Forwarding
6060 North Figueroa Street
Los Angeles, Calif. 90042

Empire Freight Company, Inc.
1039 Richmond Street
Los Angeles, Calif. 90033

Guam Freight Forwarders
  and Consolidators
2425 Porter Street
Los Angeles, Calif. 90021

Source: The American Register of Exporters and
Importers, 1978 edition. 38 Park Row,
N.Y., N.Y.

Honolulu Freight Service
2425 Porter Street
Los Angeles, Calif. 90021

James Loudon & Co.
510 W. 6th Street
Los Angeles, Calif. 90014

Lyon Household Shipping, Inc.
1950 South Vermont Avenue
Los Angeles, Calif. 90007

Mid-Pacific Forwarding Co., Inc.
5760 Ferguson Drive
Los Angeles, Calif. 90022

Pacific Freight Forwarding Co.
760 Warehouse Street
Los Angeles, Calif. 90021

Superior Fast Freight
611 North Mission Road
Los Angeles, Calif. 90033

United Transportation Co., Inc.
1910 North Main Street
Los Angeles, Calif. 90031

W.T.C. Air Freight, Inc.
P.O. Box 92923
Los Angeles, Calif. 90009

Westransco Freight Company
1910 North Main Street
Los Angeles, Calif. 90031

LONG BEACH, California
Aloha Consolidators International
2350 Dominguez Street
Long Beach, Calif. 90801

American Ensign Van Service, Inc.
2360 Pacific Avenue
Suite "D"
Long Beach, Calif. 90806

OAKLAND, California
Astron Forwarding Company
75 Market Street
Post Office Box 161
Oakland, Calif.

PALO ALTO, California
O.N.C. Forwarding
2800 W. Bayshore Road
Palo Alto, Calif. 94303

RICHMOND, California
Vanpac Carriers, Inc.
2114 MacDonald Avenue
Richmond, Calif. 94801

SAN DIEGO, California
Britton & Co.
300 W. 2nd St.
Calexico, Calif.

Enicso, Manual A.
First & Paulin
Calexico, Calif.

Four Winds Forwarding, Inc.
7035 Convoy Court
San Diego, Calif. 92138

Cantu, Cesar A.
207 Broadway Pier Bldg.
San Diego, Calif.

Dana & Co., A. E.
355 West G. Street
San Diego, Calif.

Porter, David E.
Lindberg Field, P.O. Box 81488
San Diego, Calif.

SAN DIMAS, California
Lux Art Race Horse Forwarding Co.
155 North Eucla
San Dimas, Calif. 91773

SAN FRANCISCO, California
Aero Special Air Freight, Inc.
242 Steuart Street
San Francisco, Calif. 94105

Air Sea Forwarders
512 S. Airport Blvd.
San Francisco, Calif.

Airoceanic Shippers
219 Lawrence Ave. So.
San Francisco, Calif. 94080

Asiatic Forwarders, Inc.
335 Valencia Street
San Francisco, Calif. 94103

W. C. Auger & Co.
545 Sansome St., P.O. Box 2250
San Francisco, Calif. 94126

Berry & Mc Carthy Shipping Co.
260 California St.
San Francisco, Calif.

L. E. Coppersmith, Inc.
260 California St.
San Francisco, Calif. 94111

Enterprise Shipping Corp.
58 Sutter St.
San Francisco, Calif.

Fritz Transportation International
244 Jackson Street
San Francisco, Calif. 94111

Higa Fast Pac, Inc.
465 California Street
San Francisco, Calif. 94104

Hoyt, Shepston & Sciaroni, Inc.
P.O. Box 2184
San Francisco, Calif. 94126

Nova International Air Freight
(Far East)
100 Bush Street
San Francisco, Calif. 94104

SAN MATEO, California
JCF Air Freight, Inc.
1700 South Camino Rd.
Suite 201
San Mateo, Calif. 94402

SANTA ANA, California
Jet Forwarding, Inc.
200 West Central Avenue
Santa Ana, Calif. 92707

TORRANCE, California
Columbia Export Packers, Inc.
19032 South Vermont Avenue
Torrance, Calif. 90502

CANADA

Adley Corp.
6406 Cote de Liesse Road
Dorval
Montreal, P.Q. Canada

Affiliated Customs Brokers Ltd.
450 Ste Helene St.
Montreal, P.Q. Canada

Allports Custom Brokers
407 McGill St.
Montreal, P.Q. Canada

Alwoods Customs Brokers Ltd.
501 A Cleveland Cresc.
S.E. Calgary, Alberta, Canada

Harte & Lynne Ltd., T.H. & B.
Station Hunter St., P.O. Box 124
Hamilton, Ontario, Canada

Kenney, C.R.
25 Hughson St. S.
Hamilton, Ontario, Canada

Higinbotham Ltd., H.T.
10015 103rd Ave.
Edmonton, Alberta, Canada

Johnson & Mathew Ltd.
112 11th Ave. S.E.
Calgary, Alberta, Canada

Maze, Hickey & Redman Ltd.
110 11th Ave. S.E.
Calgary, Alberta, Canada

Smith, Ltd. H.H.
10015 103rd Ave.
Edmonton, Alberta, Canada

Atlas Customs Brokers Ltd.
Toronto Int'l. Airport
Malton, Ont., Canada

Border Brokers Ltd.
60 Front St. W.
Toronto, Ont., Canada

Affiliated Custom Brokers
159 Bay St.
Toronto, Canada

COLORADO

DENVER, Colorado
Fritz & Co., Arthur J.
P.O. Box 299
Denver, Colorado 80207

Freight Forwarders Int'l. Inc.
1700 15th St.
Denver, Colorado, 80217

Schayer, Charles M.
Dedham Bldg.
1812 California
Denver, Colorado 80202

LITTLETON, Colorado
North Pacific Forwarders, Inc.
P.O. Box 192
Littleton, Colorado 80120

CONNECTICUT

BRIDGEPORT, Connecticut
Marshall, Wm. A.
P.O. Box 128
Bridgeport, Conn.

Moran Co. Inc., J. F.
P.O. Box 571
Milford, Conn.

Weiss, Murray H.
1188 Main St.
P.O. Box 757
Bridgeport, Conn.

EAST HARTFORD, Connecticut
Refrigerated Forwarders, Inc.
241 Park Avenue
East Hartford, Conn. 06108

Brian R. Glynn
Suffield Village
Suffield, Conn. 06078

WILTON, Connecticut
Emery Air Freight Corporation
P.O. Box 322
Wilton, Conn. 06897

FLORIDA

MIAMI, Florida
Air Sea Shipping Service
1955 N.W. 72nd Avenue
Miami, Florida 33122

Aircargo Brokerage Co.
P.O. Box 012019, Flagler Station
Miami, Florida 33101

Florida-Texas Freight, Inc.
777 N.W. 72nd Avenue
Miami, Florida 33126

Ports International Inc.
3730 N.W. 54th Street
Miami, Florida 33148

M & H Brokerage
P.O. Box 912, Int'l. Airport
Miami, Florida 33148

Robbins Customhouse Brokers
Bldg. 2134
Miami International Airport
P.O. Box 48 1111
Miami, Florida 33148

EVERGLADES, Florida
The Copeland Co., Inc.
P.O. Box 13064, Port Everglades
Fort Lauderdale, Florida 33316

J. P. Reynolds Co.
P.O. Box 13071
Fort Lauderdale, Florida 33316

JACKSONVILLE, Florida
E. Allen Brown International
P.O. Box 38022
Jacksonville, Florida 32206

Robert M. Mc Coy
1501 Haines St., P.O. Box 121
Jacksonville, Florida

Suddath Enterprises, Inc.
P.O. Box 6699
Jacksonville, Florida 32205

T.M.T. Trailer Ferry Inc.
1045 Bond Avenue, P.O. Box 4787
Jacksonville, Florida 32201

Sullivan & Sons Inc.
P.O. Box 512
Jacksonville, Florida 32201

Thomas L. Watkins
2080 Talleyrand Ave.
Jacksonville, Florida 32201

Reedy Forwarding Company
3730 N.W. 54th Street
Miami, Florida 33148

ST. PETERSBURG, Florida
Delcher Intercontinental
Moving Service, Inc.
4219 Central Avenue
St. Petersburg, Florida 33733

Imperial Van Lines
International, Inc.
9675 4th Street, North
St. Petersburg, Florida 33702

TAMPA, Florida
J. Cortina
York & 13th Sts. P.O. Box 603
Tampa, Florida 33601

Fillette, Green & Co. of Tampa
315 Madison St.
Tampa, Florida 33602

Hamilton Bros., Inc.
501 Jackson St.
Tampa, Florida

Hillebaum-Tampa, Inc.
501 Jackson St.
Tampa, Florida

GEORGIA

ATLANTA, Georgia
Bruce Duncan Company Inc.
2459 Roosevelt Hwy. C. Pk.
Atlanta, Georgia

Duncan Jean D. Custom House Broker
Located at the Atlanta Airport
Scott Hudgens Bldg., Hpvl.
Atlanta, Georgia

Oldstein Custom House Brokers
1664 Lenox Road, N.E.
Atlanta, Georgia

Winter, Donald R. & Co. Inc.
1005 Virginia Ave., Hpvl.
Atlanta, Georgia

Alexander V. & Co. Exports
1041 Lees Mill Rd., SW
Atlanta, Georgia

Bellair Expediting Service
2608 Charleston Dr., C. Pk.
Atlanta, Georgia

Cape Air Freight Inc.
1199 Willingham Dr., E. Pt.
Atlanta, Georgia

Nagel Corp.
1240 Truck Rd., Hpvl.
Atlanta, Georgia

Panalpina International Forwarding
Limited
1001 Virginia Ave., Hpvl.
Atlanta, Georgia

SAVANNAH, Georgia
Anderson Shipping Co.
2 Whitaker Street, P.O. Box 9805
Savannah, Georgia

W. G. Carroll & Company, Inc.
130 E. Bay Street
Savannah, Georgia 31402

Craig Jos. & Co.
2 Barnard
Savannah, Georgia

Ebberwein, Joseph K.
Suite 208-209 Realty Bldg.
Savannah, Georgia

International Forwarders, Inc.
P.O. Box 1764
Savannah, Georgia

James, Johns
312 W. Congress Street
Savannah, Georgia

Mobley, E. L.
P.O. Box 1686
Savannah, Georgia

Powers, D. J.
P.O. Box 9614
Savannah, Georgia

Southeastern Maritime Co.
310 East Bay Street
Savannah, Georgia 31402

Smith & Kelly
P.O. Box 1805
Ocean Terminal Bldg.
Savannah, Georgia

Southern Shipping Company
P.O. Box 2808
Ocean Terminal Bldg.
Savannah, Georgia

Wise, Jr. George W.
P.O. Box 2221
Savannah, Georgia

HAWAII

HONOLULU, Hawaii
HC&D Forwarders International, Inc.
911 Middle Street
Honolulu, Hawaii 96819

American Customs Brokerage Co.
P.O. Box 261
Honolulu, Hawaii 96809

S. J. Lam
P.O. Box 2713, Room 302
Arcade Bldg.
Honolulu, Hawaii

ILLINOIS

ARLINGTON HEIGHTS, Illinois
Seatrain Lines, Inc.
   Container Division
120 West Eastman Street
Arlington Heights, Illinois 60004

CHICAGO, Illinois
Action World Shippers, Inc.
4239 N. Nordica
Chicago, Ill. 60634

D. C. Andrews International, Inc.
327 South La Salle Street
Chicago, Ill. 60604

Bernard, J. E. & Co., Inc.
1111 Nicholas Boulevard
Elk Grove Village, Ill. 60007

Central Forwarding Company
509 West Roosevelt Road
Chicago, Ill. 60607

Lyons Transport, Inc.
2800 West 38th Street
Chicago, Ill. 60632

Merchant Shippers
1601 South Western Avenue
Chicago, Ill. 60608

Acme International Inc.
5106 N. Cicero
Chicago, Ill.

Fritz & Co., Arthur J.
227 W. Adams St.
Chicago, Ill.

International Customs Service Inc.
P.O. Box 6n176
O'Hare International Airport
Chicago, Ill. 60666

Mc Ginty Co., William A.
327 South La Salle Street
Chicago, Ill. 60604

DCI International
9759 W. Allen
Rosemont, Ill. 60018

Harper Robinson & Co.
529 Thomas Dr.
Bensenville, Ill. 60106

INDIANA

EVANSVILLE, Indiana
Atlas Van Lines International Corp.
1212 St. George Road
Evansville, Ind. 47711

INDIANAPOLIS, Indiana
Crest Forwarders, Inc.
863 Massachusetts Avenue
Indianapolis, Ind. 46204

American Fletcher National Bank
P.O. Box 41594
Weir Cook Airport
Indianapolis, Ind. 46241

Furniture Forwarding, Inc.
2525 East 56th Street
P.O. Box 55191
Indianapolis, Ind. 46205

International Services Inc.
Weir Cook Airport
P.O. Box 41607
Indianapolis, Ind. 46241

SOUTH BEND, Indiana
T n'T, Inc.
4000 West Sample Street
South Bend, Ind. 46621

PORTAGE, Indiana
Port Of Indiana
P.O. Box 189
Burns Waterway Harbor
Portage, Indiana 46368

NEW HAVEN, Indiana
North American International, Inc.
P.O. Box 210
New Haven, Ind. 46774

KANSAS

WICHITA, Kansas
Kingpak, Inc.
707 East Harry
Wichita, Kan. 67207

SNAWNEE MISSION, Kansas
Yellow Forwarding Co.
P.O. Box 7270
10990 Roe Avenue
Snawnee Mission, Kansas 60207

KENTUCKY

LOUISVILLE, Kentucky
Mrs. Ruth Carey
1609 Ellwood Ave.
Louisville, Kentucky

Walter F. Meuter
1203½ South 6th St.
Louisville, Kentucky 40203

NEWPORT, Kentucky
Hosea & Sons Company, H. J.
12th & Brighton
Newport, Kentucky 41071

LOUISIANA

KENNER, Louisiana
Security Forwarders, Inc.
100 West Airline Highway
Kenner, Louisiana 70062

NEW ORLEANS, Louisiana
Allen & Co., Inc., J. W.
325 Whitney Bldg.
New Orleans, Louisiana

Alltransport, Inc.
1318 Int'l Trade Mart Tower
New Orleans, Louisiana

Clipper Express Company
Alonso Shipping Company
315 Charles Street
New Orleans, Louisiana

Gulf Forwarding Company
823 Whitney Bldg.
New Orleans, Louisiana

Hampton & Co., Inc., J. W., Jr.
107 Camp Street
New Orleans, Louisiana

Harle Forwarding Co. of Louisiana
Inc., J.P.
519 Richards Bldg., 837 Gravier St.
New Orleans, Louisiana

Harper, Robinson, Inc.
Int'l Trade Mart
New Orleans, Louisiana

International Express Company, Inc.
1536 International Trade Mart
New Orleans, Louisiana 70130

Intra-Mar Shipping Corp.
332 Whitney Bank Bldg.
New Orleans, Louisiana

Jackson & Son, Inc., S.
422 Natchez Street
New Orleans, Louisiana

Judson-Sheldon Int'l Corp.
442 Canal Street
New Orleans, Louisiana

Standard Shipping Company
537 Whitney Bank Bldg.
New Orleans, Louisiana

Transoceanic Shipping Company
1505 International Trade Mart
New Orleans, Louisiana 70130

MAINE

JACKMAN, Maine
Lausier, Ronald A.
P.O. Drawer 488
Jackman, Maine 04845

PORTLAND, Maine
Hugh P. Costello
Main State Pier
Portland, Maine

Gignoux, Inc., Fred E.
10 Dana Street
Portland, Maine

Chase, Leavitt & Co.
Ten Dana St.
Portland, Maine 04112

MARYLAND

BALTIMORE, Maryland
Davidson Forwarding Company
698 Fairmount Avenue
Baltimore, Maryland 21204

Republic Household Goods
Shipping Co.
9219 Hartford Road
Baltimore, Maryland 21234

Andrews International
400 Water Street
Baltimore, Maryland

Connors Inc., John S.
33 S Gay Street
Baltimore, Maryland 21201

DCI International
507–509 Chamber of Commerce Bldg.
Baltimore, Maryland

Masson Inc., William H.
810 Keyser Bldg.
207 East Redwood St.
Baltimore, Maryland 21202

CHEVY CHASE, Maryland
Routed Thru-Pac, Inc.
7204 Wisconsin Avenue
Chevy Chase, Maryland 20015

MASSACHUSETTS

BOSTON, Massachusetts
A&M Custom Brokers
126 State Street
Boston, Mass. 02109

Advance Brokers
148 State Street
Boston, Mass. 02109

John A. Conkey & Co.
15 Broad Street
Boston, Mass. 02109

Dolliff & Company, Inc.
131 State Street
Boston, Mass. 02109

HOLYOKE, Massachusetts
Gannon, Inc., Hugh, F.
452 Dwight Street
Holyoke, Mass. 01040

Sheldon Forwarding Co.
170–190 Main Street
Holyoke, Mass. 01040

SEEKONK, Massachusetts
Providence-Philadelphia Dispatch,
Inc.
275 Pine Street
Seekonk, Mass. 02771

MICHIGAN

DETROIT, Michigan
John V. Carr & Son, Inc.
P.O. Box 479-A
Detroit, Michigan 48232

Export-Import Service Co., Inc.
2828 Howard Street
Detroit, Michigan 48226

Filbin & Co., Inc. W. R.
221 Case Avenue
Detroit, Michigan 48226

Harris & Co., I. C.
1950 David Stott Bldg.
Detroit, Michigan 48226

Nahrgang Co., V. G.
155 West Congress Street
Detroit, Michigan 48226

Richardson Co., The J. D.
1225 Lafayette Bldg.
Detroit, Michigan 48226

Schmitt & Company, Gerry
1522 Guardian Bldg.
Detroit, Michigan 48226

MINNESOTA

DULUTH, Minnesota
Buchannan Jr., Robert A.
625 Board of Trade Bldg.
Duluth, Minnesota 55802

Lakeshead Forwarding Corp.
306 Board of Trade Bldg.
Duluth, Minnesota

Svensoon Shipping Agency Inc.
625 Board of Trade Bldg.
Duluth, Minnesota 55802

MINNEAPOLIS, Minnesota
Northwest Dairy Forwarding Co.
210 9th Avenue, South
Minneapolis, Minnesota 55415

M. B. Ingham & Son
7400 24th Ave. South
Minneapolis, Minnesota 55111

Jerome Skar Inc.
7910 12th Ave. S.
Minneapolis, Minnesota 55420

MISSISSIPPI

GULFPORT, Mississippi
Albatross Shipping
P.O. Box 4093
Gulfport, Miss. 39501

Finley, Robert E. Sr.
P.O. Box 273
Gulfport, Miss.

Transworld Shipping Corp.
Bingham Bldg.
Gulfport, Miss.

MISSOURI

GRANDVIEW, Missouri
Cartwright International Van Lines
Inc.
11901 Cartwright Avenue
Grandview, Mo. 64030

KANSAS CITY, Missouri
Riss Intermodal Corporation
Suite 1200, Temple Building
903 Grand Avenue
Kansas City, Mo. 64106

James A. Green Jr. & Co.
P.O. Box 15456
Kansas City, Mo. 64106

Kaysing Co., F. H.
308 Argyle Bldg.
306 E. 12th St.
Kansas, City, Mo. 64106

Swartz, S.
P.O. Box 15126
Kansas City, Mo. 64106

ST. LOUIS, Missouri
H. N. Epstein & Co.
Box 10134
Lambert Airfield
St. Louis, Mo. 63145

L. E. Mc Cullough & Co.
6912 Bonhomme
St. Louis, Mo. 63105

Hanebrink Co. Inc.
10 Hildon Parkway
St. Louis, Mo.

Koeller-Strauss Co.
140 Weldon Parkway
St. Louis, Mo.

Springmeier Shipping Company, Inc.
1123 Hadley Street
St. Louis, Mo. 63101

FENTON, Missouri
United Foreign Shipping Company
#1 United Drive
Fenton, (St. Louis County), Mo. 63026

NEW JERSEY

CHERRY HILL, New Jersey
Shulman Air Freight, Inc.
20 Olney Avenue
Cherry Hill Industrial Park
Cherry Hill, N.J. 08002

ELIZABETH, New Jersey
Engel Storage Corporation
901 Julia Street
Elizabeth, N.J. 07201

NEWARK, New Jersey
Import Export Service of
New Jersey, Inc.
972 Broad St.
Newark, N.J. 07102

Manco International Forwarders
9 Clinton Street
Newark, N.J.

Redden, Charles A.
Port Authority Terminal
400 Delancy St.
Newark, N.J. 07105

NORTH BERGEN, New Jersey
New England Forwarding Co., Inc.
2121 91st Street
North Bergen, N.J. 07047

Puerto Rican Forwarding Co., Inc.
2121 91st Street
North Bergen, N.J. 07047

PORT NEWARK, New Jersey
Ohio Fast Freight Corp.
100 Marsh Street
Port Newark, N.J. 07114

RUTHERFORD, New Jersey
National Movers Forwarding Corp.
P.O. Box 70
Rutherford, N.J. 07070

SECAUCUS, New Jersey
Chain Deliveries Express, Inc.
One Gilbert Drive
Secaucus, N.J. 07094

TENAFLY, New Jersey
Knickerbocker Despatch, Inc.
16 Central Avenue
Tenafly, N.J. 07670

WEEHAWKEN, New Jersey
All Cargo Forwarders, Inc.
P.O. Box 4958
Weehawken, N.J. 07087

NEW YORK

ATLANTIC BEACH, New York
Triple R. Trucking Company, Inc.
101 Flamingo Street
Atlantic Beach, N.Y. 11509

Emery Air Freight Corp.
P.O. Box 201
JFK International Airport
Jamaica, N.Y. 11430

Export-Import Air Service Inc.
177–25 Rockaway Blvd.
Jamaica, N.Y. 11434

Nippon Express U.S.A. Inc.
147 32 Farmers Blvd.
Jamaica, N.Y. 11434

Profit By Air, Inc.
148–11 New York Boulevard
Jamaica, N.Y. 11434

Trans-Air Freight System, Inc.
153–40 Rockaway Blvd.
Jamaica, N.Y. 11434

Wings & Wheels Express, Inc.
World Headquarters Building
John F. Kennedy International Airport
Jamaica, N.Y. 11430

LAKE SUCCESS, L.I., New York
Republic Freight System, Inc.
2335 New Hyde Park Road
Lake Success, L.I., N.Y. 11040

MASPETH, New York
Home-Pack Transport, Inc.
57–48 49th Street
Maspeth, N.Y. 11368

NEW YORK CITY, New York
ABC Freight Forwarding Corp.
201 11th Avenue
New York, N.Y. 10001

American Freight Forwarding Corp.
11 Broadway
New York, N.Y. 10004

Alltransport Incorporated
17 Battery Place
New York, N.Y. 10004

Arrow-Lifschultz Freight
Forwarders, Inc.
386 Park Avenue, South
New York, N.Y. 10016

Baggage Transport, Inc.
516 West 207th Street
New York, N.Y. 10034

Bor-Air Freight Co., Inc.
351 West 38th Street
New York, N.Y. 10018

Byrnes, W. J. & Company of
New York, Inc.
71 Murray Street, 11th Floor
New York, N.Y. 10007

Chilean Line
29 Broadway
New York, N.Y. 10006

BROOKLYN, New York
Sea-Jet Trucking Co., Inc.
4201 First Avenue
Brooklyn, N.Y. 11232

S & F Warehouses Inc.
Building 77
Brooklyn Navy Yard
Brooklyn, N.Y. 11205

BUFFALO, New York
Century Carloading, Inc.
15 Court Street
Buffalo, N.Y. 14202

G&W International Forwarders Inc.
538 Ellicott Sq. Bldg.
Buffalo, N.Y. 14203

Quigley & Manard Inc.
100 South Elmwood Ave.
Buffalo, N.Y. 14202

Corcoran International Corp.
15 Park Row
New York, N.Y. 10038

Tower & Sons, C. J.
128 Dearborn St.
Buffalo, N.Y.

Coronet Brokers Corp.
One World Trade Center
New York, N.Y. 10048

FARMINGDALE, L.I. New York
Empire Household Shipping Company
of New York, Inc.
187 Florida Avenue
Farmingdale, L.I., N.Y. 11735

Gendco, Inc.
611 Court Street
Brooklyn, New York 11231

JAMAICA, New York
Add Air Freight Corp.
P.O. Box X
JFK International Airport
Jamaica, N.Y. 11430

Berkley Air Service Corp.
Cargo Bldg. 80
JFK International Airport
Jamaica, N.Y. 11430

Crossocean Shipping Co.
One World Trade Center
New York, N.Y. 10048

Crown Air Freight Corp.
153 27 Rockaway Blvd.
Jamaica, N.Y. 11434

Hellenic Lines Ltd.
39 Broadway
New York, N.Y. 10006

Continental Forwarders, Inc.
105 Leonard Street
New York, N.Y. 10013

Dependable Auto Shippers, Inc.
130 West 42nd Street, Suite 2004
New York, N.Y. 10036

International Freight Forwarders
1 World Trade Center
New York, N.Y. 10048

E. A. Jasper & Co.
261 Broadway
New York, N.Y. 10007

Midland Forwarding Corporation
201 11th Avenue
New York, N.Y. 10001

National Carloading Corporation
201 Eleventh Avenue
New York, N.Y. 10001

Novo Airfreight Corp.
733 Third Avenue
New York, N.Y. 10017

Ocean Freight Consultants
1 World Trade Center
New York, N.Y. 10048

Shippers Traffic Service
5 World Trade Center
New York, N.Y. 10048

Special Forwarding Corp.
630 West 26th Street
New York, N.Y. 10001

Triangle Forwarding Corp.
52 Broadway
New York, N.Y. 10004

Universal Carloading & Distributing
Co., Inc.
345 Hudson Street
New York, N.Y. 10014

ROCHESTER, New York
C & M Forwarding Company, Inc.
322 Oak Street
Rochester, N.Y. 14608

OHIO

CLEVELAND, Ohio
Wess Inc., Henry A.
Div A. W. Fenton Co. Inc.
6565 Eastland Road
Cleveland, Ohio 44142

Canales International Services
Fidelity Bldg.
Cleveland, Ohio 44114

Fox Custom House Brokers, Inc.
1617 Wrenford Rd.
Cleveland, Ohio 44121

Teimouri & Co. Inc., S.R.
One Leader Bldg.
Cleveland, Ohio 44114

CINCINNATI, Ohio
Brie International
36 E. 4th Street
Cincinnati, Ohio

OREGON

PORTLAND, Oregon
Geo. S. Bush & Co. Inc.
310 S.W. Fourth Ave.
Portland, Oregon 97208

Fritz & Co., Arthur J.
Board of Trade Bldg.
Portland, Oregon 97204

Ted L. Rausch Co. of Oregon
320 S.W. Stark St.
Oregon Pioneer Bldg.
Portland, Oregon 97204

NORTH CAROLINA

CHARLOTTE, North Carolina
Bevon International
P.O. Box 3444
Charlotte, N.C. 28203

Southern Overseas Corp.
P.O. Box 27086
Charlotte, N.C. 28208

Waters Shipping Co.
3331 East Cessna Road
Charlotte, N.C.

WILMINGTON, North Carolina
Hipage Company Inc.
P.O. Box 1624
Wilmington, N.C. 28401

Lindsey, Dorothy
P.O. Box 3312
Wilmington, N.C.

Southern Overseas Corp.
P.O. Box 3745
Wilmington, N.C.

Waters Shipping Company
P.O. Box 118
Wilmington, N.C. 28401

PENNSYLVANIA

PHILADELPHIA, Pennsylvania
Allen Forwarding Co.
4th & Chestnut Sts.
Philadelphia, Pa. 19016

Amco Customs Brokerage Co.
208 South 3rd St.
Philadelphia, Pa. 19106

Wolf D. Barth Co.
721 Chestnut St.
Philadelphia, Pa. 19106

Friedman & Co, Morris
320 Walnut St.
Philadelphia, Pa.

John A. Steer Co.
136 Chestnut St.
Philadelphia, Pa. 19106

Aghoian-Tague Inc.
44 South Second St.
Philadelphia, Pa. 19106

Alla Bros Co. Inc.
901 Poplar St.
Philadelphia, Pa.

Dunnington & Arnold of Phil.
404 Bourse Bldg.
Philadelphia, Pa.

PITTSBURG, Pennsylvania
Barge Service Corporation
1202 Benedum-Trees Building
Pittsburgh, Pa. 15222

River Forwarders, Inc.
One Oliver Plaza
Pittsburgh, Pa. 15222

Sheer, I. J. and J. A. Feldmeier
d/b/a Pittsburg Stores Fast Freight
711 Penn Avenue
Pittsburgh, Pa. 15222

Steel City Freight Forwarders, Inc.
11th and Etna Street
Pittsburgh, Pa. 15222

Western River Forwarders, Inc.
Suite #2503
Allegheny Towers
625 Stanwix Street
Pittsburgh, Pa. 15222

Swearer Co., R. L.
717 Liberty Ave.
Pittsburgh, Pa. 15222

Traffic Dispatch International
4751 Campbells Run Road
Pittsburgh, Pa.

Helm's International
P.O. Box 268
Pittsburgh, Pa.

Wood Shipping Co. Inc., J. B.
Investment Building
Pittsburgh, Pa.

SCRANTON, Pennsylvania
Acme Fast Freight, Inc.
100 Jefferson Avenue
Scranton, Pa. 18503

PUERTO RICO

SAN JUAN, Puerto Rico
International Shipping Agency
P.O. Box 2748
San Juan, Puerto Rico

Acme Fast Freight of Puerto Rico, Inc.
P.O. Box 10651, Caparra Hgts. Sta.
San Juan, Puerto Rico

Albarco Int'l (PR) Inc.
P.O. Box 3248
San Juan, Puerto Rico

Mendez & Co.
G.P.O. Box 3348
San Juan, Puerto Rico 00936

Caribe Shipping Co., Inc.
P.O. Box 3267
San Juan, Puerto Rico

Consolidated Express, Inc.
P.O. Box 2080
San Juan, Puerto Rico

OLD SAN JUAN, Puerto Rico
Air-Mar Shipping Inc.
P.O. Box 2664
Old San Juan, Puerto Rico 00903

Altieri, Inc. J. M.
P.O. Box 1781
Old San Juan, Puerto Rico

Jose M. Pietri
P.O. Box 2928
Old San Juan, Puerto Rico 00903

SOUTH CAROLINA

CHARLESTON, South Carolina
Charleston Overseas Forwarders, Inc.
16 Hasell Street
Charleston, S. C. 29402

Battery Brokers, & Forwarders
198 E. Bay St.
Charleston, S.C. 29402

Frederick Richards Inc.
12 North Adgers Wharf
Charleston, S.C. 29402

Dickinson, Mikell & Comar
4 N. Atlantic Wharf
Charleston, S.C. 29401

Rogers & Brown Customs Brokers
P.O. Box 161
Charleston, S.C. 29402

TEXAS

BROWNSVILLE, Texas
Port of Brownsville
P.O. Box 3070
Brownsville, Texas 78520

Roser Customs Service
P.O. Box 48
Brownsville, Texas 78520

Soto Forwarding Agency
223 Paradise Line Road
Brownsville, Texas

Watts, Tom J.
P.O. Box 1673
1409 E. Jefferson St.
Brownsville, Texas

DALLAS, Texas
Leslie B. Canion
P.O. Box 61045
Dallas/Ft. Worth Airport
Dallas, Texas 75261

Fritz, Arthur J. & Co.
1343 Round Table Dr.
Dallas, Texas

Harper Robinson & Co.
P.O. Box 61023
Dallas/Ft. Worth Airport
Dallas, Texas 75261

Sekin & Co., Darrell J.
P.O. Box 6249
6839 Harry Hines
Dallas, Texas

Texas Shippers Association, Inc.
5223 North Westmoreland Street
Dallas, Texas 75247

EL PASO, Texas
Brown, Alcantar & Brown, Inc.
P.O. Box 872
201 W. Seventh Ave.
El Paso, Texas 79945

Brown, Joseph H. & Son
6930 Market Street
El Paso, Texas 79915

Lightbourn, Carlos
214 W. San Antonio St.
El Paso, Texas 79901

Martin Brokerage Co.
1805 Magoflin
El Paso, Texas

Miles & Sons, Inc., Rudolph
P.O. Box 45
El Paso, Texas

Hendrix, Joseph
P.O. Box 840
Presidio, Texas

FORT WORTH, Texas
Trans-American World Transit, Inc.
8400 South Freeway
P.O. Box 6517
Fort Worth, Texas 76134

FREEPORT, Texas
Port of Freeport, Texas
1001 Pine Street
Freeport, Texas 77541

GALVESTON, Texas
Leslie B. Canion Customs
Rm. 717, U.S. Nat'l. Bank Bldg.
Galveston, Texas

L. Braverman & Co.
818 U.S. Nat'l. Bank Bldg.
Galveston, Texas

Herbein Forwarding Co., J. F.
509 37th St.
Galveston, Texas

Michels, J. R., Inc.
P.O. Box 724
Cotton Exchange Bldg.
Galveston, Texas

Stone Forwarding Co., Inc.
U.S. National Bank Bldg.
P.O. Box 118
Galveston, Texas

HOUSTON, Texas
Houston Container & Trailer
Marrying Company
d/b/a CON TRA MAR
254 McCarty
Houston, Texas 77029

Hudson International Inc.
1121 Walker Street
Houston, Texas 77002

Lone Star Shipping, Inc.
  Steamship Agents and Operators
1318 Texas Avenue
Houston, Texas 77002

Alexander G. Arroyos
P.O. Box 53162
Houston, Texas 77052

Canion Customs Brokers
Petroleum Bldg.
Houston, Texas 77002

E. R. Hawthorne & Co. Inc.
806 Great Southwest Bldg.
Houston, Texas 77002

LaBay International Inc.
P.O. Box 52170
Houston, Texas 77052

R. W. Smith & Co.
P.O. Box 52040
Houston, Texas 77052

M. G. Maher & Co. Inc.
Great Southwest Bldg.
Houston, Texas 77002

IRVING, Texas
  Swift Home-Wrap, Inc.
  618 North Beltline Road
  Irving, Texas 75060

LAREDO, Texas
  Alvarez, J. O.
  1400 Sta. Rita Ave.
  Laredo, Texas

  Carlos Chapa
  1210 Zaragoza St.
  Laredo, Texas 78040

  William G. Hovel, Jr.
  1817 Jefferson St.
  Laredo, Texas 78040

  Leal, Juan
  P.O. Box 909
  Laredo, Texas

PRESIDIO, Texas
  Hendrix, Joseph
  P.O. Box 840
  Presidio, Texas

SAN ANTONIO, Texas
  Robert F. Barnes
  International Airport
  San Antonio, Texas

  John P. Coston
  9517 Airport Blvd.
  San Antonio, Texas 78216

Soto, Steve L.
241 E. Terminal Dr.
International Airport
San Antonio, Texas

Towne International Forwarding, Inc.
P.O. Box 16156
San Antonio, Texas 78246

VERMONT

NEWPORT, Vermont
  C. W. Emery Company, Inc.
  Newport, Vermont 05855

VIRGINIA

ALEXANDRIA, Virginia
  International Export Packers, Inc.
  5360 Eisenhower Avenue
  Alexandria, Virginia 22304

NEWPORT NEWS, Virginia
  Wilfred Schade & Co., Inc.
  P.O. Box 278
  Newport News, Virginia 23514

NORFOLK, Virginia
  Anders Williams & Co., Inc.
  1 Commercial Place
  Norfolk, Virginia

  Cavalier Shipping Co., Inc.
  Law Bldg.
  Norfolk, Virginia

  Browning Co., Inc. W. J.
  626 Royster Bldg.
  Norfolk, Virginia 23510

  Cavalier Shipping Co., Inc.
  P.O. Box 3386
  Custom House Station
  Norfolk, Virginia 23514

  Martin E. Day
  301 Plume Street
  Norfolk, Virginia 23510

  Gaskell, Fred P., Co., Inc.
  Cor. Plume & Atlantic Streets
  Norfolk, Virginia 23514

  The Hipage Company, Inc.
  Citizens Bank Building
  Norfolk, Virginia 23510

  Schade, Wilfred & Co.
  P.O. Box 278
  Norfolk, Virginia 23607

  Smith & Co. Inc., W. O.
  147 Granby Street
  Norfolk, Virginia

SPRINGFIELD, Virginia
  Star World Wide Forwarders, Inc.
    Formerly Ocean Kargo Forwarders
  900 Braddock Road, Suite 153
  Springfield, Virginia 22151

  Universal Van Lines, Inc.
  117 W. Virginia Beach Blvd.
  Norfolk, Virginia

WASHINGTON

SEATTLE, Washington
  B. R. Anderson & Co.
  Custom House Brokers
  1000 Second Avenue
  Seattle, Washington 98104

  Airborne Forwarding Corporation
  5th Floor Colman Building
  Seattle, Washington 98104

  Bush & Co., Inc., Geo. S.
  259 Colman Bldg.
  Seattle, Washington 98104

  Door to Door International, Inc.
  7109 Woodlawn Avenue, N.E.
  Seattle, Washington 98115

  Dow, Frank P., Co., Inc.
  914 Second Avenue
  Olympic National Building
  Seattle, Washington 98104

  Karevan, Inc.
  Building 41, Pier 91
  Seattle, Washington 98119

  North Star Forwarding Co.
  1102 S.W. Massachusetts Street
  Seattle, Washington 98134

  Sal, Inc.
  3250 26th Avenue, S.W.
  Seattle, Washington 98106

  Sunpak Movers, Inc.
  534 Westlake Avenue, North
  Seattle, Washington 98109

  Perfect Pak Company
  2013 Airport Way, South
  Seattle, Washington 98134

  C. E. Tolonen Co., Inc.
  1000 Second Avenue
  Seattle, Washington 98114

WISCONSIN

MILWAUKEE, Wisconsin
  M. E. Dey & Co. Inc.
  759 North Milwaukee St.
  Milwaukee, Wisconsin 53202

Ray E. Fisher Co. Inc.
312 E. Wisconsin Ave.
Milwaukee, Wisconsin

Foreign Forwarding
P.O. Box 2991
Hampton Station
Milwaukee, Wisconsin

SURINAME

PARAMARIBO, Suriname
  De Boer's Veem N.V.
  P.O. Box 1041
  Paramaribo, Suriname

Appendix Six

Banks in World Trade

AKRON, *Ohio*
First National Bank of Akron
Akron, Ohio

ATLANTA, *Georgia*
First Nat'l Bank of Atlanta
1st Nat'l Bank Bldg.
Atlanta, Georgia

Citizens & Southern National Bank
Broad St. at Marcelle St.
Atlanta, Georgia

The Trust Company of Georgia
36 Edgewood Ave., N.E.
Atlanta, Georgia

BALTIMORE, *Maryland*
Equitable Trust Company
3 W. Baltimore Street
Baltimore, Maryland

First National Bank
Light & Redwood Streets
Baltimore, Maryland

Maryland National Bank
Baltimore & Light Streets
Baltimore, Maryland

Mercantile Safe Deposit & Trust Co.
2 Hopkins Plaza
Baltimore, Maryland

Union Trust Company of Maryland
Baltimore & St. Paul Streets
Baltimore, Maryland

BEAUMONT, *Texas*
American National Bank
Park & Bowie Streets
Beaumont, Texas

First Security National Bank
505 Orleans
Beaumont, Texas

BEVERLY HILLS, *California*
Beverly Hills National Bank
9600 St. Monica Blvd.
Beverly Hills, California

BOSTON, *Massachusetts*
The First National Bank of Boston
100 Federal Street
Boston, Mass.

The Nat'l Shawmut Bank of Boston
40 Water St.
Boston, Mass.

New England Merchants National Bank
1 Washington Mall
Boston, Mass. 02108

State Street Bank & Trust Co.
111 Franklin Street
Boston, Mass.

QUINCY, *Massachusetts*
South Shore National Bank
1400 Hancock Street
Quincy, Mass.

BRIDGEPORT, *Connecticut*
Connecticut National Bank
888 Main Street
Bridgeport, Conn.

City Trust Co.
961 Main Street
Bridgeport, Conn.

Source: The American Register of Exporters and
Importers, 1978 edition. 38 Park Row,
N.Y., N.Y.

BROWNSVILLE, Texas
First National Bank
835 E. Levee Street
Brownsville, Texas

Pan American Bank
1034 E. Levee Street
Brownsville, Texas

National Bank of Commerce
2300 Boca Chica Boulevard
Brownsville, Texas

BUFFALO, New York
Manufacturers & Traders Trust
1 Manufacturers & Traders Square
Buffalo, N.Y.

Liberty National Bank
424 Main Street
Buffalo, N.Y.

Marine Midland Bank West
237 Main Street
Buffalo, N.Y. 14203

CHARLESTON, Virginia
Bankers Trust of S.C.
One Broad Street
Charleston, Virginia

South Carolina National Bank
16 Broad Street
Charleston, Virginia

CHARLOTTE, North Carolina
North Carolina National Bank
Charlotte, North Carolina

First National Bank of N.C.
Charlotte, North Carolina

CHICAGO, Illinois
American National Bank & Trust
  Company of Chicago
33 N. La Salle St.
Chicago, Illinois

Continental Illinois National Bank &
  Trust Co. of Chicago
231 S. La Salle Street
Chicago, Illinois

Exchange National Bank
La Salle & Adams Streets
Chicago, Illinois

First National Bank of Chicago
1 First National Plaza
Chicago, Illinois

Harris Trust & Saving Bank
115 W. Monroe Street
Chicago, Illinois

La Salle National Bank
135 S. La Salle St.
Chicago, Illinois

Northern Trust So.
50 South La Salle Street
Chicago, Illinois

CINCINNATI, Ohio
The Central Trust Company
Fourth & Vine Streets
Cincinnati, Ohio

Fifth-Third Bank
5th & 3rd Center
Cincinnati, Ohio

The First National Bank of Cincinnati
4th & Walnut Streets
Cincinnati, Ohio

CLEVELAND, Ohio
Society National Bank
127 Public Square
Cleveland, Ohio

The Cleveland Trust Company
Euclid Avenue & East 9th Street
Cleveland, Ohio

The National City Bank of Cleveland
623 Euclid Avenue
Cleveland, Ohio

Union Bank of Commerce
917 Euclid Avenue
Cleveland, Ohio

COLUMBUS, Ohio
City National Bank & Trust
100 E Broad Street
Columbus, Ohio 43215

Huntington National Bank
17 So. High Street
Columbus, Ohio 43215

Ohio National Bank
Gay & High Street
Columbus, Ohio 43215

DALLAS, Texas
First National Bank in Dallas
1401 Main Street
Dallas, Texas

Mercantile National Bank at Dallas
Mercantile Bank Bldg.
Dallas, Texas

Republic National Bank of Dallas
Pacific & Ervay Sts.
Dallas, Texas

DAYTON, Ohio
The First National Bank
1 First National Plaza
Dayton, Ohio 45202

Third National Bank
34 North Main Street
Dayton, Ohio

Winters National Bank
Winters Bank Tower
Dayton, Ohio 45402

DENVER, Colorado
First National Bank of Denver
17th & Welton
Denver, Colorado 80202

Denver United States National Bank
P.O. Box 5247
Denver, Colorado

DETROIT, Michigan
Bank of the Commonwealth
W. Fort & Griswold
Detroit, Michigan

The Detroit Bank & Trust Co.
211 Fort Street
Detroit, Michigan

Manufacturers National Bank
of Detroit
411 Lafayette St.
Detroit, Michigan 48226

National Bank of Detroit
611 Woodward St.
Detroit, Michigan 48232

DULUTH, Minnesota
Duluth National Bank
2000 W. Superior Street
Duluth, Minnesota

National Bank of Commerce
117 Tower Avenue
Superior, Minnesota

EL PASO, Texas
State National Bank
San Antonio & Oregon Sts.
El Paso, Texas

Southwest National Bank
320 N. Stanton Street
El Paso, Texas

FORT WORTH, Texas
First National Bank
Fort Worth, Texas

GALVESTON, Texas
Moody National Bank
2302 Post Office
Galveston, Texas

United States National Bank
2201 Market Street
Galveston, Texas

HARTFORD, Connecticut
Hartford National Bank & Trust Co.
100 Constitution Plaza Office
Hartford, Connecticut

Merchants Nat'l. Bank & Trust
11 So. Meridian
Indianapolis, Indiana

HOUSTON, Texas
First City National Bank of Houston
1101 Main Street
Houston, Texas

Bank of Southwest, National Association
910 Travis Street
Houston, Texas

Texas National Bank of Commerce
712 Main Street
Houston, Texas

INDIANAPOLIS, Indiana
American Fletcher National Bank &
Trust Co.
Market & Pennsylvania Streets
Indianapolis, Indiana 46204

Indiana National Bank
1 Indiania Square
Indianapolis, Indiana

JACKSONVILLE, Vlorida
Atlantic National Bank of Jacksonville
Atlantic Nat'l Bank Bldg.
Jacksonville, Florida

Barnett National Bank
100 Laura Street
Jacksonville, Florida

Florida First National Bank
West Bay Annex
Jacksonville, Florida

KANSAS CITY, Missouri
Commerce Trust Co.
922 Walnut Street
Kansas City, Missouri 64106

First National Bank
14 West 10th St.
Kansas City, Missouri 64106

United Missouri Bank
Tenth and Grand Avenue
Kansas City, Missouri

LAREDO, Texas
Bank of Commerce
1200 San Bernardo Ave.
Laredo, Texas

Laredo National Bank
700 Bernardo Avenue
Laredo, Texas

LOS ANGELES, California
Banco Nacional de Mexico, S.A.
458 So. Spring
Los Angeles, California

Bank of America N.T. & S.A. International Banking Office
101 W. Seventh Street
Los Angeles, California

First Western Bank & Trust Co.
548 So. Spring St.
Los Angeles, California

The Hong Kong of California
9300 Wilshire Boulevard
Los Angeles, California

Security Pacific National Bank
333 South Flower St.
Los Angeles, California

LOUISVILLE, Kentucky
Citizen Fidelity Bank & Trust
Louisville, Kentucky 40201

First National Bank
First National Tower
Louisville, Kentucky 40201

Liberty National Bank
P.O. Box 1499
Louisville, Kentucky 40201

MANCHESTER, New Hampshire
Merchant's National Bank
Manchester, New Hampshire

MEMPHIS, Tennessee
First National Bank
165 Madison Avenue
Memphis, Tennessee 38103

Union Planters National Bank
P.O. Box 387
Memphis, Tennessee 38147

MIAMI, Florida
Central Bank & Trust Company
1316 N.W. 36th St.
Miami, Florida 33142

The First National Bank of Miami
10051 Biscayne Blvd.
Miami, Florida 33131

Pan American Bank of Miami
250 South East 1st St.
Miami, Florida 33131

MILWAUKEE, Wisconsin
First Wisconsin National Bank
777 North Water Street
Milwaukee, Wisconsin

Marshall & Ilsley Bank
770 N. Walter Street
Milwaukee, Wisconsin

Marine National Exchange Bank
111 E. Wisconsin
Milwaukee, Wisconsin

MINNEAPOLIS, Minnesota
First National Bank
120 So. 6th St.
Minneapolis, Minnesota

Northwestern Nat'l Bank
620 Marquette Avenue
Minneapolis, Minnesota

MOBILE, Alabama
American National Bank & Trust Co.
120 St. Joseph St.
Mobile, Alabama 36601

First National Bank of Mobile
17 North Royal St.
Mobile, Alabama

Merchants National Bank of Mobile
P.O. Box 2527
Mobile, Alabama 33622

NEW HAVEN, Connecticut
First New Haven National Bank
One Church Street
New Haven, Conn.

Second National Bank of New Haven
135 Church Street
New Haven, Conn.

NEW ORLEANS, Louisiana
The National Bank of Commerce in
New Orleans
210 Barrone Street
New Orleans, Louisiana 70112

Whitney National Bank of New Orleans
P.O. Box 61260
New Orleans, Louisiana 70130

NEWARK, New Jersey
Bank of Commerce
59 Springfield Ave.
Newark, New Jersey

Fidelity Union & Trust Company
755 Broad St.
Newark, New Jersey

First National State Bank, N.J.
550 Broad Street
Newark, New Jersey

Bank of Commerce
59 Springfield Avenue
Newark, New Jersey

Fidelity Union Trust
765 Broad Street
Newark, New Jersey

First National State Bank
550 Broad Street
Newark, New Jersey

NEWPORT NEWS, Virginia
Bank of Virginia
2803 Washington Ave.
Newport News, Va.

NEW YORK CITY, New York
American Express Company
  Overseas Banking Division
65 Broadway
New York City, N.Y. 10006

Atlantic Bank of New York
960 Avenue of the Americas
New York City, N.Y.

Bank of America International
432 Westchester Ave.
Bronx, N.Y.

Bank of China
40 Wall Street
New York City, N.Y.

Banca Commerciale Italiana
280 Park Avenue
New York City, N.Y.

Banca Nazionale del Lavoro
25 W. 51st St.
New York City, N.Y.

Banco do Brasil s.a.
550 Fifth Avenue
New York, N.Y. 10036

Banco De Ponce
10 Rockefeller Plaza
New York City, N.Y.

Banco di Napoli
62 Williams Street
New York City, N.Y.

Banco di Roma
40 Wall Street
New York City, N.Y.

Banco Nacional de Mexico
New York Agency
45 Wall Street
New York City, N.Y.

Bank of China, N.Y. Agency
2 Wall Street
New York City, N.Y.

Bank of Indonesia
25 Broadway
New York City, N.Y.

Bank Leumi le-Israel B.M.
579 Fifth Avenue
New York City, N.Y.

Bank of London & South America, Ltd.
95 Wall Street
New York City, N.Y.

Bank of Japan
1 Chase Manhattan Plaza
New York City, N.Y.

Bank of Montreal
N.Y. Agency
2 Wall Street
New York City, N.Y.

Bank of Tokyo Ltd.
100 Broadway
New York City, N.Y.

Bank of New York
48 Wall Street
New York City, N.Y.

The Bank of Nova Scotia
67 Wall Street
New York City, N.Y.

The Bank of Tokyo Trust Co.
100 Broadway
New York City, N.Y.

Bankers Trust Company
16 Wall Street
New York City, N.Y.

Barclays Bank Ltd., London
120 Broadway
New York City, N.Y.

Canadian Bank of Commerce Trust Co.
26 Exchange Place
New York City, N.Y.

Canadian Imperial Bank
  of Commerce
22 William Street
New York City, N.Y.

Chase Manhattan Bank
1 Chase Manhattan Plaza
New York City, N.Y.

Chemical Bank New York Trust Co.
20 Pine St.
New York City, N.Y.

Credito Italiano
67 Wall Street
New York City, N.Y.

Dai-ichi Bank Ltd.
1 World Trade Center
New York City, N.Y.

Federal Reserve Bank
33 Liberty
New York City, N.Y.

Fiduciary Trust Co. of New York
1 Wall Street
New York City, N.Y.

The First of Boston Int'l Corp.
2 Wall Street
New York City, N.Y.

First National City Bank
55 Wall Street
New York City, New York

French American Banking Corporation
120 Broadway
New York City, N.Y.

Fuji Bank Ltd., The
Chase Manhattan Plaza
New York City, N.Y.

Israel Discount Bank
511 Fifth Avenue
New York, N.Y. 10017

Irving Trust Company
1 Wall Street
New York City, N.Y.

Industrial Bank of Japan
1 Wall Street
New York City, N.Y.

Lloyds Bank Limited, London
95 Wall Street
New York City, N.Y.

Manufacturers Hanover Trust Co.
  International Division
350 Park Avenue
New York City, N.Y.

Marine Midland Trust Co. of N.Y.
140 Broadway
New York City, N.Y.

Merchants Bank of New York, The
434 Broadway
New York City, N.Y.

Mitsui Bank Ltd.
1 Chase Manhattan Plaza
New York City, N.Y.

Mitsubishi Bank
1 World Trade Center
New York City, N.Y.

Morgan Guaranty Trust Co. of N.Y.
23 Wall Street
New York City, N.Y.

National Bank of North America
44 Wall Street
New York, N.Y. 10005

Nippon Kango Bank Ltd.
44 Wall Street
New York City, N.Y.

Overseas Discount Corp., Inc.
551 5th Avenue
New York City, N.Y.

Philippine National Bank
5 World Trade Center
New York City, N.Y.

The Royal Bank of Canada
68 William Street
New York City, N.Y.

J. Henry Schroeder Banking
  Corporation
1 State Street Plaza
New York City, N.Y.

Standard Chartered Bank Ltd.
160 Water Street
New York, N.Y. 10038

Sterling National Bank
1410 Broadway
New York City, N.Y. 10018

Sumitomo Bank, Ltd.
80 Broad Street
New York City, N.Y.

Swiss Bank Corporation
15 Nassau Street
New York City, N.Y.

Swiss Credit Bank
100 Wall Street
New York City, N.Y.

Toronto-Dominion Bank
45 Wall Street
New York City, N.Y.

Security National Bank of L.I.
1411 Broadway
New York, N.Y. 10018

The Standard Bank Ltd.
52 Wall Street
New York City, N.Y. 10005

State Street Bank
20 Exchange Place
New York City, N.Y.

Tokai Bank Ltd., The
67 Broad Street
New York City, N.Y.

United States Trust Co. of New York
45 Wall Street
New York City, N.Y.

Wells Fargo Bank
  International Division
40 Wall Street
New York, N.Y.

NORFOLK, Virginia
Virginia National Bank
P.O. Box 600
Norfolk, Virginia 23501

OAKLAND, California
Central Valley National Bank
Oakland, California

OKLAHOMA CITY, Oklahoma
First National Bank & Trust
1st Nat'l Bank Bldg.
Oklahoma City, Oklahoma

PATERSON, New Jersey
First Nat'l Bank of Passaic County
125 Ellison Street
Paterson, New Jersey

PHILADELPHIA, Pennsylvania
Central-Penn National Bank of
  Philadelphia
5 Penn Central Plaza
Philadelphia, Pa. 19101

First Pennsylvania Banking & Trust
  Co.
15th And Walnut Streets
Philadelphia, Pa.

The Fidelity Bank
Broad & Walnut Streets
Philadelphia, Pa. 19109

Girard Trust Co.
1 Girard Plaza
Philadelphia, Pa. 19101

The Philadelphia National Bank
Broad & Chestnut Sts.
Philadelphia, Pa. 19101

Provident National Bank
Broad & Chestnut Streets
Philadelphia, Pa.

PORTLAND, Oregon
The First National Bank of Oregon
S.W. Fifth, Sixth & Stark St.
Portland, Oregon

The Oregon Bank
319 S.W. Washington Street
Portland, Oregon

United States National Bank
321 S.W. 6th Avenue
Portland, Oregon 97205

PROVIDENCE, Rhode Island
Industrial National Bank of Providence
111 Westminster Street
Providence, Rhode Island

Rhode Island Hospital Trust Co.
15 Westminster Street
Providence, Rhode Island

PHOENIX, Arizona
First National Bank of Arizona
411 N. Central Ave.
Phoenix, Arizona

Valley National Bank
141 North Central Ave.
Phoenix, Arizona

PITTSBURGH, Pennsylvania
Equibank NA
435 Smithfield
Pittsburgh, Pa.

Mellon National Bank & Trust
Mellon Square
Pittsburg, Pa. 15219

Pittsburgh National Bank
5th Ave. & Wood
Pittsburgh, Pennsylvania 15219

RICHMOND, Virginia
First and Merchants National Bank
  of Richmond
9th & Main St.
Richmond, Virginia

State–Planters Bank and Trust Co.
9th & Main St.
Richmond, Virginia

SALT LAKE CITY, Utah
Walker Bank & Trust
Main & 2nd St.
Salt Lake City, Utah

SAN JUAN, Puerto Rico
Banco Credito
P.O. Box 4467
San Juan, P.R.

Banco De Ponce
San Juan, P.R.

Banco Popular de Puerto Rico
Banco Popular Center
Hato Rey, P.R.

ST. LOUIS, Missouri
First National Bank in St. Louis
510 Locust St.
St. Louis, Missouri 83116

Mercantile Trust Co.
721 Locust Street
St. Louis, Missouri 83116

ST. PAUL, Minnesota
First National Bank of St. Paul
322 Minn. St.
St. Paul, Minnesota

SAN DIEGO, California
First National Bank of San Diego
P.O. Box 1311
San Diego, Calif.

United States National Bank
190 Broadway
San Diego, Calif.

SAN FRANCISCO, California
American Trust Company
464 California Street
San Francisco, Calif.

Bank of America N.T. & S.A.
300 Montgomery Street
San Francisco, Calif.

Bank of California
400 California Street
San Francisco, Calif.

The Barclay Group of Banks
111 Pine Street
San Francisco, Calif.

Crocker-Citizens Nat'l. Bank
1 Montgomery St.
San Francisco, Calif.

First Western Bank & Trust Co.
201 Montgomery St.
San Francisco, Calif.

Sumitomo Bank of Calif.
365 California Street
San Francisco, Calif.

United California Bank
405 Montgomery St.
San Francisco, Calif.

Wells Fargo Bank
464 California Street
San Francisco, Calif.

SAVANNAH, Georgia
Savannah Bank & Trust Co.
P.O. Box 9947
Savannah, Georgia

Liberty National Bank
P.O. Box 9586
Savannah, Georgia 31402

SEATTLE, Washington
Pacific National Bank
1215 Fourth Ave.
Seattle, Washington

Peoples National Bank of Washington
1414 4th Avenue
Seattle, Washington

Rainier National Bank
2nd Avenue & Spring St.
Seattle, Washington

Seattle-First National Bank
1001 4th Avenue
Seattle, Washington

TOLEDO, Ohio
The Toledo Trust Company
  International Department
245 Superior Street
Toledo, Ohio 43603

The National Bank of Toledo
606 Madison
Toledo, Ohio

TULSA, Oklahoma
First Nat'l Bank & Trust
15 East 5th St.
Tulsa, Oklahoma

UNION CITY, New Jersey
Hudson Trust Company
3112 Bergentline Avenue
Union City, New Jersey

WASHINGTON, D.C.
American Security & Trust Company
15th & Pennsylvania Ave., N.W.
Washington, D.C.

Riggs National Bank of Washington
1503 Pennsylvania Avenue
Washington, D.C.

WILMINGTON, North Carolina
Bank of North Carolina
36 N. Front Street
Wilmington, North Carolina

First Union National Bank
201 N. Front Street
Wilmington, North Carolina

Wachovia Bank & Trust
101 N. Front Street
Wilmington, North Carolina

WINSTON SALEM, North Carolina
Wachovia Bank & Trust Co.
Winston Salem, North Carolina

WORCESTER, Massachusetts
Mechanics National Bank of Vancouver
303 Main Street
Worcester, Mass.

Worcester County National Bank
446 Main Street
Worcester, Mass.

SPRINGFIELD, Massachusetts
Third National Bank of Hampden
  County
1391 Main Street
Springfield, Mass. 01101

Valley Bank and Trust Co.
Springfield, Mass.

Safe Deposit Bank and Trust Co.
127 State Street
Springfield, Mass.

TAMPA, Florida
First National Bank
P.O. Box 1810
Tampa, Florida

Exchange National Bank of Tampa
601 Franklin St.
Tampa, Florida 33602

Marine Bank & Trust Co.
P.O. Box 3303
Tampa, Florida 33601

Appendix Seven

State Trade Promotion Offices

Alaska

Department of Commerce and Economic Development
Office of the Commissioner (H. Phillip Hubbard, Commissioner)
Pouch D
Juneau, Alaska 99801–(907)465-2500

Services: Provides general information and assistance. An Alaska State Office in Tokyo, Japan, can provide information on Japanese importers. Address: Alaska State Office Corporation Akasaka Heights, 5/28 8 Chome, Akasaka, Minato Ku, Tokyo 107, Japan.

Arizona

Arizona Office of Economic Planning and Development, International Trade Section, (William Kane, Director).
1700 W. Washington, Suite 505
Phoenix, Arizona 85007–(602) 271-3737

Services: Publishes Export-Import Register of Arizona firms. Assists in product location, trade leads and market development for both exports and imports. Arranges visits and contacts for overseas business visitors.

Arkansas

Arkansas Industrial Development Commission (Nolan Fleming, International Consultant).
205 State Capitol Bldg.
Little Rock, Arkansas 72201–(501) 371-2563
European Office: State of Arkansas European Office of the Governor (Robert Adcock, Director).
Avenue Louise–437 BT 4
Brussels, Belgium B 1050–649-6024

Source: *Exporter's Encyclopedia*, 1978 edition, pages 1–16.
Dun and Bradstreet International, P.O. Box 3088,
Grand Central Station, New York, N.Y. 10017

Services: Provides general information and assistance, overseas business leads, conducts foreign trade missions.

Connecticut

Connecticut Department of Commerce International Division (Gary H. Miller, Director).
210 Washington St.
Hartford, Conn. 06106–(203) 566-5426

Services: As an associate office of the U.S. Department of Commerce, supports and promotes its programs and services. Collaborates with the Field Office of the U.S. Department of Commerce in in-state programs of education, public meetings, etc. to promote international trade. In addition keeps continually updated files on companies that are exporters or potential exporters and makes such lists available to firms servicing exporters. Also operates a "Sort-To-Order" System to distribute foreign business leads selectively and directly to those businessmen likely to be interested. Promotes licensing and joint ventures as a vehicle to acquire new products and technology for Connecticut manufacturers. Publishes an "International Newsletter" sent to exporters and potential exporters. Provides specific assistance by phone or field calls to particular companies according to their particular requirements. Promotes foreign investment in Connecticut, aided by services of a European representative, providing specific information about Connecticut pertinent to the inquiring overseas firm, and by personal visits abroad.

Florida

Florida Department of Commerce
Division of Economic Development
Bureau of Trade Development (Richard N. Brock, Chief)
107 W. Gaines St.
Tallahassee, Florida 32304–(904) 488-9050

Services: Operations cover a wide field of activities such as: providing technical assistance and counsel to prospective foreign traders; participating in international trade missions, mobile or floating trade exhibits and travel caravans, and solo exhibits of Florida products in foreign markets; participating in foreign trade symposia, seminars, workshops, conferences, conventions, and educational programs; working with shipping companies, airlines, freight forwarders and customs brokers' associations, and ports councils in promoting increased cargo activities via Florida's seaports and international airports; working with trade committees of local chambers of commerce, world trade associations, and other private programs for this purpose; cooperating with universities and graduate schools in developing foreign trade courses and programs; originating and conducting sales-education seminars and tours for foreign travel agents, editors and airline personnel; originating and conducting reverse investment missions; originating and distributing foreign language trade and travel promotional literature and films; and maintaining liaison with foreign consulates and government agencies in Florida, and assisting important foreign visitors and buying groups in establishing local contacts. Besides publishing a newsletter, the Department has available a "Florida World Trade Directory" (price in Florida, $8.84; outside Florida, $8.50–the cost in both instances is all inclusive).

Georgia

Georgia Department of Industry and Trade (Mr. W. Milton Folds, Commissioner)
P.O. Box 1776
Atlanta, Ga. 30301–(404) 656-3556

Services: Provides general information and assistance, overseas business leads, sponsors trade missions and reverse investment missions, assists investors, sponsors export seminars, and offers assistance for joint ventures and licensing agreements. The Department also maintains overseas offices in Brussels, Tokyo, Toronto, and Sao Paulo.

Hawaii

Department of Planning & Economic Development (Mr. Hideto Kono, Director)
Kamamalu Bldg., P.O. Box 2359
Honolulu, Hawaii 96804–(808) 548-4620

Services: Provides general information and assistance. Operates U.S. Foreign-Trade Zone No. 9 and Sub-Zone 9A, and Hawaii International Services Agency.

Illinois

Department of Business and Economic Development
International Trade Division   (John N. Gallo, Managing Director, Office of International Marketing)
Room 1122, 205 West Wacker Drive
Chicago, Ill. 60606–(312) 793-2086

Services: Provides information to Illinois organizations selling abroad, foreign business firms planning U.S. operations; conducts research and conferences and renders personal assistance, sponsors trade missions and trade shows. Maintains offices at 222 South College St., Springfield, Illinois 62706; 5 Place du Champ de Mars, 1050 Brussels, Belgium; Illinois Bureau de Servicos, Ltda., C.P. 7801, 01000 Sao Paulo, S.P., Brasil; State of Illinois, Hall of the States, Suite 210, 444 North Capitol Street, N.W., Washington, D.C. 20001; 172 Des Voeux Rd., Room 1304, Hong Kong.

Indiana

International Trade Division
Indiana Department of Commerce (F. Jay Lahr, Director)
336 State House
Indianapolis, Ind. 46204–(317) 633-4538

Services: Provides aid to foreign businessmen in contacting over 8500 Indiana manufacturers; assists foreign companies seeking plant location or joint venture and licensing partners; promotes exports, foreign investment and State's international port system through trade missions, seminars, and personal contact.

Iowa

Iowa Development Commission (Dean Arbuckle, Director, International Division)
250 Jewett Bldg.
Des Moines, Ia. 50309–(515) 281-3270 Telex: 478-466 IA DEV COM DMS

Services: Provides export assistance and information, sponsors trade missions and an annual export conference. Publishes an Iowa international trade directory and world trade guide for manufactures.

Kansas

Kansas Department of Economic Development (Marilyn Weil, World Trade Representative)
503 Kansas Avenue, Sixth floor
Topeka, Kan. 66603–(913) 296-3487

Services: Provides general information and assistance.

Kentucky

Kentucky Department of Commerce (Mr. W. Terry McBrayer, Commissioner)
International Division (Mr. William Savage, Director, and Mr. Theodore Sauer, Jr., Assistant Director)
Capitol Plaza Tower 22nd Floor
Frankfort, Ky., 40601–(502) 564-2170

Services: Export and foreign direct investment development. Also maintains an office in Brussels; European Economic Development Office, Commonwealth of Kentucky, Avenue Louise 379, 1050 Brussels, Belgium, Mr. John L. Novotny, Director, Telephone: 02-649-9895.

Louisiana

Louisiana Department of Commerce & Industry (Gilbert C. Lagasse, Secretary)
P.O. Box 44185
Baton Rouge, La. 70804–(504) 389-5371
Louisiana Department of Commerce
International Trade & Investment (Clarence T. Breaux, Manager)
343 International Trade Mart
New Orleans, La. 70130–(504) 568-5255

Services: Publishes a directory of Louisiana manufacturers; promotes industrial investment by foreign firms in Louisiana; provides general information and assistance.

Maine

State Development Office
193 State Street
Augusta, Me. 04333–(207) 289-2656

Services: General information, assistance in developing foreign trade, international marketing, and reverse investment in the State of Maine. Contact: Hadley P. Atlass, Director, State Development Office, 193 State Street, Augusta, Maine 04333.

Maryland

Department of Economic and Community Development

Division of Business and Industrial Development (Mr. James A. McComas, Jr., Director)
1748 Forest Drive
Annapolis, Md. 21401–(301) 267-5514

Services: Provides general information, assists buyers, sellers, investors, seekers of licensing agreements, etc., to find introduction to interested parties; publishes "Directory of Maryland Exporters-Importers," an International Handbook.

Massachusetts

Massachusetts Department of Commerce and Development (Commissioner, John J. Marino)
Office of New Business (Frank O'Neill, Director)
Leverett Saltonstall Bldg.
100 Cambridge St.
Boston, Mass. 02202–(617) 727-3234

Services: The Office of International Trade encourages and counsels Massachusetts manufacturers to enter international trade, promotes foreign participation and investment in Massachusetts industry and conducts a program designed to assist the Bay State's industrial complex in taking advantage of opportunities international commerce presents.

Michigan

International Division (Clifford A. Kleier, Director)
Office of Economic Expansion
Department of Commerce
P.O. Box 30225
Lansing, Mich. 48909–(517) 373-6390

Services: Responsible for all international trade and investment development activities except the export of agricultural products, which is the responsibility of the Department of Agriculture. European Office: rue Ducale 41, B-1000, Brussels, Belgium. Tel: 511.07.32. (Charles S. Besterman, Director); Asian office: Shinsaka 40 Bldg. #304, 10-24 Akasaka 8-chome, Minato-Ku, Tokyo, 107, Japan. Tel: 403 9896. (Edward S. Dubel, Director).

Minnesota

Department of Economic Development (Lee A. Vann, Commissioner)
480 Cedar St.
St. Paul, Minn. 55101–(612) 296-2755

Services: Provides information and assistance to firms in Minnesota engaged in export and import; establishes trade relations; and participates in trade missions, reverse investment missions, foreign trade shows and exhibitions.

Mississippi

Mississippi Marketing Council (Merle Fraser, Secretary)
P.O. Box 849
Jackson, Miss. 39205–(601) 354-6707 Telex: 585-489

Services: Promotion of Mississippi products in world markets. Advises exporters regarding shipping, insurance, financing, investment opportunities, etc.

Montana

Department of Community Affairs (Division of Economic Development)
Capitol Station
Helena, Mont. 59601–(406) 449-2402

Services: Provides information to firms interested in export. Encourages development of commercial and manufacturing activities. Conducts Export Seminars in cooperation with the Governor's Office, Regional Office, U.S. Department of Commerce, Montana Chamber of Commerce and the SBA.

Nebraska

Bill Wheeler, Industrial Consultant
Nebraska Department of Economic Development
Box 94666, 301 Centennial Mall South
Lincoln, Neb. 68509–(402) 471-3111

Services: Coordinates world trade activities and information from U.S. agencies and serves as a clearinghouse of educational and business material for Nebraska industries.

New Hampshire

Office of Industrial Development (Paul H. Guilderson, Director)
Department of Resources & Economic Development
P.O. Box 856
Concord, N.H. 03301–(603) 271-2591

Services: Provides general information and assistance.

New Jersey

New Jersey Office of International Trade (Joseph F. Brady, Chief)
New Jersey Department of Labor and Industry
1100 Raymond Boulevard, Room 508
Newark, N.J. 07102–(201) 648-3518, 3519

Services: Provides general information and assistance on exporting and importing; publishes "International Report," a periodic bulletin of trade leads for New Jersey businessmen; staff visits to businessmen who export or are involved in international business; serves as the initial point of contact for foreign firms locating in the State of New Jersey; has co-operative activities with the U.S. Department of Commerce District Office located in Newark; New Jersey State Chamber of Commerce; the Port Authority of New York/New Jersey and the Delaware River Port Authority including overseas offices; sponsors annual New Jersey World Trade Conference and numerous other similar events in partnership with various organizatons and associations.

New Mexico

Exports and Marketing Services (David E. Chavez, Director)
New Mexico Department of Development
113 Washington Ave.
Santa Fe, N.M. 87503–(505) 827-3101

Services: Provides information and assistance to New Mexico exporters and importers. Also provides specific information to foreign buyers on New Mexico products and data to firms wishing to locate in New Mexico. Publishes literature on exporting and an export manufacturers' directory, a cattle brochure, and other publications. Participates in trade missions and shows on behalf of New Mexico ranchers, farmers and businessmen. Is an associate office of the U.S. Dept. of Commerce.

New York

State of New York Department of Commerce (Stanley S. Newman, Associate Research Analyst)
Division of International Commerce
230 Park Ave.
New York, N.Y. 10017–(212) 949-9300

Services: Publishes foreign trade opportunities bulletins containing export sales leads developed in overseas markets and distributes such bulletins to New York State manufacturers who have registered their interests in expanding overseas sales. Counsels New York State manufacturers at export expansion workshops on procedures and techniques in entering the international sales field. Maintains branch offices in London and Tokyo.

North Carolina

North Carolina Department of Natural and Economic Resources
Division of Economic Development (Mr. Hunter A. Poole, Chief, International Section)
Box 27687
Raleigh, N.C. 27611–(919) 733-4151

Services: Provides world trade information, sponsors trade missions, conducts trade promotion events, refers trade leads, assists in reverse investment.

Ohio

Office of International Trade
Department of Economic and Community Development, State of Ohio
P.O. Box 1001
Columbus, Ohio 43216–(614) 466-5017

Services: Promotes exports among small and medium sized Ohio firms; provides overseas trade leads and market developments; and organizes Ohio Trade Missions and coordinates all international trade activities in Ohio. Manager: F. A. Sexton.

Oklahoma

Oklahoma Industrial Development Department (Scott Eubanks, Director; Estal Hart, C.I.D., Director, Industrial Divisions; Sam Ott, International Business Coordinator)
500 Will Rogers Bldg.
Oklahoma City, Oklahoma 73105–(405) 521-2401

Services: Promotes exports throughout the state of Oklahoma. Provides overseas trade leads and market developments. Organizes conferences, meetings and seminars to promote world trade. Participates in industry organized government approved trade missions.

Oregon

Department of Economic Development
International Trade Division (Howard P. Traver, Manager)
317 S. W. Alder St.
Portland, Oregon 97204–(503) 229-5535

Services: Provides general information and assistance, trade leads; sponsors trade missions, trade shows, seminars, conferences, exhibits; renders personal assistance to manufacturers to increase international trade; works in partnership activities with chamber of commerce, U.S. Department of Commerce and Port of Portland; assists important foreign visitors and buying groups in establishing local contacts; has international trade advisory committee serving the Governor and the Economic Development Commission; keeps an up-to-date library of research materials on overseas markets; encourages reverse investment, joint ventures, etc.

Pennsylvania

Bureau of International Commerce (J. Thomas Rogers, Director)
Pennsylvania Department of Commerce
408 South Office Bldg.
Harrisburg, Pennsylvania 17120–(717) 787-7190

Services: Assists Pennsylvania's manufacturers in efforts to expand their exports; assists foreign companies to find suitable locations in the state to establish wholly owned production and distribution facilities or locates Pennsylvania companies for joint ventures or cross licensing arrangements; aids in improving business procedures and investment climate to encourage the movement of foreign capitol into the Commonwealth.

Puerto Rico

Department of Commerce
Foreign Trade Program
P.O. Box 4275
San Juan, Puerto Rico 00901–(809) 723-3290

Services: Services to the exporters; trade missions and fairs, market studies of foreign countries; statistical information.

Rhode Island

Department of Economic Development
International Trade Division (Fred L. Hansen, Director)
One Weybosset Hill
Providence, R.I. 02903–(401) 277-2601

Services: Provides general information and assistance; overseas business leads.

South Carolina

South Carolina State Ports Authority (Richard E. Curran, Trade Promotion Co-
ordinator)
P.O. Box 817
Charleston, S.C. 29402– (903) 723-8651

Services: Provides general information and assistance on cargo-handling services
through ports of South Carolina.

Tennessee

Department of Economic & Community Development
International Marketing (Will G. Fisher, Acting Director)
Room 1004, Andrew Jackson Bldg.
Nashville, Tennessee 37219–(615) 749-2549 Telex: 555196 ECD NAS

Texas

International Trade Division (James H. Havey, Director)
Texas Industrial Commission
712 Sam Houston State Office Bldg.
Capitol Station, Box 12728
Austin, Texas 78711–(512) 475-5551

Services: Provides general information and assistance; overseas business leads;
trade missions.

Vermont

Economic Development Department
Agency of Development and Community Affairs
Montpelier, Vermont 05602–(802) 828-3221

Services: Provides foreign trade leads and possibilities of joint venture and/or cross
licensing as well as export opportunities. Contact Curtis Lamorey, Foreign Trade
Consultant.

Virginia

International Trade and Development Department (Fred G. Kessener, Director)
Virginia Division of Industrial Development
Governor's Office
1010 State Office Bldg.
Richmond, Virginia 23219–(804) 786-4486

Services: Assists private enterprise in Virginia in developing international trade through personal contacts; promotes joint ventures in Virginia between foreign and Virginia firms; encourages reverse investment, i.e., attracting foreign firms to Virginia; promotes exports of Virginia-manufactured products throughout the world, with emphasis upon Europe and Japan. Maintains European Office, shared with Virginia Port Authority and Virginia Department of Agriculture & Commerce, at 479 Avenue Louise, Brussels 1050, Belgium. Tel: 648-0036. Contacts in Japan and South America may be made through Virginia Port Authority offices at: Suite 763, Hotel New Japan, Tokyo 100 (Tel: 581-7006); and Av. Brigadeiro Faria Lima 1794-2/48, 10452 Sao Paulo-SP, Brazil (Tel: 81-8857).

Washington

Department of Commerce and Economic Development (John S. Larsen, Director)
101 General Administration Bldg.
Olympia, Washington 98504

Services: Provides general information and assistance on foreign trade.

Wisconsin

(Stephen W. Ludwick, Acting Director of International Business Services)
Department of Business Development
123 W. Washington Ave. Room 650
Madison, Wisconsin 53702–(608) 266-3222

Services: Provides general Wisconsin economic information and assistance; locates international industry; provides assistance in exporting and other international business matters. European Representative (Donald C. Burdon) Postfach 3525, 6000 Frankfurt am Main 1, Federal Republic of Germany. Tel.: 0611-71451, ext. 289.

Appendix Eight

Associations Fostering Foreign Trade

A. U.S. National Organizations

(a) National Foreign Trade Council, Inc., 10 Rockfeller Plaza, New York, N.Y., 10020. Robert M. Norris, President (212) 581-6420.

The National Foreign Trade Council is a private, non-profit, non-partisan organization of United States companies engaged in international trade and investment. The Council, which sponsors the annual National Foreign Trade Convention on behalf of the United States international business community, was established in accordance with a resolution of the First National Foreign Trade Convention in 1914.

Through the years its continuing purpose in an ever-changing political and economic environment has been to further the following basic objectives: to promote and expand American foreign trade and investment through private initiative; to preserve and protect the effective role of free, private, competitive enterprise in international trade and investment; to serve as an authoritative voice of the broad cross-section of United States international interests, large and small, represented by the membership of the Council; and to develop in consultation with industry and Government, measures to achieve the foregoing. The Council's membership comprises United States companies representing broad and highly diversified interests from all parts of the nation and includes manufacturers, banks, exporters and importers, and members of the shipping, airlines, insurance, communications, publishing, advertising, engineering and construction industries.

The committees of the Council are made up of experienced international executives representing member companies and meet as required to deal with technical subjects relating to foreign trade and investment and with matters of area and country concern.

The analytical and technical work of the committees and staff enables the Council to present expert testimony on proposed legislation, treaties, regulations and related matters at hearings before Congressional committees and at conferences

---

Source: *Exporter's Encyclopedia*. Annual.
        Dun & Bradstreet International,
        99 Church St., New York, N.Y.

with the Executive departments and agencies. In this connection, and for the development of sound international economic, trade and investment policies, the Council prepares and presents position papers and memoranda on a wide range of subjects dealing with the conduct of foreign trade and investment.

Bulletins, weekly news digests of European (Breve) and Latin American (Noticias) developments, Pacific-Asia Report, and other reports to members keep them informed of current developments in foreign trade policy and operation.

The annual National Foreign Trade Convention is sponsored by the Council (Nov. 14 & 15, 1977). The World Trade Dinner is the occasion for the presentation of the Annual Captain Robert Dollar Memorial Award, first awarded to Cordell Hull in 1938, for distinguished contribution to the advancement of American foreign trade. The annual Policy Declarations of the National Foreign Trade Council formulate basic policies and principles and serve as a guide to the Government and Congress on the attitude of American business to current problems affecting overseas trade and investment and related services.

(b)   Chamber of Commerce of the United States, Washington, D.C. 20062. Manager/International Division:—Mr. John Caldwell (202) 659-6114.

The Chamber of Commerce of the U.S. is the world's largest voluntary business organization. Three thousand, six hundred local and state chambers of commerce, trade and professional associations, and American chambers of commerce in 39 countries comprise the organizational membership of the federation. In addition, the Chamber's membership includes over 64,000 business members—firms and individuals. To service this widespread membership which covers commerce, industry, banking, transportation, communication, insurance, construction, agriculture and all other sectors of American business, the Chamber maintains specialists dealing with the major national and international interests of U.S. business.

The Chamber's international work is managed by the International Division, which analyzes international trade and investment legislation and government administration procedures, looking toward National Chamber policy formation and implementation in Congress and with the Executive Branch of the Government. The Division serves as the secretariat for the Chamber's International Committee, the Panel on Foreign Trade Policy, the International Investment Panel, and ad hoc task forces which work on specific problem areas of concern to the business community. It also assists members in building international business through various source handbooks and other forms of communication.

The Division is also responsible for the foreign affairs of the Chamber. Through a process of "business diplomacy" it brings together top American business leaders and their counterparts in key selected countries for ongoing discussions on international trade, investment, monetary and economic development issues. Policy recommendations stemming from these talks are submitted to respective governments.

This element of the Division's activities concentrates on Asian-Pacific affairs, European affairs, Hemispheric affairs, East-West affairs, Middle East affairs and African affairs.

It carries out its mandate on three mutually complementary levels: bilateral and multilateral councils and committees with such economies as Japan, the Near East, Canada, the European Community and Eastern European countries; American chambers of commerce abroad and intergovernmental and international business organizations.

b1.   United States Council of the International Chamber of Commerce Inc., 1212 Ave. of the Americas, New York, N.Y. 10036. Harvey Williams, President. (212) 354-4480. Telex: 14-8361 New York.

The United States Council of the International Chamber of Commerce is an association of private enterprises, all deeply interested in international business activities or finance, in which trade organizations also can participate as members. The business membership includes manufacturers, banks, insurance companies, commercial organizations, law firms, certified public accountants, management consultants, engineers and construction organizations—all with important overseas activities. The Council is the largest of 54 National Councils of the I.C.C. all served by the central I.C.C. Secretariat in Paris, France. The ICC has less formal representation in about 30 additional countries.

The officers, staff, and committees of the United States Council play an important role in the formulation of the policies of the International Chamber of Commerce. They participate in study projects undertaken by the Chamber and in the preparation of its reports and recommendations. They also initiate new projects within the I.C.C. structure. In these activities the Council works in cooperation with the other National Councils or committees of the I.C.C. The International Chamber thereby draws upon the combined experience and judgment of business executives in many nations and many occupations in reaching recommendations or conclusions concerning international economic problems.

The reports and recommendations of the I.C.C. and its member Councils are made available to businessmen, governments, intergovernmental organizations and the general public. The Chamber has been recognized for more than fifty years as the spokesman for the international business community on matters that affect the private sector.

The International Chamber maintains representation at the United Nations under a special consultative status as well as with the Commission of the E.E.C., the GATT, the Bank for International Settlements, the I.M.F., World Bank and over 150 other inter-governmental organizations. The headquarters of the I.C.C.'s, New York UN Liaison office are at the U.S. Council.

The United States Council also serves as the issuing organization for the United States in implementing the ATA Carnet Customs Convention (ATA stands for Admission Temporaire—Temporary Admission). This system of international customs clearances facilitates temporary export shipments throughout the effective area of the Convention—embracing currently 31 countries. It enables the exporter to make temporary shipments of commercial and industrial samples of professional equipment without the necessity of posting bonds or making deposits at each foreign point of entry. Instead, arrangements are made with the issuing organization in the exporter's home country.

The United States Council also represents the international segment of the American business community at U.S. Congressional hearings on matters affecting international trade and finance, taxation of overseas earnings and other legistlation related to international operations and finance. Its officers and trustees serve on various committees such as the States Department Advisory Committee on Transnational Enterprise and on such business groups as the Business Council and the Business Round Table. It attempts to assist domestic business associations in the formulation of views on international business matters. It is often represented at intergovernmental organization meetings such as the UNCTAD, the U.N. Commission on Transnational Corporations, the I.M.F. or World Bank where its members have a direct interest.

The United States Council also houses the Secretariat of the U.S.A.–B.I.A.C. –the American branch of the Business and Industry Advisory Committee to the Organization for Economic Cooperation and Development (OECD) which has its headquarters in Paris, France. The Council's President serves as Secretary–Treasurer of U.S.A.–B.I.A.C.

b2. *The Council of the Americas, 680 Park Ave., New York, N.Y. 10021. Henry R. Geyelin, President. Augustine R. Marusi, Chairman. (212) 628-3200.*

The Council of the Americas is a non-profit business association supported by member corporations. There are no individual memberships. The programs of the Council are carried out by active participation of officers and management representatives of member companies.

The mission of the Council is to further understanding and acceptance of the role of private enterprise as a positive force for the development of the Americas. The Council provides for continuing dialogue with the leaders of the Americas to increase convergence and to lessen confrontation on issues arising from change.

The organization was founded in New York City in 1958, as the United States Inter-American Council, Inc. Its name was changed in 1965 to Council for Latin America, Inc., and in 1970 to Council of the Americas, Inc. The Council is exempt from Federal income taxes under the provisions of Internal Revenue Code, Section 501(c) (6).

b3. *National Association of Manufacturers, 1776 F. St., N.W. Washington, D.C. 20006. Forrest I. Rettgers, Executive Vice President (Acting President). (202) 331-3800.*

Organized in 1895, the National Association of Manufacturers is a voluntary membership organization of industrial and business firms. Headquarters are maintained in Washington, D.C. There are seven divisional officers. Secretary, Edmund Haskins.

c. *International Executives Association, Inc., One World Trade Center, Suite 1207, New York 10048. Robert L. Roper, Executive Director. (212) 432-1860.*

The International Executives Association, Inc., is a world-wide association of executives from various companies, institutions, and agencies who are directly involved in the field of exporting. The association was founded in 1917 as the Export Managers Club of New York, and since its inception the organization has dedicated itself to the development of international trade and better economic understanding throughout the world. The I.E.A. still maintains its base of operations in New York City, but the association has members from all over the United States, as well as from several foreign countries. The I.E.A. lives up to its association motto, "Helping Each Other in International Trade," through regular luncheon meetings, seminars, and workshops, as well as a regular bulletin service, a membership questionnaire service, a placement service for members, and a spot information service. The I.E.A. holds the President's "E" Award for outstanding contributions to the export expansion program of the United States.

d.   Bankers Association for Foreign Trade

Membership in this Association is divided into four classes: U.S., International, Honorary, and Special.   Membership is confined to corporations, associations, partnerships, or other organizations substantially engaged in foreign and international banking and such individuals as may, from time to time, be elected to Honorary Membership.   U.S. Membership is limited, by invitation, to domestic banks. International Membership is limited, by invitation, to chartered Canadian banks or banks organized under the laws of the U.S. but not controlled and predominantly owned by U.S. citizens, or foreign banks which have branches, agencies or representative offices in the U.S. but not controlled and predominantly owned by U.S. citizens, or foreign banks which have branches, agencies or representative offices in the U.S.   The purpose of the Association is to promote and foster international banking and foreign trade by doing all things appropriate to the stimulation of public interest therein and to the improvement of existing practices and the development of new techniques thereof.   President, Robert N. Bee, Senior Vice President, Wells Fargo Bank, San Francisco; Vice President, Robert B. Palmer, Executive Vice President, Philadelphia National Bank, Philadelphia; Secretary-Treasurer, B. Kenneth West, Executive Vice President, Harris Trust and Savings Bank, Chicago; Counsel, Thomas L. Farmer, Esq., Washington, D.C., Public Affairs Office: 1101 Sixteenth St., N.W. Suite 501, Washington, D.C.   (202) 833-3060.

e.   National Association of Credit Management, 475 Park Ave., South, New York, N.Y. 10016.   Robert D. Goodwin, Executive Vice President; J. S. Giles, Executive Vice President of the FCIB-NACM Corp.   (212) 725-1700.

Since 1919 this organization has secretaried an International Department (FCIB) for the purpose of rendering service to those of its 40,000 members who are interested in international trade.

This Department furnishes information of a general and specific character in connection with problems of its members regarding international business and credits.   The scope of the work is not limited to problems of a strictly credit nature, but covers the entire field of export finance, exchange and collection procedure.

Through its Board of Directors, the organization is also active in the promotion of sound credit techniques throughout the world, working in close contact with credit organizations and movements in many overseas countries, all for the purpose of promoting better credit in international trade and a freer interchange of information.

The FCIB (See *FCIB-NACM Corp.*), through tabulated ledger experience reports and other credit information, provides a practical yet economical means for promoting and protecting the export business of its members on a cooperative and nonprofit basis.   The FCIB conducts conferences quarterly in various European cities to better serve its members there, has an office with a full time staff at 502 Ave Louise, Brussels, Belgium.

The World-Wide Collection Department provides for the collection of delinquent accounts anywhere in the free world. Market studies and surveys are also among the special services available to all international traders.

f.   *International Advertising Association, Inc., 475 Fifth Ave., New York, N.Y. 10017. John S. W. Wasley, Executive Director. (212) MU4-1583.*

The International Advertising Association, Inc., was organized on October 3, 1938, for the purpose of providing members of the international advertising profession with an opportunity for the interchange of ideas and experiences in order to promote the sale of goods throughout the world, by means of advertising in all its forms. The growth of the Association has been steady, with membership more than doubled in recent years, and now totaling over 2,500, divided 25–75 between the U.S. and 80 other countries and population centers.

g.   *Far East-America Council of Commerce & Industry, 1270 Ave. of the Americas, New York, N.Y. 10020. (212) 265-6375.*

A private, non-profit organization devoted exclusively to the stimulation of trade, the expansion of economic relations and the furtherance of better understanding between the countries of Asia and the United States. Executive Director and Secretary, June D. Mayer.

h.   *Association of World Trade Chamber Executives, Inc., 65 Liberty St., New York, N.Y. 10005. (212) 766-1346.*

An organization of chamber of commerce staff personnel, located in 45 major cities, engaged in providing service in the field of international trade to their respective member companies. President; Robert W. Palmer. Secretary-Treasurer; Alfred D. Payne.

i.   *American Institute of Merchant Shipping (AIMS), 1625 K St., N.W., Washington, D.C. James J. Reynolds, President. (202) 783-6440.*

Established to foster development of programs to strengthen the U.S. shipping fleet. It includes companies formerly comprising the American Merchant Marine Institute, the Committee of American Steamship Lines and the Pacific American Steamship Association.

j.   *Export Management Associations*

National Federation of Export Management Companies (FEMCO), c/o New York Chamber of Commerce and Industry, 65 Liberty St., New York, N.Y. 10005. (212) 766-1343.

This organization is composed of regional trade associations of export management companies throughout the U.S. Executive Secretary, Gilbert M. Weinstein.

National Association of Export Management Companies, Inc., 65 Liberty St., New York, N.Y. 10005. (212) 766-1343.

This is a national organization with membership limited to responsible export management companies representing two or more U.S. manufacturers. Secretary, Gilbert M. Weinstein.

Florida World Trade Association, P.O. Box 2093, Coral Gables, Florida 33134.

President, Charles F. McKay.

Overseas Sales & Marketing Association of America, 5715 North Lincoln Ave., Chicago, Illinois 60659. (312) 334-1502.

Membership limited to export management companies. President, Peter H. Reinhard.

Association of International Management Companies, c/o Tradecom International, Inc., 1276 West Third St., Cleveland, Ohio 44113. (216) 861-3754.

President, Edward S. Benhoff.

Council of Ohio Combination Export Managers, 690 Union Commerce Bldg., Cleveland, Ohio 44115.

Membership limited to combination export managers. Secretary, Harold B. Mendes.

Export Managers Association of California, 10919 Vanowen Street, North Hollywood, California 91605. (213) 627-0634.

Membership includes export management companies, company export managers and export serrvice representatives. Executive Secretary, Norma Persky.

Export Mangement Association of the Northwest, Suite 220, 200 S.W. Market St., Portland, Oregon 97207. (503) 228-4361.

Composed of a group of firms actively engaged, as well as specializing in the international trade field. The Association, among its other activities, provides FEMCO (the national association) a central point through which to funnel trade leads to the Portland-Metropolitan Area.

Southwest Association of Exporters, Inc., Box 17575, Fort Worth, Texas 76102

Membership includes combination export managers, company export managers and export representatives of banks. President, W. F. Sprinkle.

B.   International Organizations

International Chamber of Commerce, 38, Cours Albert 1er, Paris 75008, France. Secretary General, Carl-Henrik Winqwist. Tel: 359-05-92. Telex: 650770. Telegram: Incomerc Paris.

(United States Council of the ICC, Inc., 1212 Avenue of the Americas, New York, N.Y. 10036.)

The ICC's essential role is the facilitation of world trade and investment and the promotion of the market economy at the international level. To this end it has developed extensive contact with the leading inter-governmental organizations (the United States economic agencies, GATT, OECD, CCC, ICAD, EEC, etc.), while at the same time steadily extending its range of practical services offered to members and the business community in general. These include the ATA Carnet system, the ICC Court of Arbitration, Incoterms (see separate entries), and a wide variety of work designed to standardize and improve international business practices—notable results of which include the widely adopted international Codes of Advertising and market research practices. The Chamber is also noted for work on environmental affairs, particularly as regards industry.

Some forty international specialized commissions and committees composed of business men and experts appointed by member countries, with whose activities more than sixty specialized international organizations are associated, help to further the ICC's program of action.

The ICC now has National Committees in 54 countries, including all the leading market economy countries. Full meetings of its membership (Congresses) are held every three years, and more specialized Conferences and seminars are also organized regularly.

Organization of American States, Washington, D.C. 20006. Alejandro Orfila, Secretary General. (202) 331-1010.

The Organization of American States originated in 1890 at the First International Conference of American States. Its definite Charter was signed at the Ninth Conference in 1948. Its purpose is to achieve an order of peace and justice, promote American solidarity, strengthen collaboration among the Member States, and defend their sovereignty, independence and territorial integrity.

The III Special Inter-American Conference, Buenos Aires, February 27, 1967, approved the Protocol of Buenos Aires, amendments to the Charter of the OAS which became effective on February 27, 1970, when ratified by more than two-thirds of the Member States. The Protocol created a General Assembly of the OAS (meeting once a year) and established on an equal basis, the Permanent Council, the Inter-American Economic and Social Council, and the Inter-American Council for Education, Science, and Culture.

The Permanent Council is composed of one representative from each Member State with the rank of Ambassador.

The General Secretariat is maintained by means of annual quotas determined by the General Assembly of the Organization.

There are 26 member nations in the Organization: Argentina, Barbados, Bolivia, Brazil, Chile, Colombia, Costa Rica, Cuba, the Dominican Republic, Ecuador, El Salvador, Grenada, Guatemala, Haiti, Hondoras, Jamaica, Mexico, Nicaragua, Panama, Paraguay, Peru, Surinam, Trindad and Tobago, the United States, Uruguay and Venezuela.

The activities of the General Secretariat of the OAS have expanded into all fields of international cooperation, while its technical and information offices are at the service of the governments and the peoples of the hemisphere. It has the responsibility for furthering, through these offices and under the direction of the Secretary General of the Organization, economic, social, juridical, and cultural relations among the American States.

The Secretary General and the Assistant Secretary General, who acts as Secretary of the OAS Permanent Council, are elected for five-year terms by that Council and are assisted in the discharge of their duties by over 1,000 international civil servants.

The activities of the General Secretariat are divided among the Offices of the Secretary General and the Assistant Secretary General; the Executive Secretariats for Economic and Social Affairs and for Education, Science, and Culture; and the Secretariats for Development Cooperation and for Management. The General Secretariat provides secretariat services to the Inter-American Economic and Social Council, the Inter-American Council for Education, Science and Culture, the Inter-American Commission of Women, the Inter-American Statistical Institute, the Inter-American Commission on Human Rights, the Inter-American Nuclear Energy Commission, the Inter-American Peach Committee, and the Special Consultative Committee on Security. An Inter-American Export Promotion Center, headquartered in Bogota, Colombia, and reporting to the Secretary General through the Executive Secretary for Economic and Social Affairs, was created in 1968. There are Offices Away from Headquarters in 24 member countries and in Geneva.

The Columbus Memorial Library contains more than 200,000 catalogued volumes, 2,900 current periodicals, and publications of the OAS and its specialized organizations, as well as a large collection of photographs. All of these are used extensively by researchers and students of Latin America.

"Americas," monthly magazine on Inter-American affairs, issued in English, Spanish and Portuguese is one of the official publications of the Organization of American States. Special reports, surveys, and booklets on Inter-American travel, economy, law, education, social problems and other themes of interest are regularly distributed by the General Secretariat at nominal prices (free catalogue on request).

The beautiful main building of the General Secretariat is a mecca for tourists to Washington and was erected through the munificence of Andrew Carnegie and the contributions of the American Republics. Other offices are housed in an adjacent administration building, designed along the same classical lines and completed in the fall of 1949, and in office buildings elsewhere in Washington.

The Pan American Society of the U.S., Inc., 680 Park Ave., New York, N.Y. 10021. Wayland Barre Waters, Executive Secretary. (212) 628-9400.

The Pan American Society, founded in 1912, is an unofficial organization whose object is to bring the peoples of the American Republics into closer understanding and cooperative effort for the advancement of their common interests. Its major activity is to show hospitality and attention to representative citizens of the Republics of the other Americas who visit the U.S. It also seeks to stimulate public interest in the U.S. in the southern Republics. While its membership is drawn from leading business and professional men, it is neither a political nor a commercial organization, all of its activities being aimed toward the development of closer relationships among the peoples of the Americas. The society is supported by dues from a membership of approximately 300. Its headquarters are in New York City.

Consular Corps College & International Consular Academy, 1002 Mutual Building, Richmond, Virginia 23219. Walter W. Regirer, Director General. (804) 643-7126.

The Consular Corps College & International Consular Academy, a non-profit, non-political, educational society organized by Consuls, was incorporated in 1969.

Its objects are to bring the Consular Corps together and to promote its professional efficiency. The society consists of two groups: Consular Corps College to which only active Consular Officers (career and honorary) may belong; The International Consular Academy which is open to active and former consuls and those in related fields, including government, business, law, education, etc. The activities of these organizations consist of the following: (1) Planning of short seminars on Continuing Consular Education. (2) Publishing of periodic Newspapers on Current Consular Events. (3) Cooperating with organizations having interest in Consular affairs—OAS; American Society of International Law: Instituto Consular InterAmericano, etc. (4) Planning for International Consular Conferences. At the present time, members consist of Consular Officers of 72 countries.

C. Industrial

Motor Vehicle Manufacturers Association, Inc., 320 New Center Bldg., Detroit, Michigan 48202. William D. Eberle, President and Chief Executive Officer. (313) 872-4311.

The Motor Vehicle Manufacturers Association, Inc., founded in 1913, is a Trade Association composed of domestic manufacturers of motor vehicles. As a nonprofit service organization, the major activities of MVMA include: research, liaison with governmental bodies and private organizations, compilation of published data relating to the industry, and operation of public information services. Offices: Detroit, New York City, Washington, D.C.

D. Miscellaneous Organizations

1. New York Chamber of Commerce and Industry, 65 Liberty St., New York, N.Y. 10005. (212) 766-1300.

The New York Chamber of Commerce and Industry came into being in 1973, as a result of a consolidation of the Commerce & Industry Association of New York and the New York State Chamber of Commerce, thus creating the largest and oldest group of international business firms in the country. Serving the world trade community in the New York metropolitan area as a clearing house for information on all phases of import and export procedure, its World Trade Bulletin is distributed to members and provides up-to-the-minute regulation changes and current news of interest to world traders.

Gilbert M. Weinstein, Vice President International Affairs Group, (212) 766-1343; Al Payne, Director, Export/Import Department, (212) 766-1346; Daniel Curll, Port Affairs Coordinator, (212) 766-1364; Walter Vasquez, Director, Latin American Affairs, (212) 766-1348.

Trade Opportunity Division—Assists in making contacts with agents, distributors, buyers and sellers abroad; provides aid to responsible overseas businessmen seeking U.S. contacts. (212) 766-1352.

Import Division—Provides comprehensive service on problems of importers, particularly those relating to U.S. customs and tariff regulations.

Export Division—Advises members on trade problems; provides information on consular and shipping procedure, export practices and foreign import and exchange requirements; certifies export shipping documents for all countries requiring chamber of commerce certification: (a) Certificates of origin; (b) Commercial in-

voices as to export prices; (c) Affidavits, travelers identity certificates, sanitary certificates, etc., when requested. Certification of documents is handled at the One
World Trade Center office (Room 2571), at Five World Trade Center (Room 6119),
at JFK International Airport (147–29–182nd St., Jamaica, New York, N.Y. 11413),
and, if documents submitted by mail, at 65 Liberty St., New York, N.Y. 10005.

Various world trade staff services are available at 65 Liberty St., New York,
N.Y. 10005.

2.   *New York Board of Trade, Inc., International Section, 500 Fifth Avenue,
      New York, N.Y. 10036. (212) 661-6300.*

Organized to further international trade through trade promotion programs,
educational and cultural programs and related activities. William J. Sloboda, Executive Vice President.

3.   *The Chicago Association of Commerce & Industry, 130 S. Michigan Ave.,
      Chicago, Illinois 60603. Thomas H. Coulter, Chief Executive Officer.
      (312) 786-0111.*

Has World Trade Council, World Trade Policy Committee, Export Committee, International Investments Committee, International Banking Committee, and
Canadian-American Committee functioning through the Association's World Trade
Division. Seeks to promote the two-way foreign trade, international investment
and finance of the Chicago metropolitan area and the Middle West. Active in connection with legislation affecting foreign trade. Maintains foreign reference library
with trade directories. Executes certificates of origin, of free sale, of trade marks
and other export and import documents requiring authentication by a chamber of
commerce. Sponsors annual Chicago World Trade Conference, jointly with the International Trade Club of Chicago. Association's World Trade Division has conducted annual trade missions to all parts of the world as a function of its export
expansion program established in 1959. World Trade Division publishes annual
Directory of Foreign Consulates in Chicago and other Foreign Representation.
A booklet, "Invest in Chicago," is available for organizations contemplating new
facilities in the Chicago area: corporate or regional headquarters, sales offices,
industrial plants, facilities or warehouses.

4.   *Greater Detroit Chamber of Commerce, 150 Michigan Ave., Detroit, Michi-
      gan 48226. (313) 964-4000.*

The World Trade Department seeks to promote and encourage foreign trade
both from an institutional standpoint and through direct service to individual
members.

The Department maintains a foreign reference library, including trade directories from many countries, and comprehensive files containing information on
many firms in this area engaged in exporting, importing, or service fields related to
world trade. The Department sponsors International Trade Tours to all parts of the
world.

The World Trade and Port Development Council advocates and promotes
a mutual reduction of trade barriers between nations, an easing of restrictions on
American exports and tax laws permitting extension of American business in world
markets. Studies legislation involving the flow of new materials and ideas to and
from the Detroit area. It advises the Board of Directors on the mechanics of world

trade and recommends action in keeping with the Chamber of Commerce international trade policy.

The Department endorses Certificates of Origin and serves members in all phases of world trade. Dwight Havens, CCE. President; George C. Kiba, General Manager, Transportation, World Trade and Port Development Departments.

5. *The American Arbitration Association, 140 W. 51st St., New York, N.Y. 10020. Robert Coulson, President. (212) 977-2000.*

The American Arbitration Association is a nonprofit, membership organization with national headquarters at 140 W. 51st st., New York and 21 regional offices throughout the United States. The association is composed of individual and organizational members whose purpose is the advancement of the practice of commercial and labor arbitration and other forms of voluntary settlement of all kinds of disputes. It maintains for this purpose the Commercial Arbitration Tribunal, the Voluntary Labor Arbitration Tribunal, the Accident Claims Tribunal, and other specialized Tribunals. The Rules for the above Tribunals are available upon request.

The outstanding features of the work of the American Arbitration Association are: (1) it offers facilities for arbitration and a panel of approximately 40,000 qualified arbitrators; (2) it provides standard arbitration rules of procedure adaptable in trade and industrial groups requiring special services; (4) it conducts educational work in the publication of standard books on arbitration law and practice and by means of research, conferences and public meetings; (5) it issues a quarterly Arbitration Journal and other periodicals covering all kinds of voluntary dispute settlements; (6) the AAA also offers a variety of voluntary settlement services for all kinds of community and family disputes.

Through arrangements with the Inter-American Commercial Arbitration Commission and other foreign and international arbitration organizations the AAA provides facilities for the settlement of foreign trade arbitration. These services also offer the parties the opportunity to choose expert and impartial arbitrators in disputes arising in any branch of foreign trade.

6. *Inter-American Commercial Arbitration Commission, U.S. Section: Donald B. Straus, Vice President, 140 W. 51st St., New York, N.Y. 10020, (212) 977-2084. (Also: Charles Robert Norberg, Esq., Treasurer and General Counsel, Federal Bar Bldg., West, Room 310, Washington, D.C. 20006. (202) 293-1457, and Miguel M. Blasquez, President, Balderas No. 144, 1er Piso, Mexico, D.F. Tel. 512-77-83.*

The Inter-American Commercial Arbitration Commission was organized in September 1934, at the request of the Governing Board of the Pan American Union, following Resolution XLI of the Seventh International Conference of American States, for the purpose of establishing an inter-American system of commercial arbitration.

The membership of the Commission represents all of the American Republics, and its purposes are: (1) The establishment of arbitration facilities in each American Republic. For this purpose the Commission has appointed National Committees in the various Republics, responsible for organizing panels of arbitrators, and administering the standard Rules of the Commission. (2) The modification of arbitration laws in order to facilitate the conduct of arbitrations and ensure the enforcement of arbitration agreements and awards. The National Committees of the Commission are undertaking, in their respective countries, to modify arbitration laws to harmonize them with the standards approved by the Seventh International Conference of American States. (3) Familiarizing business men in all the American Republics with arbitration procedure, and its advantages to exporters and importers in inter-American trade. This work is being conducted through publicity and correspondence. (4) The arbitration or adjustment of differences or controversies, arising in the course of inter-American trade, that might interfere with the flow of goods from market to market or impair the goodwill and friendly relations of businessmen of the American Republics.

7.   *American Institute of Marine Underwriters, 14 Wall St., New York, N.Y. 10005. (212) 233-0550.*

The American Institute of Marine Underwriters, which was founded in 1898, is an association of companies writing marine insurance and individual representatives of those companies. The membership is composed not only of domestic companies but also foreign companies that are admitted to do business in the U.S. and its membership with their affiliated companies represents almost the entire American ocean marine insurance market.

The Institute does not write insurance and its functions are of an advisory or informative nature. One of the principal functions of the Institute is the release of recommended clauses, and American Institute clauses are receiving more and more recognition from financial and commercial organizations, both in the U.S. and abroad. The Institute is active in the area of cargo loss prevention with respect to ocean and air cargo. In addition to a Board of Directors, nineteen in number, the Institute has Standing Committees; namely Committee on Containers and Cargoes, Committee on Ocean Hulls, Committee on Membership, Committee on Forms and Clauses, Committee on Laws, Committee on Adjustments, and Committee on Correspondents, and Special Committees are appointed as required. The Annual Meeting of the Institute is held on the third Thursday in November and the officers are elected by the members. President: Thomas A. Fain.

8.   *American Graduate School of International Management, Thunderbird Campus, Glendale, Arizona. (Affiliated with the American Management Association.) President, William Voris. (602) 938-7200.*

A nonprofit, fully accredited graduate school, founded in 1946, which trains men and women for careers with business as well as Government and social service organizations with international operations. The tripartite curriculum offers intensive practical training in international commerce (including financing, documentation, export-import procedures, economics, marketing, accounting, advertising and general management); area studies of the history, politics, economics, custom, culture and geography of major regions (Latin America, Far East, Europe, Africa and the Middle East); and languages taught by the aural-oral method (Spanish, French, German, Portuguese, Japanese, English as second language), Chinese and Arabic. The graduate curriculum is geared to a three semester program. Special six-week concentrated language and area courses, are offered to executives bound overseas. Quarters for approximately 350 students are available on Thunderbird Campus. Official address: Thunderbird Campus, Glendale, Arizona 85306.

9.   *American Society of International Executives, P.O. Box 16444, Philadelphia, Pennsylvania 19122. President, Melvin K. Kerr. (215) 236-9494.*

A foreign trade professional society, formed in April 1964, the Society aims to give professional standing to qualified personnel engaged in international business. There are various classifications of members subject to examination: Certified Documentary Specialist, with the initials CDS; Certified International Executive (CIE) in the Fields of Export Management (EM), Traffic Management (TM), Forwarding (FF) and Air Forwarding (AF), equivalent to Assistant Manager of a foreign department in one of those fields; Qualified International Executive (QIE), equivalent to department manager in one of the above fields. There are detailed qualifications for each grade, and examinations, which are held in leading cities throughout the country, are necessary to obtain the society's certifications. Among other classes of membership without examination, the following are perhaps most noteworthy: Corporate Membership held by companies which are engaged in some division of international trade and wish to aid the activities of the Society; and Experienced International Executives admitted under a "grandfather's" provision; Senior and Cooperating members; and Associate Membership for those not qualified for other memberships.

10.   *National Export Traffic League, Inc., 507 Fifth Ave., New York, N.Y. 10017. Theodore Slahetka, President. Phone: Ortho Diagnostics Inc. (201) 524-2384.*

The National Export Traffic League was formed in May 1946, by a group of export and import traffic executives. The objectives of the League are: (a) To serve American Industry in export and import transportation and customs matters of general importance; (b) To promote cooperation between shippers, transportation companies, constituted regulatory bodies and all those interested in transportation, particularly in respect to practices, regulations and all other pertinent matters; (c) To obtain helpful legislation and the modification of such laws, rulings, or regulations as may be found harmful to international transportation; (d) To cooperate with other organizations in promoting these ends; (e) To foster educational programs and to encourage the study and discussion of subjects relating to export and import transportation and the interchange of ideas and thoughts thereon between the members.

11.   *Air Freight Forwarders Association of America, 1730 Rhode Island Avenue, N.W., Suite 607, Washington, D.C. 20036. Louis P. Haffer, Executive Vice President and Counsel. (202) 293-1030.*

A national organization of air freight forwarders.

12.   *National Committee on International Trade Documentation, 30 E. 42nd St., New York, N.Y. 10017. Executive Director, Arthur E. Baylis. (212) 687-6261. Cable–INTRADOCUM.*

A non-profit, membership organization working to simplify and to reduce documents and procedures that create paper work in international trade.

13. *National Customs Brokers & Forwarders Association of America, Inc., One World Trade Center, Suite 1109, New York, N.Y. 10048. Vincent J. Bruno, Executive Vice President. (212) 432-0050.*

The only nationwide trade association for U.S. firms which act as customs brokers, ocean and air freight forwarders, and foreign freight sales agents.

More than 400 members and associate members in the U.S. and throughout the world. Twenty-one regional and local associations in the U.S. are affiliated with the NCBFAA.

Foreign Trade Clubs

Foreign Trade Clubs

Akron, Ohio: International Tade Council, Akron Regional Development Board, Eighth Floor, One Cascade Plaza, 44308. Paul C. Livick, Manager, (216) 376-5550.

Atlanta, Ga.: The International Division, Atlanta Chamber of Commerce, 1300 Commerce Bldg., Atlanta, Ga. 30303. International Director, J. H. Wilkerson, (404) 501-0845.

Georgia International Trade Association Inc., Box 6963, Atlanta, Ga. 30315. Irvine E. Morris, President. Luncheon meetings 12:15 p.m., third Thursday, Atlanta America Motor Hotel, September to June inclusive, Secretary, Mrs. Joyce Stephens, Sidney Wolf, Life Director, P.O. Box 6963, Atlanta, Ga. 30315. (404) 622-4473.

Boston, Mass.: The International Business Center of New England, Inc., 470 Atlantic Ave., Boston, Massachusetts 02210. (A non-profit membership corporation whose principal objective is the expansion of international business.) Executive Director, Rear Admiral Harry Hull, U.N.S. (Ret.). (617) 542-0426.

The Foreign Commerce Club of Boston, Inc., 99 Buckskin Path, Centerville, Mass. 02632. Secretary and Treasurer, Sidney H. Pollard. (617) 775-7832.

Chicago, Ill.: International Trade Club of Chicago (formerly Export Managers Club of Chicago), 310 S. Michigan Ave., Chicago, Ill. 60604. Executive Administrator, Agnes C. Stenros.

Meets monthly to discuss subjects relating to international trade and investment; also conducts special interest seminars and educational projects. Sponsors annual Chicago World Trade Conference jointly with the Chicago Association of Commerce & Industry. Active in study of and recommendations regarding U.S. foreign economic and trade policy and legislation affecting world trade. Publishers of "International Trade News," monthly publication containing news of club activities and world trade matters. Also publishes annually, manual on "Principles and Techniques in Exporting." (312) 341-9021.

Source: *Exporter's Encyclopedia*. Annual.
Dun & Bradstreet International,
99 Church St., New York, N.Y.

Cincinnati, Ohio: World Trade Club of the Greater Cincinnati Chamber of Commerce, 120 West Fifth St., Cincinnati, Ohio 45202. Secretary, Charles E. Webb, Greater Cincinnati Chamber of Commerce. (513) 721-3300.

Cleveland, Ohio: International Division of the Greater Cleveland Growth Association, 690 Union Commerce Bldg., Cleveland, Ohio 44115.

The International Division is composed of the Cleveland World Trade Association which has operated the International Department of the Association's Regional Economic Development Division since 1970. The Cleveland World Trade Association, will, however, retain its identity as an organization dedicated to the enhancement of world trade. Lothar A. Koehere, Vice President of Greater Cleveland Growth Association and Staff Vice President of the Cleveland World Trade Association. (216) 621-3300.

Columbus, Ohio: International Trade Committee of the Columbus Area Chamber of Commerce. Kathleen Walsh, Department of Economic Development, The Columbus Area Chamber of Commerce. 50 W. Broad Street, Columbus Ohio 43215. (614) 221-1321.

Dallas, Texas: International Trade Association of Dallas, Inc., Box 672, Dallas, Texas 75221. Meetings held second Wednesday of the Month, September to June. For information contact M. Pentecost, (214) 658-6323 or Buddy Polser (214) 369-5825.

Dayton, Ohio: World Trade Committee of the Dayton Area Chamber of Commerce, Dayton Area Chamber of Commerce, 111 W. First St., Dayton Ohio 45402. Meetings third Wednesday of month. Dale Ross, Manager, World Trade Department, Dayton Area Chamber of Commerce, (513) 226-1444. Robert Scott, Executive Vice President, Dayton Area Chamber of Commerce.

Denver, Colo.: International Trade Association of Colorado (ITAC), P.O. Box 18398, Denver, Colo., 80218. Meetings held second Tuesday of each month. Anna Limacher, secretary-treasurer, 429 E. 14 Ave., Denver, Colo., 80203. (303) 831-1332.

Detroit, Mich.: World Trade Club of Detroit, Inc. Secretary, Gerald E. Dehn. Mail address: 14815 Lincoln, Suite 215, Oak Park, Michigan 48237. Dinner Meetings third Thursday evening each month October to May. Annual meeting in June.

Fort Washington, Pa.: International Trade Development Association. Nancy Evers, Executive Secretary. Box 113, Furlong, Pa. 18925. (215) 345-9589. Meets monthly on second Tuesday at Coach Inn, Ft. Washington, Pa.

Fort Worth, Texas: World Trade Committee of the Fort Worth Area Chamber of Commerce. 700 Throckmorton St., Ft. Worth, Texas 76102. Meetings, as called. Norman B. Robbins, Jr. (817) 336-2491.

Fort Worth Export-Import Club. Box 17372, Fort Worth, Texas 76102. Secretary, Mrs. Mabyl Miller. (817) 625-2211.

Galveston, Texas: Traffic Club of Galveston-Texas City. P.O. Box 343, Galveston, Texas 77550. Meetings held monthly. Secretary-Treasurer, Jim Naylor.

Grand Rapids, Mich.: West Michigan World Trade Club. P.O. Box 1238, Grand Rapids, Michigan. Meets fourth Tuesday of each month. September through May (except December). Secretary, Marilyn Warmels. (616) 245-9221.

Hartford, Conn.: Connecticut Business and Industry Association. Suite 1202, 60 Washington St., Hartford, Conn. 06106. Attorney, John R. Anderson.

Honolulu, Hawaii: Hawaii World Trade Association of the Chamber of Commerce of Hawaii. Dillingham Bldg., Honolulu, Hawaii 96813. Executive Secretary, J. Russell Geib. (808) 531-4111.

Houston, Texas: Houston World Trade Association. 1013 World Trade Center, Houston, Texas 77002. Executive Director, Bernard Murphy. (713) 225-0968.

Indianapolis, Ind.: World Trade Committee. Indianapolis Chamber of Commerce, 320 N. Meridian St., Indianapolis, Ind. 46204. Secretary, Robert W. Palmer. (317) 635-4747.
    World Trade Club of Indiana, Inc., 928 Chamber of Commerce Bldg., Indianapolis, Ind., 46204. Meets monthly. Executive Secretary, Robert W. Palmer. (317) 635-4747.

Kansas City, Mo.: International Trade Club of Greater Kansas City. 4530 Madison Ave., Kansas City, Mo. 64111. President, Mr. Gerard B. A. Seymour. (816) 561-8800.

Long Beach, Calif.: Long Beach Area Chamber, World Trade Information. 50´ Oceangate Plaza, Long Beach, Calif. 90802. (213) 436-1251. President, Weck Morgan.
    Economic Development Department, Long Beach Area Chamber of Commerce. 50 Oceangate Plaza, Long Beach, Calif. 90802. (213) 436-1251. Executive Vice President, Ron Watson.

Los Angeles, Calif.: Foreign Trade Association of Southern California. 333 S. Flower St., Suite 226, Los Angeles, Calif. 90017. F. V. Swanson, Executive Secretary. (213) 627-0634.

Louisville, Ky.: Foreign Trade Club of University of Louisville. Executive Director, Dr. George Brodschi. International Center, University of Louisville, Louisville, Kentucky. (502) 588-6602.
    Kentuckiana World Commerce Council, Inc. 300 W. Liberty St., Louisville, Kentucky 40202. Secretary, Carter M. Harrison. (502) 582-2421.

Melville, N.Y.: The Long Island Association of Commerce and Industry. 425 Broad Hollow Road, Suite 205, Melville, New York 11746. President, John B. Rettaliata. (516) 752-9600.

Milwaukee, Wis.: World Trade Association of Milwaukee, Inc. Room 310, 828 N. Broadway, Milwaukee, Wis. 53202. Executive Secretary, George Carini. (414) 273-3000.

Minneapolis, Minn.: Minnesota World Trade Association. 5235 Xerxes Ave. South, Minneapolis, Minn. 55410. President, Paul Strand. Business Manager, A. L. Cadieux. (612) 926-6202.

New Orleans, La.: World Trade Club of Greater New Orleans. 242 International Trade Mart, 2 Canal St., New Orleans, La. Executive Secretary, Mrs. R. M. Pe Dotti. (504) 525-7201.

The club annually cooperates in sponsoring the Mississippi Valley World Trade Conference held in New Orleans where world traders from all parts of the country and from abroad gather to discuss their mutual problems.

New York, N.Y.: Foreign Commerce Club of New York, Inc. Secretary, John E. Ward, Boise-Griffin S. S. Co. Inc., One World Trade Center, Suite 3811, New York, N.Y. 10048. (212) 432-1575.

International Industrial Marketing Club. 10 Cutter Mill Road, Great Neck, New York 10021. An informal club comprised of international marketing and sales managers. Secretary-Treasurer, Gerald E. Keller. Meetings first Thursday of each month (except July) at the Chemists Club in New York City. (516) 829-9210.

Overseas Automotive Club, Inc. 475 Park Ave., South, New York, N.Y. 10016. Formed in 1923, this organization devoted exclusively to executives of U.S. manufacturers of automotive vehicles, components and maintenance parts, organizations servicing these manufacturers—such as banks, credit, insurance companies, forwarders, steamship lines and airlines—and combination export managers who directly represent manufacturers or have their own brand names, has grown to 318 U.S. members and 430 in the International Section, which was formed in 1960. This Club publishes the "OAC News" a quarterly publication and minutes of monthly luncheon meetings usually held the second Thursday of months from September to May, inclusive. Annually OAC sponsors members and overseas guests to the (IASI) International Automotive Services Industries Show—McCormick Place, Chicago, Ill.—March 15-17, 1978. Secretary, J. Stewart Gillies. (212) 725-1700.

World Trade Club of New York, Inc. Walter Vasquez, Executive Secretary. Organized in April 1950, as The Junior World Trade Club of New York, Inc., an affiliate of the New York Chamber of Commerce and Industry. 65 Liberty St., New York 10005. Usually meets on the first Monday of each month (except July and August). (212) 766-1351.

Norfolk, Va.: Hampton Roads Foreign Commerce Club. 7432 North Shore Road, Norfolk, Va. 23505. Secretary, Mrs. Edythe Z. Fine. (804) 423-2429.

Oakland, Calif.: Oakland World Trade Club. 1939 Harrison St., # 400, Oakland, Calif. 94612. Executive Secretary, Robert W. Ross. (415) 451-7800.

Oklahoma City, Okla.: Oklahoma City International Trade Club. Oklahoma City Chamber of Commerce, One Santa Fe Plaza, Oklahoma City, Okla. 73102. Usually meets on the second Tuesday evening of each month (except July and August). Earl Nichols, Manager, World Trade Dept. (405) 232-6381.

Omaha, Nebraska: Midwest International Trade Association. P.O. Box 1434, Downtown Station, Omaha, Nebraska 68101.

Philadelphia, Pa.: World Trade Association of Philadelphia, Inc. Executive Administrator, Mrs. Marianne C. McDevitt, Land Title Bldg., Broad & Chestnut Sts. Philadelphia, Pa. 19110. Meetings monthly. Annual meeting in September. (215) 563-8887.

Providence, R.I.: World Trade Club of the Greater Providence Chamber of Commerce. Executive Office, Howard Bldg., 10 Dorrance St., Providence, R.I. Executive Director, James A. Devine. (401) 521-5000.

Reading, Pa.: Reading Foreign Traders. 607 Washington St., Reading, Pa. (Mail address: P.O. Box 142, Reading, Pa. 19603.) Secretary, Kenneth R. Sensenig. Meetings held second Wednesday of each month, Abraham Lincoln Motor Inn, 6 p.m. (except June, July and August). (215) 376-1578.

Richmond, Va.: Richmond Export-Import Club. 8010 Federal Bldg., Richmond, Va. 23240. Meetings held at noon, usually on fourth Wednesday of each month at Holiday Inn Downtown. Secretary, Joseph E. Vaden. (804) 271-5101.

St. Louis, Mo.: World Trade Club of St. Louis, Inc. 212 North Kingshighway, St. Louis, Mo. 63108. (314) 361-6009. For additional information contact the Secretary. Meetings fourth Thursday of each month.

Salt Lake City, Utah: World Trade Association of Utah. 1201 Federal Bldg., 125 S. State, Salt Lake City, Utah 84138. Meetings held monthly, except during summer. Executive Secretary, George M. Blessing, Jr. (801) 524-5116.

San Antonio, Texas: Export-Import Club of San Antonio. 221 Olmos Dr. W., San Antonio, Texas 78212. President, J. L. McPherson. Affiliate of Texas International Trade Association (TITA). (512) 826-3400.

San Francisco, Calif.: World Trade Association of the San Francisco Chamber of Commerce. 465 California St., San Francisco, Calif. 94104. Richard L. Harcourt, Executive Director, W.T.A. (415) 392-4511.

    International Trade and Industries Association of the Western United States. 303 World Trade Center, San Francisco, Calif. 94111. James P. Wilson, President. (415) 986-5698.

    Junior World Trade Association of the San Francisco Chamber of Commerce. 465 California St., San Francisco, Calif. 94104. Thomas M. Molton, President. (415) 392-4511.

San Juan, P.R.: The International Trade Association of Puerto Rico, c/o Manuel T. Hidalgo, Membership Chairman. 1319 Ashford Ave., Santurce, P.R. 00907. (809) 724-4918.

Seattle, Wash.: World Trade Club of Seattle. Mayflower Park Hotel, 405 Olive Way, Seattle, Wash. 98101. (206) 682-6986.

South Bend, Ind.: Michiana World Trade Club. 230 W. Jefferson Blvd., South Bend, Ind. 46601. Executive Director, Eli D. Miller. (219) 234-0051.

Syracuse, N.Y.: World Commerce Association of Central New York, c/o Greater Syracuse Chamber of Commerce. 1700 One MONY Plaza, 100 Madison St., Syracuse, N.Y. 13202. Meetings last Tuesday of each month. Robert F. Valentine, Secretary-Treasurer. (315) 422-1343.

Tampa, Fla.: Tampa World Trade Council, International Department of the Greater Tampa Chamber of Commerce. P.O. Box 420, Tampa, Fla. 33601. Executive Director, Eugene E. Paredes. (813) 228-7777.

Tulsa, Okla.: Tulsa World Trade Association. 616 South Boston, Tulsa, Okla. 74119. Meetings held monthly (except June, July and August). Mike Williams, President. (918) 585-1201.

York, Pa.: World Trade Council of the York Area Chamber of Commerce. P.O. Box 1229, York, Pa. 17405. Carl F. Nev. (717) 854-3814.

Miscellaneous Clubs and Bureaus

Chicago, Ill.: Foreign Trade Credit Group of the Chicago Midwest Credit Management Association. 315 South Northwest Highway, Park Ridge, Ill. 60068. Secretary, Mr. W. L. Haney. (312) 696-3000.

Long Island, New York: Long Island Association of Commerce and Industry. 131 Jericho Turnpike, Jericho, New York 11753. Robert C. Sellers, Executive Vice President. (516) 333-9300.

Rochester, N.Y.: World Trade Council, Rochester Area Chamber of Commerce, Inc. 55 St. Paul St., Rochester, N.Y. 14604. Director, W. F. Freiert. (716) 454-2220.

St. Louis, Mo.: World Trade Department, St. Louis Regional Commerce & Growth Association. 10 Broadway, St. Louis, Mo. 63102. Joseph M. de Rotaeche, Manager, World Trade. (314) 231-5555.

International Federation of Purchasing. 1 Rue aux Laines, Brussels, Belgium. Dr. John Hyde, Secretary General. Membership consists of 19 national associations of purchasing and supply management executives in 17 nations. (No Current Information Available.)

Appendix Ten

Chambers of Commerce

American Chambers of Commerce Abroad

Argentina: The American Chamber of Commerce in Argentina, Avenida R. Saenz Pêna 567, 1352 Buenos Aires. Tel.: 33-5591. J. Baldwin Robinson, General Manager.

Australia: American Chamber of Commerce in Australia, 8th Floor, 50 Pitt St., Sydney, New South Wales 2000. Tel.: 241-1907. Kevin Bannon, Executive Director.
American Chamber of Commerce in Australia, 8th Floor, Guardian Assurance Bldg., 50 Grenfell St., Adelaide, S.A. 5000. Tel.: 87.5781. Secretary, Miss L. Cannon.
American Chamber of Commerce in Australia, Room 4, 4th Floor, 139 Leichhardt St., Brisbane, Qld., 4000. Tel.: 221-8542. Brisbane Manager, Mrs. I. O'Brien.
American Chamber of Commerce in Australia, 3rd Floor, 186 Exhibition St., Melbourne, Victoria, 3000. C. W. Miller, Manager. Tel.: 662.3535.
American Chamber of Commerce in Australia, 9th Floor, 16 St. George's Terrace, Perth, W. A. 6000. Tel.: 25.9540. Perth Manager, Mrs. P. Maxwell.

Austria: American Chamber of Commerce in Austria, Severingasse 1, A-1090, Vienna. Tel.: 421271. Manager: Dkfm. Dr. Patricia A. Helletzgruber.

Belgium: American Chamber of Commerce in Belgium, Rue du Commerce 21, 1040 Brussels, Mr. Wayne W. Fisher, Executive Director. Tel.: (02) 512.12.62.

Bolivia: American Chamber of Commerce of Bolivia, Casilla de Correo 8268, La Paz. Tel.: 54355.

Brazil: American Chamber of Commerce for Brazil-Rio de Janeiro, Avenida Rio Branco, 123 - 21st floor, Caixa Postal 916-ZC-00, Rio de Janeiro, Augusto de Moura Diniz, Jr., Executive Vice President. Tel.: 222-1983.
American Chamber of Commerce for Brazil-Sao Paulo, Rua Formosa, 367, 29° andar, 01049 Sao Paulo, SP. (Postal Address: Caixa 8109, 01000 Sao Paulo, SP.) Tel.: 37-7181.

Source: *Exporter's Encyclopedia*. Annual.
        Dun & Bradstreet International,
        99 Church St., New York, N.Y.

American Chamber of Commerce for Brazil-Porto Alegre, Branch Office of Sao Paulo, Av. Borges de Medeiros, 410 6th floor, rooms 612/613, Porto Alegre, R.S. (Mail Address: P.O. Box 1572, 90.000 Porto Alegre). Tel.: 25-0356. Curt Schroeder, President.

American Chamber of Commerce for Brazil-Recife Branch, Caixa Postal 3351, 30.000, Recife, Pernambuco, Brazil. Tel.: 24-5988. Executive Secretary, M.S. de Azevedo.

American Chamber of Commerce for Brazil-Salvador Branch, Conselheiro Dantas, 8, Sala 904, Edificio Paraguassu, Salvador, Bahai. Tel.: 2-0284.

Chile: Chamber of Commerce of the U.S.A. in the Republic of Chile, Bandera 84, Office 408, Santiago. (Postal address: P.O. Box 4131, Santiago.) Tel.: 86348. Juan Breit, Executive Secretary. Bernard J. Curtis, Executive Manager.

China: American Chamber of Commerce in the Republic of China, Room N-1012, Chia Hsin Bldg. II, 96 Chung Shan N. Rd., Sec. 2, Taipei, Taiwan, Republic of China, P.O. Box 17-277, Tel.: 5512515. President Marinus van Gessel. Executive Director, Herbert Gale Peabody.

Colombia: Colombian-American Chamber of Commerce, Bogota Hilton Hotel, Suite 701, Apartado Aereo 8008, Bogota. Tel.: 329701, 329791. Telex: 044326. Oscar A. Bradford, President.

Colombian-American Chamber of Commerce, Edificio Banco Comercio Antioqueno, Apartado Aereo 5943, Cali, Valle. Tel.: 771012, Srta. Maria Cecilia Monsalve C, Executive Director.

Costa Rica: American Chamber of Commerce of Costa Rica, P.O. Box 4946, San Jose, Costa Rica. Manager, Felicia M. Morales, Te.: 23-24-97.

Dominican Republic: American Chamber of Commerce of the Dominican Republic, Hotel El Embajador, First Floor, P.O. Box 95-2, Santo Domingo. Tel.: 533-7292. Lic. Eduardo Fernandez P., President. Wilson A. Rood, Executive Director.

Ecuador: Ecuadorian-American Chamber of Commerce, P.O. Box 2432, Quito. Tel.: 543-512. Executive Director, Karl Newlands.

England: American Chamber of Commerce (United Kingdom), 75 Brook St., London, WIY 2 EB, Eric J. Forbes, Secretary-Treasurer. Tel.: 01-493-0381.

France: American Chamber of Commerce in France, 21 Ave. George V, 75008 Paris. W. Barrett Dower, Executive Director. Tel.: 225-01-54.

Germany: American Chamber of Commerce in Germany, Rossmarkt 12, D-6000 Frankfurt 1. Tel.: (0611)-282554. Executive Secretary, Paul G. Baudler.

American Chamber of Commerce in Germany. 1000 Berlin 12, Fasanenstrasse 4. Tel.: (030)-317001. Robert H. Lochner.

American Chamber of Commerce in Germany, 8000 Munich 22, Zweibruckenstrasse 6. Tel.: (0811)-295953. Dr. Leo Goodman.

Greece: American-Hellenic Chamber of Commerce, 17 Valaoritou and Amerikis Sts., Athens 134. D. Georgiopoulos, General Manager. Tel.: 3618-385 or 3636-407.

Guatemala: American Chamber of Commerce of Guatemala (Cámara de Comercio Norteamericana de Guatemala), 9a. Calle 5-54, Zona 1, Guatemala City. (Mail Address: c/o Apartado Postal 833, Guatemala City.) Executive Manager, Belton W. Rudder. Tel.: 82020.

Hong Kong: American Chamber of Commerce in Hong Kong, 322 Edinburgh House, Hong Kong. Tel.: 5-260165. Executive Director, Stanley Young.

Indonesia: American Chamber of Commerce in Indonesia, Tromol Pos 3449/JKT— Jakarta. Tel.: 353-194. Robert L. Houser, President.

Iran: Iran—American Chamber of Commerce, Iranians' Bank Bldg., 7th Floor, Takhte Jamshid Ave., Tehran. Tel.: 895149. F. T. Burroughs, Executive Director.

Ireland: The United States Chamber of Commerce in Ireland. 16 Eustace St., Dublin 2, Ireland. Tel.: Dublin 77 55 54. Executive Director, Robert P. Chalker.

Israel: Israel-America Chamber of Commerce and Industry (1965), Ltd., America House, 35 Shaul Hamelech Blvd., P.O. Box 33174 Tel-Aviv, Israel. Tel.: 252341/2. Telex: 32139. Executive Director, Elisha Galon.

Italy: American Chamber of Commerce in Italy, Via Agnello 12, 20121 Milan. Herman H. Burdick, General Secretary. Tel.: 807955. A branch office is maintained at: Via Lombardia 40, 00187 Rome. Tel.: 4754540.

Japan: American Chamber of Commerce in Japan, 701 Tosho Bldg., 2-2, Maranouchi 3-chome, Chiyoda-ku, Tokyo 100, Japan. Tel.: (03) 211-5861/3. William T. Panttaja, Executive Director.

American Chamber of Commerce in Okinawa, Manneng Bldg., 136 Oyama, Ginowan-shi, Okinawa-ken, Japan 901-22. Tel.: 09889-7-2118/6634. Duncan Tucker, President.

Korea: American Chamber of Commerce in Korea. Third Floor, Chosun Hotel, Seoul. Mr. Richard C. Witt, President; Brig. Gen Frederick C. Kraus (Ret.) Executive Director. Tel.: 23-6471.

Mexico: American Chamber of Commerce of Mexico, Lucerna No. 78, Mexico 6, D.F. (Mail Address: Apartado 82-bis, Mexico 1, D.F.) Tel.: 566-0866. Al R. Wichtrich, President; John M. Bruon, General Manager; Jose Luis Newman, Director, Commercial Information Unit.

American Chamber of Commerce of Mexico, Guadalajara Branch, Condominio Guadalajara, 16 de Septiembre 730-301, Guadalajara, Jalisco. Tel.: 12-26-49. General Manager, Eugene Delgado-Arias.

American Chamber of Commerce of Mexico, A.C., Condominio Acero, Desp. 213, Monterrey, Nuevo Leon. Tel.: 44-00-90/91. Lic. Guillermo Marcos, Manager.

Morocco: American Chamber of Commerce in Morocco, Hotel El Mansour, 27, Ave. des F.A.R., Casablanca. President, Henry F. Batchelder II, General Manager, First National City Bank Maghreb, Mrs. Gladys Levy, Executive Sec. Tel.: 22-14-48.

Netherlands: American Chamber of Commerce in the Netherlands, Carnegieplein 5, The Hague, Tel.: 659808. Miss A. J. van der Graaf, General Manager.

New Zealand: American Chamber of Commerce in New Zealand, P.O. Box 3408, Wellington. Tel.: 727549. H. A. Purcell, Executive Manager.

Nicaragua: American Chamber of Commerce of Nicaragua, Apartado 2720, Managua, Nicaragua. Tel.: 8765 or 8796. Ing. Oscar Stradthagen, Executive Director.

Peru: American Chamber of Commerce of Peru, P.O. Box 2888, Lima 1. Tel.: 40-3425. President, Alan D. Rogers, General Manager, Bank of America. Manager, Edwin McCain.

Philippines: American Chamber of Commerce of the Philippines, Inc., 6th Floor, Security Bank Building, Ayala Avenue, Makati, Metro Manila. Mail Address: P.O. Box 1578 MCC, Makati, Metro Manila. Tel.: 86-51-15. Lt. Gen. Jesus M. Vargas AFP (Ret.), Executive Vice President.

Portugal: Portuguese-American Chamber of Commerce, Rua de D. Estefania, 155, 5°-E, Lisbon 1, Portugal.

El Salvador: American Chamber of Commerce of El Salvador, Apartado Postal (5) 9, San Salvador, El Salvador. Tel.: 23-9704/24-2056. Manager, Bill Chinchilla.

Singapore: American Business Council of Singapore, 9th Floor, Shaw House, Orchard Road, Singapore 9. Tel.: 2350077. John A. Siniscal, Honorary Secretary.

Spain: American Chamber of Commerce in Spain with following offices: Avda. Generalisimo Franco, 477, Barcelone-11. Tel.: 321 81 95/6, and Eurobuilding, Oficina 9A, Padre Damián 23 Madrid-14, Tel.: 458 65 20.

Switzerland: Swiss-American Chamber of Commerce, Talacker 41, 8001 Zurich. Tel.: 01/211 24 55. Executive Director, Walter H. Digglemann.

Thailand: The American Chamber of Commerce in Thailand, P.O. Box 11-1095, Bangkok. Tel.: 2519266/7, Jack Scott, Executive Director.

Uruguay: The Chamber of Commerce of the U.S.A. in Uruguay, P.O. Box 389, Montevideo. Tel.: 906052. John L. Micheloni, Manager.

Venezuela: Venezuelan-American Chamber of Commerce and Industry, Centro Plaza, Torre A, Nivel 15, Av. Francisco de Miranda, Los Palos Grandes, Apartado 5181, Caracas 101. Frank J. Amador, Executive Director.

Foreign Chambers of Commerce in the United States and Puerto Rico

African-American Chamber of Commerce, Inc., 65 Liberty St., New York 10005. Gilbert M. Weinstein, Executive Director. Tel.: (212) 766-1343.

Chamber of Commerce of the Americas, Tampa International Airport, Suite 309, Tampa, Fla. 33607. Tel.: (813) 870-2934. Charles F. McKay, President. Professor John M. Dyer, World Trade Committee Chairman.

U.S.-Arab Chamber of Commerce, One World Trade Center, Suite 4657, New York, N.Y. 10048. Tel.: (212) 432-0655, M. A. Baghal, Executive Director.

American-Arab Association for Commerce & Industry, Inc., 342 Madison Ave., Suite 1060, New York, N.Y. 10017. Tel.: (212) 986-7229. Executive Director: Robert G. Barnes; Director of Research: I. Yusif.

American-Arab Chamber of Commerce, 319 World Trade Bldg., Houston, Texas 77002. Tel.: (713) 222-6152. Dr. Atef Gamal-Eldin, President and Chief Executive Officer.

Mid America-Arab Chamber of Commerce, 135 South LaSalle St., Suite 2050, Chicago, Ill. 60603. Tel.: (312) 782-4654. Mr. Owais Succari, Director.

U.S.-Arab Chamber of Commerce (Pacific), Inc., 230 California St., Suite 201, San Francisco, Calif. 94111. Tel.: (415) 397-5663.

Argentine-American Chamber of Commerce, Inc., 11 Broadway, New York 10004. Tel.: (212) 943-8753. P. E. Sibilia, Secretary.

United States-Austrian Chamber of Commerce, Inc., 165 W. 46th St., New York 10036. Tel.: (212) 757-0117. Ernst A. Rott, Executive Secretary.

Belgian American Chamber of Commerce in the United States, Inc., 50 Rockefeller Plaza, Suite 1003-1005, New York, 10020. Tel.: (212) 247-7613. In Belgium: 117 Avenue des Nerviens, Boite 40, B-1040, Brussels. Tel.: (02) 733.93.08. Gustave E. Pairoux, Executive Secretary.

The Belgian American Chamber of Commerce, Midwest Chapter, 12900 S. Metron Drive, Chicago, Ill., 60633. Tel.: (312) 646-4000. Andrew A. Athens, Chairman.

Brazilian American Chamber of Commerce, Inc., 22 W. 48th St., New York, 10036. Tel.: (212) 575-9030, Mrs. S. Kincaid Barner, Executive Director.

The Brazilian-American Chamber of Commerce in New Orleans, International Trade Mart Bldg., New Orleans, La. 70103. James M. Farley, Secretary.

British-American Chamber of Commerce, 10 E. 40 St., New York 10016, Tel.: (212) 889-0680. David Farquharson, Executive Director.

British American Chamber of Commerce, 350 South Figueroa Street, Suite 562, Los Angeles, Calif. 90071. Tel.: (213) 622-7124. Evelyn M. Parson, Executive Secretary.

British-American Chamber of Commerce, 68 Post St., Suite 714, San Francisco, Calif. 94104. Frank Elton, Manager. Tel.: (415) 624-7493.

Central American Chamber of Commerce in the U.S., Inc., 65 Liberty St., New York 10005. Tel.: (212) 766-1348. Walter Vasquez, Secretary-Treasurer.

Chile-American Association, Inc., 220 E. 81st St., New York 10028. Tel.: (212) BU 8-5691. Executive Secretary, Lester Ziffren.

The Chamber of Commerce, Industries and Tourism of Chile and California, 303 World Trade Center, San Francisco, Calif. 94111. Tel.: (415) 986-5698. Founder-President, James P. Wilson.

The Chinese Chamber of Commerce of New York Inc., 180 Park Row, New York 10038, Tel.: (212) 962-2798. Chairman, Y. T. Huang.

Chinese Chamber of Commerce of San Francisco, 730 Sacramento St., San Francisco, Calif. 94108, Tel.: (415) 982-3000. Harry S. Y. Leong, Executive Secretary.

Colombian-American Association, Inc., 55 Liberty St., New York 10005. Tel.: (212) 233-7776. Paul E. Calvet, Secretary.

Ecuadorean American Association, Inc., 55 Liberty St., New York 10005. Tel.: (212) 233-7776. Paul E. Calvet, Secretary.

Finnish American Chamber of Commerce, Finland House, 540 Madison Ave., New York 10022. Tel.: (212) 832-2588. Jukka Vihersaari, Executive Secretary.

Finnish American Chamber of Commerce of the Midwest, One IBM Plaza, Suite 3205, Chicago, Ill. 60611. Tel.: (312) 467-6767. John Saari, President. Antti Wuorenjuuri, Executive Secretary.

Finnish-American Chamber of Commerce on the Pacific Coast., Inc., 3600 Wilshire Blvd., Suite 1720, Los Angeles, Calif. Tel.: (213) 385-1779.

French-American Chamber of Commerce in the United States, Inc., 1350 Ave. of the Americas, New York 10019. Tel.: (212) 581-4554. Bernard A. Friedrich, General Manager. Paris address: 7, rue Jean-Goujon, 75008 Paris, France. Michel Darde, Secretaire General des Services Français.

German American Chamber of Commerce, Inc., 666 Fifth Ave., New York, N.Y. 10019. Tel.: (212) 582-7788. Werner Walbrol, Executive Director.

German American Chamber of Commerce of Chicago, 77 E. Monroe St., Chicago, Ill. 60603. Tel.: (312) 782-8557. Niels G. Friedrichs, Managing Director.

German-American Chamber of Commerce, Two Houston Center, Suite 3418, Houston, Texas 77002. Tel.: (713) 658-8230. Kurt W. de Boer, Manager.

German American Chamber of Commerce of Los Angeles, 3250 Wilshire Blvd., Los Angeles, 90010. Tel.: (213) 381-2236. Peter M. Weyrauch, Acting Managing Director.

German-American Chamber of Commerce of the Pacific Coast, 465 California St., San Francisco, Calif. 94104. Tel.: (415) 392-2262. Adm J. Heidenreich, Managing Director.

American Chamber of Commerce in Germany, 517 Meridian St., Falls Church, Va. 22046. E. F. Becker, Washington Representative.

Hellenic-American Chamber of Commerce, 25 Broadway, New York 10004. Tel.: (212) WH 3-8594.

India Chamber of Commerce of America, Inc. (As of press date, the organization is being reorganized.)

American Indonesian Chamber of Commerce, Inc., 120 Wall St., New York, 10005. Tel.: (212) 344-1808. Ladd I. Johnson, Secretary.

Iran American Chamber of Commerce, Inc., 555 Fifth Ave., Suite 500, New York 10017. Tel.: (212) 986-9560. Executive Director.

Ireland-United States Council for Commerce and Industry, 460 Park Ave., New York 10022. Tel.: (212) 751-2660.

American-Israel Chamber of Commerce & Industry, Inc., 500 Fifth Ave., New York 10036. Dr. Philip Opher, Executive Vice President. Tel.: (212) 354-6510.

American-Isreal Chamber of Commerce & Industry, Inc., Midwest, 180 N. Michigan Ave., Chicago, Ill. 60601. Roberta Lipman, Executive Director. Tel.: (312) 641-2937.

American-Israel Chamber of Commerce & Industry, Inc., Cleveland Chapter, 10800 Brookpark Road c/o Foreign City Enterprises Inc., Cleveland Ohio 44130. Tel.: (216) 267-1200. Mr. Max Ratner.

American-Israel Chamber of Commerce and Industry, Inc., The Executive Club Bldg., Suite 601, 1776 South Jackson, Denver, Colorado 80210.

American-Israel Chamber of Commerce & Industry, Philadelphia Chapter, c/o Jack Hirsch, President, 5th Floor, 1500 Walnut St., Philadelphia, Pa. 19107. Tel.: (215) 545-4100.

American-Israel Chamber of Commerce & Industry, Pittsburgh Chapter, c/o Vanguard Sunglasses Inc., 2417 Smallman St., Pittsburgh, Pa. 15222. Tel.: (412) 471-9730. Gerald Wilson.

California-Israel Chamber of Commerce, 6399 Wilshire Blvd., Suite 806, Los Angeles, 90048. Tel.: (213) 658-7910. Murray Codman, President. Martin A. Rose, Executive Director.

Florida-Israel Chamber of Commerce, 3950 Biscayne Blvd., Miami 33137. Tel.: (305) 576-4000. Executive Director, Milton M. Hecker.

San Diego-Israel Chamber of Commerce, 10760 Atrium Drive., San Diego, Calif. 92131. Tel.: (714) 235-6634.

Italy-America Chamber of Commerce, Inc., 350 Fifth Ave., New York 10001. Tel.: (212) 279-5520. Arthur A. DeSantis, Executive Secretary.

Italian Chamber of Commerce of Chicago, 327 S. LaSalle St., Chicago, Ill. 60604. Tel.: (312) HA 7-3014. Leonora LiPuma Turner, Executive Secretary.

Italian-American Chamber of Commerce of Western United States (formerly IACCPC), World Trade Center, San Francisco, Calif. 94111. Tel.: (415) 392-3387. Telex: 67649 Italtrade. Dr. Sergio Masocco, President.

Japanese Chamber of Commerce of New York, Inc., 39 Broadway, New York 10006. Tel.: (212) 425-2513. H. Okada, Executive Director.

Japanese Chamber of Commerce & Industry of Chicago, 230 N. Michigan Ave., Chicago, Ill. 60601. Tel.: (312) 332-6199. Michihiro Matsumoto, General Manager.

Japanese Chamber of Commerce of Northern California, World Trade Center, Ferry Building, San Francisco, Calif. 94111. Tel.: (415) 986-6140. Ms. Kinuko Kobayashi, Managing Secretary.

Japanese Chamber of Commerce of Southern California, 355 East First Street, Los Angeles, Calif. 90012. Tel.: (213) 626-5116, Edward M. Matsuda, President; Tsunemi "Hank" Nakamura, Executive Secretary.

U.S.-Korea Economic Council, Inc., Suite 2-L, 88 Morningside Drive, New York 10027. Tel.: (212) 749-4200. Dr. William Henderson, Executive Director.

Korean-American Midwest Association of Commerce and Industry (KAMACI), c/o Swift Agricultural Chemicals Corp., 111 W. Jackson Blvd., Chicago, Ill. 60604. Tel.: (312) 431-2533. Edward R. Urablik, President.

Chamber of Commerce of Latin America in the United States, Inc., One World Trade Center, Suite 3549, New York, 10048. Tel.: (212) 432-9313. Executive Secretary, Hernando Ramirez.

United States Lebanese Chamber of Commerce, Inc., Five World Trade Center, New York, 10048. Admiral John M. Will, President, George G. Shiya, Director-Counsel. Tel.: (212) 432-1133.

Association of Asian-American Chambers of Commerce, P.O. Box 2801, Washington, D.C. 20013. Tel.: (202) 638-5593. Co-Executive Director, Bernard B. Blazes; Co-Director, K. Nakatsukasa.

Mexican Chamber of Commerce of the U.S., Inc., Five World Trade Center, Suite 6343, New York 10048. Tel.: (212) 432-9332. Louis D. Balseiro, Executive Vice President.

Mexican American Chamber of Commerce and Industry of Chicago, One South Wacker Drive, Suite 400, Chicago, Ill. 60606. Tel.: (312) 236-1082. Jose Carlos Gomez, President.

Mexican Chamber of Commerce of Los Angeles, 125 Paseo de la Plaza, Los Angeles, Calif. 90012. Tel.: (213) 688-7330. Ben Conant, President.

United States-Mexico Chamber of Commerce, 1800 "K" St., N.W., Suite 410, Washington, D.C. 20006. Tel.: (202) 296-5198. Mr. J. James Kuhn, Executive Vice President.

The Netherlands Chamber of Commerce in the U.S., Inc., One Rockefeller Plaza, New York 10020. Tel.: (212) 265-6460. J. Martin Bakels, Executive Secretary.

Nigerian American Chamber of Commerce, 65 Liberty St., New York 10005. Gilbert Weinstein, Executive Secretary. Tel.: (212) 766-1343.

Norwegian American Chamber of Commerce, Inc., 800 Third Ave., New York 10022. Tel.: (212) 421-9210. Bjorn Kvisgaard, Chief Executive.

Norwegian American Chamber of Commerce, Inc., Midwest-Chicago Chapter, 360 N. Michigan Ave., Chicago, Ill. 60601. Tel.: (312) 782-7751. Mr. Per Melhoos, Director.

Norwegian American Chamber of Commerce, 800 Foshay Tower, Minneapolis, Minn. 55402. Tel.: (612) 336-3338.

Norwegian American Chamber of Commerce Inc., World Trade Center, 350 S. Figueroa St., Suite 360, Los Angeles, Calif. 90071. Tel.: (213) 626-0338. Knut-Ivar Halvorsen, Secretary-Treasurer.

Norwegian American Chamber of Commerce, One Embarcadero Center, Suite 2609, San Francisco, Calif. 94111. Tel.: (415) 986-0766/7/8. T. Norendal, Vice-Consul.

Norwegian American Chamber of Commerce, 1120-4th Ave., Seattle, Washington 98101. Tel.: (206) 682-5250. Einar Sivertsen, President.

Pakistani-American Chamber of Commerce, Inc., c/o R. L. Britchard & Co. Inc., 21 Vernon St., Floral Park, New York 11002. Tel.: (516) 488-4100, Mr. Robert M. Baisley, President.

Peruvian-American Association, Inc., 11 Broadway, New York 10004. Tel.: (212) 943-8753. P. E. Sibilia, Secretary.

Philippine American Chamber of Commerce, Inc., 565 Fifth Ave., New York, N.Y. 10017. Tel.: (212) 972-9326. Miss Lucie Toehl, Executive Director and Secretary.

Puerto Rico Chamber of Commerce in the U.S. Inc., 65 Liberty St., New York, N.Y. 10005. Tel.: (212) 766-1348. Walter Vasquez, Executive Director.

Spain-U.S. Chamber of Commerce, Inc., 500 Fifth Ave., New York, N.Y. 10036. Tel.: (212) 354-7848/9. Mariano Baguena, Executive Director.

Spain-U.S. Chamber of Commerce of the Middle West, 180 N. Michigan Ave., Chicago, Ill. 60601. Tel.: (312) 782-7663. Executive Secretary, Joaquin R. Mata.

Spain-U.S. Chamber of Commerce of the Pacific Coast, Inc., World Trade Center, 350 S. Figueroa St., Suite 944, Los Angeles, Calif. 90071. Tel.: (213) 489-4459.

Cámara Oficial Española de Comercio en Puerto Rico, Comercio 452-2 San Juan, P.R. 00902. (Mail Address: Apartado 894, San Juan, P.R. 00902.) Tel.: (809) 725-5178. President, Francisco Pérez, Jr.

Swedish-American Chamber of Commerce, Inc., 1 Dag Hammarskjold Plaza, New York, 10017. Tel.: (212) 838-5530. Tomas Ericson, President.

Swedish American Chamber of Commerce of the Western United States, Inc., World Trade Center, San Francisco, Calif. 94111. Tel.: (415) 781-4188. Lars Lewendal, Managing Director.

Trinidad and Tobago Chamber of Commerce of the United States of America, Inc., 400 Madison Ave., New York 10017. Tel.: (212) PL 5-9360. Ted M. Levine, Secretary. Clyde S. Namsoo, President.

The Venezuelan American Association of the U.S., Inc., 55 Liberty St., New York 10005. Tel.: (212) 233-7776. Paul E. Calvet, Secretary.

Foreign Trade Departments and/or Bureaus in Chambers of Commerce throughout the United States

The Chambers of Commerce in the following list maintain foreign trade bureaus or render a specific foreign trade service(s). The department (and official within the department) having direction of international trade affairs (when known) is indicated.

Revised with the assistance of the Chamber of Commerce of the U.S.

Alabama:—Birmingham Area Chamber of Commerce, 1914 6th Avenue, North, Birmingham, Alabama 35203. Contact:—Trade Development Division Director, Tel: (205) 323-5461. Mobile Area Chamber of Commerce, P.O. Box 2187, Mobile, Alabama 36601. Contact:—Trade Development Manager. Tel: (205) 433-6951. Alabama State Chamber of Commerce, P.O. Box 76, Montgomery, Alabama 36101. Contact:—Agricultural & Industrial Divisions Director. Tel: (205) 834-6000. Selma and Dallas County Chamber of Commerce, P.O. Drawer D. Selma, Alabama 36701. Contact:—Manager. Tel. (205) 875-7241.

Alaska:—Greater Juneau Chamber of Commerce, 200 N. Franklin Street, Juneau, Alaska 99801. Contact:—Executive Vice President. Tel: (907) 586-2201.

Arizona:—Nogales-Santa Cruz County Chamber of Commerce, P.O. Box 578, Nogales, Arizona 85621. Contact:—Manager, Tel: (602) 287-3685. Phoenix Metropolitan Chamber of Commerce, P.O. Box 1, Phoenix, Arizona 85001. Contact:—Industrial Development Department Manager. Tel.: (602) 254-5521.

Arkansas:—Fort Smith Chamber of Commerce, 613 Garrison Avenue, Forth Smith, Arkansas 72901. Contact:—Manager. Tel: (501) 783-6118. Little Rock Chamber of Commerce, Continental Building, Little Rock, Arkansas 72201. Contact:—Transportation Department Director. Tel: (501) 374-4871.

California:—Greater Bakersfield Chamber of Commerce, P.O. Box 1947, Bakersfield, California 93303. Contact:—General Manager. Tel: (805) 327-4421. Culver City Chamber of Commerce, P.O. Box 707, Culver City, California 90230. Contact:—Executive Vice President. Tel: (213) 838-3139. Gardena Valley Chamber of Commerce, 1320 W. Gardena Blvd., Gardena, Calif. 90247. Contact:—Manager. Tel: (213) 323-1103. Hayward Chamber of Commerce, 22300 Foothill Blvd., Suite 303, Hayward, California 94541. Contact:—General Manager. Tel: (415) 536-2424. Huntington Beach Chamber of Commerce, 18582 Beach Blvd., Huntington Beach, California 92648. Contact:—Executive Manager. Tel.: (714) 962-6661. Long Beach Area Chamber of Commerce, 121 Linden Avenue, Long Beach, California 90802. Contact:—Executive Vice President. Tel: (213) 436-1251. Los Angeles Area Chamber of Commerce, P.O. Box 3696, Los Angeles, California 90051. Contact:—World Trade and Maritime Department Manager. Tel: (213) 482-4010. Oakland Chamber of Commerce, 1320 Webster Street, Oakland, California 94612. Contact:—Business and Government Relations Division Manager. Tel: (415) 451-7800. Orange County Chamber of Commerce, 401 Bank of America Tower—Suite 401, One City Blvd., W., Orange, California 92668. Contact:—Foreign Trade Legislation Subcommittee Chairman. Tel: (714) 639-6460. Pomona Chamber of Commerce, P.O. Box 941, Pomona, California 91766. Contact:—Executive Vice President. Tel: (714) 622-1256. California Chamber of Commerce, P.O. Box 1736, Sacramento, California 95808. Contact:—Economic Stabilization Group Director. Tel: (916) 444-6670. Sacramento Metropolitan Chamber of Commerce, P.O. Box 1017, Sacramento, California 95805. Contact:—International Trade Committee Manager. Tel: (916) 443-3771. San Diego Chamber of Commerce, 233 A Street, Suite 300, San Diego, California 92101. Contact:—International Trade Department Manager. Tel: (714) 232-0124. San Fernando Chamber of Commerce, 502 S. Brand Blvd., San Fernando, California 91340. Contact:—Executive Manager. Tel: (213) 361-1184. San Francisco Chamber of Commerce, 465 California Street, San Francisco, California 94104. Contact:—International Department Director. Tel: (415) 392-4511, Ext. 33. Torrance Area Chamber of Commerce, 1510 Cravens Avenue, Torrance, California 90501. Contact:—Executive Vice President. Tel: (213) 328-2814. Van Nuys Chamber of Commerce, 6728 Van Nuys Blvd., Van Nuys, California 91407. Tel: (213) 785-6571.

Colorado:—Boulder Chamber of Commerce, P.O. Box 73, Boulder, Colorado 80301. Contact:—Manager. Tel:(303) 442-1044. Denver Chamber of Commerce, 1301 Welton Street, Denver, Colorado 80204. Contact:—Staff Project Manager. Tel: (303) 534-3211. Longmont Chamber of Commerce, P.O. Box 667, Longmont,

Colorado 80501. Contact:—Executive Vice President. Tel: (303) 776-5295. Rocky Ford Chamber of Commerce, P. O. Box 232, Rocky Ford, Colorado 81067. Contact:—Executive Director. Tel: (303) 254-7483.

Connecticut:—Bridgeport Area Chamber of Commerce, Chapel Street, Bridgeport, Connecticut 06604. Contact:—Executive Vice President. Tel: (203) 335-3145. Danbury Chamber of Commerce, 20 West Street, Danbury Connecticut 06810. Contact:—President. Tel: (203) 743-5565. Greater Meriden Chamber of Commerce, 17 Church Street, Meriden, Connecticut 06450. Contact:—Executive Vice President. Tel: (203) 235-7901. New Britain Chamber of Commerce, Central Park Plaza, 127 Main Street, New Britain, Connecticut 06051. Contact:—Executive Vice President. Tel: (203) 229-1665. Greater New Haven Chamber of Commerce, 152 Temple Street, New Haven, Connecticut 06510. Contact:—Research and Development Manager. Tel: (203) 787-6735.

Delaware:—Delaware State Chamber of Commerce, Inc., 1102 West Street, Wilmington, Delaware 19801. Contact:—Transportation and World Trade Director. Tel: (302) 665-7221.

Florida:—Manatee Chamber of Commerce, Inc., P.O. Box 321, Bradenton, Florida 33506. Contact:—Executive Vice President. Tel: (813) 744-3411. Greater Fort Lauderdale Chamber of Commerce, P.O. Box 14516, Fort Lauderdale, Florida 33302. Contact:—President. Tel: (305) 522-4721. Greater Hollywood Chamber of Commerce, P.O. Box 2345, Hollywood, Florida 33022. Contact:—President. Tel: (305) 920-3330. Jacksonville Area Chamber of Commerce, P.O. Drawer 329, Jacksonville, Florida 32201. Contact:—Economic Development Director. Tel: (904) 353-6161. Orlando Area Chamber of Commerce, P.O. Box 1913, Orlando, Florida 32804. Contact:—Economic Development Department Manager. Tel: (305) 425-5563. Pensacola Area Chamber of Commerce, P.O. Box 889, Pensacola, Florida 32593. Contact:—Port Manager. Tel: (904) 438-8537. Florida Chamber of Commerce, P.O. Box 5497, Tallahassee, Florida 32301. Contact:—General Manager. Tel: (904) 222-2831. Greater Tampa Chamber of Commerce, P.O. Box 420, Tampa, Florida 33601. Contact:—Tampa World Trade Council Executive Director. Tel: (813) 228-7777.

Georgia:—Atlanta Chamber of Commerce, P.O. Box 1740, Atlanta, Georgia 30301. Contact:—International Director. Tel: (404) 521-0845. Georgia Chamber of Commerce, 1200 Commerce Building, Atlanta, Georgia 30303. Contact:—International Council Manager. Tel: (404) 524-8481. Gordon County Chamber of Commerce, P.O. Box 344, Calhoun, Georgia 30701. Contact:—Executive Vice President. Tel: (404) 629-6912. DeKalb Chamber of Commerce, 515 Decatur Federal Building, Decatur, Georgia 30030. Contact:—Executive Vice President. Tel: (404) 378-3691. Douglas Coffee County Chamber of Commerce, P.O. Box 112, Douglas, Georgia 31533. Contact:—Executive Director. Tel: (912) 384-1873. Savannah Area Chamber of Commerce, P.O. Box 530, Savannah, Georgia 31402. Contact:—Executive Vice President. Tel: (912) 233-3067. Emanuel County Chamber of Commerce, 124 N. Main Street, Swainsboro, Georgia 30401. Contact:—Executive Secretary. Tel: (912) 237-6426.

Hawaii:—Chamber of Commerce of Hawaii, Dillingham Transportation Building, Honolulu, Hawaii 96813. Contact:—President. Tel: (808) 533-7491.

Idaho:—Greater Boise Chamber of Commerce, P.O. Box 2368, Boise, Idaho 83701. Contact:—Executive Vice President. Tel: (208) 344-5515.

Illinois:—Chicago Association of Commerce and Industry, 130 South Michigan Avenue, Chicago, Illinois 60603. Contact:—World Trade Division Director. Tel: (312) 786-0111. Chicago South Chamber of Commerce, 11145 S. Michigan Avenue, Chicago, Illinois 60628. Contact:—President. Tel: (312) 928-3200. Evanston Chamber of Commerce, 807 Davis Street, Evanston, Illinois 60201. Contact:—Executive Vice President. Tel: (312) 328-1500. Moline Chamber of Commerce, 622 19th Street, Moline, Illinois 61265. Contact:—Executive Vice President. Tel: (309) 762-3661. Ottawa Chamber of Commerce, P.O. Box 787, Ottawa, Illinois 61350. Contact:—Executive Vice President. Tel: (815) 433-0084. Rockford Area Chamber of Commerce, 815 East State Street, Rockford, Illinois 61101. Contact:—Industrial and Economic Affairs Manager. Tel: (815) 968-5855. Skokie Chamber of Commerce, 8322 Lincoln Avenue, Skokie, Illinois 60076. Contact:—Manager. Tel: (312) 673-0240.

Indiana:—Anderson Chamber of Commerce, P.O. Box 469, Anderson, Indiana 46015. Contact:—Executive Vice President. Tel: (317) 642-0264. Columbus Area Chamber of Commerce, P.O. Box 29, Columbus, Indiana 47201. Contact:—Executive Vice President. Tel: (812) 379-9579. Elkhart Chamber of Commerce, P.O. Box 428. Elkhart, Indiana 46514. Contact:—Executive Vice President. Tel: (219) 293-1531. Metropolitan Evansville Chamber of Commerce, 329 Main Street, Evansville, Indiana 47708. Contact:—Transportation and Environmental Management Division Director. Tel: (812) 425-8147. Greater Fort Wayne Chamber of Commerce, 826 Ewing Street, Fort Wayne, Indiana 46802. Contact:—Executive Vice President. Tel: (219) 742-0135. Indianapolis Chamber of Commerce, 320 N. Meridian Street, Indianapolis, Indiana 46204. Contact:—World Trade and Economic Research Director. Tel: (317) 635-4747. Kokomo Chamber of Commerce, P.O. Box 731, Kokomo, Indiana 46901. Contact:—Executive Vice President. Tel: (317) 457-5301. Greater Lafayette Chamber of Commerce, P.O. Box 348, Lafayette, Indiana 47901. Contact:—Executive Vice President. Tel: (317) 742-4041. Logansport Area Chamber of Commerce, 109 Fifth Street, Logansport, Indiana 46947. Contact:—Executive Vice President. Tel: (219) 753-6388. Marion Area Chamber of Commerce, 325 S. Adams Street, Marion, Indiana 46952. Contact:—Executive Vice President. Tel: (317) 664-5107. New Castle Chamber of Commerce, P.O. Box 485, New Castle, Indiana 47362. Contact:—Manager. Tel: (317) 529-5210.

Iowa:—Boone Chamber of Commerce, 811 Keeler Street, Boone, Iowa 50036. Contact:—Manager. Tel: (515) 432-3342. Cedar Falls Chamber of Commerce, P.O. Box 367, Cedar Falls, Iowa 50613. Contact:—Foreign Trade Committee Chairman. Tel: (319) 266-3593. Cedar Rapids Chamber of Commerce, 127 3rd Street, N.E., Cedar Rapids, Iowa 52401. Contact:—International Trade Bureau Manager. Tel: (319) 364-5135. Greater Des Moines Chamber of Commerce, 800 High Street, Des Moines, Iowa 50307. Contact:—World Trade Department Manager. Tel: (515) 283-2161. Fort Dodge Chamber of Commerce, P.O. Box T, Fort Dodge, Iowa 50501. Contact:—Executive Vice President. Tel: (515) 576-2108. Fort Madison Chamber of Commerce, P.O. Box 277, Fort Madison, Iowa 52627. Contact:—Manager. Tel: (319) 372-5471. Waterloo Chamber of Commerce, P.O. Box 749, Waterloo, Iowa 50704. Contact:—Business Development Manager. Tel: (319) 233-8431.

Kansas:—Kansas City Chamber of Commerce, P.O. Box 1310, Kansas City, Kansas 66117. Contact:—Economic Research Manager. Tel: (913) 371-3070. Liberal Chamber of Commerce, P.O. Box 676, Liberal Kansas 67901. Contact:—Executive Vice President. Tel: (316) 624-3855. Wichita Area Chamber of Commerce, 350 W. Douglas Avenue, Wichita, Kansas 67202. Contact:—Industrial Development Assistant Manager. Tel: (316) 265-7771.

Kentucky:—Ashland Chamber of Commerce, Henry Clay Hotel Building, Ashland, Kentucky 41101. Contact:—Executive Secretary. Tel: (606) 324-5111. Louisville Area Chamber of Commerce, 300 W. Liberty Street, Louisville, Kentucky 40202. Contact:—Urban Affairs Department Manager. Tel: (502) 582-2421.

Louisiana:—Jeanerette Chamber of Commerce, 1522 W. Main Street, Jeanerette, Louisiana 70544. Contact:—Manager. Tel: (318) 276-4293. Greater Lafayette Chamber of Commerce, P.O. Box 51352 OCS, Lafayette, Louisiana 70501. Contact:—Executive Vice President. Tel: 233-2705. Lake Charles Chamber of Commerce, P.O. Box 3109, Lake Charles, Louisiana 70601. Contact:—Executive Vice President. Tel: (318) 433-3632. Chamber of Commerce of New Orleans Area, P.O. Box 30240, New Orleans, Louisiana 70190. Contact:—International Business Development/Economic Development Manger. Tel: (504) 524-1131.

Maine:—Biddeford-Saco Chamber of Commerce, P.O. Box 305, Biddeford, Maine 04005. Contact:—Executive Vice President. Tel: (207) 282-1513. Concord Chamber of Commerce, 1/2 Main Street, Concord, Maine 01742. Contact:—Executive Director. Tel: (617) 369-3120. Maine State Chamber of Commerce, 477 Congress Street, Portland, Maine 04111. Contact:—Executive Vice President. Tel: (207) 774-9871.

Maryland:—Maryland State Chamber of Commerce, 22 Light Street, Baltimore, Maryland 21202. Contact:—Legislative Services Manager. Tel: (301) 539-7600. Chamber of Commerce of Metropolitan Baltimore, 22 Light Street, Baltimore, Maryland 21202. Contact:—Economic Development Manger. Tel: (301) 539-7600. Hagerstown Area Chamber of Commerce, 92 W. Washington Street, Hagerstown, Maryland 21740. Contact:—Executive Vice President. Tel: (301) 739-2105. Salisbury Area Chamber of Commerce, P.O. Box 510, Salisbury, Maryland 21801. Contact:—Executive Director. Tel: (301) 749-0144.

Massachusetts:—Massachusetts State Chamber of Commerce, Inc., 10 Post Office Square, Suite 1230, Boston, Massachusetts 02109. Contact:—President. Tel: (617) 482-4615. Greater Fall River Area Chamber of Commerce, P.O. Box 1871, Fall River, Massachusetts 02772. Contact:—Executive Manager. Tel: (617) 676-8226. South Middlesex Area Chamber of Commerce, 109 Concord Street, Framingham, Massachusetts 01701. Contact:—Executive Vice President. Tel: (617) 879-5600. Greater Gardner Chamber of Commerce, 301 Central Street, Gardner, Massachusetts 01440. Contact:—Vice President. Tel: (617) 632-1780. Nantucket Chamber of Commerce, Pacific Club Building, Nantucket, Massachusetts 02554. Contact:—President. Tel: (617) 228-1700. New Bedford Area Chamber of Commerce, P.O. Box G-827, New Bedford, Massachusetts 02742. Contact:—Executive Vice President. Tel: (617) 999-5231. Greater Northampton Chamber of Commerce, 115 Main Street, Northampton, Massachusetts 01060. Contact:—Executive Director. Tel: (413) 584-1934. Greater Springfield Chamber of Commerce, Baystate West Plaza, Suite 600, Springfield, Massachusetts 01115. Contact:—Executive Vice Presi-

258

dent. Tel: (413) 734-5671. Waltham West Surburban Chamber of Commerce, 663 Main Street, Waltham, Massachusetts 02154. Contact:—Executive Vice President. Tel: (617) 894-4700. Worcester Area Chamber of Commerce, 100 Front Street, Suite 350, Worcester, Massachusetts 01608. Contact:—Industry Services Manager. Tel: (617) 753-2924.

Michigan:—Belleville Area Chamber of Commerce, 116 Fourth Street, Belleville, Michigan 48111. Contact:—Executive Secretary. Tel: (313) 697-7151. Greater Detroit Chamber of Commerce, 150 Michigan Avenue, Detroit, Michigan 48226. Contact:—World Trade and Port Development Departments General Manager. Tel: (313) 964-4000. Michigan State Chamber of Commerce, 501 S. Capitol Avenue, Lansing, Michigan 48933. Contact:—President. Tel: (517) 371-2100. Greater Mount Clemens Chamber of Commerce, 31½ N. Walnut St., Mount Clemens, Michigan 48043. Contact:—Manager. Tel: (313) 463-1528. Greater Port Huron-Marysville Chamber of Commerce, 920 Pine Grove Avenue, Port Huron, Michigan 48060. Contact:—Executive Director. (Tel: (313) 985-7101.

Minnesota:—Duluth Area Chamber of Commerce, 220 Medical Arts Building, Duluth, Minnesota 55802. Contact:—Executive Vice President. Tel: (218) 722-5501. Greater Minneapolis Chamber of Commerce, 15 S. Fifth Street, Minneapolis, Minnesota 55402. Contact:—World Trade Program Manager. Tel: (612) 339-8521. St. Paul Area Chamber of Commerce, Osborn Building, Suite 300, St. Paul, Minnesota 55102. Contact:—Economic Action Group. Tel: (612) 222-5561. St. Peter Chamber of Commerce, 214 Grace Street, St. Peter, Minnesota 56082. Contact:—Manager. Tel: (507) 931-3400.

Mississippi:—Gulfport Area Chamber of Commerce, P.O. Drawer FF, Gulfport, Mississippi 39501. Contact:—Manager. Tel: (610) 863-2933. Jackson Chamber of Commerce, P.O. Box 22548, Jackson, Mississippi 39205. Contact:—Res. Manager. Tel: (601) 948-7575.

Missouri:—Missouri State Chamber of Commerce, P.O. Box 149, Jefferson City, Missouri 65101. Contact:—Executive Vice President. Tel: (314) 634-3511. Chamber of Commerce of Greater Kansas City, 600 TenMain Street, Kansas City, Missouri 64105. Contact:—International Department Mangager. Tel: (816) 221-2424. St. Louis Regional Commerce and Growth Association, 10 Broadway, St. Louis, Missouri 63102. Contact:—World Trade Department. Tel: (314) 231-5555.

Montana:—Montana Chamber of Commerce, Box 1730, Helena, Montana 59601. Contact:—Director. Tel: (406) 442-2405.

Nebraska:—Beatrice Chamber of Commerce, P.O. Box 703, Beatrice, Nebraska 68310. Contact:—Executive Vice President. Tel: (402) 223-2338. Crete Chamber of Commerce, P.O. Box 426, Crete, Nebraska 68338. Contact:—Manager. Tel: (402) 826-3100. Lincoln Chamber of Commerce, 1221 N. Street, Lincoln, Nebraska 68508. Contact:—Transportation Department Manager. Tel: (402) 432-7511. Greater Omaha Chamber of Commerce, 1620 Dodge Street, Omaha, Nebraska 68102. Contact:—Economic Development Council Executive Director. Tel: (402) 341-1234.

Nevada:—Nevada State Chamber of Commerce, 152 Water Street, Henderson, Nevada 89015. Contact:—Executive Director. Tel: (702) 565-8951. Greater Las Vegas Chamber of Commerce, 3201 E. Sahara Avenue, Las Vegas, Nevada 89105. Contact:—Executive Vice President. Tel: (702) 457-4664. Greater Reno Chamber of Commerce, P.O. Box 3499. Reno, Nevada. Contact:—General Manager. Tel: (702) 786-3030.

New Hampshire:—Greater Nashua Chamber of Commerce, One Main Street, Nashua, New Hampshire 03060. Contact:—Executive Vice President. Tel: (603) 882-8106.

New Jersey:—Atlantic City Chamber of Commerce, 10 Central Pier, Atlantic City, New Jersey 08401. Contact:—Executive Director. Tel: (609) 345-2251. Eastern Union County Chamber of Commerce, P.O. Box 300, Elizabeth, New Jersey 07207. Contact:—International Affairs Committee/Port of Economic Development Department Manager. Tel: (201) 352-0900. Hoboken Chamber of Commerce, 20 Hudson Place, Hoboken, New Jersey 07030. Contact:—Executive Vice President. Tel: (201) 659-0500. Jersey City Chamber of Commerce, 911 Bergen Avenue, Jersey City, New Jersey 07306. Contact:—Executive Vice President. Tel: (201) 653-7400. Morris County Chamber of Commerce, P.O. Box 122M, Morristown, New Jersey 07960. Contact:—Executive Vice President. Tel: (201) 539-3882. New Jersey State Chamber of Commerce, 54 Park Place, Newark, New Jersey 07102. Contact:—Secretary. Tel: (201) 623-7070. Passaic Area Chamber of Commerce, 625 Main Avenue, Passaic, New Jersey 07055. Contact:—Executive Vice President. Tel: (201) 777-0700. Greater Paterson Chamber of Commerce, 253 Main Street, Paterson, New Jersey 07505. Contact:—Executive Vice President. Tel: (201) 881-7300. South Jersey Chamber of Commerce, North Park Drive, Pennsauken, New Jersey 08109. Contact:—Planning and Research Director. Tel: (609) 964-3400. Plainfield Central Jersey Chamber of Commerce, 119 Watchung Avenue, Plainfield, New Jersey 07060. Contact:—President. Tel: (201) 754-7250. Vineland Chamber of Commerce, P.O. Box 489, Vineland, New Jersey 08360. Contact:—Executive Vice President. Tel: (609) 691-7400. Woodbridge Area Chamber of Commerce, 655 Amboy Avenue, Woodbridge, New Jersey 07095. Contact:—Executive Vice President. Tel: (201) 636-4040.

New Mexico:—Greater Albuquerque Chamber of Commerce, 401 Second Street, N.W., Albuquerque, New Mexico 87102. Contact:—Trade Expansion Program Project Director. Tel: (505) 842-0220.

New York:—Albany Area Chamber of Commerce, 510 Broadway, Albany, New York 12207. Contact:—World Trade Council Chairman. Tel: (518) 434-1214. Capital District Chamber of Commerce, 3 Computer Drive, Albany, New York 12205. Contact:—Chief Executive Officer. Tel: (518) 458-1500. Broome County Chamber of Commerce, P.O. Box 995, Binghamton, New York 13902. Contact:— Industrial Development Department Manager. Tel: (607) 772-8860. Brooklyn Chamber of Commerce, 26 Court Street, Brooklyn, New York 11242. Contact:— Foreign Trade Secretary. Tel: (212) 875-1000. Buffalo Area Chamber of Commerce, 238 Main Street, Buffalo, New York 14202. Contact:—Transportation and World Trade Director. Tel: (716) 852-5400. St. Lawrence County Chamber of Commerce, P.O. Drawer A, Canton, New York 13617. Contact:—Executive Vice President. Tel: (315) 386-4000. Long Island Association of Commerce and Industry, 131 Jericho Turnpike, Jericho, L.I., New York 11753. Contact:—Executive Vice President. Tel: (516) 333-9300. Chamber of Commerce of the Borough of Queens, 24 16 Bridge Plaza South, Long Island City, New York 11101. Contact: —Executive Vice President. Tel: (212) 784-7700. Orange County Chamber of

Commerce, 26 North Street, Middletown, New York 10940. Contact:—Executive Vice President. Tel: (914) 342-2522. Mount Vernon Chamber of Commerce, 10 South Second Avenue, Mt. Vernon, New York 10550. Contact:—Executive Vice President. Tel: (914) 664-7500. New York Chamber of Commerce and Industry. 65 Liberty Street, New York, New York 10005. Contact:—Import-Export Department Director. Tel: (212) 766-1346. Niagra Falls Area Chamber of Commerce, 224 First Street, Niagara Falls, New York 14303. Contact:—Vice President. Tel: (716) 285-9141. Chamber of Commerce of Tonawandas, 84 Sweeny Street, North Tonawanda, New York 14120. Contact:—Executive Vice President. Tel: (716) 692-5120. Port Chester-Town of Rye Chamber of Commerce and Civic Association, 10 Pearl Street, Port Chester, New York 10573. Contact:—Executive Director. Tel: (914) 939-1900. Rochester Area Chamber of Commerce, Inc., 55 St. Paul Street, Rochester, New York 14604. Contact:—Department of Transportation and World Trade Manager. (716) 454-2220. Schenectady County Chamber of Commerce, 101 State Street, Schenectady, New York 12305. Contact:—Economic Development Director. Tel: (518) 372-5656. Syracuse Chamber of Commerce. 1700 One Mony Plaza, Syracuse, New York 13202. Contact:—Economic Development Director. Tel: (315) 422-1343. Greater Troy Chamber of Commerce, 28 Second Street, Troy, New York 12180. Contact:—Executive Vice President. Tel: (518) 274-7020. Westfield Chamber of Commerce, P.O. Box 25, Westfield, New York 14787. Contact:—Executive Secretary. Tel: (716) 326-3211.

North Carolina:—Asheboro Chamber of Commerce, P.O. Box 519, Asheboro, North Carolina 27203. Contact:—Executive Vice President. Tel: (919) 625-6121. Charlotte Chamber of Commerce, P.O. Box 1867, Charlotte, North Carolina 28233. Contact:—Economic Development Manager. Tel: (704) 377-6911. Greensboro Chamber of Commerce, P.O. Box 3246, Greensboro, North Carolina 27402. Contact:—Urban Action Group Manager. Tel: (919) 275-8675. High Point Chamber of Commerce, P.O. Box 5025, High Point, North Carolina 27262. Contact:—Executive Vice President. Tel: (919) 882-8151. Raleigh Chamber of Commerce, P.O. Box 2978, Raleigh, North Carolina 27602. Contact:—Economic Development Director. Tel: (919) 833-3005. Winston-Salem Chamber of Commerce, P.O. Box 1408, Winston-Salem, North Carolina 27102. Contact:—Economic Development Department Manager. Tel: (919) 725-2361.

North Dakota:—Greater North Dakota Association, Box 2467, Fargo, North Dakota 58102. Contact:—Agriculture Department Manager. Tel: (701) 237-9461.

Ohio:—Akron Regional Development Board, 137 S. Main Street, Room 210, Akron, Ohio 44308. Contact:—Executive Director. Tel: (216) 253-9181. Ashland Area Chamber of Commerce, 43 W. Main Street, Ashland, Ohio 44805. Contact:—General Manager. Tel: (419) 324-4584. Ashtabula Area Chamber of Commerce, P.O. Box 96, Ashtabula, Ohio 44004. Contact:—Executive Vice President. Tel: (216) 997-9756. Greater Canton Chamber of Commerce, 229 Wells Avenue, N.W. Canton, Ohio 44703. Contact:—Executive Vice President. Tel: (216) 456-7253. Greater Cincinnati Chamber of Commerce, 309 Vine Street, Cincinnati, Ohio 45202. Contact:—Membership Services Director. Tel: (513) 721-3300. Greater Cleveland Growth Association, 690 Union Commerce Building, Cleveland, Ohio 44115. Contact:—Executive Director. Tel: (216) 621-3300. Columbus Area Chamber of Commerce, P.O. Box 1527, Columbus, Ohio 43216. Contact:—Department of Economic Development Vice President. Tel: (614) 221-1321. Ohio

Chamber of Commerce, 17 S. High Street, 8th Floor, Columbus, Ohio 43215. Contact:—Industrial Development—Social Legislation Director. Tel: (614) 228-4201. Dayton Area Chamber of Commerce, 111 W. First St., Suite 200, Dayton, Ohio 45402. Contact:—World Trade Department Manager. Tel: (513) 226-1444. Defiance Area Chamber of Commerce, P.O. Box 130, Defiance, Ohio 43512. Contact:— Executive Manager. Tel: (419) 782-7946. East Liverpool Area Chamber of Commerce, P.O. Box 94, East Liverpool, Ohio 43920. Contact:—Executive Manager. Tel: (216) 385-0845. Lima Area Chamber of Commerce, 53 Public Square, Lima, Ohio 45801. Contact:—Executive Vice President. Tel: (419) 222-6045. Greater Lorain Chamber of Commerce, 204 5th Street, Lorain, Ohio 44052. Contact:— Executive Manager. Tel: (216) 244-2292. Middletown Area Chamber of Commerce, Manchester Inn Building, Middletown, Ohio 45042. Contact:—Secretary-Treasurer. Tel: (513) 422-4551. Toledo Chamber of Commerce, 218 Huron Street, Toledo, Ohio 43604. Contact:—Transportation and International Commerce Director. Tel: (419) 243-8191. Youngstown Area Chamber of Commerce, 200 Wick Building, Youngstown, Ohio 44503. Contact:—Executive Vice President. Tel: (216) 744-2131.

Oklahoma:—Oklahoma City Chamber of Commerce, One Santa Fe Plaza, Oklahoma City, Oklahoma 73102. Contact:—International Trade Development Manager. Tel: (415) 232-6381. Metropolitan Tulsa Chamber of Commerce, 616 South Boston Avenue, Tulsa, Oklahoma 74119. Contact:—Economic Development Division. Tel: (918) 585-1201.

Oregon:—Portland Chamber of Commerce, 824 S.W. 5th Avenue, Portland, Oregon 97204. Contact:—World Trade and Transportation Department Manager. Tel: (503) 228-9411.

Pennsylvania:—Allentown-Lehigh County Chamber of Commerce, 462 Walnut Street, Allentown, Pennsylvania 18105. Contact:—Staff Associate. Tel: (215) 437-9661. Bradford Area Chamber of Commerce, 15 Main Street, Bradford, Pennsylvania 16701. Contact:—Executive Vice President. Tel: (814) 368-7115. Butler Area Chamber of Commerce, P.O. Box 1082, Butler, Pennsylvania 16001. Contact: —Manager. Tel: (412) 285-3208. Coatesville Area Chamber of Commerce, P.O. Box 872, Coatesville, Pennsylvania 19320. Contact:—Secretary. Tel: (215) 384-9550. Greater Downingtown Area Chamber of Commerce, 15 E. Lancaster Avenue, Downingtown, Pennsylvania 19335. Contact:—Secretary. Tel: (215) 269-1523. Easton Area Chamber of Commerce, 157 South 4th Street, Easton, Pennsylvania 18042. Contact:—Executive Vice President. Tel: (215) 253-4211. Lower Bucks County Chamber of Commerce, 409 Hood Boulevard, Fairless Hills, Pennsylvania 19030. Contact:—Executive Vice President. Tel: (215) 943-7400. Hanover Area Chamber of Commerce, 146 Broadway, Hanover, Pennsylvania 17331. Contact:— Executive Vice President. Tel: (717) 637-6130. Steel Valley Chamber of Commerce, 805 Ann Street, Homestead, Pennsylvania 15120. Tel: (412) 461-4141. Huntingdon Business and Industry, Inc., 320½ Penn Street, Huntingdon, Pennsylvania 16652. Contact:—Executive Director. Tel: (814) 643-4322. Jenkintown Chamber of Commerce, P.O. Box 172, Jenkintown, Pennsylvania 19046. Contact: —Executive Director. Tel: (215) TU7-5122. Greater Philadelphia Chamber of Commerce, 1528 Walnut Street, 9th Floor, Philadelphia, Pennsylvania 19102. Contact:—Executive Vice President. Tel: (215) 732-7324. Northeast Philadelphia Chamber of Commerce, 8601 E. Roosevelt Blvd., Philadelphia, Pennsylvania

19152. Contact:—Executive Director. Tel: (215) 332-3400. Chamber of Commerce of Greater Pittsburgh, 411 7th Avenue, Pittsburgh, Pennsylvania 15219. Contact:—Community Development Manager. Tel: (412) 391-3400. Chamber of Commerce of Reading and Berks County, 541 Court Street, Reading, Pennsylvania 19601. Contact:—Executive Director. Tel: (215) 376-6766. Greater Scranton Chamber of Commerce, Chamber of Commerce Building, 426 Mulberty Street, Scranton, Pennsylvania 18503. Contact:—Industrial Development Manager. Tel: (717) 342-7711. State College Area Chamber of Commerce, 129 West Beaver Avenue, State College, Pennsylvania 16801. Contact:—Executive Director. Tel: (814) 237-7644. Uniontown Area Chamber of Commerce, P.O. Box 2124, Downtown Station, Uniontown, Pennsylvania 15401. Contact:—Executive Vice President. Tel: (412) 437-4571. Warren County Chamber of Commerce, P.O. Box 942. Warren, Pennsylvania 16365. Contact:—Executive Vice President. Tel: (814) 723-3050. Greater Washington Area Chamber of Commerce, The George Washington, Washington, Pennsylvania 15301. Contact:—Executive Director. Tel: (412) 225-3010.

Rhode Island:—Greater Providence Chamber of Commerce, Howard Bldg., Box 1, Providence, Rhode Island 02903. Contact:—Economic Development Vice President. Tel: (401) 521-5000.

South Carolina:—Bamberg Area Chamber of Commerce, P.O. Box 907, Bamberg, South Carolina 29003. Tel: (803) 245-4427. Greater Greenville Chamber of Commerce, P.O. Box 10048, Greenville, South Carolina 29603. Contact:—Economic Development Manager. Tel: (803) 242-1050. Spartanburg Chamber of Commerce, P.O. Box 1636, Spartanburg, South Carolina 29301. Contact:—Executive Vice President. Tel: (803) 585-8722.

South Dakota:—Sioux Falls Chamber of Commerce, P.O. Box 1425, Sioux Falls, South Dakota. Contact:—Assistant Manager. Tel: (605) 336-1620.

Tennessee:—Cleveland/Bradley Chamber of Commerce, P.O. Box 1018, Cleveland, Tennessee 37311. Contact:—Executive Vice President. Tel: (615) 472-6587. Greater Knoxville Chamber of Commerce, 705 Gay Street, Knoxville, Tennessee 37902. Contact:—Community Development Director. Tel: (615) 522-6111. Memphis Area Chamber of Commerce, P.O. Box 224, Memphis, Tennessee 38101. Contact:—Business and Industrial Services Department Associate Manager. Tel: (901) 523-2322. Nashville Area Chamber of Commerce, 161 Fourth Avenue, N., Nashville, Tennessee 37219. Contact:—International Affairs Director. Tel: (615) 259-3900.

Texas:—Abilene Chamber of Commerce, P.O. Box 2281, Abilene, Texas 79604. Contact:—Foreign Trade Manager. Tel: (915) 677-7241. West Texas Chamber of Commerce, P.O. Box 1561, Abilene, Texas 79604. Contact:—Executive Vice President. Tel: (915) 677-4325. Beaumont Chamber of Commerce, P.O. Box 3150, Beaumont, Texas 77704. Contact:—Traffic & Transportation Department Manager. Tel: (713) 838-6581. Corpus Christi Chamber of Commerce, P.O. Box 640, Corpus Christi, Texas 78403. Contact:—Assistant General Manager. Tel: (512) 882-6161. Dallas Chamber of Commerce, Fidelity Union Tower, 1507 Pacific, Dallas, Texas 75201. Contact:—World Trade Department Manager. Tel: (214) 651-1020. Denton Chamber of Commerce, P.O. Drawer F, Denton, Texas 76201. Contact:— Executive Vice President. Tel: (817) 382-9693. El Paso Chamber of Commerce,

10 Civic Center Plaza, El Paso, Texas 79944. Contact:—Executive Director. Tel: (915) 544-7880. Forth Worth Area Chamber of Commerce, 700 Throckmorton Street, Forth Worth, Texas 76102. Contact:—Economic Development Division Assistant Manager. Tel: (817) 336-2491. Gainesville Chamber of Commerce, P.O. Box 518, Gainesville, Texas 76240. Contact:—Industrial Division Executive Vice President. Tel: (817) 665-2831. Galveston Chamber of Commerce, 315 Tremont Street, Galveston, Texas 77550. Contact:—General Manager. Tel: (713) 763-5326. Harlingen Chamber of Commerce, P.O. Box 189, Harlingen, Texas 78550. Contact:—President. Tel: (512) 423-5440. Houston Chamber of Commerce, P.O. Box 53600, Houston, Texas 77052. Contact:—International Business Manager. Tel: (713) 227-5111. Jacksonville Chamber of Commerce, P.O. Box 1231, Jacksonville, Texas 75766. Contact:—Executive Vice President. Tel: (214) 586-2217. Laredo Chamber of Commerce, P.O. Box 790, Laredo, Texas 78040. Contact:—Port of Laredo Committee. Tel: (512) 722-9895. East Texas Chamber of Commerce, P.O. Box 1592, Longview, Texas 75601. Contact:—President. Tel: (214) 757-4444. Nacogdoches County Chamber of Commerce, P.O. Box 974, Nacogdoches, Texas 75961. Contact:—Executive Vice President. Tel: (713) 564-7351. Odessa Chamber of Commerce, P.O. Box 3626, Odessa, Texas 79760. Contact:—President. Tel: (915) 332-9111. Port Arthur Chamber of Commerce, P.O. Box 460, Port Arthur, Texas 77640. Contact:—Executive Vice President. Tel: (713) 985-9373. San Antonio Chamber of Commerce, P.O. Box 1628, San Antonio, Texas 78296. Contact: —International Affairs Manager. Tel: (512) 227-8181. Greater Texas City-La Marque Chamber of Commerce, 625 8th Avenue, Texas City, Texas 77590. Contact:—Executive Vice President and General Manager. Tel: (713) 945-2306. Waco Chamber of Commerce, P.O. Box 1220, Waco, Texas 76703. Contact:—Industrial Development Department Manager. Tel: (817) 752-6551.

Utah:—Salt Lake Area Chamber of Commerce, # 19 East Second South, Salt Lake City, Utah 84111. Contact:—Economic Development Department Director. Tel: (801) 364-3631.

Vermont:—Rutland Region Chamber of Commerce, 1 Mead Building, Rutland, Vermont 05701. Contact:—Executive Vice President. Tel: (802) 773-2747.

Virginia:—Charlottesville-Albemarle Chamber of Commerce, P.O. Box 1654, Charlottesville, Virginia 22901. Contact:—Executive Vice President. Tel: (804) 295-3141. Fairfax County Chamber of Commerce, 8550 Arlington Boulevard, Fairfax, Virginia 22030. Contact:—Executive Vice President. Tel: (703) 560-4000. Richmond Chamber of Commerce, 201 E. Franklin Street, Richmond, Virginia 23219. Contact:—Executive Manager. Tel: (703) 643-7491. Winchester-Frederick County Chamber of Commerce, P.O. Box 667, Winchester, Virginia 22601. Contact:—Executive Director. Tel: (703) 662-4118.

Washington:—Renton Chamber of Commerce, 300 Rainier Avenue, Renton, Washington 98055. Contact:—Manager. Tel: (206) 226-4560. Seattle Chamber of Commerce, 215 Columbia Street, Seattle, Washington 98104. Contact:—Commerce Department Manager. Tel: (206) 447-7268. Tacoma Area Chamber of Commerce, P.O. Box 1933, Tacoma, Washington 98401. Contact:—Economic Development Department Manager. Tel: (206) 627-2175.

West Virginia:—West Virginia Chamber of Commerce, P.O. Box 2789, Charleston, West Virginia, 25330. Contact:—Executive Vice President. Tel: (304) 342-1115.

Wisconsin:—Area Chamber of Commerce, 111 West Front Street, Ashland, Wisconsin 54806. Contact:—Executive Secretary. Tel: (715) 682-2500. Fond Du Lac Area Association of Commerce, 207 N. Main Street, Fond Du Lac, Wisconsin 54935. Contact:—Executive Vice President. Tel: (414) 921-9500. Janesville Area Chamber of Commerce, P.O. Box 998, Janesville, Wisconsin 53545. Contact:— Executive Vice President. Tel: (608) 752-7459. Greater La Crosse Chamber of Commerce, P.O. Box 842, La Crosse, Wisconsin 54601. Contact:—Executive Vice President. Tel: (608) 784-4880. Greater Madison Chamber of Commerce, P.O. Box 71, Madison, Wisconsin 53701. Contact:—Executive Director. Tel: (608) 256-8348. Wisconsin State Chamber of Commerce, P. O. Box 1143, Madison, Wisconsin 53701. Contact:—Executive Vice President. Tel: (608) 257-1088. Marinette Area Chamber of Commerce, P.O. Box 512, Marinette, Wisconsin 54143. Contact:—Manager. Tel: (715) 735-6681. Metropolitan Milwaukee Association of Commerce, 828 North Broadway, Milwaukee, Wisconsin 53202. Contact:—Trade/ Transportation/Air Service Division Manager. Tel: (414) 273-3000. Racine Area Chamber of Commerce, 731 Main Street, Racine, Wisconsin 53403. Contact:— Vice President. Tel: (414) 326-5426. Sheboygan Area Chamber of Commerce, P.O. Box 687, Sheboygan, Wisconsin 53801. Contact:—President. Tel: (414) 457-9491. Superior Chamber of Commerce, 1213 Tower Avenue, Superior, Wisconsin 54880. Contact:—Executive Manager. Tel: (715) 394-7716. Wausau Area Chamber of Commerce, P.O. Box 569, Wausau, Wisconsin 54401. Contact:—Executive Vice President. Tel: (715) 845-6231.

Wyoming:—Casper Area Chamber of Commerce, P.O. Box 399, Casper, Wyoming 82601. Contact:—Executive Manager. Tel: (307) 234-5311. Greater Cheyenne Chamber of Commerce, P.O. Box 1147, Cheyenne, Wyoming 82001. Contact:— Executive Director. Tel: (307) 638-3388.

Appendix Eleven

Service Organizations

Sources of Commercial and/or Credit Information

Export Information Division, Domestic & International Business Administration: U.S. Department of Commerce, Room 1033, Washington, D.C. 20230. (202) 377-4203: World Traders Data Reports on foreign firms, supplying information useful in judging the suitability of prospective agents, distributors, and suppliers. Each WTDR contains detailed commercial information, including financial references, on an individual firm and must be ordered with complete name and address of the firm and advance payment of $15.

Dun & Bradstreet International, a division of Dun & Bradstreet, Inc., 99 Church Street, New York. (212) 285-7191: Credit reports on business concerns throughout the world. Over 218 offices in the leading cities in the United Kingdon, Europe, North and South America, Australia, South Africa, and Israel. Publishers of Market Guides for continental Europe and Latin America, and domestic credit Reference Books for Argentina, Brazil, Mexico, Great Britain and South Africa. These volumes list the names of manufacturers, wholesalers, retailers, agents and service organizations in countries named, with local data for benefit of American exporters. The Reference Books include payment code and capital code on almost all accounts listed.

Dun & Bradstreet, International publishes an annual encyclopaedia, kept up to date with twice monthly supplements, *E.E.-World Marketing Guide*; and a twice-monthly Newsletter *World Marketing*. Also publishes *World Products* and Dun & Bradstreet Marketing Directory of *Principal International Businesses*. International Commercial Collections Division provides an integrated worldwide collection service for subscribers.

FCIB-NACM Corp., (formerly Foreign Credit Interchange Bureau), 475 Park Ave., South, New York 10016. (212) 725-1700: FCIB-NACM is an association of Executives in Finance, Credit and International Business which was organized in 1919 and has continued its operation since that time. Its membership comprises many leading banks and exporters in all parts of the world. Its method of operation is based upon the mutual interchange of ledger information on overseas accounts, and its files contain information on over 300,000 firms in international business.

Source: *Exporter's Encyclopedia*. Annual.
    Dun & Bradstreet International,
    99 Church St., New York, N.Y.

The FCIB is a cooperative, nonprofit organization supervised by a Board of Directors of its members. Among its activities, in addition to issuing interchange reports are: Trade Groups, the Bulletins which contain a resume of credit and collection conditions in foreign markets, World-Wide collection service on delinquent buyers, and monthly Round-Table conferences on international credit, collection and exchange conditions. Participation in the FCIB's activities is based upon a membership plan and the fees are nominal. The Association has set up a European chapter (FCIB Europe) and opened an office at Ave Louise, 502, Brussels, Belgium to serve some 160 manufacturing members in Europe. Executive Vice President, J. Stewart Gillies, Secretary and Manager Ira Mermer.

Retail Credit Co., Atlanta, Ga.; New York Office, 747 Third Ave.: This company has facilities for reporting on individuals throughout the world. They make reports for use in determining credit status and for considering agency, representative and employment connections. They also serve insurance and bonding companies, reporting on original applications, and on claims which later arise from insurance contracts, in addition to furnishing market information services and studies to industry. They maintain branch offices throughout the U.S. and Canada; also offices in Kingston, Jamaica; San Juan, P.R.; and Mexico, D.F. They also have correspondents covering all other points of the civilized world. Information and terms will be furnished on application to the home office in Atlanta at P.O. Box 4081, Atlanta, Ga., 30302, or to the New Yorkoffice at P.O. Box 427, Grand Central Station, New York, 10017. Mr. W. Lee Burge, President and Chief Executive Officer, may be reached by telephone at either Atlanta (404) 875-8321 or New York (212) 832-6800 or by mail at either of the preceding addresses.

Appendix Twelve

Guide to Information Sources

This appendix has been prepared to provide the reader with a guide to the extensive amount of useful published material available for isolating opportunities in foreign markets and planning a strategy to approach these opportunities. For the most part, only examples are presented in this appendix since it would be impossible to present a comprehensive list of the material available. In addition, any attempt at a "comprehensive" list would become rapidly out of date as new material becomes available. However, from a review of the examples given, you will be in a position to search for that information which most closely suits your particular needs.

International Statistics

1.   General Reference Works (which are not *sources of actual statistics).*

a.   Trade Statistics:
International Trade Statistics edited by R. G. D. Allen and J. Edward Ely, New York, John Wiley & Sons, 1953. An excellent discussion of the trade statistics gathered by all major countries which includes a valuable appendix entitled "Primary National Publications of International Trade Statistics." Pages 149–151 describe the use of trade statistics to locate export markets for U.S. razor blades.
Manual on the Compilation of Basic Information on Export Markets, GATT, Geneva. A pratical guide for statistical analysis which contains a number of illustrated suggestions on "how to analyze."

b.   Economic Statistics:
International Economic Statistics. A memorandum prepared for the Subcommittee on Economic Statistics of the Joint Economic Committee on Economic Statistics of the Joint Economic Committee by the Office of Statistical Standards of the Bureau of the Budget. U.S. Government Printing Office, Washington, D.C. Out of print but available in many libraries, this useful reference work describes the development and availability of international economic statistics, particularly those of the United Nations.

Source: *Export Marketing for Smaller Firms*, 3d Ed.,
        August 1971. Small Business Administration,
        Washington, D.C.

c.   *U.S. Government Statistics:*

Guide to Foreign Trade Statistics. Bureau of the Census, U.S. Department of Commerce. Helpful in understanding various sources of foreign trade statistics and the content and the general arrangement of the data they contain in U.S. imports and exports, gives examples of all trade statistical tables.

U.S. Foreign Trade Statistics: Classifications and Cross-Classifications. Bureau of the Census, Washington, D.C., 20233. A volume for use in relating imports, exports to domestic output of various commodities as well as relating U.S. foreign trade to the trade of other nations.

d.   *Statistics Collected by International Organizations:*

The United Nations and its related organizations such as the World Health Organization issue a comprehensive series of international trade and economic statistics. Although the United Nations is the most important source of international statistics, other groups such as GATT, The General Agreement on Tariffs and Trade, also publish statistical material.

A useful bibliography of international publications containing statistics and a comprehensive catalogue of the statistical series collected by international organizations is:

A Compendium of Sources: International Trade Statistics. GATT, Geneva.

Since the United Nations provides the most comprehensive and readily available international trade and economic statistics, only its statistical publications are included in this section. These statistical publications are available in most libraries.

e.   *Trade Statistics:*

Commodity Trade Statistics, 196_. Series D. Imports and Exports of member nations according to SITC Classification, Annual.

Yearbook of International Trade Statistics. Volume I, imports and exports by unit and value for 132 countries. Annual.

World Trade Annuals–Vols. I-IV. (Published for 1963 and 1964; PC, Vols, I-IV; English.) Detailed trade for *23 major trading countries*, showing commodities (SITC 4-5 digit) by countries of origin/destination; yearly figures; values in U.S. dollars.

Supplement to the World Trade Annual–Vols. I-V. (Published for 1964; PC: Clothbound; English.) Detailed trade of *23 major trading countries* with Eastern Europe (Vol. 1), *South and Central America*, including the *Caribbean* (Vol. II), *Africa* (Vol. III), the *Near East* (Vol. IV) and the *Far East* (Vol. V) by commodities (SITC sections, divisions, groups and selected sub-groups—4 digit— and items—5 digit) in commodity by country order; figures refer to 1964; values in U.S. dollars.

f.   *Economic Statistics:*

Statistical Yearbook. Annual publication providing comprehensive data for over 250 countries on a wide range of social and economic subjects.

Monthly Bulletin of Statistics. A monthly supplement to the *Yearbook* which includes data from more than 150 countries on more than 60 subjects in the social and economic area.

Current Economic Indicators. A quarterly publication providing data on approximately 500 economic indicators for the world, major regions, underdeveloped areas, and seven industrial countries (Canada, France, Germany, Japan, United Kingdom, and United States).

The potential exporter/importer will probably find that economic statistics provided by the United Nations are more valuable in isolating attractive markets than are the trade statistics. These trade statistics must by necessity summarize the statistics provided by individual countries. Since the value of trade statistics diminishes rapidly as they become more general, many exporters/importers will find the United Nations' trade statistics of little value.

After international organizations, the next important source of statistical data are regional groups such as the Organization for Economic Cooperation and Development, the European Economic Community and the Council of Europe. As might be expected regional organizations which include the Western European countries are the most significant statistical sources.

2. Statistics Collected by Regional Organizations:

The number of regional organizations providing statistical material makes it impossible to list them all here. However, the most important regional organization is the Organization for Economic Cooperation and Development which includes the European countries, Greece and Turkey and Japan. The United States and Canada are associate members. The important statistical publications of this organization are listed here along with examples of statistical data from two other regional groups, the European Common Market or EEC—the European Economic Community—and EFTA—the European Free Trade Association.

a. Trade Statistics:

O.E.C.D. Foreign Trade Bulletins. Series C. A semi-annual publication in two volumes (imports and exports) with details on quantity and value by countries of origin and destination given for 272 commodity categories. Annual subscriptions. (Organization for Economic Cooperation and Development.)

Foreign Trade (red series), Monthly Statistics and Analytical Tables (European Common Market). Further details from Service des Publications des Communautes Europeens, Bureau de vente: 2, place de Metz-Luxembourg.

b. Economic Statistics:

General Statistics. Published six times each year and includes data on industrial production, population, wholesale and retail indexes, salaries and wages, finance and economics. Annual subscription includes monthly supplement giving seasonally adjusted series for the main economic indicators. (Organization for Economic Cooperation and Development.)

General Statistical Bulletin. Published 11 times per year by the European Common Market Organization. For details, same as above. Annual subscription.

Main Economic Indicators. 1959-69, O.E.C.D., Paris. Historical statistics of the 23 O.E.C.D. countries. *Statistical Data.* Handbook published by the Council of Europe providing data on industry, trade, finance, transport and population. U.S. sales agent is Manhattan Publishing Co., New York, New York.

3.   Statistics Published by National Governments:

National governments are undoubtedly the most significant source of detailed but generally available statistics. Most foreign governments *summarize* their statistics in periodic bulletins and yearbooks. Refer again to *A Compendium of Sources: International Trade Statistics*. GATT, Geneva for a bibliography of these sources.

The Library of Congress has prepared two useful bibliographies of these publications which are:

Statistical Bulletins, Census Library Projects, U.S. Library of Congress, Washington, 1954. An annotated bibliography of the general statistical bulletins of major political subdivisions of the world.

Statistical Yearbooks, Phyllis G. Carter, U.S. Library of Congress, Washington, D.C. 1953. An annotated bibliography of the general statistical yearbooks of major political subdivisions of the world.

However, the bulletins and yearbooks are only summaries of more detailed information which is *also* available. For example, detailed foreign trade statistics (imports and exports) are published separately by most governments although they may be summarized in the bulletins and yearbooks. A list of these publications entitled "Primary National Publications of International Trade Statistics" is included as an appendix in the book entitled *International Trade Statistics* mentioned at the beginning of this section.

Information about more detailed statistics may be obtained directly from the foreign government, through its consulate in this country or from the appropriate country desk, in the Office of International Regional Economics, U.S. Department of Commerce.

4.   Statistics Published by Groups within Foreign Countries:

The most detailed statistics available originate with sources very similar to their U.S. counterparts. These are trade associations and to a lesser extent trade publications. Unfortunately these statistics may be difficult to obtain since trade associations in foreign countries are likely to be quite secretive when dealing with nonmembers.

However, generalizations are of little value and the individual firm must attempt to locate the appropriate organizations and publications in the country being studied and then correspond to determine whether any statistical material is available.

Here are two examples of statistical publications from trade associations which would be of interest to smaller firms in the electrical and electronic area:

Die westdeutsche Elektroindustries, Statistischer Bericht 1960. Zentralverband der Elektrotechnischen Industrie E. V. Frankfurt/Main, Federal Republic of Germany. A very comprehensive statistical publication from the central association of the West German electrical industry (includes electronics).

Etudes Economiques Documentation. Federation Nationale des Industries Electroniques. A very detailed survey by the association of the French electronic industry which includes a considerable amount of narrative data in addition to statistics.

This concludes the section on statistics. The next section will deal with non-statistical material.

Data on Foreign Markets

Information about foreign markets may be obtained from a great variety of sources and it is usually difficult to predict in advance which sources will be the most useful. Therefore, this section is presented in the form of an annotated list of different sources. Examples are included whenever appropriate to illustrate the type of material which may be found. Emphasis is placed on published material but the reader is reminded that correspondence with the sources of this published material may prove valuable.

1. Bibliographical Services:

A considerable amount of important information can often be obtained from reviewing the important bibliographical services which are available. Most public libraries have the *Business Periodicals Index* and the *Public Affairs Information Service*, both of which should be reviewed for significant material.

One bibliographical service deserves special mention. This is *The International Executive* which reviews books and articles of significance to those concerned with international business. Published quarterly by the Foundation for the Advancement of International Business Administration, 64 Ferndale Drive, Hastings-on-Hudson, New York. Annual subscription.

Three important bibliographical services are published in Europe. These three services are oriented toward broad economic and political questions but all of them include a considerable number of useful commercial references. These services are:

Economic Abstracts. (Library of the Economic Information Service, 95 Bezuidenhoutseweg, The Hague, Netherlands). A semimonthly review (with annual index of articles and books on economics, finance, trade and industry, management and labor).

Research, Bibliographical and Documentary Information Bulletin. (Documentation Section, Council of Europe, Strasbourg. Published six times per year). This bibliography covers finance, politics, economics, transport, law, population and refugees, labor and social questions, culture and publications of international bodies.

Bibliographies d'etudes et d'articles selectionnes. Catalogue Permanent des derniers documents entres. Bibliotheque de la Chambre de Commerce et d'Industrie de Paris, 16, Rue Chateaubriand, Paris VIIIe), France. A very complete bibliographical service with a commercial and economic orientation.

2. Regional Organizations:

Bodies such as the Organization for Economic Cooperation and Development and the European Economic Community already mentioned as sources of statistical information publish material of a narrative nature which may be of value to the exporter. The Organization for Economic Cooperation and Development is a particularly worthwhile source of general material on particular industries, consumer habits and other subjects. A review of their publications catalogue will indicate which if any of their published studies should be read.

3. Foreign Governments:

Most of the interesting material available from foreign governments has been published to aid the country's business community in the same way that material from the U.S. Department of Commerce assists the American business community. The importance of this material cannot be overstressed. For example, the British Ministry of Labour has published a *Family Expenditure Survey* which provides detailed information about the breakdown of consumer spending. A publication from the British Board of Trade entitled *Women's Measurements and Sizes* would certainly be of interest to the exporter of wearing apparel.

The way to learn about such publications is by corresponding with the foreign government's printing office requesting lists of available publications. For example, a list of publications by the British Board of Trade is entitled *Government Publications Sectional List* and is available without charge.

Besides individual studies, certain foreign governments publish periodicals which although aimed at export promotion, also contain information on the local business situation. Two examples of these are the *Pakistan Exports* and the *Kenya Trade and Suppliers Bulletin*.

Material prepared to assist the country's exporters is also useful and readily available. For example, the British Board of Trade publishes an excellent series entitled *Hints to Businessmen Visiting* (various countries). Pamphlets in this series are available for a very nominal fee, a characteristic of all government publications both in this country and abroad.

Finally foreign governments prepare a certain amount of material designed to interest foreign investors. One of the finest examples of this type of publication is is the *Guide to Investment in Greece* available from the Industrial Development Corporation in Athens. Another example is *Investing in India—Objects and Functions* from the Indian Investment Center in New Delhi and in New York.

4. Consulates and Official Trade Promotion Groups:

Foreign consulates in this country frequently publish periodicals for special reports of interest to the exporter. The Nigerian Consulate General in New York issues the *Nigeria Trade Journal*. The Belgian Industrial Information Service (New York) has prepared *Reaching New Markets from a Business Base in Belgium*, and the commercial office of the Italian Embassy sends out the monthly *Italian Trade Topics*.

Although these publications are of a general nature, they provide a satisfactory introduction to the question of doing business in the foreign country.

5.   *Chambers of Commerce:*

Many foreign chambers of commerce maintain offices in the United States and the publications of this group often contain material of value to the exporter. The usual publications of this group are a monthly magazine such as the *Belgian Trade Review* (The Belgian Chamber of Commerce in the United States) and the *German-American Trade News* (German-American Chamber of Commerce). In addition, these magazines may be supplemented with a newsletter published on a weekly or monthly basis.

Other publications from this group are also useful. For example, the membership directory of the French Chamber of Commerce in the United States contains extensive material on the subject of doing business in France.

6.   *Commercial Banks:*

The publications of commercial banks in foreign countries represent an outstanding source of general information about the country. These publications may appear as periodicals, usually on a monthly or quarterly basis and as general booklets which appear at irregular intervals. Some banks offer a combination of publications to their customers. For example, Barclays Bank publishes two periodicals, the *Barclays Bank Review* and the *Overseas Review* which has an annual summary entitled the *Overseas Survey* which includes a number of the new African countries.

Some examples of the periodicals issued by other banks throughout the world (and all in English) are *Review of the Economic Situation of Mexico* (Banco National de Mexico), *Monthly Economic Report* (Banco Exterior de Espana), *Quarterly Review* (Amsterdamsche Bank, Netherlands), and *The Quarterly Survey* (Australia and New Zealand Bank Limited).

Some examples of individual studies prepared by foreign banks are *Belgium: Key to the Common Market* (Kredietbank, Brussels), *Spanish Industry as seen by the Banco Vizcaya* (Banco de Vizcaya) and *Possibilities for Establishing Foreign Companies in the Netherlands* (Rotterdamsche Bank).

Many of these bank periodicals have indexes and are available in larger libraries.

7.   *Investment Banking Firms:*

In recent years, investment banking firms in foreign countries where there are active securities markets, have undertaken investment surveys very similar to those prepared by U.S. investment bankers. Such surveys, usually on an industry basis, provide a wealth of information about the industry and leading firms in it. Two examples of such studies are:

The Electrical Engineering Industry in the Common Market. Eurosyndicat Investment Research Bureau, Brussels, Belgium.

Japan's Chemical Industry and Its Outlook. Yamaichi Securities Company, Tokyo, Japan.

Locating these investment studies is likely to be difficult and one of the best ways to proceed is by contacting a U.S. investment banker. In many instances, the foreign firm has circulated copies of these studies among the U.S. investment banking community.

8.   *Trade Journals:*

The value of reviewing appropriate trade journals published in foreign countries and corresponding with their editorial staffs cannot be overstated. These magazines are extremely useful sources of information in terms of both editorial and advertising content. *Ulrich's International Periodical Directory* is an excellent source for isolating the names of appropriate publications.

9.   *Trade Associations:*

Trade associations in foreign countries have already been mentioned as a source of detailed statistical information. These associations also collect other types of information and the potential exporter should definitely get in touch with whatever trade association is concerned with his particular types of products.

The consulates in this country will be helpful in providing the names of appropriate trade associations and these names are often included at the rear of Trade Lists published by the U.S. Department of Commerce.

10.   *General Periodicals of a Commercial, Financial or Economic Nature:*

Almost every industrially advanced country has its equivalent to *Business Week, Barrons* or the *Wall Street Journal*. These newspapers and periodicals are an extremely valuable source of up-to-date events. These newspapers and periodicals are listed in *Ulrich's International Periodical Directory, The Newspaper Press Directory* and *The Europa Yearbook*. Also useful is *Management Checklist for Foreign Operations*, published by Buiness International, 757 Third Ave., New York.

Many larger libraries subscribe to these important periodicals which include *The Economist* and numerous others. If you are unable to find sample copies of these items, they may usually be obtained directly from the publisher. Most of these periodicals maintain some type of index which may be used to locate important articles while others offer formalized clipping and reference services.

11.   *Periodicals on Marketing and Related Subjects:*

General periodicals on marketing and related subjects often contain valuable material particularly for exporters of consumer goods. Some of these magazines deal with specialized areas such as *South African Sales Promotion and Packaging* or the *New Zealand Retailer*. Others dealing with the general subject of marketing are *Det Danski Marked* (Denmark), *Studi De Mercata* (Italy) and *Vendre* (France).

12. *Export Magazines:*

Two distinct types of export publications originate from a number of different sources and may, therefore, be used for different purposes by the exporter. The first type of magazine is directed toward the exporter and seeks to help him by providing information about foreign markets, trade restrictions and other important factors. Almost without exception these magazines are issued by governments and contain reports from the governments' overseas commercial representatives. As such, they are similar to *Business America* published biweekly by the U.S. Department of Commerce. Outstanding examples of this type of export magazine include *Foreign Trade* (Canada), *Board of Trade Journal* (Great Britian), *Bulletin Commercial Belge* (Belgium), and *Overseas Trading* (Australia). The market reports appearing in these magazines are as useful to exporters in the U.S. as to exporters in the country publishing the magazine.

The other type of export magazine is directed primarily toward overseas customers and is prepared by private publishing firms, export associations and government organizations. In essence these magazines contain advertisements and notices of products which the manufacturer would like to export. Export magazines of this type are sometimes useful for learning about the product offered by competitors in foreign markets. Firms advertising in these magazines may be expected to forward complete details about their product line upon request.

Among the magazines published by private firms are *Made in Europe* with an annual *Buyers' Guide, Overseas Post, Export-Anzeiger, Export Market* and *The German Exporter*, all of which are published in Germany. Others include *The Ambassador* (Great Britian), *The British Trade Journal and Export World, Oriental America, Japan Trade Monthly, Trade Channel Magazines, Asian Buyers Guide, Taiwan Buyers Guide,* and *Hong Kong Buyers Guide.*

Those issued by groups of exporters include *The South African Exporter, Featuring Sweden,* the *Finnish Trade Review* and *The Israel Export and Trade Journal.*

The last group are those published by foreign governments and semiofficial organizations. These include *Italy Presents*; three from Japan, *Japan Commerce and Industry, Merchandise That Japan Offers* and *Quality Goods on Parade*; and also *Polish Foreign Trade*, and *Canada Commerce*.

In addition to looking at sample copies of these magazines, the reader should consider corresponding with the editorial staffs which are usually in a position to provide information for exporters to their country as well as importers from it.

13. *Commercial and Economic Publications of a Regional Nature:*

Useful information about markets in the developing countries can often be obtained from commercial and economic publications of a regional nature. An outstanding example of such a publication is the *Far Eastern Economic Review* published weekly in Hong Kong. This publication has a formal reference service available through which questions about doing business in the area may be answered for a fee.

Other publications of a regional nature are *Far East Trade, East African Trade and Industry, West Africa, African Trade and Development.*

14. Corporate Publications:

In addition to their annual reports, certain large foreign corporations publish journals intended for circulation outside the company and therefore, without the personal touches usually present in house organs. One of the best of these corporate journals is the *Statistical and Economic Review* published by the United Africa Company and containing useful articles and statistics on those areas of Africa in which the company operates.

15. Research Institutes:

Research institutes concerned with business and economic matters often prepare and publish detailed studies about industries, consumption of various products and other subjects of interest to the exporter. *The Europa Yearbook* lists many of these organizations and correspondence with them will indicate the availability of useful material.

16. Businessmen's Organizations in Foreign Countries:

These groups often publish periodicals and special studies which would be of assistance to the exporter. Although the material is usually of a general nature, articles and pamphlets on specific industries and sectors of the economy are not uncommon. Examples of two periodicals from such groups are *The Manufacturer* (South African Federated Chamber of Industries) and the *Journal of the Indian Merchant's Chamber.*

The Economic Picture of Japan was published as a single pamphlet by the Federation of Economic Organizations.

17. Promotional Brochures for Publications, Advertising Agencies and Market Research Firms:

These organizations often publish promotional booklets on a variety of subjects in order to attract new business. These promotional pieces are of particular interest because of their marketing orientation. An example of such a publication is *Norway: A prospering market, an informative publication for exporters to Norway*, published jointly by the newspaper *Aftenposten* and *Den norske Creditbank.*

18. Publications of Professional Firms:

Consulting or accounting firms often publish information on various aspects of doing business overseas. An example is: *Information Guides for doing Business in (country)*, Price-Waterhouse and Co., a series on the legal and tax aspects of business operations in specific foreign countries.

Material on the Mechanics of Exporting

A variety of books on the general subject of foreign trade are available to the potential exporter. The titles of these books vary but their content is essentially similar and most contain a considerable amount of detail on the mechanics of exporting. Anyone concerned with developing a serious export program would be well advised to borrow as many of these books as can be found in his local library. A quiet weekend reviewing all of them will help the potential exporter decide which (if any) would make a worthwhile addition to his business library.

In alphabetical order, these books are:

Adventures in Export. A. W. and W. C. King. Marsit Publishing Co., 711 East B St., Belleville, Ill.

Foreign Trade Handbook. 1963. The Dartnell Corporation, Chicago.

Handbook of International Marketing. A. O. Stanley. McGraw-Hill Book Co., 1963.

International Marketing. John M. Hess and Philip R. Cateora, Richard D. Irwin, Homewood, Ill., 1966. Text edition.

International Marketing. John Fayerweather, Prentice-Hall, Englewood Cliffs, N.J., 1965, paperback.

Marketing for the Developing Company, John Winkler, Hutchinson and Co., London, 1969.

International Marketing Management. Michael J. Thomas, Houghton-Mifflin Co., Boston, Mass., 1969, paperback.

World Marketing–a Multinational Approach. John K. Ryans and James C. Baker, John Riley and Son, New York, 1967.

Principals of World Business. Lawrence P. Dowd, incorporating the work of E. E. Pratt, Allyn & Bacon, 150 Tremont St., Boston, Mass. 1965.

All of these books have been rewritten several times and many libraries will have them in earlier editions which sometimes bear a different title. These earlier postwar editions are not basically different and should be used if the latest edition is not available.

An extremely useful export library can be started for very little cost if one takes advantage of the many inexpensive publications which are available. The following list includes publications which are frequently referenced in the manual and are available for a very small cost.

One source of such materials is the U.S. Department of Commerce. The following titles are available from the Department's regional field offices or directly from the Superintendent of Documents, U.S. Government Printing Office, Washington, D.C. 20402.

Introductory Guide to Exporting, 1971.
Ocean Freight Rate Guidelines for Shippers.
Foreign Business Practices, 1970.
Marketing Aids for Higher Export Profit, 1968, Free.
Marketing Information Guide.

Sources of Credit Information on Foreign Firms, 1967.

A number of useful and inexpensive publications are available from other sources. These include:

World Trade Data Yearbook. Dun & Bradstreet, Inc., 99 Church St., New York, New York. Published annually, contains information on mail, phone, radio and cable message rates and regulations, electric current, conversion factors, credit terms survey, sales terms, etc.

Unz & Co., 24 Beaver St., New York, New York, publishes a series of inexpensive pamphlets on export documentation. List available on request.

Foreign Commerce Handbook and *Introduction to Doing Import and Export Business.* From the International Department, Chamber of Commerce of the United States, Washington, D.C. *Foreign Commerce Handbook* is particularly useful as a source of references.

Marine Insurance: Notes and Comments on Ocean Cargo Insurance and *Ports of the World.* Both available on request from the Insurance Company of North America, 1600 Arch St., Philadelphia, Pennsylvania. These useful booklets contain information on foreign trade terms, insurance, packing and port conditions throughout the world.

This list is by no means comprehensive but it does suggest a number of basic references which are available without charge or for very little cost. The serious exporter should consider obtaining most if not all of these publications for his library.

Three basic reference services are available to assist the exporter in coping with the mechanics of export trade. The exporter should review each of these services carefully before reaching any decision about their relative merits. These are:

The Chase Manhattan Foreign Trade Service. Available on request from The Chase Manhattan Bank, 1 Chase Manhattan Plaza, New York, New York. An excellent service on trade restrictions and exchange controls throughout the world.

Exporter's Encyclopedia. Annual with supplements by Dun & Bradstreet, Inc., 99 Church St., New York, New York.

Exporters Year Book (197_.), Donald H. Dodds, Marine Publications, London, U.K. Lists documentary requirements for trading with all the countries of the world and gives additional information on each country.

Appendix Thirteen

Uniform Customs and Practice for Documentation Credits

General Provisions and Definitions

a.   These provisions and definitions and the following articles apply to all documentary credits and are binding upon all parties thereto unless otherwise expressly agreed.

b.   For the purposes of such provisions, definitions and articles the expressions "documentary credit(s)" and "credit(s)" used therein mean any arrangement, however named or described, whereby a bank (the issuing bank), acting at the request and in accordance with the instructions of a customer (the applicant for the credit),

i is to make payment to or to the order of a third party (the beneficiary), or is to pay, accept or negotiate bills of exchange (drafts) drawn by the beneficiary, or

ii authorizes such payments to be made or such drafts to be paid, accepted or negotiated by another bank,

against stipulated documents, provided that the terms and conditions of the credit are complied with.

c.   Credits, by their nature, are separate transactions from the sales or other contracts on which they may be based and banks are in no way concerned with or bound by such contracts.

d.   Credit instructions and the credits themselves must be complete and precise. In order to guard against confusion and misunderstanding, issuing banks should discourage any attempt by the applicant for the credit to include excessive detail.

e. The bank first entitled to exercise the option available under Article 32 b. shall be the bank authorized to pay, accept or negotiate under a credit. The decision of such bank shall bind all parties concerned.

A bank is authorized to pay or accept under a credit by being specifically nominated in the credit.

A bank is authorized to negotiate under a credit either

i by being specifically nominated in the credit, or

ii by the credit being freely negotiable by any bank.

f. A beneficiary can in no case avail himself of the contractual relationships existing between banks or between the applicant for the credit and the issuing bank.

A. Form and Notification of Credits

Article 1

a. Credits may be either

i revocable, or

ii irrevocable.

b. All credits, therefore, should clearly indicate whether they are revocable or irrevocable.

c. In the absence of such indication the credit shall be deemed to be revocable.

Article 2

A revocable credit may be amended or cancelled at any moment without prior notice to the beneficiary. However, the issuing bank is bound to reimburse a branch or other bank to which such a credit has been transmitted and made available for payment, acceptance or negotiation, for any payment, acceptance or negotiation complying with the terms and conditions of the credit and any ammendments received up to the time of payment, acceptance or negotiation made by such branch or other bank prior to receipt by it of notice of amendment or of cancellation.

Article 3

a. An irrevocable credit constitutes a definite undertaking of the issuing bank, provided that the terms and conditions of the credit are complied with:

i to pay, or that payment will be made, if the credit provides for payment, whether against a draft or not;

ii to accept drafts if the credit provides for acceptance by the issuing bank or to be responsible for their acceptance and payment at maturity if the credit provides for the acceptance of drafts drawn on the applicant for the credit or any other drawee specified in the credit;

   iii to purchase/negotiate, without recourse to drawers and/or bona fide holders, drafts drawn by the beneficiary, at sight or at a tenor, on the applicant for the credit or on any other drawee specified in the credit, or to provide for purchase/negotiation by another bank, if the credit provides for purchase/negotiation.

b.   An irrevocable credit may be advised to a beneficiary through another bank (the advising bank) without engagement on the part of that bank, but when an issuing bank authorizes or requests another bank to confirm its irrevocable credit and the latter does so, such confirmation constitutes a definite undertaking of the confirming bank in addition to the undertaking of the issuing bank, provided that the terms and conditions of the credit are complied with:

   i to pay, if the credit is payable at its own counters, whether against a draft or not, or that payment will be made if the credit provides for payment elsewhere;

   ii to accept drafts if the credit provides for acceptance by the confirming bank, at its own counters, or to be responsible for their acceptance and payment at maturity if the credit provides for the acceptance of drafts drawn on the applicant for the credit or any other drawee specified in the credit;

   iii to purchase/negotiate, without recourse to drawers and/or bona fide holders, drafts drawn by the beneficiary, at sight or at a tenor, on the issuing bank, or on the applicant for the credit or on any other drawee specified in the credit, if the credit provides for purchase/negotiation.

c.   Such undertakings can neither be amended nor cancelled without the agreement of all parties thereto. Partial acceptance of amendments is not effective without the agreement of all parties thereto.

Article 4

a.   When an issuing bank instructs a bank by cable, telegram or telex to advise a credit, and intends the mail confirmation to be the operative credit instrument, the cable, telegram or telex must state that the credit will only be effective on receipt of such mail confirmation. In this event, the issuing bank must send the operative credit instrument (mail confirmation) and any subsequent amendments to the credit to the beneficiary through the advising bank.

b.   The issuing bank will be responsible for any consequences arising from its failure to follow the procedure set out in the preceding paragraph.

c.   Unless a cable, telegram or telex states "details to follow" (or words of similar effect), or states that the mail confirmation is to be the operative credit instrument, the cable, telegram or telex will be deemed to be the operative credit instrument and the issuing bank need not send the mail confirmation to the advising bank.

Article 5

When a bank is instructed by cable, telegram or telex to issue, confirm or advise a credit similar in terms to one previously established and which has been the subject of amendments, it shall be understood that the details of the credit being issued, confirmed or advised will be transmitted to the beneficiary excluding the amendments, unless the instructions specify clearly any amendments which are to apply.

Article 6

If incomplete or unclear instructions are received to issue, confirm or advise a credit, the bank requested to act on such instructions may give preliminary notification of the credit to the beneficiary for information only and without responsibility; in this event the credit will be issued, confirmed or advised only when the necessary information has been received.

B.   Liabilities and Responsibilities

Article 7

Banks must examine all documents with reasonable care to ascertain that they appear on their face to be in accordance with the terms and conditions of the credit. Documents which appear on their face to be inconsistent with one another will be considered as not appearing on their face to be in accordance with the terms and conditions of the credit.

Article 8

a.   In documentary credit operations all parties concerned deal in documents and not in goods.

b.   Payment, acceptance or negotiation against documents which appear on their face to be in accordance with the terms and conditions of a credit by a bank authorized to do so, binds the party giving the authorization to take up the documents and reimburse the bank which has effected the payment, acceptance or negotiation.

c.   If, upon receipt of the documents, the issuing bank considers that they appear on their face not to be in accordance with the terms and conditions of the credit, that bank must determine, on the basis of the documents alone, whether to claim that payment, acceptance or negotiation was not effected in accordance with the terms and conditions of the credit.

d.   The issuing bank shall have a reasonable time to examine the documents and to determine as previously mentioned whether to make such a claim.

e.   If such claim is to be made, notice to that effect, stating the reasons therefore, must, without delay, be given by cable or other expeditious means to the bank from which the documents have been received (the remitting bank) and such notice must state that the documents are being held at the disposal of such bank or are being returned thereto.

f.   If the issuing bank fails to hold the documents at the disposal of the remitting bank, or fails to return the documents to such bank, the issuing bank shall be precluded from claiming that the relative payment, acceptance or negotiation was not effected in accordance with the terms and conditions of the credit.

g.   If the remitting bank draws the attention of the issuing bank to any irregularities in the documents or advises such bank that it has paid, accepted or negotiated under reserve or against a guarantee in respect of such irregularities, the issuing bank shall not thereby be relieved from any of its obligations under this article. Such guarantee or reserve concerns only the relations between the remitting bank and the beneficiary.

Article 9

Banks assume no liability or responsibility for the form, sufficiency, accuracy, genuineness, falsification or legal effect of any documents, or for the general and/or particular conditions stipulated in the documents or superimposed thereon; nor do they assume any liability or responsibility for the description, quantity, weight, quality, condition, packing, delivery, value or existence of the goods represented thereby, or for the good faith or acts and/or omissions, solvency, performance or standing of the consignor, the carriers or the insurers of the goods or any other person whomsoever.

Article 10

Banks assume no liability or responsibility for the consequences arising out of delay and/or loss in transit of any messages, letters or documents, or for delay, mutilation or other errors arising in the transmission of cables, telegrams or telex. Banks assume no liability or responsibility for errors in translation or interpretation of technical terms, and reserve the right to transmit credit terms without translating them.

Article 11

Banks assume no liability or responsibility for consequences arising out of the interruption of their business by Acts of God, riots, civil commotions, insurrections, wars or any other causes beyond their control or by any strikes or lockouts. Unless specifically authorized, banks will not effect payment, acceptance or negotiation after expiration under credits expiring during such interruption of business.

Article 12

a.   Banks utilizing the services of another bank for the purpose of giving effect to the instructions of the applicant for the credit do so for the account and at the risk of the latter.

b.   Banks assume no liability or responsibility should the instructions they transmit not be carried out, even if they have themselves taken the initiative in the choice of such other bank.

c.   The applicant for the credit shall be bound by and liable to indemnify the banks against all obligations and responsibilities imposed by foreign laws and usages.

Article 13

A paying or negotiating bank which has been authorized to claim reimbursement from a third bank nominated by the issuing bank and which has effected such payment or negotiation shall not be required to confirm to the third bank that it has done so in accordance with the terms and conditions of the credit.

C.   Documents

Article 14

a.   All instructions to issue, confirm or advice a credit must state precisely the documents against which payment, acceptance or negotiation is to be made.

b.   Terms such as "first class," "well known," "qualified" and the like shall not be used to describe the issuers of any documents called for under credits and if they are incorporated in the credit terms banks will accept documents as tendered.

*C.1   Documents Evidencing Shipment or Dispatch
or Taking in Charge (Shipping Documents)*

Article 15

Except as stated in Article 20, the date of the Bill of Lading, or the date of any other document evidencing shipment or dispatch or taking in charge, or the date indicated in the reception stamp or by notation on any such document, will be taken in each case to be the date of shipment or dispatch or taking in charge of the goods.

Article 16

a.   If words clearly indicating payment or prepayment of freight, however named or described, appear by stamp or otherwise on documents evidencing shipment or dispatch or taking in charge they will be accepted as constituting evidence of payment of freight.

b.   If the words "freight pre-payable" or "freight to be prepaid" or words of similar effect appear by stamp or otherwise on such documents they will not be accepted as constituting evidence of the payment of freight.

c.   Unless otherwise specified in the credit or inconsistent with any of the documents presented under the credit, banks will accept documents stating that freight or transportation charges are payable on delivery.

d.   Banks will accept shipping documents bearing reference by stamp or otherwise to costs additional to the freight charges, such as costs of, or disbursements incurred in connection with loading, unloading or similar operations, unless the conditions of the credit specifically prohibit such reference.

Article 17

Shipping documents which bear a clause on the face thereof such as "shipper's load and count" or "said by shipper to contain" or words of similar effect, will be accepted unless otherwise specified in the credit.

Article 18

a.   A clean shipping document is one which bears no superimposed clause or notation which expressly declares a defective condition of the goods and/or the packaging.

b.   Banks will refuse shipping documents bearing such clauses or notations unless the credit expressly states the clauses or notations which may be accepted.

C.1.1 Marine Bills of Lading

Article 19

a.   Unless specifically authorized in the credit, Bills of Lading of the following nature will be rejected:

i Bills of Lading issued by forwarding agents.

ii Bills of Lading which are issued under and are subject to the conditions of a Charter-Party.

iii Bills of Lading covering shipment by sailing vessels.

However, subject to the aforementioned and unless otherwise specified in the credit, Bills of Lading of the following nature will be accepted:

i "Through" Bills of Lading issued by shipping companies or their agents even though they cover several modes of transport.

ii Short Form Bills of Lading (i.e., Bills of Lading issued by shipping companies or their agents which indicate some or all of the conditions of carriage by reference to a source or document other than the Bill of Lading).

iii Bills of Lading issued by shipping companies or their agents covering unitized cargoes, such as those on pallets or in Containers.

Article 20

a. Unless otherwise specified in the credit, Bills of Lading must show that the goods are loaded on board a named vessel or shipped on a named vessel.

b. Loading on board a named vessel or shipment on a named vessel may be evidenced either by a Bill of Lading bearing wording indicating loading on board a named vessel or shipment on a named vessel, or by means of a notation to that effect on the Bill of Lading signed or initialled and dated by the carrier or his agent, and the date of this notation shall be regarded as the date of loading on board the named vessel or shipment on the named vessel.

Article 21

a. Unless transhipment is prohibited by the terms of the credit, Bill of Lading will be accepted which indicate that the goods will be transhipped en route, provided the entire voyage is covered by one and the same Bill of Lading.

b. Bills of Lading incorporating printed clauses stating that the carriers have the right to tranship will be accepted notwithstanding the fact that the credit prohibits transhipment.

Article 22

a. Banks will refuse a Bill of Lading stating that the goods are loaded on deck, unless specifically authorized in the credit.

b. Banks will not refuse a Bill of Lading which contains a provision that the goods may be carried on deck provided it does not specifically state that they are loaded on deck.

C.1.2. Combined Transport Documents

Article 23

a. If the credit calls for a combined transport document, i.e., one which provides for a combined transport by at least two different modes of transport, from a place at which the goods are taken in charge to a place designated for delivery, or if the credit provides for a combined transport, but in either case does not specify the form of document required and/or the issuer of such document, banks will accept such documents as tendered.

b. If the combined transport includes transport by sea the document will be accepted although it does not indicate that the goods are on board a named vessel, and although it contains a provision that the goods, if packed in a Container, may be carried on deck, provided it does not specifically state that they are loaded on deck.

C.1.3. Other Shipping Documents, Etc.

Article 24

> Banks will consider a Railway or Inland Waterway Bill of Lading or Consignment Note, Counterfoil Waybill, Postal Receipt, Certificate of Mailing, Air Mail Receipt, Air Waybill, Air Consignment Note or Air Receipt, Trucking Company Bill of Lading or any other similar document as regular when such document bears the reception stamp of the carrier or his agent, or when it bears a signature purporting to be that of the carrier or his agent.

Article 25

> Where a credit calls for an attestation or certification of weight in the case of transport other than by sea, banks will accept a weight stamp or declaration of weight superimposed by the carrier on the shipping document unless the credit calls for a separate or independent certificate of weight.

C.2 Insurance Documents

Article 26

a. Insurance documents must be as specified in the credit, and must be issued and/or signed by insurance companies or their agents or by underwriters.

b. Cover notes issued by brokers will not be accepted, unless specifically authorized in the credit.

Article 27

> Unless otherwise specified in the credit, or unless the insurance documents presented establish that the cover is effective at the latest from the date of shipment or dispatch or, in the case of combined transport, the date of taking the goods in charge, banks will refuse insurance documents presented which bear a date later than the date of shipment or dispatch or, in the case of combined transport, the date of taking the goods in charge, as evidenced by the shipping documents.

Article 28

a. Unless otherwise specified in the credit, the insurance document must be expressed in the same currency as the credit.

b. The minimum amount for which insurance must be effected is the CIF value of the goods concerned. However, when the CIF value of the goods cannot be determined from the documents on their face, banks will accept as such minimum amount the amount of the drawing under the credit or the amount of the relative commercial invoice, whichever is the greater.

Article 29

a.   Credits should expressly state the type of insurance required and, if any, the additional risks which are to be covered. Imprecise terms such as "usual risks" or "customary risks" should not be used; however, if such imprecise terms are used, banks will accept insurance documents as tendered.

b.   Failing specific instructions, banks will accept insurance cover as tendered.

Article 30

Where a credit stipulates "insurance against all risks," banks will accept an insurance document which contains any "all risks" notation or clause, and will assume no responsibility if any particular risk is not covered.

Article 31

Banks will accept an insurance document which indicates that the cover is subject to a franchise or an excess (deductible), unless it is specifically stated in the credit that the insurance must be issued irrespective of percentage.

C.3   Commercial Invoices

Article 32

a.   Unless otherwise specified in the credit, commercial invoices must be made out in the name of the applicant for the credit.

b.   Unless otherwise specified in the credit, banks may refuse commercial invoices issued for amounts in excess of the amount permitted by the credit.

c.   The description of the goods in the commercial invoice must correspond with the description in the credit. In all other documents the goods may be described in general terms not inconsistent with the description of the goods in the credit.

C.4 Other Documents

Article 33

When other documents are required, such as Warehouse Receipts, Delivery Orders, Consular Invoices, Certificates of Origin, of Weight, of Quality or of Analysis, etc., and when no further definition is given, banks will accept such documents as tendered.

D. Miscellaneous Provisions

Quantity and Amount

Article 34

a.   The words "about," "circa" or similar expressions used in connection with the amount of the credit or the quantity or the unit price of the goods are to be construed as allowing a difference not to exceed 10% more or 10% less.

b.   Unless a credit stipulates that the quantity of the goods specified must not be exceeded or reduced a tolerance of 3% more or 3% less will be permissible, always provided that the total amount of the drawings does not exceed the amount of the credit. This tolerance does not apply when the credit specifies quantity in terms of a stated number of packing units or individual items.

Partial Shipments

Article 35

a.   Partial shipments are allowed, unless the credit specifically states otherwise.

b.   Shipments made on the same ship and for the same voyage, even if the Bills of Lading evidencing shipment "on board" bear different dates and/or indicate different ports of shipment, will not be regarded as partial shipments.

Article 36

If shipment by instalments within given periods is stipulated and any instalment is not shipped within the period allowed for that instalment, the credit ceases to be available for that or any subsequent instalments, unless otherwise specified in the credit.

Expiry Date

Article 37

All credits, whether revocable or irrevocable, must stipulate an expiry date for presentation of documents for payment, acceptance or negotiation, notwithstanding the stipulation of a latest date for shipment.

Article 38

The words "to," "until," "till" and words of similar import applying to the stipulated expiry date for presentation of documents for payment, acceptance or negotiation, or to the stipulated latest date for shipment, will be understood to include the date mentioned.

Article 39

a. When the stipulated expiry date falls on a day on which banks are closed for reasons other than those mentioned in Article 11, the expiry date will be extended until the first following business day.

b. The latest date for shipment shall not be extended by reason of the extension of the expiry date in accordance with this Article. Where the credit stipulates a latest date for shipment, shipping documents dated later than such stipulated date will not be accepted. If no latest date for shipment is stipulated in the credit, shipping documents dated later than the expiry date stipulated in the credit or amendments thereto will not be accepted. Documents other than the shipping documents may, however, be dated up to and including the extended expiry date.

c. Banks paying, accepting or negotiating on such extended expiry date must add to the documents their certification as follows: "Presented for payment (or acceptance or negotiation as the case may be) within the expiry date extended in accordance with Article 39 of the *Uniform Customs*."

Shipment, Loading or Dispatch

Article 40

a. Unless the terms of the credit indicate otherwise, the words "departure," "dispatch," "loading" or "sailing" used in stipulating the latest date for shipment of the goods will be understood to be synonymous with "shipment."

b. Expressions such as "prompt," "immediately," "as soon as possible" and the like should not be used. If they are used, banks will interpret them as a request for shipment within thirty days from the date on the advice of the credit to the beneficiary by the issuing bank or by an advising bank, as the case may be.

c. Expression "on or about" and similar expressions will be interpreted as a request for shipment during the period from five days before to five days after the specified date, both end days included.

Presentation

Article 41

Nothwithstanding the requirement of Article 37 that every credit must stipulate an expiry date for presentation of documents, credits must also stipulate a specified period of time after the date of issuance of the Bills of Lading or other shipping documents during which presentation of documents for payment, acceptance or negotiation must be made. If no such period of time is stipulated in the credit, banks will refuse documents presented to them later than 21 days after the date of issuance of the Bills of Lading or other shipping documents.

Article 42

Banks are under no obligation to accept presentation of documents outside their banking hours.

Date Terms

Article 43

The terms "first half," "second half" of a month shall be construed respectively as from the 1st to the 15th, and the 16th to the last day of each month, inclusive.

Article 44

The terms "beginning," "middle," or "end" of a month shall be construed respectively as from the 1st to the 10th, the 11th to the 20th, and the 21st to the last day of each month, inclusive.

Article 45

When a bank issuing a credit instructs that the credit be confirmed or advised as available "for one month," "for six months" or the like, but does not specify the date from which the time is to run, the confirming or advising bank will confirm or advise the credit as expiring at the end of such indicated period from the date of its confirmation or advice.

E.   Transfer

Article 46

a.   A transferable credit is a credit under which the beneficiary has the right to give instructions to the bank called upon to effect payment or acceptance or to any bank entitled to effect negotiation to make the credit available in whole or in part to one or more third parties (second beneficiaries).

b.   The bank requested to effect the transfer, whether it has confirmed the credit or not, shall be under no obligation to effect such transfer except to the extent and in the manner expressly consented to by such bank, and until such bank's charges in respect of transfer are paid.

c.   Bank charges in respect of transfers are payable by the first beneficiary unless otherwise specified.

d. A credit can be transferred only if it is expressly designated as "transferable" by the issuing bank. Terms such as "divisible," "Fractionable," "assignable" and "transmissible" add nothing to the meaning of the term "transferable" and shall not be used.

e. A transferable credit can be transferred once only. Fractions of a transferable credit (not exceeding in the aggregate the amount of the credit) can be transferred separately, provided partial shipments are not prohibited, and the aggregate of such transfers will be considered as constituting only one transfer of the credit. The credit can be transferred only on the terms and conditions specified in the original credit, with the exception of the amount of the credit, of any unit prices stated therein, and of the period of validity or period for shipment, any or all of which may be reduced or curtailed.

Additionally, the name of the first beneficiary can be substituted for that of the applicant for the credit, but if the name of the applicant for the credit is specifically required by the original credit to appear in any document other than the invoice, such requirement must be fulfilled.

f. The first beneficiary has the right to substitute his own invoices for those of the second beneficiary, for amounts not in excess of the original amount stipulated in the credit and for the original unit prices if stipulated in the credit, and upon such substitution of invoices the first beneficiary can draw under the credit for the difference, if any, between his invoices and the second beneficiary's invoices. When a credit has been transferred and the first beneficiary is to supply his own invoices in exchange for the second beneficiary's invoices but fails to do so on first demand, the paying, accepting or negotiating bank has the right to deliver to the issuing bank the documents received under the credit, including the second beneficiary's invoices, without further responsibility to the first beneficiary.

g. The first beneficiary of a transferable credit can transfer the credit to a second beneficiary in the same country or in another country unless the credit specifically states otherwise. The first beneficiary shall have the right to request that payment or negotiation be effected to the second beneficiary at the place to which the credit has been transferred, up to and including the expiry date of the original credit, and without prejudice to the first beneficiary's right subsequently to substitute his own invoices for those of the second beneficiary and to claim any difference due to him.

Article 47

The fact that a credit is not stated to be transferable shall not affect the beneficiary's rights to assign the proceeds of such credit in accordance with the provisions of the applicable law.

Revised American Foreign Trade Definitions—1941

Adopted July 30, 1941, by a Joint Committee representing the Chamber of Commerce of the United States of America, the National Council of American Importers, Inc., and the National Foreign Trade Council, Inc.

The following *Revised American Foreign Trade Definitions—1941* are recommended for general use by both exporters and importers. These revised definitions have no status at law unless there is specific legislation providing for them, or unless they are confirmed by court decisions. Hence, it is suggested that sellers and buyers agree to their acceptance as part of the contract of sale. These definitions will then become legally binding upon all parties.

Adoption by exporters and importers of these revised terms will impress on all parties concerned their respective responsibilities and rights.

General Notes of Caution

1. As foreign trade definitions have been issued by organizations in various parts of the world, and as the courts of countries have interpreted these definitions in different ways, it is important that sellers and buyers agree that their contracts are subject to the *Revised American Foreign Trade Definitions—1941* and that the various points listed are accepted by both parties.

2. In addition to the foreign trade terms listed herein, there are terms that are at times used, such as Free Harbor, C.I.F. & C. (Cost, Insurance, Freight, and Commission), C.I.F.C. & I. (Cost, Insurance, Freight, Commission, and Interest), C.I.F. Landed (Cost, Insurance, Freight, Landed), and others. None of these should be used unless there has first been a definite understanding as to the exact meaning thereof. It is unwise to attempt to interpret other terms in the light of the terms

given herein. Hence, whenever possible, one of the terms defined herein should be used.

3. It is unwise to use abbreviations in quotations or in contracts which might be subject to misunderstanding.

4. When making quotations, the familiar terms "hundredweight" or "ton" should be avoided. A hundredweight can be 100 pounds of the short ton, or 112 pounds of the long ton. A ton can be a short ton of 2,000 pounds or a metric ton of 2,204.6 pounds, or a long ton of 2,240 pounds. Hence, the type of hundredweight or ton should be clearly stated in quotations and in sales confirmations. Also, all terms referring to quantity, weight, volume, length, or surface should be clearly defined and agreed upon.

5. If inspection, or certificate of inspection, is required, it should be agreed, in advance, whether the cost thereof is for account of seller or buyer.

6. Unless otherwise agreed upon, all expenses are for the account of seller up to the point at which the buyer must handle the subsequent movement of goods.

7. There are a number of elements in a contract that do not fall within the scope of these foreign trade definitions. Hence, no mention of these is made herein. Seller and buyer should agree to these separately when negotiating contracts. This particularly applies to so-called "customary" practices.

Definitions of Quotations

(I) EX (Point of Origin)

"Ex Factory," Ex Mill," "Ex Mine," "Ex Plantation," "Ex Warehouse," etc. (named point of origin)

Under this term, the price quoted applies only at the point of origin, and the seller agrees to place the goods at the disposal of the buyer at the agreed place on the date or within the period fixed.

Under this quotation:

Seller must

(1)   bear all costs and risks of the goods until such time as the buyer is obliged to take delivery thereof;

(2)   render the buyer, at the buyer's request and expense, assistance in obtaining the documents issued in the country of origin, or of shipment, or of both, which the buyer may require either for purposes of exportation, or of importation at destination.

Buyer must

(1)   take delivery of the goods as soon as they have been placed at this disposal at the agreed place on the date or within the period fixed;

(2)   pay export taxes, or other fees or charges, if any, levied because of exportation;

(3)   bear all costs and risks of the goods from the time when he is obligated to take delivery thereof;

(4)   pay all costs and charges incurred in obtaining the documents issued in the country of origin, or of shipment, or of both, which may be required either for purposes of exportation, or of importation at destination.

(II) F.O.B. (Free on Board)

Note: Seller and buyer should consider not only the definitions but also the "Comments on All F.O.B. Terms" given at end of this section in order to understand fully their respective responsibilities and rights under the several classes of "F.O.B." terms.

(II-A) "F.O.B. (named inland carrier at named inland point of departure)"

Under this term, the price quoted applied only at inland shipping point, and the seller arranges for loading of the goods on, or in, railway cars, trucks, lighters, barges, aircraft, or other conveyance furnished for transportation.

Under this quotation:

Seller must

(1)   place goods on, or in, conveyance, or deliver to inland carrier for loading;

(2)   provide clean bill of lading or other transportation receipt, freight collect;

(3)   be responsible for any loss or damage, or both, until goods have been placed in, or on, conveyance at loading point, and clean bill of lading at other transportation receipt has been furnished by the carrier;

(4)   render the buyer, at the buyer's request and expense, assistance in obtaining the documents issued in the country of origin, or of shipment, or of both, which the buyer may require either for purposes of exportation, or of importation at destination.

Buyer must

(1)   be responsible for all movement of the goods from inland point of loading, and pay all transportation costs;

(2)   pay export taxes, or other fees or charges, if any, levied because of exportation;

(3)   be responsible for any loss or damage, or both, incurred after loading at named inland point of departure;

(4)   pay all costs and charges incurred in obtaining the documents issued in the country of origin, or of shipment, or of both, which may be required either for purposes of exportation, or of importation at destination.

(II-B) "F.O.B. (named inland carrier at named inland point of departure) Freight Prepaid to (named point of exportation)"

Under this term, the seller quotes a price including transportation charges to the named point of exportation and prepays freight to named point of exportation, without assuming responsibility for the goods after obtaining a clean bill of lading or other transportation receipt at named inland point of departure.

Under this quotation:

Seller must

(1)   assume the seller's obligations as under II-A, except that under (2) he must provide clean bill of lading or other transportation receipt, freight prepaid to named point of exportation.

Buyer must

(1)   assume the same buyer's obligations as under II-A, except that he does not pay freight from loading point to named point of exportation.

(II-C) "F.O.B. (named inland carrier at named inland point of departure) Freight Allowed to (named point)"

Under this term, the seller quotes a price including the transportation charges to the named point, shipping freight collect and deducting the cost of transportation, without assuming responsibility for the goods after obtaining a clean bill of lading or other transportation receipt at named inland point of departure.

Under this quotation:

Seller must

(1)   assume the same seller's obligations as under II-A, but deducts from his invoice the transportation cost to named point.

Buyer must

(1)   assume the same buyer's obligations as under II-A, including payment of freight from inland loading point to named point, for which seller has made deduction.

(II-D) "F.O.B. (named inland carrier at named point of exportation)"

Under this term, the seller quotes a price including the costs of transportation of the goods to named point of exportation, bearing any loss or damage, or both, incurred up to that point.

Under this quotation:

Seller must

(1)   place goods on, or in, conveyance, or deliver to inland carrier for loading;

(2)   provide clean bill of lading or other transportation receipt, paying all transportation costs from loading point to named point of exportation;

(3)   be responsible for any loss or damage, or both, until goods have arrived in, or on, inland conveyance at the named point of exportation;

(4)   render the buyer, at the buyer's request and expense, assistance in obtaining the documents issued in the country of origin, or of shipment, or of both,

which the buyer may require either for purposes of exportation, or of importation at destination.

Buyer must

(1)　be responsible for all movement of the goods from inland conveyance at named point of exportation;

(2)　pay export taxes, or other fees or charges, if any, levied because of exportation;

(3)　be responsible for any loss or damage, or both, incurred after goods have arrived in, or on, inland conveyance at the named point of exportation;

(4)　pay all costs and charges incurred in obtaining the documents issued in the country of origin, or of shipment, or of both, which may be required either for purposes of exportation, or of importation at destination.

(II-E) "F.O.B. Vessel (named port of shipment)"

Under this term, the seller quotes a price covering all expenses up to, and including, delivery of the goods upon the overseas vessel provided by, or for, the buyer at the named port of shipment.

Under this quotation:

Seller must

(1)　pay all charges incurred in placing goods, actually on board the vessel designated and provided by, or for, the buyer on the date or within the period fixed;

(2)　provide clean ship's receipt or on-board bill of lading;

(3)　be responsible for any loss or damage, or both, until goods have been placed on board the vessel on the date or within the period fixed;

(4)　render the buyer, at the buyer's request and expense, assistance in obtaining the documents issued in the country of origin, or of shipment, or of both, which the buyer may require either for purposes of exportation, or of importation at destination.

Buyer must

(1)　give seller adequate notice of name, sailing date, loading berth of, and delivery time to, the vessel;

(2)　bear the additional costs incurred and all risks of the goods from the time when the seller has placed them at his disposal if the vessel named by him fails to arrive or to load within the designated time;

(3)　handle all subsequent movement of the goods to destination;

　　(a)　provide and pay for insurance;

　　(b)　provide and pay for ocean and other transportation;

(4)   pay export taxes, or other fees or charges, if any, levied because of exportation;

(5)   be responsible for any loss or damage, or both, after goods have been loaded on board the vessel;

(6)   pay all costs and charges incurred in obtaining the documents, other than clean ship's receipt or bill of lading, issued in the country of origin, or of shipment, or of both, which may be required either for purposes of exportation, or of importation at destination.

(II-F) "F.O.B. (named inland point in country of importation)"

Under this term, the seller quotes a price including the cost of the merchandise and all costs of transportation to the named inland point in the country of importation.
Under this quotation:

Seller must

(1)   provide and pay for all transportation to the named inland point in the country of importation;

(2)   pay export taxes, or other fees or charges, if any, levied because of exportation;

(3)   provide and pay for marine insurance;

(4)   provide and pay for war risk insurance, unless otherwise agreed upon between the seller and buyer;

(5)   be responsible for any loss or damage, or both, until arrival of goods on conveyance at the named inland point in the country of importation;

(6)   pay the costs of certificates of origin, consular invoices, or any other documents issued in the country of origin, or of shipment, or of both, which the buyer may require for the importation of goods into the country of destination and, where necessary, for their passage in transit through another country;

(7)   pay all costs of landing, including wharfage, landing charges, and taxes, if any;

(8)   pay all costs of customs entry in the country of importation;

(9)   pay customs duties and all taxes applicable to imports, if any, in the country of importation.

Note: The seller under this quotation must realize that he is accepting important responsibilities, costs, and risks, and should therefore be certain to obtain adequate insurance. On the other hand, the importer or buyer may desire such quotations to relieve him of the risks of the voyage and to assure him of his landed costs at inland point in country of importation. When competition is keen, or the buyer is accustomed to such quotations from other sellers, seller may quote such terms, being careful to protect himself in an appropriate manner.

Buyer must

(1)   take prompt delivery of goods from conveyance upon arrival at destination;

(2)   bear any costs and be responsible for all loss or damage, or both, after arrival at destination.

Comments On All F.O.B. Terms

In connection with F.O.B. terms, the following points of caution are recommended:

1. The method of inland transportation, such as trucks, railroad cars, lighters, barges, or aircraft should be specified.

2. If any switching charges are involved during the inland transportation, it should be agreed, in advance, whether these charges are for account of the seller or the buyer.

3. The term "F.O.B. (named port)," without designating the exact point at which the liability of the seller terminates and the liability of the buyer begins, should be avoided. The use of this term gives rise to disputes as to the liability of the seller or the buyer in the event of loss or damage arising while the goods are in port, and before delivery to or on board the ocean carrier. Misunderstandings may be avoided by naming the specific point of delivery.

4. If lighterage or trucking is required in the transfer of goods from the inland conveyance to ship's side, and there is a cost therefore, it should be understood, in advance, whether this cost is for account of the seller or the buyer.

5. The seller should be certain to notify the buyer of the minimum quantity required to obtain a carload, a truckload, or a barge-load freight rate.

6. Under F.O.B. terms, excepting "F.O.B. (named inland point in country of importation)," the obligation to obtain ocean freight space, and marine and war risk insurance, rests with the buyer. Despite this obligation on the part of the buyer, in many trades the seller obtains the ocean freight space, and marine and war risk insurance, and provides for shipment on behalf of the buyer. Hence, seller and buyer must have an understanding as to whether the buyer will obtain the ocean freight space, and marine and war risk insurance, as is his obligation, or whether the seller agrees to do this for the buyer.

7. For the seller's protection, he should provide in his contract of sale that marine insurance obtained by the buyer include standard warehouse to warehouse coverage.

(III) F.A.S. (free along side)

Note: Seller and buyer should consider not only the definitions but also the "Comments" given at the end of this section, in order to understand fully their respective responsibilities and rights under "F.A.S." terms.

"F.A.S. Vessel (named port of shipment)"

Under this term, the seller quotes a price including delivery of the goods along side overseas vessel and within reach of its loading tackle.

Under this quotation:

Seller must

(1) place goods along side vessel or on dock designated and provided by, or for, buyer on the date or within the period fixed; pay any heavy lift charges, where necessary, up to this point;

(2) provide clean dock or ship's receipt;

(3) be responsible for any loss or damage, or both, until goods have been delivered along side the vessel or on the dock;

(4) render the buyer, at the buyer's request and expense, assistance in obtaining the documents issued in the country of origin, or of shipment, or of both, which the buyer may require either for purposes of exportation, or of importation at destination.

Buyer must

(1) give seller adequate notice of name, sailing date, loading berth of, and delivery time to, the vessel;

(2) handle all subsequent movement of the goods from along side the vessel;

   (a) arrange and pay for demurrage or storage charges, or both, in warehouse or on wharf, where necessary;

   (b) provide and pay for insurance;

   (c) provide and pay for ocean and other transportation;

(3) pay export taxes, or other fees or charges, if any, levied because of exportation;

(4) be responsible for any loss or damage, or both, while the goods are on a lighter or other conveyance along side vessel within reach of its loading tackle, or on the dock awaiting loading, or until actually loading on board the vessel, and subsequent thereto;

(5) pay all costs and charges incurred in obtaining the documents, other than clean dock or ship's receipt, issued in the country of origin, or of shipment, or of both, which may be required either for purposes of exportation, or of importation at destination.

F.A.S. Comments

1. Under F.A.S. terms, the obligation to obtain ocean freight space, and marine and war risk insurance, rests with the buyer. Despite this obligation on the part of the buyer, in many trades the seller obtains ocean freight space, and marine and war risk insurance, and provides for shipment on behalf of the buyer. In others, the buyer notifies the seller to make delivery along side a vessel designated by the buyer and the buyer provides his own marine and war risk insurance. Hence, seller and buyer must have an understanding as to whether the buyer will obtain the ocean freight space, and marine and war risk insurance, as is his obligation, or whether the seller agrees to do this for the buyer.

2. For the seller's protection, he should provide in his contract of sale that marine insurance obtained by the buyer include standard warehouse to warehouse coverage.

(IV) C.&F. (cost and freight)

Note: Seller and buyer should consider not only the definitions but also the "C.&F. Comments" and the "C.&F. and C.I.F. Comments", in order to understand fully their respective responsibilities and rights under "C.&F." terms.

"C.&F. (named point of destination)"

Under this term, the seller quotes a price including the cost of transportation to named point of destination.

Under this quotation:

Seller Must

(1)   provide and pay for transportation to named point of destination;

(2)   pay export taxes, or other fees or charges, if any, levied because of exportation;

(3)   obtain and dispatch promptly to buyer, or his agent, clean bill of lading to named point of destination;

(4)   where received-for-shipment ocean bill of lading may be tendered, be responsible for any loss or damage, or both, until the goods have been delivered into the custody of the ocean carrier;

(5)   where on-board ocean bill of lading is required, be responsible for any loss or damage, or both, until the goods have been delivered on board the vessel;

(6)   provide, at the buyer's request and expense, certificates of origin, consular invoices, or any other documents issued in the country of origin, or of shipment, or of both, which the buyer may require for importation of goods into country of destination and, where necessary, for their passage in transit through another country.

Buyer must

(1)   accept the documents when presented;

(2)   receive goods upon arrival, handle and pay for all subsequent movement of the goods, including taking delivery from vessel in accordance with bill of lading clauses and terms; pay all costs of handling, including any duties, taxes, and other expenses at named point of destination;

(3)   provide and pay for insurance;

(4)   be responsible for loss of or damage to goods, or both, from time and place at which seller's obligations under (4) and (5) above have ceased;

(5)   pay the costs of certificates of origin, consular invoices, or any other documents issued in the country of origin, or of shipment, or of both, which may be required for the importation of goods into the country of destination and, where necessary, for their passage in transit through another country.

C. & F. Comments

1. For the seller's protection, he should provide in his contract of sale that marine insurance obtained by the buyer include standard warehouse to warehouse coverage.

2. The comments listed under the following C.I.F. terms in many cases apply to C. & F. terms as well, and should be read and understood by the C. & F. seller and buyer.

(V) C.I.F. (cost, insurance, freight)

Note: Seller and buyer should consider not only the definitions but also the "Comments" at the end of this section, in order to understand fully their respective responsibilities and rights under "C.I.F." terms.

"C.I.F. (named point of destination)"

Under this term, the seller quotes a price including the cost of the goods, the marine insurance, and all transportation charges to the named point of destination.
Under this quotation:

Seller must

(1)   provide and pay for transportation to named point of destination;

(2)   pay export taxes, or other fees or charges, if any, levied because of exportation;

(3)   provide and pay for marine insurance;

(4)   provide war risk insurance as obtainable in seller's market at time of shipment at buyer's expense, unless seller has agreed that buyer provide for war risk coverage (See Comment 10 (c));

(5)   obtain and dispatch promptly to buyer, or his agent, clean bill of lading to named point of destination, and also insurance policy or negotiable insurance certificate;

(6)   where received-for-shipment ocean bill of lading may be tendered, be responsible for any loss or damage, or both, until the goods have been delivered into the custody of the ocean carrier;

(7)   where on-board ocean bill of lading is required, be responsible for any loss or damage, or both, until the goods have been delivered on board the vessel;

(8)   provide, at the buyer's request and expense, certificates of origin, consular invoices, or any other documents issued in the country of origin, or of shipment, or both, which the buyer may require for importation of goods into country of destination and, where necessary, for their passage in transit through another country.

Buyer must

(1)   accept the documents when presented;

(2)   receive the goods upon arrival, handle and pay for all subsequent movement of the goods, including taking delivery from vessel in accordance with bill of lading clauses and terms; pay all costs of landing, including any duties, taxes, and other expenses at named point of destination;

(3)   pay for war risk insurance provided by seller;

(4)   be responsible for loss of or damage to goods, or both, from time and place at which seller's obligations under (6) or (7) above have ceased;

(5)   pay the cost of certificates of origin, consular invoices, or any other documents issued in the country of origin, or of shipment, or both, which may be required for importation of the goods into the country of destination and, where necessary, for their passage in transit through another country.

C. & F. and C.I.F. Comments

Under C. & F. and C.I.F. contracts there are the following points on which the seller and the buyer should be in complete agreement at the time that the contract is concluded:

1. It should be agreed upon, in advance, who is to pay for miscellaneous expenses, such as weighing or inspection charges.

2. The quantity to be shipped on any one vessel should be agreed upon, in advance, with a view to the buyer's capacity to take delivery upon arrival and discharge of the vessel, within the free time allowed at the port of importation.

3. Although the terms C. & F. and C.I.F. are generally interpreted to provide that charges for consular invoices and certificates of origin are for the account of the buyer, and are charged separately, in many trades these charges are included by

the seller in his price. Hence, seller and buyer should agree, in advance, whether these charges are part of the selling price, or will be invoiced separately.

4. The point of final destination should be definitely known in the event the vessel discharges at a port other than the actual destination of the goods.

5. When ocean freight space is difficult to obtain, or forward freight contracts cannot be made at firm rates, it is advisable that sales contracts, as an exception to regular C. & F. or C.I.F. terms, should provide that shipment within the contract period be subject to ocean freight space being available to the seller, and should also provide that changes in the cost of ocean transportation between the time of sale and the time of shipment be for account of the buyer.

6. Normally, the seller is obligated to prepay the ocean freight. In some instances, shipments are made freight collect and the amount of the freight is deducted from the invoice rendered by the seller. It is necessary to be in agreement on this, in advance, in order to avoid misunderstanding which arises from foreign exchange fluctuations which might affect the actual cost of transportation, and from interest charges which might accrue under the letter of credit financing. Hence, the seller should always prepay the ocean freight unless he has a specific agreement with the buyer, in advance, that goods can be shipped freight collect.

7. The buyer should recognize that he does not have the right to insist on inspection of goods prior to accepting the documents. The buyer should not refuse to take delivery of goods on account of delay in the receipt of documents, provided the seller has used due diligence in their dispatch through the regular channels.

8. Sellers and buyers are advised against including in a C.I.F. contract any indefinite clause at variance with the obligations of a C.I.F. contract as specified in these Definitions. There have been numerous court decisions in the United States and other countries invalidating C.I.F. contracts because of the inclusion of indefinite clauses.

9. Interest charges should be included in cost computations and should not be charged as a separate item in C.I.F. contracts, unless otherwise agreed upon, in advance, between the seller and buyer; in which case, however, the term C.I.F. and I. (Cost, Insurance, Freight, and Interest) should be used.

10. In connection with insurance under C.I.F. sales, it is necessary that seller and buyer be definitely in accord upon the following points:

(a) The character of the marine insurance should be agreed upon in so far as being W.A. (With Average) of F.P.A. (Free of Particular Average), as well as any other special risks that are covered in specific trades, or against which the buyer may wish individual protection. Among the special risks that should be considered and agreed upon between seller and buyer are theft, pilferage, leakage, breakage, sweat, contact with other cargoes, and others peculiar to any particular trade. It is important that contingent or collect freight and customs duty should be insured to cover Particular Average losses, as well as total loss after arrival and entry but before delivery.

(b) The seller is obligated to exercise ordinary care and diligence in selecting an underwriter that is in good financial standing. However, the risk of obtaining settlement of insurance claims rests with the buyer.

(c) War risk insurance under this term is to be obtained by the seller at the expense and risk of the buyer. It is important that the seller be in definite accord with the buyer on this point, particularly as to the cost. It is desirable that the goods be insured against both marine and war risk with the same underwriter, so that there can be no difficulty arising from the determination of the cause of the loss.

(d) Seller should make certain that in his marine or war risk insurance, there be included the standard protection against strikes, riots and civil commotions.

(e) Seller and buyer should be in accord as to the insured valuation, bearing in mind that merchandise contributes in General Average on certain bases of valuation which differ in various trades. It is desirable that a competent insurance broker be consulted, in order that full value be covered and trouble avoided.

(VI) "Ex Dock (named port of importation)"

Note:Seller and buyer should consider not only the definitions but also the "Ex Dock Comments" at the end of this section, in order to understand fully their respective responsibilities and rights under "Ex Dock" terms.

Under this term, seller quotes a price including the cost of the goods and all additional costs necessary to place the goods on the dock at the named port of importation, duty paid, if any.

Under this quotation:

Seller must

(1)   provide and pay for transportation to named port of importation;

(2)   pay export taxes, or other fees or charges, if any, levied because of exportation;

(3)   provide and pay for marine insurance;

(4)   provide and pay for war risk insurance, unless otherwise agreed upon between the buyer and seller;

(5)   be responsible for any loss or damage, or both, until the expiration of the free time allowed on the dock at the named port of importation;

(6)   pay the costs of certificates of origin, consular invoices, legalization of bill of lading, or any other documents issued in the country of origin, or of ship-

ment, or of both, which the buyer may require for the importation of goods into the country of destination and, where necessary, for their passage in transit through another country;

(7)   pay all costs of landing, including wharfage, landing charges, and taxes, if any;

(8)   pay all costs of customs entry in the country of importation;

(9)   pay customs duties and all taxes applicable to imports, if any, in the country of importation, unless otherwise agreed upon.

Buyer must

(1)   take delivery of the goods on the dock at the named port of importation within the free time allowed;

(2)   bear the cost and risk of the goods if delivery is not taken within the free time allowed.

Ex Dock Comments

This term is used principally in United States import trade. It has various modifications, such as "Ex Quay," "Ex Pier," etc., but it is seldom, if ever, used in American export practice. Its use in quotations for export is not recommended.

Glossary Two

Commercial Terms

A.B. or AKtb: for Aktiebolager, a Swedish joint stock company.

A.G.: for Aktien-Gesellschaft, German joint stock company.

A/P—Authority to Pay: a letter, used primarily in the Far East, addressed by a bank to a seller of merchandise, authorizing the purchase, with or without recourse, of draft(s) and document(s) to a stipulated amount drawn on a foreign buyer in payment of specified merchandise shipment(s).

A.S. or AKts: Aktieselskabet, a Danish joint stock company (Aktieselskabet in Norway).

Acceptance: a draft, payable at a determinable future date, upon the face of which the drawee acknowledges his obligation to pay it at maturity.

(a) **Banker's Acceptance**: a draft of which a bank is drawee and acceptor;

(b) **Trade Acceptance**: a draft, usually arising from the sales of merchandise, of which the drawee and acceptor is an individual or a mercantile concern.

Ad Valorem Duty: see Duty.

Advisory Capacity: a term designating the limited power of a shipper's agent or representative abroad not authorizing him to make definite decisions and adjustments without reference to his principals.

After Date: the time begins to run from the date of a draft bearing this phrase: the fixed date of maturity does not depend upon the date of acceptance of the draft.

After Sight: time begins to run from the date of acceptance of a draft bearing this phrase.

Agio: the premium paid to exchange one currency for another.

Allenge: a slip of paper attached to a bill of exchange, acceptance or note, providing space for additional endorsements.

Source: Crocker National Bank,
   International Division,
    44 Montgomery St., San Francisco, CA 94104.

Arbitrage: the buying of foreign exchange, securities, or commodities in one market and the simultaneous selling in another market, in terms of a third market. By this manipulation a profit is made because of the difference in the rates of exchange or in the prices of securities or commodities involved.

Average: see Ocean Marine Insurance Policy.

Back-to-Back Credit: a term used to denote a letter of credit issued for the account of a buyer of merchandise already holding a letter of credit in his favor. The "back-to-back" letter of credit is issued in favor of the supplier of the merchandise to cover the same shipment stipulated in the credit already held by the buyer. The terms of both letters of credit, with the exception of the amount and expiration date, are so similar that the same documents presented under the "back-to-back" credit are subsequently applied against the credit in favor of the buyer. However, the buyer or beneficiary of the first credit, substitutes his draft and invoice for those presented by the supplier.

Barter: the exchange of commodities using merchandise as compensation, instead of money. Countries having blocked currencies often use this "method."

Beneficiary: the person in whose favor a draft is issued or a letter of credit opened.

Bill of Exchange (or Draft): an unconditional written order addressed by one person to another, signed by the donor and requiring the addressee to pay on demand or at a fixed date a certain sum in money to the order of a specified person.

Bill of Lading (Ocean): a document signed by the captain, agents, or owners of a vessel, furnishing written evidence for the conveyance and delivery of seaborne merchandise to a destination, it represents a receipt for merchandise and contract to deliver it as freight.

(a) **Clean**: a term describing a bill a lading when the transportation company had not noted irregularities in the packing or general condition of the shipment.

(b) **Straight**: a non-negotiable bill of lading that consigns the goods directly to a stipulated consignee.

(c) **Order**: a bill of lading usually issued to the shipper, whose endorsement is required to effect its negotiation.

(d) **Order "Notify"**: a bill of lading issued usually to the order of the shipper with the additional clause that the consignee is to be notified upon arrival of the merchandise, however, without giving the consignee title to the merchandise.

(e) **Through Bill of Lading**: a bill of lading used when several carriers, normally connecting, are involved.

Binder: a temporary insurance coverage pending the later issuance of an insurance policy or certificate.

Blocked Exchange: exchange not freely convertible into other currencies.

Bonded Warehouse: a building for storing goods authorized by customs officials until removal, without the payment of duties.

Both to Blame Collision Clause: see Ocean Marine Insurance Policy.

Carrier: freight company, air, ocean, inland, truck, rail.

C. & F.–Cost & Freight: see revised American Foreign Definitions.

C.I.F.–Cost, Insurance & Freight: see revised American Foreign Definitions section.

Certificate of Inspection: a document often required with shipments of perishable or other goods, when certification notes the good condition of the merchandise immediately prior to shipment.

Certificate of Manufacture: a statement sometimes notarized by a producer, usually also the seller, or merchandiser that indicates the goods have been manufactured and are at the disposal of the buyer.

Certificate of Origin: a special document certifying the country of origin of the merchandise required by certain foreign countries for tariff purposes, it sometimes requires the signature of the consul of the country to which it is destined.

Charges Forward: a banking term used when foreign and domestic bank commission charges, interest and government taxes in connection with the collection of a draft are for the drawee's account.

Charges Here: a banking term used when foreign and domestic bank commission charges, interest and government taxes in connection with the collection of a draft are for the drawer's account.

Charter Party: a written contract between the owner of a vessel and the one (the charterer) desiring to empty the vessel, setting forth the terms of the arrangement, i.e., freight rate and ports involved in the contemplated trip.

Clean Draft: a draft without attached documents.

Commercial Invoice: a statement of a transaction between a seller and buyer prepared by the seller, and a description of the merchandise, price, terms, etc.

Consignee: the person, firm or representative to which a seller or shipper sends merchandise.

Consignment: merchandise shipped to a foreign agent or customer when an actual purchase has not been made, but under an agreement obliging the consignee to pay the consignor for the goods when sold.

Consignor: the seller or shipper of merchandise.

Consular Documents: bills of lading, certificates of origin or special invoice forms that are officially signed by the consul of the country of destination.

Consular Invoice: a detailed statement of goods shipped certified by the consul at the point of shipment.

Consular Visa: an official signature the consul of the country of destination affixes to certain shipping documents.

Cover Note: the British equivalent of the United States "Binder."

Customs Broker: licensed by U.S. Customs to clear shipments for clients, also can forward goods "In Bond" to your port.

D/A—Documents Against Acceptance: instructions from a shipper to his bank that the documents attached to a time draft for collection are deliverable to the drawee against his acceptance of the draft.

D/P—Documents Against Payment: instructions a shipper gives to his bank that the documents attached to a draft for collection are deliverable to the drawee only against his payment of the draft.

Date Draft: a draft drawn to mature on a fixed date, irrespective of its acceptance date.

Delivery Order: a delivery order issued to or by a warehouse, a railroad, a steamship company or airline, or anyone with the authority and legal right to claim or order delivery of merchandise.

Discount:

    (a) **Commercial:** an allowance from the quoted price of goods, made usually by the deduction of a certain percentage from the invoice price.

    (b) **Financial:** a deduction from the face value of commercial paper, such as bills of exchange and acceptances, in consideration of receipt by the seller of cash before maturity date.

Dishonor: refusal on the part of the drawee to accept a draft or to pay it when due.

Dock Receipt: receipt issued by an ocean carrier or its agent for merchandise delivered at its dock or warehouse awaiting shipment.

Documentary Credit: a commercial letter of credit providing for payment by a bank to the name beneficiary, usually the seller or merchandise, against delivery of documents specified in the credit.

Documents: papers customarily attached to foreign drafts, consisting of ocean bills of lading, marine insurance certificates, and commercial invoices, and where required, including certificates of origin and consular invoices.

Domicile: the place where a draft or acceptance is made payable.

Draft: see Bill of Exchange.

Drawback: see Duty.

Drawee: the address of a draft, i.e., the person on whom the draft is drawn.

Drawer: the issuer, or signer, of a draft.

Drop Ship: shipment by foreign shipper directly to your domestic customer. Price includes freight and postage.

Duty:

    (a) **ad valorem** duty means an assessed amount at a certain percentage rate on the monetary value of an import.

(b) **Specific duty**: an assessment on the weight or quantity of an article without preference to its monetary value or market price.

(c) **Drawback**: a recovery in whole or in part of duty paid on imported merchandise at the time of exportation, in the same or different form.

E. & O.E.—Errors and Omissions Excepted: a phrase accompanying the shipper's signature on an invoice, by which he disclaims final responsibility for typographical errors or unintentional omissions.

Endorsement: a signature on the reverse of a negotiable instrument made primarily for the purpose of transferring the holder's rights to another person, it constitutes a contract between the holder and all parties to the instrument. Each endorser thus orders the prior parties to fulfill the contract to his endorsee and also agrees with the endorsees that, if they do not, he will.

English and Colonial Clause: a clause used in connection with drafts drawn in sterling (£) on the British Commonwealth and Colonies, requiring the drawee of a draft to pay exchange (plus English and Colonial stamps) at the current London exchange rate for the negotiation of drafts on the colonies.

Expiration Date: the final date upon which draft(s) under a letter of credit may be presented for negotiation.

Extension: an additional period granted by the drawer for payment of a draft when the drawee is unable or unwilling to make payment on the maturity date.

F.A.S.—Free Alongside Vessel: see Revised Foreign Trade Definitions.

F.O.B.—Free on Board: (destination) (named point) (vessel)—see Revised Foreign Trade Definitions.

F.P.A.—Free of Particular Average: see Ocean Marine Insurance Policy.

First of Exchange: the original of a draft drawn in original and duplicate.

Foreign Exchange: a general term applied to transactions involving foreign currencies.

Future Exchange Contract: usually a contract between a bank and its customer to purchase or sell foreign exchange at a fixed rate with delivery at a specified time, generally used because the customer desires to preclude the risk of fluctuations in foreign exchange rates.

G.m.b.H.: the abbreviation for the German term "Gesellschaft mit beschraenkter Haftung," meaning a limited liability company. The equivalent of "incorporated."

Go-Down: a warehouse in the Far East where goods are stored and delivered when warranted.

In Bond: a term applied to the status of merchandise admitted provisionally to a country without payment of duties—either for storage in a bonded warehouse or for trans-shipment to another point, where duties will eventually be imposed.

In Case of Need: a term used of the agent or representative of a shipper abroad, to whom a bank may apply for instructions, when the shipper directs.

Inherent Vice: a condition causing damage to merchandise by reason of its own inherent defects.

Insurance Certificate: see Ocean Marine Insurance Policy.

Jettison: the throwing overboard of part of a craft's cargo or equipment in order to save the remainder.

Letter of Credit-Commercial: a letter addressed by a bank, at the instance and responsibility of a buyer of merchandise, to a seller, authorizing him to draw drafts to a stipulated amount under specified terms and undertaking conditionally or unconditionally to provide eventual payment for drafts.

(a) **Confirmed Irrevocable Letter of Credit:** a letter to which has been added the responsibility of a bank other than the issuing bank.

(b) **Irrevocable Letter of Credit:** a letter of credit which can neither be modified nor cancelled without the agreement of all concerned.

(c) **Revocable Letter of Credit:** a revocable credit may be modified or cancelled at any time without notice to the beneficiary. However, payment or acceptances made by the negotiating bank within the terms of the credit prior to receipt of cancellation notice from the issuing bank validly bind all concerned parties.

(d) **Revolving Credit:** a letter from the issuing bank notifying a seller of merchandise that the amount involved when utilized will again become available, usually under the same terms and without issuance of another letter.

Special Clauses:

(a) **Red Clause:** a clause authorizing the drawing of clean drafts without documents accompanied by a statement that pertinent shipping documents will be furnished later.

(b) **Telegraphic Transfer Clause:** a clause including an undertaking by the issuing bank to pay the draft amount to the negotiating bank upon receipt of an authenticated cablegram from the latter indicating it has received the required documents.

Letter of Credit—Traveler's (Circular): a letter addressed by a bank to its correspondent banks authorizing them to honor drafts of the holder to the amount of credit.

Lighterage: the cost of loading or unloading a vessel by barges.

Lloyd's Registry: an organization maintained for the classification of ships in order that interested parties may know the quality and condition of the vessels offered for insurance or employment.

Ltd.–Limited: originally a British abbreviation denoting a company that limits the owner's liability to the amount of invested or subscribed capital.

M/V: motor vessel.

Mate's Receipt: receipt signed by the mate of a vessel acknowledging receipt of cargo. This type of receipt is not usually encountered except in case of chartered vessels.

Maturity Date: the date when a note, draft, or acceptance becomes due for payment.

Ocean Marine Insurance Policy: an indemnity contract designed to reimburse an insured for the loss because of unforeseen circumstances or damage to merchandise shipped. The basic marine policy insures transportation perils but can be amended to cover additional hazards.

(a) **Open Policy**: a marine insurance contract in which the insurer agrees that all shipments moving at the insured's risk are automatically covered under the policy and the insured agrees to report the shipments and to pay premium thereon to the insurer.

(b) **Special Marine Policy**: sometimes referred to as a marine insurance certificate—this is a policy covering a specific shipment, most frequently used to provide evidence of insurance.

Marine Insurance Terms:

(a) **Average**: a term of marine insurance meaning loss or damage.

(b) **General Average**: a loss arising from a voluntary sacrifice made of any part of the vessel or cargo, or expenditure to prevent loss of the whole and for the benefit of all persons at interest. The loss is apportioned not only among all the shippers including those whose property is lost, but also to the vessel itself. Until the assessment is paid, a lien lies against the entire cargo.

(c) **Particular Average**: a marine insurance term meaning a partial loss, or damage.

(d) **With Average (W.A.) or With Particular Average (W.P.A.)**: provides protection for partial loss by perils of the sea if it amounts to a certain percentage, usually 3 percent of the insured value. The 3 percent, a franchise, is not a deductible percentage, rather the minimum amount of claim. The franchise does not apply when a vessel is involved in a fire, stranding, sinking, burning, or a collision, or in General Average losses.

(e) **Free of Particular Average, American Conditions—(FPAAC)**: covers only those losses directly resulting from fire, stranding, sinking or collision of the vessel.

(f) **Free of Particular Average, English Conditions—(FPAEC)**: this resembles PFAAC except that partial loss resulting from any peril of the sea becomes recoverable when the vessel has been stranded, sunk, burned, on fire or in a collision with the insured cargo aboard. The actual damage need not directly result from these specified perils—only that one of them has occurred.

(g) **Average Irrespective of Percentage**: the broadest "with Average" clause permits full recovery, regardless of percentage, or of partial losses due to perils of the sea.

The foregoing clauses may be broadened by adding coverage for theft, pilferage, non-delivery, breakage, or leakage, for example.

(h) **All Risks**: the broadest marine insurance coverage insures merchandise against all risks of physical loss or damage from any external cause which may arise. Delay, deterioration, loss of market, inherent vice, capture and seizure, war, strikes, riots and civil commotion represent various exclusions.

(i) **Warehouse to Warehouse**: a common marine insurance term referring to coverage which attaches to the goods upon their leaving the shipper's warehouse. It continues during the ordinary course of transit until delivery of the merchandise at the consignee's warehouse, within specified time limits.

(j) **Both to Blame Collision Clause**: this constitutes protection against a disclaimer of liability and it appears in some bills of lading when damage results from negligence of both vessels that are parties to an accident.

(k) **Strikes, Riots, and Civil Commotion—(S.R. & CC.)**: the marine policy does not cover the risks of strikes, riots, and civil commotion, except on endorsement.

(l) **Free of Capture and Seizure—(F.C. & S.)**: this clause excludes the risks of war and warlike operations from the marine policy.

(m) **War Risk**: although not covered under any of the foregoing terms of average, the risks of war may be covered under a separate open War Risk only Policy or by endorsement of the Special or Individual Marine Policy.

Open Policy: See Ocean Marine Insurance Policy.

Par of Exchange: the equivalent of the unit of money in one country expressed in the currency of another country, using gold as the standard value.

Parcel Post Receipt: a signed postal acknowledgment of delivery of a shipment made by parcel post.

Particular Average: see Ocean Marine Insurance.

Payee: the person to whom a draft or check is made payable.

Per Mille: per 1000. a basis upon which quotations are frequently made in foreign countries, instead of fractional percentage, e.g. one per mille ($1^\circ/00$) is equal to one tenth per cent (1/10%).

Per Pro (p.pl): an abbreviation for per procuration, applied to the signature of an authorized agent on behalf of his principal.

Perils of the Sea: a marine insurance policy phrase referring to accidents or casualties of the sea against which a simple marine policy insures.

Protest: this represents a certificate of dishonor provided by a consul, vice consul, notary public, or other person so authorized when an instrument presented for acceptance or payment is refused.

Pty: "proprietary," signifying a privately owned company in Great Britian and the Commonwealth.

Rate of Exchange: an expression signifying the basis upon which the money of one country will be exchanged for that of another.

Rebate Rate: the rate per cent deductible if a bill of exchange or draft is paid before its maturity date.

Red Clause: see Letters of Credit.

S.A.: Sociedad Anonima, Societe Anonyme and for Societa Anomima, joint stock companies in Spanish-and-French-speaking countries and Italy, respectively.

S/S: steamship.

S. en C.: Sociedad en Comandita, a silent partnership in Spanish-speaking countries.

Second of Exchange: the duplicate of a draft drawn in original and duplicate.

Security Agreement: an agreement that creates or provides for a security interest.

Security Interest: indicates an interest in personal property or fixtures securing payment or performance of an obligation.

Ship's Manifest: a written instrument duly signed by the captain, containing a true list of the individual shipments comprising a vessel's cargo.

Sight Draft: a draft payable upon presentation to the drawee.

Specific Duty: see Duty.

Tare: the weight of the container or package holding merchandise.

Telegraphic Transfer Clause: see Letters of Credit.

Tenor: the term fixed for payment of a draft.

Time Draft: a draft maturing at a fixed or terminable future date.

Transit Shipment: a term designating a shipment destined for an interior point or a place best reached by reshipment from another port.

Trust Receipt: a written agreement, signed and delivered by the trustee in a trust receipt transaction, designating the goods, documents or instruments concerned and signifying that the entruster has a security interest therein.

Usance: the same as tenor.

W.A. (W.P.A.): With Average. (With Particular Average.)

Warehouse Receipt: a receipt supplied by a warehouseman for goods he has placed in storage.

    (a) **Negotiable:** transferable by endorsement and requiring surrender of a receipt to the warehouseman for delivery of the goods.

    (b) **Non-Negotiable:** indicates the non-transferability of goods will be delivered only to the person named therein or to a third party only on written order, i.e., delivery order.

Weight:

    (a) **Gross:** generally, the total weight of the shipped merchandise including all containers and packing material.

    (b) **Legal:** generally, the weight of the merchandise plus the immediate container, a definition that varies somewhat by country.

    (c) **Net:** generally, the weight of the merchandise unpacked, exclusive of containers. This definition also varies somewhat in other countries.

Wharfage: a charge assessed by docks for the handling of incoming or outgoing merchandise.

Without Recourse: a form of endorsement specifying that the endorser does not agree to pay a dishonored instrument, it does not otherwise affect the general warranties by an endorser.

Bibliography

Pamphlets

All of the following are introductory pamphlets that are either free or cost only a few dollars. There are stars by the ones that I have found most useful.

A Basic Guide to Exporting, August 1976. U.S. Department of Commerce, Washington, D.C., and 43 district offices.

A Business Guide to the Near East and North Africa, July 1976. U.S. Department of Commerce, Washington, D.C.

Introductory Guide to Exporting, 1971. U.S. Department of Commerce, Washington, D.C.

Export and Import Procedures. Morgan Guaranty Trust Company, International Banking Division, 23 Wall St., New York, N.Y. 10008.

Export Information Services for U.S. Business Firms. U.S. Department of Commerce, Washington, D.C.

Export Marketing for Smaller Firms, August 1971, Third Edition. Small Business Administration, Washington, D.C.

Exporting to the United States, September 1977. U.S. Customs Service, Washington, D.C.

A Guide to Financing Imports, December 1976. U.S. Department of Commerce, Washington, D.C.

Guide to Foreign Information Sources, March 1974. Chamber of Commerce of the U.S., Washington, D.C.

Guidelines for Importers (Exporting to the United States), 1975. American Importers Association, 420 Lexington Ave., New York, N.Y. 10017.

How to Become Financially Independent in the Import Business, 1974. D. D. Klinger.

Overseas Export Promotion Calendar, October 1977–December 1978. U.S. Department of Commerce, Washington, D.C.

Paying for Imports with Foreign Currencies. American Importers Association, 420
   Lexington Ave., New York, N.Y. 10017.
Source Book: The "How To" Guide for Importers and Exporters. UNZ & Co., 190
   Baldwin Ave., Jersey City, N.J. 07306.
A Summary of U.S. Export Administration Regulations, Revised June 1975. U.S.
   Department of Commerce, Washington, D.C.
U.S. Importing Requirements. U.S. Customs Service, Washington, D.C.

Books

The following books provide the beginner with a solid nucleus for an import/export
library. Each entry is annotated to give the reader information about the contents
and benefits of each book.

Foreign Trade Marketplace, 1977. Edited by George Schuttz. Gale Research Co.,
   Detroit, Michigan 84226.
   Reduces many complicated aspects of importing and exporting to simpler
   terms. Excellent source for lists of advertising agencies, public relations firms,
   schools and courses on foreign trade, and foreign agents.
*How to Market Overseas Successfully—A Basic Guide to Profitable International
   Business*, 1973. F. R. Lineaweaver, Jr. The Dartnell Corporation.
   Good workbook on important aspects of export trade. Second half of book
   especially helpful for beginner; it lists major ingredients for successful export
   program.
International Trade: A Management Guide, 1972. Harold J. Hech, American Man-
   agement Association, New York, N.Y.
   Simple and practical information on both importing and exporting. Good ex-
   planation of how to use statistics.
Practical Exporting and Importing, 1959. Philip MacDonald, The Ronald Press,
   New York, N.Y.
   Excellent guide. Contains sample import and export transactions.

Directories and Bibliographies

The following are reference works with which the beginner should be familiar.

American Register of Exporters and Importers. 90 West Broadway, New York, N.Y.
   10007.
   Lists over 25,000 importers and exporters, along with the products each handles.
   Good reference for the beginner.
Business International Corporation Master Key Index, quarterly, with annual cumu-
   lations. New York.
   Contains research reports, management reports, and a periodicals list. Some of
   these reports are quite helpful because they contain surveys of product categories in numerous countries.

Custom House Guide. North American Publishing Company, 134 N. 13th, Philadelphia, PA 19107.

Most important reference for the potential importer. Lists the text of the Tariff Schedules of the U.S., plus complete information on custom house brokers, steamship lines, and agents. Monthly supplement entitled "American Import and Export Bulletin" contains important news and current customs regulations.

Exporter's Encyclopedia, Annual. Dun & Bradstreet International, 99 Church St., New York, N.Y.

Most comprehensive reference work for the potential exporter. Gives important marketing, shipping, banking, communications, and exchange regulations for most of the countries of the world. Has a semimonthly news sheet entitled "World Marketing" on current events related to international trade.

Foreign Commerce Hand Book, 17th Edition, 1976. Chamber of Commerce of the U.S., Washington, D.C.

Useful and inexpensive guide to foreign commerce sources. Very complete and easy to use for the beginner.

Books—General

The following provides the beginner with assistance in establishing a business when he or she has never run one before.

How to Make Money in Your Own Small Business, 1977. Metcalf, Bunn, and Stigelman, The Entrepreneur Press, Fairfield, CA.